Ronald Vaughan

BLACK
MONDAY'S
CHILDREN

GLORIA J. POWELL, M.D.

Director of Mental Health Services
Community-University Health Care Center
Minneapolis, Minnesota;
Assistant Professor, Division of Child Psychiatry
University of Minnesota Medical School;
Assistant Professor, Institute of Child Development
University of Minnesota

with special assistance of

MARIELLE FULLER
Research Associate, Department of Psychiatry
U.C.L.A. Center for the Health Sciences

BLACK MONDAY'S CHILDREN

*A Study of the Effects
of School Desegregation
on Self-Concepts
of Southern Children*

APPLETON-CENTURY-CROFTS / New York
A Publishing Division of Prentice-Hall, Inc.

Copyright © 1973 by APPLETON-CENTURY-CROFTS
A Publishing Division of Prentice-Hall, Inc.

74 75 76 77 78 79 / 10 9 8 7 6 5 4 3 2

Library of Congress Catalog Card Number 70-181736

PRINTED IN THE UNITED STATES OF AMERICA 0-8385-0717-4

BLACK
MONDAY'S
CHILDREN

GLORIA J. POWELL, M.D.

Director of Mental Health Services
Community-University Health Care Center
Minneapolis, Minnesota;
Assistant Professor, Division of Child Psychiatry
University of Minnesota Medical School;
Assistant Professor, Institute of Child Development
University of Minnesota

with special assistance of

MARIELLE FULLER
Research Associate, Department of Psychiatry
U.C.L.A. Center for the Health Sciences

BLACK MONDAY'S CHILDREN

*A Study of the Effects
of School Desegregation
on Self-Concepts
of Southern Children*

APPLETON-CENTURY-CROFTS / New York
A Publishing Division of Prentice-Hall, Inc.

74 75 76 77 78 79 / 10 9 8 7 6 5 4 3 2

Library of Congress Catalog Card Number 70-181736

Preface

This book represents an attempt to study the psychologic effects of school desegregation in the South vis-à-vis an analysis of the self-concept of children. Before the 1954 Supreme Court decision much evidence was advanced to support the negative psychologic effects of school segregation in the South. Since, then, few efforts have been made to examine the psychologic consequences of school desegregation in the South. Self-concept testing was used because what a person thinks and feels about himself is largely determined by what others think and feel about him. For young children parental attitudes play the most significant role in self-concept development, in young adolescents the peer group begins to take on more importance.

In order to understand the total picture of desegregation and its effects on young people, one needs to understand the developmental history of the process and, hence our excursions into history in order to better understand the dynamics of the present. As a child psychiatrist, it is difficult for me to avoid developmental history; I am not an historian and do not attempt to be. However, the psychodynamic factors operating in present day desegregation practices in the South have their beginnings deeply rooted in the past.

I have purposely omitted any attempt to study the effects of I.Q. or achievement as a result of school desegregation although mention of other studies related to that area are discussed. Black children are always part of any study on intellectual performance, very few studies focus primarily on their emotional growth and development. Inasmuch as black children, like white children, spend a great deal of their youth in school, it would seem appropriate to examine the effect of their new school life, school desegregation, on their emotional growth and development.

Finally, Black Monday's Children are not only the black and white children who participated in this study, but they are all the children, black and white, whose lives were affected by the May 17, 1954 decision. School desegregation is a vital issue confronting communities all over the country. I have chosen to study the South because that is where school desegregation has resulted in dramatic social change. By choosing the South to study, I do not mean to imply that the emotional consequences of school desegregation are more or less significant than in the North. I am currently in the process of completing the data on several Northern cities. The comparison should be interesting.

I wish to express my very special appreciation to Mrs. Marielle Fuller, who has been my most valuable assistant in preparing this book. Without her loyalty, patience, and scholarship this book could not have been written. I also wish to express my appreciation to the Department of Psychiatry at U.C.L.A., Mount Holyoke College, and Meharry Medical College who provided me with moral and financial support.

G.J. Powell

Minneapolis, Minnesota 1972

Contents

vii

PART FOUR: GREENSBORO

PART FIVE: BLACK MONDAY'S CHILDREN

PART ONE

Self-Concept and School Desegregation

1

Introduction

The question "Who am I?" is basic to the psychologic issue of identity and self-concept, but is also deeply rooted in man's eternal religious and philosophic search for meaning. William James' *The Consciousness of Self*, published in 1890, is a classic in that it begins to bridge the gap between the philosophic discussion of self and the psychologic reality of self, from navel contemplation, as it were, to involvement and action in the real world.[1] That a person's self comprises the experience of his identity as a distinct individual is an existential ideology as well as a psychologic axiom.

When Erik Erikson first arrived in this country and began to practice as an analyst, he made many references to the prevailing problems of identity which so many of his American patients seemed to have in contrast to his European patients.[2] Although the concept of America as the great "melting pot" still persists, the actual heterogeneity of America representing various nationalities, and racial and ethnic groups produces many subcultures, different ideologies, as well as class distinctions. To resolve one's identity in the face of a variety of subgroups, class distinctions, and ideologies accentuated by rapid social changes and rapid changes in technology is, indeed, difficult for a young American.

Myrdal, however, pointed out that it has been the "American Creed" that has served as "the cement in the structure of this great and disparate nation."[3] What is this American Creed? The essence of it has been defined by Myrdal:

These ideals of the essential dignity of the individual human being, of the fundamental equality of all men, and of certain inalienable rights to freedom, justice, and a fair opportunity represent to the American people the essential

3

meaning of the nation's early struggle for independence. In the clarity of and intellectual boldness of the Enlightenment period these tenets were written into the Declaration of Independence, the Preamble of the Constitution, the Bill of Rights, and into the constitutions of the several states. The ideals of the American Creed have thus become the highest law of the land. The Supreme Court pays its reverence to these general principles when it declares what is constitutional and what is not.[4]

Nowhere else in American institutions has the American Creed been more embedded in its very foundation than in the American institution of free public schools. Each morning millions of school children begin their school day with the Pledge of Allegiance—"one nation, under God, with liberty and justice for all." The institution of public schools in this country was created to facilitate socioeconomic mobility and to promote equal opportunities. Yet the institution of segregation of the races, especially in the South, mitigated against the very principles on which free education was established and, indeed, against the credulence of the American Creed. Before 1954, 17 Southern and border states and the District of Columbia operated completely separate schools for whites and blacks. On May 17, 1954, the Supreme Court held that such separate schools were inherently unequal. This decision ushered in an era of American social revolution. May 17, 1954, was recorded and written about by white Southern politicians as "Black Monday" — the beginning of the demise of the Southern way of life. (It is interesting to note that the word "black" in that context was used to connote mourning, doom, and despair.)

The psychosocial ills arising from segregation have been explored by many social scientists and social psychologists. A review of this subject will be presented in a subsequent chapter. Since the 1954 decision, many have investigated the results of school desegregation on academic achievement, I.Q. scores, as well as on racial attitudes and social accommodations. The Group for the Advancement of Psychiatry states:

> Desegregation is not merely a legal problem; it is also a social problem; an economic one, and above all, a psychological one. . . . Desegregation also means that, irrespective of racial proportions, many children find themselves in new groups. In all these instances the reactions of the individual who finds himself a stranger in a group, as well as the reactions of the group as it tries to cope with the newcomer, assume great importance.[5]

There is no doubt that the Supreme Court ruling has made a significant social and political impact on American communities. If the sociocultural milieu to which a child is exposed influences his self-concept development, which entails understanding how and what he learns about himself, what he thinks about himself, and how he feels about himself, then what impact has "Black Monday" made on the people so vitally involved in this social revolution, the children themselves?

As school desegregation proceeds across the country, those who are concerned about the maintenance of mental health and the prevention of mental illness in children need to take a more careful look at how desegregation affects the psychologic development or retardation of the children involved. It is essential to evaluate the "when" and "how" of school desegregation in order to promote the psychologic and educational development of the children involved.

This study attempts to evaluate the psychologic effects of school desegregation on seventh-, eighth-, and ninth-grade students in three Southern cities by using a standardized self-concept scale. The psychologic effects of school segregation on seventh-, eighth-, and ninth-grade students in the South prior to 1954 has not been studied systematically by self-concept scales. Strong and Feder reviewed 15 instruments used in self-concept studies.[6] The methodologies used included Q technique, Likert-type rating methods, free-response methods, and check tests. Crowne and Stephens have pointed out that since the instruments cannot be assumed to be equivalent, the comparability across studies using different instruments presents many difficulties.[7] Thus, we are left with the basic assumptions from what available research data there is in spite of the lack of comparability, that prior to 1954 black children in seventh, eighth, and ninth grades in public schools in the South had low self-concepts when compared with white children of similar age and grade. This thesis underlies the hypotheses of this study.

Inasmuch as the assessment of personality and psychologic development by self-concept testing is still controversial in many clinical circles and studies dealing with black children present a vast array of results, then the first task of this book will be to review the literature on identity, racial awareness and preference, and self-concept studies of black children done in the 1950's and 1960's (Chapter 2).

Another assumption underlying the hypotheses of this study is that the social changes resulting from the 1954 decision have had an effect on self-concept changes in Southern black children. Therefore, the second task will be to review that decision and the historical events preceding and following it in order to understand present problems and the data that will be presented (Chapter 3). The data from each city which comprises Parts 2, 3, and 4 of the book will be presented separately, but the conclusions, Part 5, will be drawn from the data retrieved from the three cities.

School desegregation presents many problems in many areas. As a multi-facet problem it needs to be viewed from many perspectives. Although the concern of this study is mainly psychologic, where historical, social, and political data is needed to give more insight into the psychologic problems and explain the results of the study, they will be included.

In the introduction to *An American Dilemma*, Myrdal states that "America is continuously struggling for its soul."[8] As the study of school desegregation is unraveled in these chapters it may well be said that that struggle is as true today as it was when Myrdal wrote.

1. Wolman, B., ed. Handbook of Clinical Psychology, New York, McGraw-Hill, Inc., 1965.
2. Erikson, E. Reflections on American identity, Chap. 8. *In* Childhood and Society, 2nd ed. New York, W.W. Norton and Co., 1963, pp. 285-324.
3. Myrdal, G. An American Dilemma, Vol. I. New York, McGraw-Hill, Inc., 1964, p. 4.
4. Ibid.
5. Group for Advancement of Psychiatry. Psychiatric aspects of school desegregation, Report No. 37. May, 1957, p. 5 and 58.
6. Strong, D.J., and Feder, D.D. Measurement of self-concept: A critique of the literature. Journal of Counseling Psychology, 1961, 8:170-178.
7. Crowne, D.P., and Stephens, N.W. Self-acceptance and self-evaluative behavior: A critique of methodology. Psychological Bulletin, 1961, 58:104-121.
8. Myrdal. Op. cit., p. 4.

2

Black Monday Revisited: The History of School Desegregation

Monday is decision day in the Supreme Court of the United States. It is the day when the eyes and ears of the legal world are turned toward Washington and the marbled temple of justice which houses the most powerful judicial body in the world today.

. . . Vacation and recess periods excepted, no Monday can draw to a close without some judicial dictate that affects the life, liberty or property of tens of thousands—or tens of millions—of people in the United States.

One Monday morning in the year 1954 was destined to be more important, more historic, more dramatic than any of the others.

. . . At 12:52 p.m., May 17, 1954, 335 years after the first Negro slaves arrived in America in chains and 91 years after the Emancipation Proclamation, Earl Warren, Chief Justice of the United States, began reading the Supreme Court opinion in *Brown* v. *Board of Education.* . . . The reading of the unanimous decision ended precisely at 1:20.[1]

The Supreme Court had spoken and the words uttered that day constituted "the most controversial and far-reaching decision of the twentieth century."[2]

The concluding paragraph of the decision read as follows:

We conclude that in the field of public education the doctrine of "separate but equal" has no place. Separate educational facilities are inherently unequal. Therefore, we hold that the plaintiffs and others similarly situated for whom the actions have been brought are, by reason of the segregation complained of, deprived of the equal protection of the laws guaranteed by the Fourteenth Amendment.

Why did the Supreme Court come to such a decision? Why was the decision so monumental? What were the events leading to the decision? Who were the plaintiffs and what were their complaints? In what way did that

7

decision affect the lives of the peoples of the United States? In order to answer and, indeed, to understand those and many other questions, the reader must take a winding historical journey into the American past and review a few landmarks.

NEGRO EDUCATION IN THE 1800's

In the late 1700's and in the early 1800's, before the Civil War, separate schools were set up in some communities for the education of free blacks. Some colleges, such as Bowdoin, Oberlin, Franklin, Rutland Colleges, and Harvard University, admitted Negro students. A few black colleges began to operate, for example, Lincoln University in Pennsylvania in 1854, Wilberforce University in Ohio in 1856. Although the demand for free public schools even for white children followed substantially the same pattern in both the North and South, the development in the South did not begin to gain momentum until about 1850, twenty years after that in the North. The reasons for the somewhat slower development in the South could be explained by the more rural character of the South as well as the different regional attitudes toward state assistance. Compulsory school attendance laws were not adopted until after the ratification of the Fourteenth Amendment and it was not until 1918 that such laws were in force in all the states.

Education for blacks had a low status in all sections of the country before and immediately after the Civil War. After the Civil War former slaves turned to education as a means to a better life, and in some states school facilities were provided for the newly freed blacks of all ages who were eager for book-learning. These schools set up by state and local governments and by church groups, with few exceptions, were always separate from the whites. Shortly after the war the federal government established the Freedman's Bureau with the sole purpose of helping blacks, and under its jurisdiction 4,000 schools for blacks were set up. Though vastly inferior to the educational facilities for whites, schools and colleges for blacks multiplied and improved. Under the Bureau's jurisdiction such well known institutions as Howard University, Hampton Institute, Atlanta University, and Fisk University were established. In 1870 when the Bureau was ended there were nearly 250,000 blacks in more than 4,000 schools. However, it must be remembered that for the most part in the South the Civil War had stopped virtually all progress in public education.

A more vigorous prosecution of the idea of universal education was one of the results of the inauguration of radical re-construction in the ex-confederate states in 1867. Negro spokesmen called for free public education for the newly enfranchised freedman. Leaders from the North, the so-called carpetbaggers, believed that an expanded educational program in the South would do much to improve the cultural and political life of the region.

... Universal education, even among carpetbaggers and Negroes, did not necessarily mean racially integrated schools. Most Freedman Bureau schools were segregated, in the sense that most of them were Negro schools. And the existent public schools were segregated, in the sense that most of them were white schools, with a gesture here and there toward Negroes. But there was some reluctance to be explicit about segregated schools in the face of the equal provisions of the Fourteenth Amendment.[3]

The Fourteenth Amendment originated in the thirty-ninth Congress which convened in December, 1865, as the first post-Civil War Congress. There was a Republican Senate and a Republican House, and within the majority party a vicious power struggle between the moderates and radicals had begun. John Bingham of Ohio, a Radical Republican, proposed a constitutional amendment restricting the power of the states to deny equal protection of the laws to any citizen. The "equal protection" clause was objected to because it was argued that Congress would have the power to force the states to provide the same schools for white and black children. The amendment was defeated, but for reasons other than the school segregation argument. In April, 1866, Thaddeus Stevens offered a proposal to the Joint Committee on Reconstruction which in essence was a Radical Republican Plan for reconstruction of the South. Stevens included additions that contained the language of the Fourteenth Amendment, i.e., privileges and immunities, due-process and equal-protection clauses. Congress, under the leadership of the Republic whips, approved the Fourteenth Amendment without change in the Bingham language: "No state shall deprive any person of life, liberty, or property without due process of law, or deny to any person within its jurisdiction the equal protection of the laws."

On July 28, 1868, the Secretary of State declared the Fourteenth Amendment ratified by three fourths and more of the states of the Union. In the first cases applying the Fourteenth Amendment, decided shortly after the adoption, the Supreme Court interpreted it as denouncing all state-imposed discrimination against the black race. However, the status of public education at the time of the ratification of the amendment was such that the real intent of Congress and the state legislatures with respect to segregated schools is inconclusive.

At the time of the Fourteenth Amendment public school education had advanced further in the North, but even in the North the conditions of public education did not approximate those of today. The curriculum was rudimentary; ungraded schools were common in rural areas; the school term was but three months a year; a compulsory school attendance was virtually unknown.

In the South the movement toward free common schools, supported by general taxation, had not yet taken hold. Education of white children was largely in the hands of private groups; education of blacks was almost non-existent. In some states any education of blacks was forbidden by law. Opposition to the education of blacks was widespread. J.H. Franklin points out that whites did not regard it necessary to include blacks in any programs of public education, that most white Southerners were opposed to any education for blacks and relentless in their fight to oppose mixed schools even in the face of the equal protection provisions of the Fourteenth Amendment.[4]

In Alabama the legislators were opposed to mixed schools but also "seemed to realize that it would be indiscreet to forbid them." The Board of Education established a law stating that " . . . in no case shall it be lawful to unite in one school both colored and white children, unless it be by the unanimous consent of the parents and guardians of such children."[5]

J.H. Franklin also points out that in the constitutional conventions of Mississippi, Georgia, North Carolina, and Virginia there were no references to segregation in the articles on education nor were any color distinctions made. The issue of mixed schools was avoided, although the legislators were basically opposed to the idea. Arkansas and Tennessee established separate schools from the beginning of Reconstruction. Louisiana and South Carolina were the only two ex-Confederate states that tried to establish laws for mixed schools.

> It would not be too much to say that attempts to integrate schools were generally unsuccessful either in the states that where the provisions were sufficiently vague to countenance them or where they were expressedly authorized by law. The initial hostility of white Southerners to schools of any kind had been the most effective weapon against mixed schools. If Negro teachers were burned, if white teachers of Negroes were ostracized, threatened, whipped, and chased from the community, any kind of schools for Negroes had little chance of succeeding. Mixed schools had no chance whatever. Even the friends of Negro education and many of those who frowned on separation were forced to the unpleasant but inescapable conclusion that the only real chance for success in the education of Negroes lay in the establishment and maintenance of separate schools.[6]

After Reconstruction, the white Southerner, returning to the control of his government, began to withdraw voting rights from the blacks, and a pattern of separation of the races began to develop in churches, hotels, restaurants, and trains. One by one more and more states began to follow the earlier examples of Florida, Tennessee, and Arkansas in establishing segregated schools.

Once Jim Crow was firmly established in the public schools of the South, the inequities persisted and increased; and the conditions most destructive to the educative process in a democracy were created. White children were taught, if not directly then indirectly by their superior advantages, that they belonged to some kind of a master race. Even the rather dull minded among them, moreover, could see that they lived lives that contradicted the basic democratic tenets of equality and justice. For the Negro children the task was an almost impossible one: to endure the badge of inferiority imposed on them by segregation, to learn enough in inferior Jim Crow schools to survive in a highly complex and hostile world, and, at the same time keep faith in democracy. For both Negro and white children, one of the most effective lessons taught in Jim Crow schools was that even in institutions dedicated to training the mind a greater premium was placed on color than on brains. True education in the South was languishing. Only Jim Crow was flourishing and making steady gains in the generation after the Civil War.[7]

THE "SEPARATE BUT EQUAL" DOCTRINE

In addition to the Fourteenth Amendment, another legal landmark also surfaced in the post-Civil War days; the case of *Plessy* v. *Ferguson*, thereafter referred to as "the separate but equal doctrine." Both legal landmarks were of the utmost importance in the May 17, 1954, decision.

Homer Plessy was one-eighth black and seven-eighths white and was arrested in Louisiana when he refused to ride in the "colored" coach of the train as required by Louisiana law. Plessy then tried to prevent enforcement of the law on the grounds that it violated the Thirteenth and Fourteenth Amendments. Ferguson was the Louisiana judge selected to conduct the trial, although Plessy had entered a plea that Ferguson be prohibited from hearing the case. Plessy argued that state-enforced segregation stamped blacks with a badge of inferiority. The Supreme Court disagreed, stating that such laws did not necessarily imply the inferiority of either one of the races. Plessy, therefore, could suffer no damage as a result of mere separation so long as the facilities furnished were equal to those from which he was excluded. Thus, in 1896 the Supreme Court upheld the principles of separate but equal facilities for whites and blacks in the case of *Plessy* v. *Ferguson*.

Justice John Harlan, the sole dissenter, declared: "Our constitution is color blind, and neither knows or tolerates classes among citizens . . . In my opinion the judgment this day rendered will, in time, prove to be quite as pernicious as the decision of the Dred Scott case."[8]

In the *Plessy* case the court had ignored the impact of the Fourteenth Amendment and had made the "separate but equal" doctrine the law of the Constitution. Although the *Plessy* v. *Ferguson* case involved intrastate transportation, in the years to follow the situation was to be interpreted as applying to other situations. "Although *Plessy* v. *Ferguson* did not involve education, there is no doubt that the Supreme Court had bestowed its blessings on the state-maintained segregated school systems."[9]

Three years after *Plessy* v. *Ferguson* the court faced its first school segregation case, *Cummings* v. *Board of Education of Richmond County, Georgia,* in 1899. The black plaintiffs asked for an injunction closing the white schools until a separate school was provided for black children. The court decided that the remedy requested was improper and the suit was dismissed.

"Thus in its first education case the Supreme Court not only avoided passing on the validity of separate but equal but also failed to indicate any appropriate standards for measuring equality."[10]

In the 1908 case of *Berea College* v. *Kentucky* the Supreme Court had under analysis the "Day Law" of Kentucky which required that whites and blacks could not be taught in any private school unless that school maintained separate buildings for each race at least 25 miles apart. The Court allowed the "Day Law" to stand without reconsidering the separate but equal doctrine. As in *Plessy* v. *Ferguson,* Justice Harlan registered a dissent.

The third case presented before the court after *Plessy* v. *Ferguson* was the 1927 decision of *Gong Lum* v. *Rice* in which Martha Lum, a Chinese resident of Mississippi objected to attending a black school. In the Lum case the Supreme Court accepted the finding of the Mississippi courts which had stated that for purposes of public education laws, those who were not white were considered colored. Once again the Court had avoided the separate but equal doctrine. In the only three school cases that had arisen between 1895 to the 1940's questions regarding the constitutionality of the separate but equal doctrine were not considered by the Court.

> Failure to act resulted in the continuation of separate school systems all over the South and in some parts of the North. It was clear that such schools would continue to exist until the Supreme Court squarely faced the issue. For all practical purposes, the separate but equal concept had achieved de facto constitutionality in the field of public education as a minimum requirement.[11]

The separate but equal doctrine came before the Court again in the first 40 years following *Plessy* v. *Ferguson,* but it was upheld only in transportation cases.

SEPARATE BUT UNEQUAL

The ideal of equal education opportunity was a goal to be considered only after the needs of white children were met. By 1933 more than 200

Southern counties with black populations of 12.5 percent or more had no black high schools.[12]

In the 1930's and 1940's a great proportion of the total budgets of cities and an increasingly greater part of the state and federal budgets were ear-marked for public education. There were no financial statistics for the North that separated the amount spent on the education of blacks as compared with that spent on whites. In actual practice, however, schools in needy districts, where there were a large concentrations of blacks, tended to be somewhat older, less well equipped, and often more overcrowed. In many instances school authorities were reluctant to increase the incentive for black migration from the South to schools in Northern black districts, and had been slower to increase school facilities in black districts than they had been in white districts. Racial discrimination in the apportionment of school facilities in the South was as spectacular as it was well known by the 1940's. In 1935 the expense per pupil in daily attendance per year in elementary and secondary schools in ten Southern states was $17.04 for blacks and $49.30 for white children.[13] In Mississippi and Georgia only $9.00 was spent on a black school child and $45.00 spent on the average white child.[14] It should be mentioned, however, that Delaware, Missouri, and Oklahoma did not discriminate against blacks in this way.[15] In Washington, D.C., Negro schools received only slightly smaller appropriations per pupil than did white schools.

The most important factor in the great differential in expenditures for black and white schools was teachers' salaries. In the South, before the *Brown* decision, more than 5 percent of the Negro female workers were in professional categories; school teaching has been one of the major profes-sions among blacks. In the South a black teacher had a heavier teaching load than a white teacher. In 1934 black teachers in elementary schools had classes with 43 pupils compared with classroom size of 34 in white schools.[16] In order for the pupil load in black schools to equal that in white schools, 26 percent more black teachers were needed in Southern elementary and secondary schools. The average salary in Southern elementary schools in 1935–1936 was $510 for black teachers and $833 for white teachers. In Mississippi black teachers earned $247 and white teachers earned $783. The exceptions were in Washington, D.C., Delaware, and Missouri.

Aside from teachers' salaries and pupil-teacher ratios, the third difference in expenditure per black pupil compared with that for a white pupil was in transportation. Less transportation was provided for black children; in 10 Southern states, where black children were 28 percent of the total enroll-ment, only 3 percent of the expenditures for school transportation were for black children in 1935. The differential in school expenditures was often greatest in states in which the proportion of blacks was the highest, and a similar tendency could be noted among counties within each state. In such instances the temptation to take monies allotted to the black schools and give them to white schools was tremendous and indeed this was done; every dollar per pupil taken from the black group meant two dollars per pupil for the white group. School segregation increased the cost of the educational system for a given average.

The New Deal greatly increased education benefits to blacks. However, although the Public Works Administration paid 55 percent of the costs of building new schools, the South saw to it that schools were provided for whites first. Of some 91 million dollars of federal funds spent for new schools in 16 Southern states, a little over 7 million dollars went for black schools.[17] When the federal government did give aid for education, it allowed the states to allocate it and spend it which then permitted discrimination against blacks.

Another issue to be explored in the inequality of education for blacks before the *Brown* decision is the subject of the qualifications of black teachers. In many instances black teachers were teaching who had not had a high school education or had just finished high school. This difference of credentials aided and abetted the discrepancy in salaries between white and black teachers.

The status of education for blacks prior to the *Brown* decision can be summed up by Schrieke:

> . . . although there is some sort and some amount of Negro education everywhere. Negro education still does not have a fixed, legitimate, acknowledged place. It is realized that something must be done in order to keep the Negro satisfied and in order to uphold the American slogan of free schools for every child, but it is rare that a community has any real interest in planning or building a wise system of education for the race. Politically, it is not generally admitted that the Negro has a right to schools or to other public services . . . The Negro is still not recognized as a citizen despite the Civil War amendments.[18]

With the end of World War II Americans showed increasing concern over racial discrimination. In the South, segregation laws separated the races in schools, restaurants, theaters, and other public places. In the North, blacks faced discrimination in jobs, in housing, and in many other areas.

> By the middle of the twentieth century, the pattern of segregation was as irregular as it was complex. Every conceivable form of segregation had been evolved. Although one would have to visit many places to observe all the variations. . . . The law had created two worlds so separate that communication between them was almost impossible.[19]

In the mid-1940s several important Supreme Court decisions attacked the problem of segregation. Although the Fourteenth Amendment, adopted after the Civil War, guaranteed equal protection under the law to all citizens, for many years after the Reconstruction period proposals for federal legislation to enforce this principle were defeated. In 1946 the Supreme Court ruled that a Virginia law requiring segregation on interstate buses was invalid and in 1948 the Court ruled that restrictive real estate covenants could not be enforced by federal or state courts. In a series of decisions extending over several years the Court ruled that black colleges in several states were not equal to white colleges within these states and that those states should therefore admit blacks to white colleges.

If indeed forthcoming events cast their shadows ahead of them, then the decisions of several cases dealing with the separate but equal doctrine in higher education that were brought before the Court began to lay the legal groundwork for 1954. The details of these cases will not be reviewed here, but mention of the cases and the significance of them will be alluded to in the following paragraphs. Of the following cases, four had to do with the legality and equality of segregation of Negroes in law schools and one in graduate school.

The first case was that of *Pearson* v. *Murray* in 1936. Murray had applied to the University of Maryland Law School but was denied admission. The Maryland Court of Appeals held (1) that Maryland's offer of an out-of-state tuition scholarship was inadequate and (2) that "he could not there have the advantages of study of law of this state primarily, and of attendance on state courts where he intends to practice."[20] The Maryland Court of Appeals had answered decisively two critical questions involved in the separate but equal doctrine: the measure of equality and the proper remedy.

The second case dealt with admission to a state-supported law school, the University of Missouri, in the case of *Gaines* v. *Canada* in 1938. The U.S. Supreme Court held that in the absence of a separate equal law school, the plaintiff had the right to attend the University of Missouri Law School.

In the 1948 case of *Sipvel* v. *Board of Education*, the Court ordered the immediate admission of the black applicant, Sipvel, to the University of Oklahoma Law School noting that the unequality was blatant.

In the fourth case of *Sweatt* v. *Painter* in 1950, Herman Sweatt was denied admission to all-white University of Texas Law School and was referred to a separate law school for blacks. The Supreme Court found substantial inequality between Texas's white and black law schools and further declared: "What is more important, the University of Texas Law School possesses to a greater degree those qualities which are incapable of objective measurement but which make for greatness in a law school."

In the 1950 case of *McLaurin* v. *Oklahoma State Regents*, McLaurin had been admitted to the graduate school but was assigned a special seat in each classroom and the library and had to eat in a segregated section of the cafeteria. The Supreme Court declared such discriminatory practices unconstitutional.

It should be noted that in the four cases presented before the U.S. Supreme Court and the one case presented to the Maryland Court of Appeals desegregation had been ordered to achieve equality of education. There had been six cases involving the "separate but equal" doctrine since the 1896 *Plessy* v. *Ferguson* decision presented to the U.S. Supreme Court. In each instance the question whether *Plessy* v. *Ferguson* "should be held inapplicable to public education" was avoided. However, for most Southern states these cases were convincing proof that the Court would in time open all public institutions of higher education to blacks.

"Both friends and foes of segregation in education conceded that the bitter fight would be waged on the level of the elementary and secondary schools, and the fight was not long in coming."[21]

In a desperate effort to forestall "that day" the Southern states desperately spent funds on black schools and pledged themselves to equalize the white and black schools; but in most states the educational needs of black children had been so neglected during the decades following Reconstruction that it would have taken decades to achieve even a semblance of equality.

By 1951 the National Association for the Advancement of Colored People had decided to strike at the very core of segregation as unconstitutional, unethical, and immoral. And, so it was that in 1952 the NAACP on behalf of five cases began to test the validity of segregated public schools. Fifty-five years after its first educational decision in the Cummings case, the Supreme Court decided to call for a very full argument and consideration of the question of the constitutionality of school segregation.

THE SCHOOL DESEGREGATION CASES

Oliver Brown was the father of an eight-year-old girl, Linda Carol, who had been prohibited by state law from attending an elementary school within five blocks of her home in Topeka, Kansas, because that school was reserved for white students. (Interestingly enough, at that time in Topeka the high schools were desegregated.) Thus, the Brown child had to walk through railroad yards to take a bus to a black school 21 blocks away. Early in 1951, Mr. and Mrs. Brown as well as 12 other parents of black children in similar situations asked the U.S. District Court for the District of Kansas to enjoin the Board of Education from maintaining segregation of elementary schools. The United States District Court for Kansas ruled against Mr. Brown et al., in favor of the Board of Education because the physical facilities, curricula, courses of study, qualifications and quality of teachers, as well as other educational facilities in the two sets of schools were considered to be comparable. Thus, the Court considered itself bound by the "separate but equal" doctrine of *Plessy* v. *Ferguson.* Although the Kansas Court felt compelled to rule against the black plaintiffs, the effect of this separation on the plaintiff's educational opportunities was well stated:

Segregation of white and colored children in public schools has a detrimental effect upon the colored children. The impact is greater when it has the sanction of the law; for the policy of separating the races is usually interpreted as denoting the inferiority of the Negro group. A sense of inferiority affects the motivation of a child to learn. Segregation with the sanction of law, therefore, has a tendency to retard the educational and mental development of Negro children and to deprive them of some of the benefits they would receive in a racially integrated school system.

To bring the issue of segregation in public schools before the U.S. Supreme Court additional suits were needed to be filed in lower courts and so it was that Mr. Brown's NAACP lawyers were to use his battle with the Topeka school board to fight for desegregation.

The Browns and other black parents were not the only black families contesting state school desegregation laws. Indeed, in 1949, black parents of children attending the overcrowded black high school in Summerton, South Carolina, had begun to meet and discuss their grievances. When their grievances to the school board went unanswered, an NAACP lawyer prepared a formal petition which 107 parents and children signed and filed with the school board. In 1950, the NAACP lawyers filed suit in behalf of 10-year-old Harry Briggs, Jr., and 66 other black children against the Summerton School District of Clarendon County in South Carolina. Six weeks before the *Brown* case was first heard, the District Federal Court in Charleston, South Carolina, denied relief and invoked the "separate but equal" doctrine of *Plessy* v. *Ferguson.* The segregated black schools in Clarendon County were found to be far inferior to those provided for white children. The court ordered the Clarendon County School Board No. 22 to take steps to equalize the public school facilities and to report back to the court in six months. The plaintiffs, however, were denied admission to the white schools during the equalization. On remand, the district court found that substantial equality had been achieved except for buildings and that the defendants were proceeding to rectify the inequality as well. The NAACP lawyers then took the *Harry Briggs, Jr.* v. *R.W. Elliot* case to the Supreme Court on January 28, 1952. The Court decided that it would not decide the case until the views of the lower court on the six-month progress report were obtained.

Meanwhile in Virginia on March 7, 1952, Dorothy Davis and other black children of high-school age residing in Prince Edward County in Virginia asked the court to declare invalid the state's constitutional and statutory provisions requiring segregation or, as an alternative, to require equalization of existing school facilities. The court found the black school inferior in physical plant, curricula, and transportation and ordered the school board to right these inequalities; but the court denied the plaintiffs admission to the schools during the equalization program. On advice of NAACP counsel, the plaintiffs appealed the case to the U.S. Supreme Court.

The fourth case on the docket to be decided on May 17, 1954, was a suit brought by the parents of Ethel Louise Belton and Barbara Bulah, and other black children of elementary and high-school age of New Castle County in Delaware. The plaintiffs sought to enjoin constitution and statutory provisions requiring segregation. On April 1, 1952, Delaware Chancellor Collins J. Seitz ordered the immediate admission of black children to schools previously attended only by white children. He contended that:

> . . . state imposed segregation in education itself results in the Negro children, as a class, receiving educational opportunities which are substantially inferior to those available to white children otherwise similarly situated.[22]

He expressed the personal belief that the separate but equal doctrine in education should be rejected, noting that the rejection must come from the U.S. Supreme Court.

The defendants contended that the Delaware courts had erred in ordering the immediate admission of the black plaintiffs to the white schools and appealed to the U.S. Supreme Court.

The case of *Bolling* v. *Sharpe* was also one of the five cases to be considered on May 17, 1954. This case came from the District of Columbia, where Spottswood Bolling and others had sought to be admitted to a brand-new white high school in Washington, D.C., and had been denied. The case was taken to the United States Court of Appeals for the District of Columbia Circuit. Judicial notice was taken of *Bolling* v. *Sharpe* and on November 10, 1952, the lower court was instructed to submit the case to the high tribunal for review.

By the October term in 1952, the Supreme Court had on the docket the appeals in the *Brown, Briggs*, and *Davis* cases and on November 24, 1952, the *Bighart* v. *Bolton* case was placed on the docket, bringing all cases together for review by the Supreme Court. It is the custom that the name of the first person in the list of plaintiffs in the first cases to reach the Court is given the title of the case to be decided. Linda Carol Brown was the first name in the list of alphabetized plaintiffs in the Topeka suit, and thus the case of the eight-year-old little girl became Case No. 1 on the Supreme Court docket; the other cases (including *Bolling* v. *Sharpe*) were submitted in a packet labeled *Oliver Brown et al.* v. *Board of Education of Topeka*.

Since *Bolling* v. *Sharpe* came from the District of Columbia where the school system is operated directly under federal authority, the case was to be heard at the same time but would receive a separate ruling. The four cases in

Brown et al. v. *Board of Education of Topeka* were contested under the Fourteenth Amendment; *Boiling* v. *Sharpe* was contested under the Fifth Amendment.

In addition to the five cases stated above there were other cases in various stages of litigation in federal district courts by the time the five reached the Supreme Court docket. From Clinton, Tennessee, came the case of *McSwain* v. *County Board of Education of Anderson County* which was filed April 26, 1950. In 1952, the case of *Bush* v. *Orleans Parish School Board* was filed. These cases were suspended pending Supreme Court action on the five mentioned.

The five were argued before the Supreme Court in December, 1952. Between the 1952 and 1953 hearings there was a change of administration, as well as the death of Chief Justice Fred M. Vinson. Earl Warren, a Republican and Governor of California at the time was appointed Chief Justice in time for the December, 1953, re-argument. The associate justices included the following: Justice Harold Barton of Ohio, a Republican; Justice Stanley Reed from Kentucky, a Democrat; Justice Tom Clark from Texas, a Democrat; Justice Hugo Black of Alabama, a Democrat; Justice William O. Douglas of Connecticut, a Democrat; Justice Felix Frankfurter from Massachusetts, a Democrat; Justice Robert H. Jackson of New York, a Democrat; and Justice Sherman Menton from Indiana, a Democrat.

The principal spokesman for the South arguing for segregation was John W. Davis, Democratic nominee for President of the United States in 1924, former Ambassador to Great Britain, and "veteran of more Supreme Court battles than any other lawyer in American history." Counsel for the plaintiffs was Thurgood Marshall, Chief Counsel of the National Association for the Advancement of Colored People and a key figure for 25 years in legal battles on behalf of blacks.

On Monday, June 8, 1953, the Supreme Court made its first significant statement in the school segregation cases: No judgment was rendered. Instead, the case was scheduled for re-argument on October 12, 1953, to discuss and answer five questions in order to guide the thinking of the Supreme Court in reaching its decision. The questions are stated in detail by Blaustein and Ferguson in their legal analysis of the meaning and effect of the school desegregation cases.[23] The substance of those questions, as outlined by Muse, in general dealt with the following issues: whether or not the Congress that had submitted the Fourteenth Amendment, and the state legislatures and conventions that had ratified it, understood that it would abolish segregation in education; whether Congress or the Supreme Court had the power under the amendment to move against public school segregation; in the event desegregation should be ordered, whether a gradual transition should be permitted and how.[24]

On December 7, 1953, the case was re-argued in the light of the questions posed. Five months of Mondays passed. Then came Monday, May 17, 1954, the South's "Black Monday," for laws requiring racial segregation in public schools were held to be unconstitutional.[25]

1. Blaustein, A.P., and Ferguson, Jr., C.C. Desegregation and the Law: The Meaning and Effect of the School Desegregation cases, 2nd ed. New York, Vintage Books, 1962, pp. 3-5.

2. Ibid.

3. Franklin, J.H. Jim Crow goes to school: The genesis of legal segregation in the south. *In* The Negro in the South Since 1865: Selected Essays in American Negro History. Wynes, C.E., ed. New York, Harper Colophon, 1968, pp. 140-141.

4. Ibid.

5. Franklin, J.H. Op cit., 1968, p. 144.

6. Ibid., p. 142.

7. Ibid., p. 147.

8. Blaustein and Ferguson. Op. cit., 1962, p. 98.

9. Ibid.

10. Blaustein and Ferguson. Op. cit., 1962, p. 100.

11. Blaustein and Ferguson. Op. cit., p. 103.

12. Muse, B. The Years of Prelude: The Story of Integration Since the Supreme Court's 1954 Decision. New York, The Viking Press, 1964.

13. Myrdal, G. Op. cit., Chap. 15, p. 339.

14. Ibid.

15. Ibid.

16. Myrdal, G. Op. cit., Chap. 14, p. 319.

17. Ibid., Chap. 15, p. 343, footnote No. 26.

18. Ibid., Chap. 41, p. 902, footnote No. 39.

19. Franklin, J.H. History of racial discrimination in the United States. *In* The Making of Black America, Vol. II. Meier, A., and Rudwick, E. eds. New York, Atheneum Publishers, 1969, p. 3.

20. Blaustein and Ferguson. Op. cit., 1962, p. 106.

21. Franklin, J.H. From Slavery to Freedom: A History of Negro Americans, 3rd ed. New York, Vintage Books, 1969, p. 555.

22. Blaustein and Ferguson. Op. cit., 1962, p. 49.

23. Ibid., p. 51.

24. Muse. Op. cit., 1964, p. 13.

25. "Black Monday" was first used by Mississippi's Congressman Williams in a 1954 speech before the House of Representatives. Mississippi's Circuit Judge Tom P. Brady adopted "Black Monday" as the title of his prosegregation tract which was widely circulated in the South.

3

Self-Concept Development in Black Children: A Review and Critique

It is indeed an ambitious task to try to present an overview of self-concept development in black children, to review most, albeit not all, of the pertinent studies that have been done in this area, and to try to present to the reader a more succinct comprehensive view of the emotional status of black children in view of their self-perception and racial identity. However, in order for the reader to understand better the research data as well as the historical, political, and social factors that must be presented in order for the reader to interpret the data, it is necessary to take a long, circuitous journey through two very controversial subjects—self-concept testing and the emotional status of black children in this country. Hence this review.

THE PROBLEM AND THE PURPOSE

The last decade has watched Black America learn, as indeed black grandparents and black great-great-grandparents already knew, that there are many dimensions to being black in America. Perhaps the most exacting dimension of being a black, in the intrapsychic sense, is that every hour of one's life is spent in "being" a black, "existing" as a black, defining and redefining that existence as a black, and struggling to find the selfness and the individual identity as distinct from the group identity.

The feeling quality of being black is an existential phenomenon. Indeed, identity and selfness tug at the very core of existentialism, the task of which is to make every man aware of what he is and to make the full responsibility of his existence rest on him. The searching into the black self brings awareness of the black self and the other internal selves (for blackness is not the totality of a black man's self). It also brings awareness of other external selves—white people and other black people and, eventually, the existential reality of the "angst" of black existence—the anguish, the dread, and despair. The existential dimensions of being black leads one through various stages— the despair at not being willing to be a black self, the wishing to be another than one's self, and sometimes not willing to be a self. Such despair, which for Kierkegaard is "the sickness unto death," was there for the black slave ancestors, there for black grandparents and their black children, and is still present for black parents and their children today.

In *Nobody Knows My Name* James Baldwin eloquently presents the existential dilemma of the black man in America—the phenomenon of name-lessness and the problem of identification. The most important anchorage to one's identity throughout life remains in one's own name. One's name, though only a symbol, is tied to one's self-esteem as well as to one's sense of identity. How closely names and self-esteem are related was shown in a study by Strunk, who found that people who disliked their names generally did not like themselves.[1]

In exploring the issue of the black man's identity, Silberman observes:

> ... It is not just the white man who does not know the Negro's name, however; the Negro does not know either. In the literal sense the Negro American has never been able to decide what to call himself ...
>   ... In the last analysis, the confusion and controversy over name is bound up with the most fundamental question of identity: the flight from blackness, the hatred of self, the yearning to be white ...[2]

It is almost impossible to read any contemporary book or article on black America without there being some reference to the issue of identity. Indeed, identity has been a major theme for black writers and scholars for many years. The word "identity" comes from the Latin word "idem" mean-ing "the same" and is defined by Webster as "sameness of essential character; sameness in all that constitutes the objective reality of a thing." The second definition that Webster gives is "unity and persistence of personality; individ-uality." Most of the literature written about the new black mood and black consciousness refers to the first definition of identity which is used in such a context to connote a social and external definition, a group phenomenon, a classification. The latter definition is one that pervades the psychodynamic literature and many times is discussed in terms of "ego identity." The ego is that part of personality structure which serves as an integrating function in relation to the self and a mediating function between the self and the envi-ronment. An important aspect of the ego is the concept of self or of one's own identity which develops gradually throughout childhood.[3] Erik Erikson very eloquently and comprehensively reviews the past and present psychoanalytic theories of identity in *Identity, Youth and Crisis*, and the reader is referred to that astute discussion which points out the persistent association of identity with crisis.[4]

Indeed, identity has become a critical social, political, and personal issue for black people in America, and especially for black youth. For many black parents the issue of racial identity and racial awareness is overdone. For others it is ignored—the forbidden subject, confusing and anxiety-producing. In most instances the subject is handled with ambivalence and inconsistency. In the final analysis what impact does the confusion and ambivalence have on the growing black child? How does he deal with the question of "Who am I?" and evolve a sense of self, for "the one and only sure criterion of our personal existence and identity lies in our sense of self."[5]

A group of white adolescents were asked to answer the question "Who are you?" in three brief statements that would express the spiritual essence of who they were.[6] The majority of the group answered in terms of "I am a boy" or "I am a girl" and then in terms of their attributes—"I am kind," "I am often uncertain," and so forth—or in terms of their aspirations. They were also asked to answer the question "Who is Ralph Bunche?" in the very same way. Ninety percent answered that he was black; 50 percent gave black as his only characteristic. Then the group was asked, "Who is John Kennedy?" No one mentioned that John Kennedy was white. They described him in terms of his beliefs and in terms of his deeds and his relationship to other people.

The same questions were given to a group of black adolescents. In answer to "Who are you?" 95 percent mentioned that they were Negro or black; 85 percent mentioned their racial identity in conjunction with their sexual identity—i.e., "I am a Negro boy," "I am a Negro girl." Less than 50 percent of the group could identify themselves in terms of other than physical or bodily descriptions—e.g., "I am tall," "I am short or stocky." Only 15 percent described themselves in terms of their beliefs, their aspirations, or their relationship to other people in contrast to the group of white adolescents in which 40 percent were able to describe themselves in more abstract terms.

The black group was also asked who Ralph Bunche is. One hundred percent identified him as black, and 60 percent identified him according to his accomplishments. When asked about John Kennedy, no one identified him as white. He was identified in terms of what he had done.

Although the research design of this study could be criticized readily in terms of technique and statistical analysis and the like, one theme rings out loud and clear and that is in 1959 for black youth in this society the most outstanding essence of self, spiritually and physically, was being black. Beyond the blackness there was very little else of self that was important enough to mention. We can also surmise that for those black youth a great deal of emotional energy was used to resolve the black identity and perhaps little was left over for other abstractions. For the white youth who were not bound by the color bar, abstractions at another level could go on and the self was allowed to evolve beyond the external boundaries, i.e., more introspection was allowed. Both groups recognized that being white was not part of the essence of who one is but being black certainly was—an important aspect of who Ralph Bunche is is that he is black, but John Kennedy's whiteness was not essential to who he was. The important issue or question that this study poses, however, is how children learn about themselves in this way and how this knowledge is used in the intrapsychic development of the self.

In order to answer these questions, for the remainder of this chapter we shall talk in terms of self-concept rather than identity, which very briefly means how an individual thinks and feels about himself. The term "concept" connotes a thought or a mental image formed by generalizations from particular aspects. This definition is, in a sense, very comprehensive in that it includes the social and psychodynamic concepts of identity as well as the cognitive development of awareness of self as an internal and external reality.

The self-concept has become a popular and important way of studying and understanding human behavior, for the individual's concept of himself is related to his general personality and his state of mental health. The scope of this chapter is intended to cover not only a review of self-concept studies that have been done on black children, but also to give an overview of the status of the emotional growth and development of black children and the status of the literature as well. Our discussion will lead us to the status of self-concept development as a psychologic issue in child development in general and then in the development of black children in particular. In reviewing the studies that have been done on the black child, we will try to take a more critical look at the data and the conclusions as well as the psychosocial implications.

The subject of self-concept development in black children has become a crucial issue in child rearing—an inescapable issue for black parents and for those who would concern themselves with the emotional well-being of black children. Therefore, the real task of this chapter is to elucidate, if possible, the developmental task of the black child who must define, conceptualize, and incorporate a sense of self into himself within the context of American society with its racism and racial confrontations. In the face of and in spite of such odds the black child must try to reach the fulfillment of "the self" whatever that "self" is conceived finally to be.

THE THEORY OF SELF-CONCEPT DEVELOPMENT

How does the individual, any individual, go about defining himself? When does a child become aware of himself as a distinct self or individual? Is the process different for a black child than it is for a white child and, if so, in what way? As of this writing, we are not aware of any data that would indicate that the process is determined by biologic or genetic differences for a black child, but there are most certainly social factors that influence this process and allow racial differences. Perhaps these questions can be answered by watching the young infant grow and develop. By recapitulating the cycle of childhood, and especially black childhood, we can more closely examine the processes involved in defining the self for black children.

The ideas and attitudes which make a "self" aware of its own existence take shape as a child. A child understands or realizes different aspects of himself with varying degrees of understanding at different points in time. The development of self involves the process of differentiation; an individual makes the distinction between himself and other objects, animate and inanimate. Sometime during the first half of the first year of life the infant discovers himself and begins to separate his bodily physical boundaries from those of his mother. Various studies have been done that document the overt signs of self-awareness in the very young child.[7, 8, 9]

Allport describes seven aspects of selfhood which together comprise the self as felt and known. He lists them as

1. Sense of bodily self
2. Sense of continuing self-identity
3. Self-esteem, pride
4. The extension of self
5. The self-image
6. The self as a rational coper
7. The self as a propriate striver.[10]

He feels that the first three aspects of self-awareness gradually evolve during the first three years of life. During the period from four to six years aspects 4 and 5 begin to develop. The development of long-range purposes adds another dimension to the sense of selfhood (propriate striving) which occurs later on in latency.

It is important to remember that (1) these processes of self-discovery are actively continuous as long as the child is developing or discovering new potentialities and (2) self-concept development is dependent on certain variables whose absence or presence impede or enhance self-discovery.

A significant phase in the process of differentiation and development of self begins when a child asserts himself, opposes others, and compares himself with his peers. Harry Stack Sullivan emphasized that a young child's self-esteem comes into being through a process of "reflected appraisals."[11] That is to say that a child is appraised by significant others and in time begins to appraise himself. Approval by others who are significant in his life plants the seeds of self-approval. The significant others in a child's life vary according to his age. Very early in life the most significant person in a child's life is the primary mothering figure, and later on the significant people may be his peers or other adults. Some empirical studies have indicated that there is likely to be a direct correlation between a child's self-evaluation and the way he is regarded by his parents.[12] We shall consider this concept in regard to black parents and black children later on in this chapter.

A part of self-differentiation occurs when a child is able to compare himself with his peers, at which time he also begins to form a more or less clear conception of his family's socioeconomic status or social class.[13]

It is safe to say that a growing person's view of himself is shaped by everything that affects the entire scope of his development from his genetic makeup to obvious social influences in the society in which he lives.

G.H. Mead perceives the self in all its aspects as a predominately social self.[14] The cultural influences on a growing child have been described by Linton as being (1) what other people do to the child; (2) what other people consciously teach the child; (3) the behavior of other people observed by the child.[15] We need to ask ourselves, then, from the black child's point of view what does he see other people doing to him; what is he learning from other people; and what is he seeing in the behavior of other people. How do the experiences of a black child compare with those of a white child? Based on his experiences and his comparisons, how does a black child evaluate himself and conceptualize himself as a self of person?

SELF-CONCEPT THEORY, THE SOCIAL SCIENCES, AND THE BLACK EXPERIENCE

In addition to psychology and philosophy there are other disciplines that have contributed to the understanding of the dynamics of self-concept development in general and self-concept development in black children in particular. We have alluded to the influence of existentialism with its emphasis on "being" and "self" and have explored the psychodynamics of self-concept theory. The past decades have witnessed decided trends in sociology and anthropology that have expanded the theoretic considerations of man and his sociocultural milieu.

The sociologic implications of the black man's assigned second-class status have been explored by many. We shall mention only a few here. Dollard, in his *Caste and Class in a Southern Town*, explored the social dynamics of being black in the post-depression U.S.A. He found that the relationships of whites and blacks in the South were systematically ordered and upheld by a caste structure and the status of the individual within each caste system was determined by social class. The process of socialization for a black child reared in this system required a conceptualization of his caste and then his class, and then the appropriate behavior and responses for each. Having learned this, the black child then would know who he was, how he was to fit into this system (if, indeed, he had a place), and how his life would be ordered from birth to death (and the black child's survival was dependent on how well he learned these circumscribed and prescribed roles).

In *Children of Bondage* by Allison Davis and John Dollard, originally published in 1940, the personality development of black youth in an urban Southern city was explored. The book relies on the field studies of W. Lloyd Warner (*Yankee City*) as well as Allison Davis and Gardner Burleigh (*Deep South*). The authors attempt to answer such questions as: "What effect does this American Caste system, issuing out of slavery, have upon the personality development of such lower caste children? What degree of character torsion does systematic oppression exert upon human personality?"[16]

The personality development of eight black adolescents is examined in depth and their experiences are used to illustrate the controls exercised by each class over the socialization of its members and the pressures of the caste-like limitations of being black upon the personality formation of black children. Twenty years later a follow-up study was done of the adolescents described in *Children of Bondage*; 90 of 107 subjects were found and 20 were studied in depth.[17] The purpose of the study was to determine whether the subjects were perpetuating in their relations with their own children the methods by which they themselves had been trained. Most of the children of the original subjects did not reflect the self-hatred reported to be so prevalent among blacks.

Other social scientists have attempted to study the personality development of black children utilizing the in-depth interview and social class technique. Some of the more notable studies include *Negro Youth at the Crossways: Their Personality Development in the Middle States* by E. Franklin Frazier; Charles S. Johnson's *Growing Up in the Black Belt: Negro Youth in the Rural South*; as well as *Color and Human Nature: Negro Personality Development in a Northern City* by W. Lloyd Warner, Buford N. Junker, and Walter A. Adams.

Although self-concept development per se is not the major theme, the implications can be extrapolated. The culture and personality conceptualizations—i.e., that cultures exist on a psychologic and behavioral level, that learned cultural patterns are inherent in the formation of the ethnic personality, and that individuals acting in a culturally prescribed way influence the development of the growing black child—are embedded in the dynamic formulations of the studies presented.

What an individual thinks and feels about himself is mediated through his perception of what others think and feel about him. Within a given culture and society an individual's self-perception is mediated via his status and role, which are acquired or assigned to him by the dominant members of that society. In America the dominant group has been the white majority—the "WASP" and the Protestant ethic. The most amateur analyst can deduce the psychologic implications of being born black in the early part of this century and have at least a meager perception of the psychologic "bag" of a generation or so ago and the psychologic inheritance of today's black youth. Malcolm X put it very simply when he said that the worst crime the white man has committed has been to teach us to hate ourselves.[18] The psychosocial inheritance of the blackman today is summarized more sophisticatedly by Kardiner and Ovesey as

1. Degradation of self-esteem.
2. Destruction of cultural forms and forced adoption of foreign culture traits.
3. Destruction of the family unit with particular disparagement of the male.
4. Relative enhancement of the female status.
5. The destruction of social cohesion among Negroes by the inability to have their own culture.
6. The idealization of the white master but with this ideal was incorporated an object which was at once revered and hated.[19]

However, the decades of the 1950's and 1960's have seen another resurgence of black consciousness and black identity which points out still another existential dimension, and also dilemma, of being black. This is that for the black man the full responsibility of his existence in America has not rested with him, he has not been allowed to be responsible for his own individuality and selfness. The new pride in Africa's achievements, the interest in the discovery of ancestral roots, the assertion that "black is beautiful," and the demands for "black power" are cries for self-determination and self-definition. The new black consciousness with the impetus of the civil rights movement and the Black Muslim ideologies has helped the black world confront itself and deal with the meaning of its blackness; it has forced a confrontation between whites and blacks who would deny the harsh reality of 20th century racism and wallow in the sanguine unreality of the "American Dream." If it is true that the relationship between the individual and the culture of his society is a reciprocal one in that he is both shaped by it and in turn contributes to its shaping, then there is nowhere a more vivid example of this truism than in the history of the American black. Indeed the blackman himself has become the focus of major changes in American society—witness the Supreme Court decision of May 17, 1954, and the subsequent impact.

Yet in spite of the changes in American society that black awareness has brought, as C. Vann Woodward points out, "There are, unhappily, less desirable consequences conceivable for the preoccupation with Africa as a clue to racial identity. For in the hands of nationalist cults, it can readily become a mystique of skin color and exclusiveness, of alienation and withdrawal."[20]

The new black consciousness has brought group solidarity and group identity by rejection of the white devil, but it has not helped the black man confront the other internal selves within the black body. In some instances the emphasis on black consciousness has led to a fragmentation of the self or a denial of the other selves and needs that exist in the total black individual. In this context we are speaking of the Eriksonian "core of that inner unification . . . an experience of an increased unity of the physical and mental, moral and sensual selves, and of a oneness in the way one experiences oneself and the way others seem to experience us."[21] This is an individual task—an individual journey in the words of the old spiritual: "You must walk this lonesome journey. You have to walk it by yourself for nobody else can walk it for you; you'll have to walk it by yourself."

In essence being black is not the sum total of an individual's self. The exploration of the other aspects of the self is a task that must ultimately be accomplished by the individual if he is to attain that "core of inner unification" which can only be achieved through a unity of personal and cultural identity.

> . . . But we can also see that this is a matter of growth, both personal and communal. For a mature psychosocial identity presupposes a community of people whose traditional values become significant to the growing person even as his growth and his gifts assume relevance for them. More 'roles' which can be 'played' interchangeably are not sufficient; only an integration of roles which foster individual vitality within a vital trend in the existing or developing social order can support identities.[22]

SELF-CONCEPT RESEARCH: A REVIEW OF THE LITERATURE

The field of psychology has witnessed the development of a variety of methods to measure the self-concept. Children's ideas and attitudes regarding themselves have been studied by records of what young children say about themselves while doing various tasks, or in informal interviews, projective procedures, brief written compositions, and elaborate inventories or tests. One widely used scale is the Tennessee Self-Concept Scale, in which a phenomenologic system was devised based on what people had said about themselves. The statements were arranged in a classification system in terms of how the individual perceives himself in a two-dimensional 3-by-5 scheme.[23]

For instance, an individual may perceive himself in terms of (1) identity, what he is; (2) self-satisfaction, how he feels about himself; and (3) behavior, what he does. Within each of these three major categories an individual may describe (a) his physical self, (b) his moral-ethical self, (c) his personal self, (d) his family self, (e) his social self.

Although such an instrument may seem more pedagogic and rhetorical than real, it does help to form a framework by which one can begin to look at the particular aspects by which an individual forms a general conceptualization of who he is in the external world of his environment and in the internal world that consists of his own mental image of himself. It is an attempt to look at how an individual perceives himself in the totality of his existence. Many similar scales have been devised in an attempt to more objectively and succinctly analyze the conceptualizations of the individual.

We shall not attempt here to give a critique of the various instruments used to assess self-concept, but some of the serious shortcomings have been: (1) the results do not in themselves show how candid or forthright persons are in rating themselves; (2) there are inevitable discrepancies between the "real" and "ideal" self and there are many variables involved in that discrepancy; (3) many of the ideas and attitudes children have with regard to themselves are beyond the reach of measures that tell how true or how realistic these attitudes are. Then, too, many of the original self-concept scales and personality tests which evaluate self-concept were not standardized on population samples that included black children or adults.

In spite of the chance of inaccuracy of self-perception as determined by objective instruments, we shall review very briefly some of the more pertinent research on self-concept and self-perception in black children. We shall concentrate on those studies that deal with (1) comparative studies of self-concept in black and white children; (2) clinical studies dealing with identity in black children; and (3) the development of race awareness and racial preference.

COMPARATIVE STUDIES OF SELF-CONCEPT IN BLACK AND WHITE CHILDREN

Self-concept studies comparing blacks and whites done during the period 1943-1958 showed that the differences were marked, with self-concept being less adequate in blacks.[24] Many more recent studies of racial comparisons, utilizing a variety of measures, also support the earlier findings that blacks have more negative self-concept.[25] Many have focused primarily on children, with the findings being very similar to those reported for adults.

The Minnesota Multiphasic Personality Inventory was given to black and white ninth-graders in an integrated school.[26] The black students tended to have more serious difficulty than white students. In another study the MMPI was given to black and white senior students from segregated schools.[27] The white students scored higher on the clinical scales than did the black students, again indicating more psychologic problems among black children.

Gibbey and Gabler investigated self-concept in black and white sixth-graders by using self-ratings of intelligence.[28] Each subject was asked to make judgments as to how intelligent he believed himself to be; how intelligent he believed his parents, teachers, and friends believed him to be; and how intelligent he would like to be. Black children achieved significantly greater discrepancies between their actual IQ scores and their ratings on the self-scale and had higher levels of aspirations and higher verbalized ambitions than the whites. The investigators concluded that the hypothesis of the damaged self-percept of black children was supported by their data because the white children tended to see themselves more accurately and realistically, while the black children tended to overrate their intellectual abilities. They further concluded that the self-concepts developed by black children as a result of caste sanctions impinge on the development of intellectual abilities.

Needless to say, in this study the measures used were not specific enough for actual assessment of self-concept in black children from their intellectual assessment. The difference between a child's IQ test score and how intelligent or capable he may think he is and then what he aspires to be may call upon variables that cannot be assessed by paper and pencil inventories.

> After all, an intelligence test is a middle-class, white man's instrument; it is a device whites use to prove their capabilities and get ahead in the white world. Achieving a high test score does not have the same meaning for a lower status Negro child, and it may even carry a definite connotation of personal threat. In this sense, scoring low on intelligence measures may for some talented Negro children be a rational response to perceived danger.[29]

Byars and Williams attempted to study the self-concept of black adolescents in a period of increasing social and academic integration.[30] The Tennessee Self-Concept Scale utilized in the study reported in this book was given to 134 black and 176 white senior high-school students. On 12 of the 17 self-evaluation dimensions the black students obtained scores significantly below those of white students; and on all 17 scales the black students obtained mean scores below the corresponding normative means. They found that the black students were low in self-confidence, defensive in self-descriptions, confused concerning self-identity and similar in performance to neurotic and psychotic people. Thirty-five of their 134 black students were in desegregated schools; however, those black students attending desegregated schools did not differ significantly from those in segregated schools. The study was conducted in a rural or small urban Southern community. The investigators concluded that the emphasis of the civil rights movement on pride and self-respect may have accounted for the defensiveness seen in the responses of the black students. They felt the refusal to admit derogatory self-perceptions was particularly pronounced among the black males, which had been noted in previous studies done by Radke, Sutherland and Rosenberg. The black females were more inclined to accept self-derogatory statements. They also noted that though there was no significant difference between the performance of black students in desegregated schools and those in the segregated schools those black students in recently desegregated schools showed some trend toward improvement in self-esteem. They concluded that it is difficult to upgrade academic achievement of black students without providing an atmosphere where they can discover and respect themselves.

A small matched study of 22 poor black and white New Haven boys during their last three years in high school showed that the black boys stabilized their identities prematurely, much earlier than the white boys. It was felt that because of this too rapid stabilization the self-images of black boys were not as strong and fully developed as they could have been. In fact, the self-image of the black boys was found to be quite negative in comparison to the self-images of the white boys. The study was conducted in a neighborhood setting using projective tests, interviews, and Q sort to measure self-perception. The conclusions drawn from the study were that for the white boys at least the formation of an identity or self-image is a progressive sort of activity, changing and constantly building through childhood and adolescence. This is not so with black boys. Using absolute standards of fullest development for psychic health the chances that black boys will have such health are substantially reduced. The diminished psychologic growth for the black boy was thought to be a probable consequence of decades of oppression.[31]

It is interesting to note, however, that a comparison of self-attitudes of eighth-grade Southern rural black and white students tends to contradict the pervasive assertion of the damaged self-percept of the black child. The eighth-grade black students in Baughman and Dahlstrom's study more frequently reported themselves as being popular with their peers, satisfied being the kind of person they were, and having a happier home life than that of the average child. Dahlstrom and Baughman admit that their methodology for assessing self-perception was neither comprehensive nor penetrating but conclude:

... clearly if the self concepts of these Negro children have been unduly damaged, this fact is not reflected in their interview statements about themselves nor in the educational and vocational aspirations which they report for themselves (and which they seem optimistic about realizing).[32]

Likewise, a more recent study by Simmons and Rosenberg of 1,900 children from grades 3 through 12 showed that black students had a higher self-esteem than white students, and that in secondary schools black students had higher self-esteem if they attended more segregated schools.[33]

There are many correlates of self-concept—age, sex, intelligence, achievement, race, socioeconomic status, peer relationships, and parental attitudes— and many more recent studies have demonstrated the importance of controlling for these variables.[34, 35, 36, 37] Many of these same studies, however, have focused primarily on the sociocultural determinants of low IQ scores and low self-esteem in disadvantaged school beginners. Such studies have added momentum to compensatory educational programs for "culturally deprived" children.

Although Rosenberg and Coopersmith have found that higher social class is directly related to favorableness of self-concept, the study of Soares and Soares shows that disadvantaged children do not necessarily reflect more negative self-perceptions or lower self-esteem than advantaged children.[38, 39, 40] A comparison of the self-perceptions of disadvantaged children with those of advantaged children in grades four through eight in a public school of a New England city indicated more positive self-images on all measures (self-concept, ideal concept, reflected-self-classmates, reflected-self-teacher, reflected-self-parent) for disadvantaged children over advantaged children. The disadvantaged children lived in low-rent tenements or subsidized housing. The ethnic composition was about two-thirds black and Puerto Rican and one-third white. The family incomes were less than $4,000 per year and many families received state aid or welfare funds. The children who were not disadvantaged came from a middle-class neighborhood in the same city. There was usually at least one adult working in a steady job or profession with an income of over $7,000 per year. The families of these students tended to live in one-family homes which they themselves owned. The ethnic makeup was about 90 percent white and 10 percent various minority groups.

In our most recent study of self-concept of white and black students, 157 white students and 149 black students in public junior high schools in a Northern city were given the Tennessee Self-Concept Scale. Both groups scored well below the normative mean for the Self-Concept Scale, indicating negative self-concept.[41] However, inasmuch as 50 percent of the black students were disadvantaged and 60 percent of the white students were advantaged, and there was no significant difference in mean total positive scores (both groups scoring below the normative mean), the assumption that higher socioeconomic status is directly related to favorableness of self-concept can be questioned. There may be other variables more directly correlated with positive self-concept than upper socioeconomic status. Also, it is important to know when a study was done and where; these are changing times and we are a heterogeneous country, which makes it necessary to consider regional variables.

There is still a great need for more hard data on the different kinds of life experiences that lead to different self-concept profiles on longitudinal studies, as well as a need for studies that focus on the development of healthy self-concepts in black children and the variables that operate to achieve such self-perception.

CLINICAL STUDIES CONCERNED WITH SELF-CONCEPT PROBLEMS IN BLACK CHILDREN

To begin with, there are very few clinical studies that deal with the emotionally disturbed black child and fewer still that deal with the problems of identity conflict in treatment. Some of the best clinical descriptions of emotionally disturbed black children are presented by Hertha Reise of the Educational Therapy Center in Richmond, Virginia, where there were 40 children in a day care treatment program, of whom 90 percent were blacks. The children ranged in age from 6 years to 17 years. In describing the children Dr. Reise writes:

> Furthermore, in my many years of work with the Negro child, I have not found "the Negro" in him. What I found was a greater despondency than in the white child, a deeper muteness when in a state of depression, also a deeper hopelessness that talking will not heal. . . . But all such more marked negative attitudes are not caused by any "Negro-ness" in these young people—it is generated by particularly damaging pressures and deprivations imposed on them as Negroes.[42]

If Dr. Reise means that being black does not make a black child a different species than a white child, and thereby a black child is susceptible to the pangs of human suffering, this is so. However, it is naive to deny that a black child in treatment has emotional problems that are due to the very fact of his Negroness. This thesis is more eloquently stated by Franz Fanon, a black psychiatrict from Algeria, and black American psychiatrists such as Pouisant, Spurlock, Gullattee, Pierce, Grier, and Cobbs, who are prepared to deal with the issue of blackness more directly.[43, 44, 45, 46, 47, 48, 49] Pierce deals with this issue very perceptively:

Now a minority person, of course, has many difficulties from a psychological viewpoint. The one which is probably the most oppressing is the fact that I don't believe that many Blacks can live a total of an hour of their conscious life without recognizing the fact of their blackness and being reminded of it in all sorts of ways. This takes a great deal of energy and a great deal of concern and it depletes a further resource that might possibly contribute more to the nation because every Black has to be hung up on these kinds of issues.[50]

A more realistic clinical view of the emotionally disturbed black child has been presented by other therapists. For example, Chetnick, Fleming, and Morris describe the effects of the distorted self-concept of two black children in a residential treatment center for 100 emotionally disturbed children of whom seven were black. The therapists felt that the distortions of the self-concept are seen in their daily behavior as well as in their treatment sessions. They describe and characterize the children's modes of reaction to this self-picture. The first is a period of hyper-race consciousness in which the children demonstrated special sensitivity, as if they expected constant blame for being black. The second period described is one of "color-blind-ness" in which the children try to deny any differences and try to be like any white child. The third period is one of loyalty conflict during which the child passes through an identity crisis. "The new 'good white' environment becomes symbolic of health while the old 'bad black' culture becomes pathology. It is as if the child were saying 'Each time I improve I get a little whiter.' "[51]

It has been the author's experience in treating emotionally disturbed black children that to deny the issue of blackness and to neglect to unravel the inherent problem of racial identity with a black child is to leave part of the therapeutic task undone. The role of the therapist must be to make the child aware of his own distorted self-image and to continue to evaluate the child's progress in the area of cultural identification as a part of the total treatment process which deals with many other aspects of the child's internal and external world. As clinicians involved in treatment of children, we must not fail to remember that children of minority groups are a special mental health risk. The Joint Commission on Mental Health for Children recognized that.

The mental health problems of minority group children are so severe that they warrant immediate and drastic attention. Only rarely does the child of an ethnic minority escape the damaging effects of racism. Often racism and poverty combine to cripple the minority group child in body, mind, and spirit.[52]

Spurlock enumerates the consequences of racism for both white and black children in the 1970's and very adequately reviewed previous studies done indicating the adverse psychologic effects of racism and discrimination on black children in this country.[53] She makes special reference to Kenneth Clark's studies which we will review in subsequent chapters.[54]

According to Ausubel, healthy ego development must be preceded by orderly development in a child's self-concept, self-attitudes, motives, aspirations, and sources of self-esteem.[55] The fact that very early in life the black child learns to depreciate his skin color and resent identifying with his own racial group results in ego deflation. Consequently, it is difficult for black children to identify with their parents and to obtain from such identification the status that provides the basis for self-esteem during childhood. Gregor and Armstrong observed the behavior of black children and concluded that those who were exposed to protracted contacts with whites during critical phases of ego development showed many similarities to the delusional system of adult black schizophrenics: "This disposition to such delusional defenses is undoubtedly preconditioned by circumstances attending primary socialization when the black child fails to establish an adequate identity relationship with the adult members of his family."[56]

Psychiatric experiences show that most of the personality disturbances of children come from their relationship with parents or parent substitutes and siblings. It is in the process of social interaction in this primary group that a child forms his first or basic conception of himself. In this respect, black children are no exception. However, where black children do differ in the development of an adequate self-system the effect is due to the peculiar social position their parents occupy in this society which interferes with this very basic primary social interaction. Hence, a study of the personality problems of black children entails an enquiry into the obstacles in the development of this basic parent-child relationship. We propose that the major obstacle to adequate personality development and adequate parenting for black children is white racism with the sociologic concomitances of poverty and family instability.

> White racism is not only the biggest problem in America, but, also, the biggest mental health and public health problem. A public health problem is one which meets these four criteria: It affects masses of people; it costs a great deal of money to eradicate; it is one which can't be treated on a one-to-one basis; and it is one which causes chronic, sustained disability.[57]

RACE AWARENESS AND RACIAL PREFERENCE

It seems fitting that this review of the literature on self-concept and race awareness begin with a review of Clark's 1939 study on the development of consciousness of self in black preschool children.[58] The study demonstrated that the process of racial identification begins very early in the preschool years. It was one of the first empirical studies to focus on the fact that young black children are very aware of race. The Clarks' study was a significant beginning in the research awareness of the psychologic development of black children.

Clark then reported on his comparative study on racial preference and identification between black children in a biracial nursery school and those in a black nursery school.[59] He found that 71 percent of the black children in the biracial school made negative responses to a colored doll. In the black nursery school, only 49 percent of the black children made a similar response. Clark concluded that black children in a racially insulated school situation had a more substantial sense of self than those in a biracial situation. Not only did this study point out the early development of race awareness, but it also underscored the following: (1) racial preference in young black children is a function of their social and racial context; (2) black children in racially insulated (21 percent) and biracial settings (51 percent) make an outgroup identification.

Goodman's work supported Clark's findings.[60] Her study setting was a biracial nursery school and both the white and black children expressed negative feelings toward "Negroness." Indeed, the black children not only agreed that whites were "prettier," "nicer," and more desirable playmates, but also felt that blacks were "dirty," "ugly," and, in general, undesirable. Black children also assessed their color as lighter than it was and made up stories to explain their dark skins; e.g., some thought that they would outgrow it or that it could be washed out. Goodman concluded that Negro children not yet five years old sensed that they were "marked" and "grow uneasy."

Morland's work confirmed findings in the previous studies mentioned above, but also noted an increased rate of growth of racial awareness at about four years of age.[61] A second study by the same investigator confirmed the outgroup identification in black children but also noted that Southern black children were least likely to identify with or prefer their race, and that Southern white children had the highest racial recognition ability.[62] These findings suggest that regional variables involving prevailing racial attitudes within a community may be brought to bear on the degree of racial awareness in children.

There are numerous more recent studies that demonstrate that the majority of black preschoolers express a preference for light-skinned over dark-skinned figures in various choice situations.[63] The Greenwald and Oppenheim study demonstrates, however, that the inclusion of an intermediate mulatto alternative doll or figure reduces black children's misidentification significantly.[64] When asked which doll looked like them, only 13 percent of the black children misidentified themselves while 44 percent of the white children misidentified themselves. We know that during the preschool years, when awareness of race is developing, children, white and black, are also learning the evaluative meaning of black as "bad" and white as "good." This kind of negative color connotation was noted in Goodman's study in 1952, and in spite of the "black is beautiful" theme the same learned negative meaning of black is still perpetuated in many instances seventeen years later as evidenced by the data from Renniger and Williams[65] as well as from Greenwald and Oppenheim. By the same token, Butts noted that those black children who perceived themselves less accurately in terms of skin color also revealed low self-esteem.[66] From the data presented thus far it would appear that the combination of early racial awareness, outgroup identification, misidentification, and negative learned meaning of black would have serious implications in the development of self-perception and self-concept in black children.

It is interesting to note that although Clark's study on racial preference and identification between black children in a biracial setting and black children in a black setting showed that the black children in a racially insulated school had a more substantial sense of self than those in a biracial setting, Ausubel concluded that black children who attended schools with a heterogenous social and racial population were in a more favorable developmental situation.[67] This diversity of opinion in terms of the psychologic effects of school racial settings is still to be argued.

In a preliminary study in 1969 by Spurlock, whose purpose was to determine if black children (all younger than 12) felt more positively about their color since the growing emphasis on black consciousness, the data suggest that socioeconomic issues and family stability are major factors in determining racial preference.[68] Black children from stable families appeared to feel more comfortable about their racial identity than did children from unstable backgrounds.

It becomes obvious that there is a desperate need for more longitudinal controlled studies in this area to assess the effects of sociopolitical and regional factors as well as class status, parental attitudes, and child-rearing attitudes on the development of racial identity.

There is a paucity of information on race awareness and racial preference among children of interracial marriages, and very few studies have been done concerning racial preferences among black children who have been adopted by white families. Teicher's observations on identity problems in children of black-white marriages should be mentioned.[69] He felt that for the mulatto child there is likely to be resentment of both parents, inability to identify with either, and resentment of siblings whose racial characteristics are different. His preliminary study showed that in general the greater a child's problem of racial identification, the greater was his problem of sexual identification. It would seem, however, that the ability of a child from an interracial marriage to accept his identity would be dependent upon the degree of ambivalence one or both parents have concerning the marriage. Needless to say, this whole area needs more definitive research.

THE BLACK CHILD, HIS FAMILY AND HIS SELF-CONCEPT

There has been a great deal written about the black family and, indeed, there has been some heated discussion generated over the issue. The brief discussion here will concentrate on the psychodynamics of the early interaction between the black child and his mother as well as socioeconomic factors and the subsequent implications of both on the development of self-concept.

The emotional and attitudinal climate into which a child is born has its beginnings long before his arrival. The mother's fantasies about babies and motherhood, the marital relationship, the experience of the mother during pregnancy, labor, and delivery all play a role in her functioning as a mother. Out of the interaction between the mother and infant, the ego and mental organization of the infant begin to develop. By the end of the first 18 months or so the infant normally should have acquired a feeling of trust as a result of his experience with his mother. When one starts to understand the early mother-child interaction in black families, it is wise to consider some variables that may have a profound effect on whatever psychodynamic factors may be operating.

The Joint Commission on Mental Health of Children has already pointed out the strong link between poverty and minority ethnic status in this country. Powell goes on to ask pertinent questions about this persistent correlation: "What's wrong with a country in which twice as many black babies die in infancy, four times as many black mothers die in childbirth, and twice as many of our black men die between the ages of 40 and 50 as white men?"[70] Most certainly these kinds of statistics would contribute significantly to the obstacles in adequate development of parent-child relationships in black families.

The modern family is subjected to unique stresses and strains, but even when socioeconomic status is held constant, the stresses imposed upon a black family are qualitatively different from those in a white family in a number of ways. The black family is much more likely than the white family to be on the lowest economic rung and a small percentage of black families is more than one generation removed from abject poverty. This means that most black children inherit a family that is economically insecure. It is well documented that the black slum child is far more liable to experience an unstable home than a white slum child.[71] Thus the emotional and attitudinal climate into which a black child is born may be one of a deeply ingrained impoverishment.

Children and young people who grow up in a community in which a large proportion of families have no father in the home, a community in which 40 percent of the men and 47 percent of the women aged 14 or over are unmarried, find it difficult, if not almost impossible, to know what an "adequate" family is like. The cycle of family instability continues uninterrupted.[72]

The impact of family instability makes it difficult for those involved in the rearing of children to accomplish the task of complementing and supplementing the ego of the child. Without this kind of nurturance, the feeling of trust referred to in previous paragraphs, as well as subsequent psychologic landmarks, may not be accomplished by the child. Thus, the self that a black child may experience is a self that may have many unmet dependency needs, a self that may have little faith that his needs will be met, a self that may be fearful of making commitments to any relationship. Such a child will be more susceptible to aggression, violence, and delinquency or to apathy and depression. Impoverished circumstances may make it more difficult for the child to identify with his parents and to obtain from such identification the status that provides the basis for self-esteem during childhood.

However, many black children do survive and do "overcome." More recently, many social scientists are taking a second look at the family life of black people and are presenting an updated view of the black family. In a volume edited by Willie many aspects of black families are presented, their strengths and their weaknesses.[73] Likewise, Billingsley presents data that contravene the Moynihan report of pervasive social disorganization in lower-class black families as well as document many different life styles of black families.[74] This is not to deny or to overlook the many problems that do exist, but social scientists and clinicians would do well to investigate coping mechanisms in the face of extreme adversity in order to plan more realistic programs for black children.

SUMMARY

The study of self-concept development in children concerns itself with the emotional and cognitive development of the child. It entails understanding how a child learns about himself, what he thinks about himself, and how he feels about himself. Although identity (what an individual is) is an important part of self-concept development, conceptualization of the self includes other aspects such as self-satisfaction (how an individual feels about himself) and behavior (what an individual does).

The majority of the research findings stated in these paragraphs suggest that (1) for the vast majority of black children self-concept development is characterized by serious deficiencies which in turn lead to a variety of sustained disabilities and (2) for a small minority of black children increased family stability, educational level of parents, and higher socioeconomic status may offset the effects of second-class citizenship, with subsequent healthy self-concept development. Other, more recent studies indicate that the damaged self-percept of the black child may be changing. Pierce notes that there is a new mood in Black America which is marked by a reduction of self-abasement and corollary feelings of worthlessness and uselessness; black people no longer believe the negative attitudes about themselves that white America has perpetrated.[75]

Do black children today feel more negative or more positive about themselves? In the face of persistent racism and the adversity of poverty how can we tell?

This study will try to address itself to these questions.

1. Strunk, O. Attitudes toward one's name and one's self. Journal of Individual Psychology, 14:64-67, 1958.
2. Silberman, C.E. Crisis in Black and White. New York, Vintage Books, 1965, p. 111.
3. Erikson, E. Childhood and Society. New York, W.W. Norton and Co., 2nd ed., 1963.
4. Erikson, E. Identity, Youth and Crisis. New York, W.W. Norton and Co., 1968, pp. 15-43.
5. Allport, G.W. The evolving sense of self. *In* Pattern and Growth in Personality. New York, Holt, Rinehart, and Winston, 1963, p. 111.
6. The data reported here are the results of a pilot study done by the author in Nashville, Tennessee, in 1959.
7. Horowitz, E. Spatial localization of the self. Journal of Social Psychology, 6:379-387, 1935.
8. Dixon, J.C. Development of self-recognition. Journal of Genetic Psychology, 91:251-256, 1957.
9. Lasso, R. Images du corps et conscience de soi. Enfance I, pp. 29-43, 1948.
10. Allport, G. Op. cit., pp. 120-127.
11. Wolman, B., ed. Handbook of Clinical Psychology. New York, McGraw-Hill Inc., 1965, pp. 364-366.
12. Khon, A.R. Self-evaluation as related to evaluations by parents and peers at pre-adolescence and adolescence. Dissertation Abstracts, 22(5) 1716-1717, 1961.
13. Clausen, J.A., and Williams, J.R. Sociological correlates of child behavior. Child Psychology: The 62nd Yearbook of the National Society for the Study of Education. Chicago, University of Chicago Press, 1963, pp. 62-107.
14. Mead, G.H. Mind, Self and Society. Chicago, University of Chicago Press, 1934.
15. Linton, R. Culture and Mental Disorders. Springfield, Ill., Charles C Thomas, 1956, p. 10.
16. Davis, A., and Dollard J. Children of Bondage: The Personality Development of Negro Youth in the Urban South. New York, Harper and Row, 1964, p. xix.
17. Rohner, J.H., and Edmonson, M.S. The Eighth Generation, New York, Harper, 1960.
18. Quoted in Crisis in Black and White. Op. cit., p. 68.
19. Kardiner A., and Ovesey L. The Mark of Oppression: Explorations in the Personality of the American Negro. Cleveland, World Publishing Co., 1968, p. 47.
20. Woodward, C.V. Clio with Soul. *In* Black Studies, Myths and Realities. A Philip Randolph Educational Fund, September, 1969, p. 25.
21. Erikson, E. The concept of identity. Daedalus. The American Academy of Arts and Sciences, Winter, 1966, pp. 150-151.

22. Ibid., p. 149.

23. Fitts, W. Tennessee Self-Concept Scale Manual, Box 6184 Acklen Station, Nashville, Tennessee.

24. Dreger, R.M., and Miller, K.S. Comparative psychological studies of Negroes and whites in the United States. Psychological Bulletin, 1960, 57:361-402.

25. Dreger, R.M., and Miller, K.S. Comparative psychological studies of Negroes and whites in the United States: 1959-1965. Psychological Bulletin Monograph Supplement, Vol. 70, No. 3, Part 2, 1968.

26. Ball, J.C. Comparison of MMPI profile of differences among Negro-white adolescents. Journal of Clinical Psychology, 1960, 16:304-307.

27. McDonald, R.L., and Gynther, M.D. MMPI differences associated with sex, race, and class in two adolescent samples. Journal of Consulting Psychology, 1963, 27:112-116.

28. Gibby, R.J., and Gabler, R. The self-concept of Negro and white children. Journal of Clinical Psychology, 1967, 23:144-150.

29. Pettigrew, T.S. A Profile of the Negro American. Princeton, N.J. Princeton University Press, 1964, p. 115.

30. Williams, R.L., and Byars H. Negro self-esteem in a transitional society. Personnel and Guidance Journal, 47:120-125, 1968.

31. Black identity formation. Reports on Higher Education. June 1970, p. 5: (summary of a study done by Stuart T. Hauser, M.D., Harvard).

32. Baugham, E.E., and Dahlstrom, W.G. Negro and White Children: A Psychological Study in the Rural South. New York, Academic Press, 1968, p. 462.

33. Personal communication from Dr. Robert Simmons, Department of Sociology, University of Minnesota. Co-investigator is Dr. Morris Rosenberg of NIMH.

34. Bledsoe, J.C., and Garrison, K.C. The self-concepts of elementary school children in relation to their academic achievement, intelligence, interest, and manifest anxiety. Research Project No. 1008, 1962, U.S. Office of HEW, Washington, D.C.

35. Henton, C.L., and Johnson, E.E. Relationship between self-concepts of Negro elementary school children and their academic achievement, intelligence, interests, and manifest anxiety. Comparative Research Project No. 1592, 1964, U.S. Office of Education, Washington, D.C.

36. McDonald, R.L. Effects of sex, race, and class on self, ideal self and parental ratings in southern adolescents. Perceptual Motor Skills, 1968, 27:15-25.

37. Long, B.H., and Henderson, E.H. Self-concept of disadvantaged school beginners. Journal of General Psychology, 1968, 113:41-51.

38. Coopersmith, S. The Antecedents of Self-Esteem. San Francisco, W.H. Freeman and Co., 1967.

39. Rosenberg, M. Society and the Adolescent Self-Image. Princeton, N.J., Princeton University Press, 1965.

40. Soares, A.T., and Soares, L.M. Self-perceptions of culturally disadvantaged children. American Educational Research Journal, Vol. 6 No. 1, 1969, pp. 31-45.

41. Powell, G.J. Self-concept in white and black children. Paper presented at the Conference on Racism and Mental Health, Department of Sociology, Syracuse University, Syracuse, N.Y., April 19, 1971.

42. Reise, H. Heal the Hurt Child. Chicago, University of Chicago Press, 1962, p. xiii.

43. Fanon, F. Wretched of the Earth. New York, Grove Press, Inc., 1966.

44. Pouisant, A.F. A Negro psychiatrist explains the Negro psyche. New York Times Magazine, pp. 52-58, August 20, 1967.

45. Spurlock, J. Consequences of racism for children. Paper presented at the Conference on Racism and Mental Health at Syracuse University, Syracuse, N.Y., April 19, 1971.

46. Gullatee, A. The Negro psyche: Fact, fiction, and fantasy. Journal of the National Medical Association. 61 (March, 1969):119-129.

47. Pierce, C. The effects of racism. Presented at AMA 15th Annual Conference of State Mental Health Representatives, Chicago, March 14-15, 1969.

48. Grier, W.H. Some special effects of Negroness on the oedipal conflict. Journal of the National Medical Association, 58(November 1966):416-418.

49. Grier, W.H., and Cobbs, P.M. Black Rage. New York, Basic Books, 1968.

50. Pierce. Op. cit., 1969.

51. Chetnick, M., Fleming, E., Morris, T.M., and McCoy, J.W. A quest for identity: Treatment of disturbed Negro children in a predominantly white treatment center. American Journal of Orthopsychiatry 37:71-77, Jan, 1967.

52. Report of the Joint Commission of Mental Health of Children. Crisis in Child Mental Health: Challenge for the 1970's. New York, Harper and Row, 1970, pp. 215-216.

53. Spurlock. Op. cit., 1971.

54. Clark, K. Prejudice and Your Child, 2nd ed. Boston, Beacon Press, 1963. Book version of the manuscript, Effect of Prejudice and Discrimination on Personality Development, prepared by Dr. Clark for the Mid-century White House Conference on Children and Youth, 1950.

55. Ausubel, D.P. Ego development among segregated Negro children. Mental Hygiene, 42:362-369, 1958.

56. Armstrong, C.P., and Gregor, A.J. Integrated schools and Negro character development: Some considerations of the possible effects. Psychiatry 27, February, 1964, p. 69.

57. Pierce, C. White racism. Journal of the American Orthopsychiatric Association, 39(4), July, 1969, p. 553.

58. Clark, K.B., and Clark, M.K. The development of consciousness of self and the emergence of racial identification in Negro preschool children. Journal of Social Psychology, 10:591-599, 1939.

59. Clark, K.B., and Clark, M.K. Racial identification and preference in Negro children. *In* Readings in Social Psychology, Eleanor Maccoby, ed. New York, Holt, Rinehart, and Winston, 1959.

60. Goodman, M.E. Race Awareness in Young Children. Cambridge, Addison-Wesley Press, 1952.

61. Morland, J.K. Racial recognition by nursery school children in Lynchburg, Va. Social Forces, 1958, 37:132-137.

62. Morland, J.K. A comparison of race awareness of Northern and Southern children. American Journal of Orthopsychiatry, 1966, 36:22-31.

63. Dreger and Miller. Op. cit., 1968.

64. Greenwald, H.J., and Oppenheim, D. Reported magnitude of self-misidentification among Negro children: Artifact. Journal of Personality and Social Psychology, 1968. 81:49-52.

65. Renninger, C.A., and Williams, J.C. Black and white color connotations and racial awareness in pre-school children. Perceptual Motor Skills, 1966, 22:771-785.

66. Butts, H.F. Skin color perception and self-esteem. Journal of Negro Education, 1963, 32:122-128.

67. Ausubel. Op. cit., 1958.

68. Spurlock, J. The problems of identification in young black children—static or changing. Read at the 74th Annual Meeting of the National Medical Association in San Francisco, August, 1969.

69. Teicher, J.D. Some observations on identity problems in children of Negro-white marriages. Journal of Nervous and Mental Disease, March, 1968, 146:249-256.

70. Powell, R.N. Research for social change. Paper presented at the 15th Annual Student Research Day Lecture, Nashville, Meharry Medical College, April 21, 1971.

71. Harrington, M. The Other American: Poverty in the United States. New York, The Macmillan Company, 1963.

72. Clark, K.B. Dark Ghetto: Dilemmas of Social Power. Harper Torchbooks, Harper and Row Publishers, Inc., 1967, p. 48.
73. Willie, C.V., ed. The Family Life of Black People. Columbus, Ohio, Charles E. Merrill Books, Inc., 1970.
74. Billingsley, A. Black Families in White America. Englewood, N.J., Prentice-Hall, 1968.
75. Pierce. Op. cit. 1969.

4

The Problem and the Purpose: The Hypotheses and Methodology of the Study on the Effects of School Desegregation on Self-Concept

THE HYPOTHESES OF THE STUDY

In *McLaurin* v. *Oklahoma State Regents*, supra, the Court in requiring that a Negro admitted to a white graduate school be treated like all other students, again resorted to intangible considerations: " . . . his ability to study, to engage in discussions and exchange views with other students, and, in general, to learn his profession." Such considerations apply with added force to children in grade and high schools. To separate them from others of similar age and qualifications solely because of race generates a feeling of inferiority as to their status in the community that may effect their hearts and minds in a way unlikely ever to be undone.[1]

The concept of inequality of separate school facilities for black children set forth in the above quotation from the text of the May 17, 1954, decision by Chief Justice Warren of the U.S. Supreme Court referred not only to the legal inequities, but also to the educational and psychologic inequities that accrue to black children because of segregated schools. Indeed, it is well known that the court was influenced in making its momentous decision by the testimony of and the carefully prepared appendix to the appellant's brief by noted social scientists and social psychologists who cited evidence regarding the adverse psychologic consequences on black children in segregated school facilities. We shall review this data in detail in a subsequent chapter. Indeed, as noted in Chapter 2 of this book, the Kansas court in deciding the original case of *Brown* v. *Board of Education* in Topeka made an elaborate reference to the psychologic damage to black children as a result of segregated schools. A reference to this was made by Justice Warren in the text of his speech:

Segregation of white and colored children in public schools has a detrimental
effect upon the colored children. The impact is greater when it has the sanction
of the law; for the policy of separating the races is usually interpreted as denoting the inferiority of the Negro group. A sense of inferiority affects the
motivation of a child to learn. Segregation with the sanction of the law, therefore, has a tendency to retard the educational and mental development of Negro
children and to deprive them of some of the benefits they would receive in a
racially integrated school system.[2]

The U.S. Supreme Court and the Kansas court both make reference to
"feelings of inferiority" engendered in black children because of segregated
schools and, indeed, the studies of psychologists and social scientists stressed
that black children experienced low self-esteem as well as self-hatred as a
result of discrimination, prejudice, and segregation.[3, 4, 5] The inference one
derives from these studies and the Court's statement is that, inasmuch as
segregation of black children in public schools leads to low self-esteem and
perpetuates self-hatred, the desegregation of public schools will lead to
higher self-esteem and help affect the self-hatred that accrues as a result of
segregation. Thus, the first hypothesis of this study is that as a result of
school desegregation, the self-concepts of black children in those states
where de jure segregation existed will have improved.

The second hypothesis is that, in fact, in the South black students in
desegregated schools will have higher self-concept scores on a standardized
self-concept scale than black students in segregated or predominantly black
schools.

Adolescence in American society has always been a time of breaking
away from or joining with established modes of living. During this time of
life the adolescent is extra-sensitive to inner psychic pressures or outer en-
vironmental pressures. His reaction to these pressures will have much to do
with shaping his adult ego-identity and his future goals. Most certainly the
sociocultural milieu to which the adolescent is exposed influences his self-
concept development which entails understanding how and what he learns
about himself, what he thinks about himself, and how he feels about himself.
Coopersmith has noted that in studying the children of preadolescent age the
likelihood that family experiences will be an important source of self-esteem
is very high.[6] Preadolescent children are more highly dependent upon their
parents and are very likely to use the family context with its values to judge
their own worth, much more so than adolescents. Coopersmith also noted
that preadolescents make little distinction about self-worth in different areas
of experience, rather such distinctions are made within the general appraisal
of self-worth. For the adolescent, however, there is a push-pull phenomenon
in which his self-perception may vary from area to area depending upon his
experiences in the outside world. His entire system of self-appraisal is in flux;

thus, he will be more susceptible to changes in the environment, especially political, social, and cultural changes. In his struggle for independence he will struggle to evaluate and even to incorporate some of the changing values he is encountering.

The winds of change are blowing particularly hard in the South, shaking the roots of old mores and laws almost out of their soil, leaving them exposed and tender. Southern adolescents as they struggle for the Eriksonian core of "inner unification" are perhaps the most vulnerable to these changes. There is a new consciousness evolving from these changes, especially for black people who are becoming more aware of their identity and potential as Black Americans.

This thesis has been articulated by Pierce[7] and we have alluded to it in our review of self-concept development in black children. Hence, our third hypothesis, and, indeed, our justification for testing young adolescents is that in spite of the concept of the damaged self-percept of the black child, pervasive throughout the literature even during the time of increased civil rights activities in the South during the 1960s[8] the self-concept of Southern black adolescents as compared with white adolescents will have improved.

In an effort to clarify how school desegregation should be implemented, a group of social scientists headed by Kenneth Clark reviewed the available data on the effects of desegregation throughout the country. This data was presented to the Supreme Court before their implementation decision of May 30, 1955.[9] That document proceded to outline clearly how desegregation could be implemented with the best opportunity for success and minimal turmoil. Hence, our fourth and final hypothesis is that where school desegregation was implemented as suggested by the social scientists (and we shall review that data in a subsequent chapter) the black adolescents will have higher self-concepts than in areas in which these guidelines were ignored. Basic to that hypothesis is the assumption that the changing social and political milieu in the South is affecting self-concept development for white and black children and that the amount and degree of self-concept change will not only be dependent on the degree of family stability and educational, occupational, and economic status of parents, but will also be dependent on the amount, degree, and kind of social, cultural, and political change within the community.

METHODOLOGY

Self-concept research has grown out of a trend in modern personality theory that the ways in which man perceives himself and how he evaluates what he perceives are determinants of individual personality. The use of such constructs demands the development of adequate methods of measuring them. The majority of self-concept studies have utilized some kind of self-report instrument. However, it is well known that data from such instruments are subject to the influence of many variables other than those the researcher wishes to measure.[10] There are subject variables and situational variables, which contribute significantly to the responses an individual subject will make; this is as true with self-concept testing as it is with other kinds of psychologic testing.

The data derived from a self-concept scale can only be as reliable as the instrument used to assess self-concept. Some of the deficiencies in self-concept testing have been reviewed in the previous chapter. For purposes of this study several self-concept scales were reviewed prior to final selection of the scale used.

SELECTION OF INSTRUMENTS AND TECHNIQUES USED IN TESTING

The self-concept scale used in this study was the Tennessee Self-Concept Scale developed by William Fitts.[11] This scale was chosen because it has been used as a research instrument in far more studies than any other self-concept scale available. It was originally standardized on Southern whites and blacks from 12 years of age to 68,[12] although since 1962 the normative means have been standardized on a national sample with various racial and age groups (as young as 12 years old) represented with equal numbers from both sexes. The scale, which contains 100 items, was devised on a phenomenologic system and the subject is asked to rate himself in terms of (1) what he is (identity); (2) how he feels about himself (self-satisfaction); and (3) what he does (behavior). Within these dimensions he also rates (a) his physical self, (b) his moral ethical self, (c) his personal self, (d) his family self, and (e) his social self. Ten of the items are taken from the Lie Scale of the Minnesota Multiphasic Personality Inventory and make up the self-criticism score of the scale. The ten items are mildly derogatory statements about the self which most people admit to be true about themselves, thus they are designed to measure the tendency of a subject to bias responses in a favorable direction.

In addition to the self-criticism score, there is the total positive score which is the most important score on the scale. It reflects the overall level of self-esteem. The respondents with high scores tend to like themselves and feel that they are persons of value and worth. Those with low scores are doubtful about their own worth and have little faith or confidence in themselves. However, a high total positive score becomes suspect if the self-criticism score is low indicating some defensiveness. The three subscores, identity, self-satisfaction, and behavior, represent an internal frame of reference within which the respondent is describing himself. When the three subscores are added, the sum represents the total positive score.

Within each of the three categories there are statements referring to what the individual thinks of himself physically, morally, socially, personally, and in regard to his family. These five subdivisions within each of the three categories represent the external frame of reference within which the respondent is describing himself.

The variability score is a measure of the amount of consistency from one area of self-perception to another. High scores mean that the subject is quite variable in this respect, but low scores, if below the first percentile, indicate low variability but also rigidity. The distribution score represents the way the respondent distributes his answers among the five available choices in responding to the items on the scale. It is also a measure of certainty about the self-perception. High scores mean that the individual is very definite and certain about how he sees himself; low scores, the reverse.

A small pilot study was conducted on seventh-, eighth-, and ninth-graders in a Southern community to assess the suitability in terms of reading ability and comprehension of the test items.[13] The average student could finish the test in less than 30 minutes with few questions regarding vocabulary.

The second instrument used was a questionnaire devised to assess the socioeconomic status, occupational and educational level of the parents, as well as degree of family stability. Sentence-completion items were also used to assess attitudes toward school, attitudes toward self, and aspirational levels. Other items were used to determine if the subject was experiencing any gross emotional problems.

In addition to the Tennessee Self-Concept Scale (TSCS) and the Powell-Fuller Questionnaire, interviews were conducted in order to assess the social and political climate at the time of the testing, as well as prevailing racial attitudes. Interviews were obtained with the faculty at each school, and, whenever possible, with school administrators in the superintendent's office or with members of the boards of education. Interviews were also conducted with people in the white and black communities—housewives, store clerks, people on the street, as well as designated community leaders. Students and parents at the participating schools were not interviewed. Although racial attitudes were obtained from the interviews, it should be noted that there were no questions regarding race or racial attitudes on the TSCS or on the questionnaire, both of which were coded prior to the testing indicating race, sex, and type of school. The scales were passed out by members of the research team who, in desegregated schools, made the judgment regarding race of the student. Wherever there was some doubt, confirmation of racial identity was made after the testing by a member of the faculty who would know. If a school was all white, then a white investigator did the testing. If a school was completely black, then a black investigator did the testing. At mixed schools white and black investigators did the testing. Likewise, in the interviews with whites a white interviewer was used, and with blacks a black interviewer was used.

At each school prior to the administration of the scales the individual from the research team administering the test introduced himself and stated the purpose of the test. The students were told that the papers given to them were not part of a school examination, that they would not receive grades, nor would their teachers or parents see their papers. They were asked not to put their names on the scales and not to consult their friends. They were told that the purpose of the procedure was for them to help us understand better what young people were thinking and feeling about themselves.

SELECTION OF CITIES

Inasmuch as the purpose of the study was to assess the impact of school desegregation in the South and in former school districts that had operated under de jure segregation, only Southern cities were considered. Time and finances would permit only a sample of students from five different Southern school districts. It was arbitrarily decided to omit rural areas and concentrate on urban centers with at least 50,000 people, and to have each of the five cities come from various parts of the South, representing various ways in which implementation had occurred.

In the spring of 1966 correspondence was started with more than 35 Southern cities. Finally, in May of 1968 after two refusals permission was received to test in Nashville; and in the spring of 1969 permission was received to test in New Orleans and Greensboro. Because of the passage of time, it was decided to limit the study in the South to those three cities. Thus, the testing of the three cities occurred during a period of one year—Nashville, Tennessee in May, 1968; New Orleans, Louisiana, in March, 1969; and Greensboro, North Carolina, in May, 1969.

The responses from many of the school districts who refused indicated that, inasmuch as the study concerned school desegregation, they were fearful of the dissension it might cause, although each was sent a copy of the scales and an outline of the study.

SELECTION OF STUDENTS AND SCHOOLS

Students in public schools in seventh, eighth, and ninth grades were tested. The schools chosen in each city were to include (1) one white segregated school, (2) one black segregated school, and (3) three desegregated schools with various percentages of black students, from 10 percent to 60 percent. The schools were also to be chosen or matched according to socioeconomic status of the students. It was hoped that as much as possible each school chosen would represent a cross section of socioeconomic groups. The students were to be selected at random, by the principal at each school, 50 boys and 50 girls from seventh, eighth, and ninth grades. In the desegregated schools, a minimum of 30 black students were to be included depending on the black student enrollment.

Although initially five public junior high schools in each city were to participate, in Nashville and in New Orleans, the public school population seemed to be overloaded with lower-class socioeconomic students. In order to get a middle-class sampling as well, permission was secured to test in Catholic parochial schools. In Greensboro the request was never acknowledged and, inasmuch as there was a time factor involved, the testing in Greensboro proceeded without participation of Catholic parochial schools.

Another major difficulty that arose in addition to the socioeconomic sampling was the definition of a segregated school and a desegregated school. Is a school that has 6 percent black enrollment a desegregated school? Is a school that has 85 percent black enrollment a desegregated school? Hence, the whole issue of racial balance and imbalance had to be decided. In Greensboro and New Orleans school districts there were several all-black junior high schools, but there were no all-white junior high schools. There were several that had less than 10 percent black enrollment.

The prevailing Southern view has been that the admission of a handful of black students or even a single one to an all-white school desegregates it. The New York Board of Education classifies an elementary school as segregated if its Negro or Puerto Rican population is either 90 percent or higher or 10 percent or lower.[14] The comparable figures for junior high schools are 85 percent and 15 percent. California's State Board of Education has ruled that any school is "imbalanced" if its minority enrollment varies more than 15 percent from the percentage of minority students in the school district.[15] Massachusetts requires local action against "racial imbalance" and will cut off state aid to schools over 50 percent black.[16]

During the school year 1965-1966, the United States Office of Education's compliance section, the Equal Educational Opportunities section, concentrated on evaluating the desegregation process in the 17-Southern-state region. In collecting the data a disparity developed between what is called "technical desegregation" and "actual desegregation." The statistics showed that in the South 92 percent of the 2,877 school districts were in technical compliance with federal regulations, but only 25 percent of the black students were attending biracial schools and about 700 all-white or all-black districts were included in the "in compliance" group.[17]

The prevailing philosophy in terms of racial balance and desegregation is aptly stated by Will Maslow:

Desegregation cannot be viewed solely in terms of arbitrary Negro-white ratios but must be related to the racial composition of the area . . .

If integration is to be achieved, school authorities must have up-to-date information about the racial and ethnic composition of their schools and the neighborhoods they serve.[18]

Inasmuch as all three school districts had black enrollments well above 10 percent, and in view of the confusion and debate in official circles, it was decided that for purposes of this study the following classification of schools would be used: (1) a segregated white school is one in which there is an all-white enrollment or a black enrollment less than 10 percent; (2) a segregated black school is one in which the student enrollment is all black or 80 percent or more black; (3) desegregated schools are those schools in which the black student enrollment is at least 10 percent but no more than 80 percent; (4) those white students attending a predominantly black school classified as segregated black would be included in the analysis of the data as desegregated white; (5) those black students attending a predominantly white school classified as segregated white would be included in the analysis of the data as a desegregated black.

With this classification there were only two instances in all of the three cities where numbers 4 and 5 of the classification schema had to be applied. In Greensboro one black student at a "segregated" white school (less than 10 percent black) is included among the desegregated black group and in Nashville 50 white students at a "segregated" black school (more than 80 percent black) are included among the desegregated white group.

Thus, six main groups of students emerge for comparison of mean scores in each of the cities: (1) segregated white students; (2) segregated black students; (3) desegregated white students; (4) desegregated black students; (5) all the black students; (6) all the white students. These groups are further divided according to sex, and comparisons are made based on sex, race, and type of school. The data is analyzed according to analysis of variance and regression techniques considering other independent variables such as family stability, education of parents, occupation and income of parents, and family size. The data from each city is considered separately first and then intracity comparisons are made.

1. Clark, K. Prejudice and Your Child, 2nd ed. Boston, Beacon Press, 1963, p. 159.
3. Clark and Clark. Op. cit., 1939; Clark and Clark. Op. cit., 1958; Davis, A. The socialization of the American Negro child and adolescence. Journal of Negro Education 8:264-275, 1939.
4. Deutscher, M., and Chein, I. The psychological effects of enforced segregation: A survey of social science opinion. Journal of Psychology, 26:259-287, 1948.
5. Clark, K. Op. cit., 1963, p. 168.
6. Coopersmith. Op. cit., 1967.

7. Pierce, Op. cit., 1969.

8. Dreger and Miller. Op. cit., 1968.

9. Clark, K., ed. Desegregation: An appraisal of the evidence. Journal of Social Issues, 9:2-76, Fall, 1953.

10. Jones, M.R. The influence of situational variables on truthfulness of responses to a self-concept scale. Paper read at the Xth Congress of the Interamerican Society of Psychology, Lima, Peru, April 3, 1967.

11. Fitts. Op. cit., 1965.

12. Jones. Op. cit., 1966.

13. Powell, G.J., and Fuller, M. School desegregation and self-concept: A pilot study on the psychological impact of school desegregation on 7th, 8th, and 9th graders in a Southern city. Paper presented at the 47th Annual Meeting of the American Orthopsychiatry Meeting, San Francisco, Calif., March, 1970.

14. Maslow, W. De factor school desegregation. Villanova Law Review, Vol. 6, Spring, 1961, p. 360.

15. Why school busing is in trouble. U.S. News and World Report, Oct. 13, 1969, p. 44.

16. Ibid., p. 43.

17. Leeson, J. Guidelines and a new count. Southern Education Report. Jan.-Feb., 1967, p. 31.

18. Maslow. Op. cit., 1961, pp. 360-362.

PART TWO

Nashville

5

Profile of a City:
Some Historical and Social Notes

The 1960 census reported that the state of Tennessee had 3,567,089 people, an increase of 8 percent over the 1950 census. By 1965 the census was estimated at 3,692,000 with about half the people living in towns and the other half living in rural areas. Most Tennesseeans are American-born descendants of British, Scotch-Irish, French Huguenot, and German immigrants. Although about 19 percent of the state's population are blacks, a lower percentage than in most Southern states, about 40 percent of the blacks live in Shelby County, in the southwestern corner of the state. (Memphis is in Shelby County.) About 47 out of 100 live in the state's four largest metropolitan areas—Memphis, Knoxville, Nashville, and Chattanooga, with Memphis being the largest and Nashville the second largest.

The first settlers came to the Nashville area in 1779 and the following year Fort Nashborough was built. The town was incorporated in 1784 at which time the name was changed to Nashville. Soon after the settlement began, the town drew up the Cumberland Compact which provided the community with a written constitutional charter. Nashville received its city charter in 1806 and became the official capital of Tennessee in 1843 with the completion of the capitol there in 1855. During the Civil War the people of Tennessee were divided in their loyalty between the North and the South. Tennessee was the last state to secede from the Union and the first to re-enter and Andrew Jackson was the only Southern Senator not to secede with his state. Union troops occupied the city and General John Bell Hood's Confederate army suffered a disastrous defeat there in 1864. It is a little-known fact that more Civil War battles were fought in Tennessee than in any other state except Virginia.

By the 1960 census the population of Nashville within corporate city limits was 399,743 with 80 percent residing in their state of birth. The proportion of black to total population, which is widely regarded as a useful measure of the magnitude of local race-relations problems, was 37.9 percent. In 1962 Nashville and Davidson County adopted a metropolitan form of government. By 1965 the estimated population of Nashville, the second-largest city in the state (Memphis is the largest) was 463,628, with 80 percent white and 20 percent black.

A replica of the Athenian Parthenon which stands in Nashville's Centennial Park helps account for the city's nickname, the Athens of the South. Nashville is a commercial and educational center occupying hilly ground along the Cumberland River in north-central Tennessee. The state of Tennessee has 33 universities and colleges accredited by the Southern Association of Colleges and Schools. Those located in Nashville include Belmont College, David Lipscomb College, Fisk University, George Peabody College, Meharry Medical College, Scarritt College, Tennessee Agricultural and Industrial State University, and Vanderbilt University. By 1965 the estimated number of students enrolled in Nashville colleges was 3,750. The city has about 60 printing firms including large religious publishing establishments. It is also a renowned study center for Southern problems; both the *Southern School News* and the *Race Relations Law Reporter* are located there. Other industries include aircraft parts, barges, cellophane, clothing, foods, footwear, heating apparatus, hosiery, plastics, rayon, and textiles. The median income in Nashville in 1960 was $3,816 with 39.9 percent earning under $3,000 and 5.7 percent earning over $10,000. The median school year completed was 8.9, with 29.3 percent of the students completing four years of high school or more, and 84.4 percent of children between 14 to 17 years old in school. Manufacturing is the state's leading source of income instead of agriculture and new industries continue to move into the state. The gross national product of the state is $3,817,627,000 with manufactured products accounting for 79 percent, agricultural products (Tennessee ranks among the leading cotton states) 18 percent, and fish and mineral products 3 percent. Average yearly number of people employed in the state is 1,231,801. However, many Tennesseeans are leaving the state and moving to the more industrialized East and North; this migration began right after the Civil War and still continues. The state is losing many skilled and semiskilled men and women between the ages of 20 to 44, but the population continues to increase slightly because the birth rate is higher than the death rate.

Education in Tennessee began with privately owned schools, usually controlled by churches and run by ministers. Samuel Dook, a Presbyterian minister, started the state's first school in about 1780. Public schools were established in the early 1800's to educate the children of the poor, and in

1873 the legislature made free public education available to all children. The history of school desegregation has been reviewed elsewhere in this book. Suffice it to say that the pattern of segregating black and white children in the state of Tennessee was like that of segregation patterns in other Southern states. Indeed, Tennessee is noted to have enacted the first Jim Crow Law.[1, 2]

NASHVILLE AFTER THE BROWN DECISION

As of May 17, 1954, the state of Tennessee was among the 17 states plus the District of Columbia that operated separate public schools for whites and blacks. In 1957 black children were admitted for the first time to previously all-white public schools in Nashville, Tennessee. The desegregation operation in Nashville was not conspicuously disorderly. In many respects the orderly desegregation of the public schools could have been expected, for Nashville had successfully desegregated the Catholic schools even before the Brown Decision. The public library, the municipal golf courses, and the railroad station were desegregated. Longer and more thorough efforts were made in Nashville to condition the public for the change. William A. Bass, the Superintendent of Schools, began meeting in April with principals, supervisors, and both white and black parent-teacher associations to inform, elucidate, and help solve problems that might grow out of the effort to comply with the ruling. Many Nashville clergymen asked their congregations to comply in a Christian spirit. The Nashville Ministers' Association and the Association of Churches, urged by the Vanderbilt Divinity School and several church-related colleges, addressed letters to all Protestant clergymen asking their help in preparing the public. Television programs were arranged. The Nashville Community Relations Conference, a biracial organization, helped mobilize parents to support the desegregation process. They secured 600 signatures of well-known citizens and civic leaders who supported school desegregation, who in turn encouraged 16 other organizations to do the same, and presented these signatures to the school board. Nashville's morning paper, the *Tennesseean*, was outstanding in its support and admonishments for orderly adherence. It should also be noted that Governor Clement was considered by many to have been more forthright than any other Southern governor in upholding the Supreme Court decision.[3]

With the admission of black pupils to white schools the initiation of "The Nashville Plan" was started. The federal district court gave tentative approval to the school board's proposal to begin compliance by desegregating all first-grade pupils in September, 1957. Although Governor Clement had vetoed earlier pro-segregation bills, when the legislature met in January,

1957, he endorsed the one-grade-a-year desegregation plan which also included a "pupil assignment plan" or "School Preference Law." This law allowed parents to choose for their children between white, black, or desegregated schools. However, this liberal transfer privilege reduced the impact of the desegregation plan and meant that little or no change in school segregation occurred. In fact, it was not unlike the "Freedom of Choice Plan" adopted in Alabama the year before which was intended to resist desegregation. For the first year of the Nashville Plan, first-grade students were assigned to schools in their neighborhood areas without regard to race. However, black students assigned to previously all-white schools were permitted, if they so desired, to transfer back to predominantly black schools and the same privilege was extended to white students. By September 9, 1957, when schools opened, only 19 Negro pupils elected to attend the seven white elementary schools assigned to them.[4] Thus, five previously all-white elementary schools were desegregated with minor incidents.

A federal court order was issued to the Nashville school board to submit a plan for desegregating the remaining 11 grades by December 31, 1957. The board tried to abandon the grade-a-year desegregation plan and adopted a plan similar to the School Preference Law which had been invalidated the previous September by a federal district court. In the meantime, while the school board was busy trying to submit an acceptable plan, the black plaintiffs in the original Nashville school desegregation suit petitioned the court to order an end to segregation in all grades by September, 1958. By April, 1958, the board committed itself to a plan of desegregating one higher grade each year until all segregation was eliminated and the plan was approved by the Federal courts. In September, 1958, schools opened without turmoil with both first and second grades desegregated with 34 black pupils in previously white schools.[5] Although only a few black pupils accepted assignments to previously all-white schools during the first two years, the leaders in the black community made a concerted effort to encourage black parents to accept assignments in desegregated schools. By 1963, almost 10 years after the *Brown* v. *Board of Education* decision, 773 black children had desegregated seven grades.[6] The evolution of the Nashville Plan would be widely studied and copied. The progress made in Nashville in the elimination of segregation in public schools would keep it in the forefront of Southern cities in the desegregation process.

THE NATURE OF RESISTANCE AND COMPLIANCE IN THE STATE

In spite of the moderate approach to desegregation, and for the most part the elimination of segregated schools by orderly process, the 1954 decision left some scars in Tennessee. Tennessee was unique among Southern states in that not only the governor, but also the two state senators, Estes Kefauver and Albert Gore, had consistently expressed moderate views on the desegregation issue. Immediately after the Supreme Court ruling, Oak Ridge, Tennessee, had been one of the first school districts in a former Confederate state to desegregate the federally operated junior and senior high schools in September, 1955. On January 23, 1956, 300 segregationists converged on Nashville and demanded an audience with the governor. Governor Clement listened for an hour, lectured them, and made no concessions to their demands. A Parents' School Preference Committee and the Tennessee Federation for Constitutional Government, both segregationist organizations, demanded that the school board abandon its desegregation plan. Ku Klux Klan activities, although minor, had resumed shortly after the 1954 decision. Asa Carter, an archsegregationist from Alabama, came to segregationist rallies in Nashville. Representative Davis of Georgia addressed the Tennessee Federation for Constitutional Government and urged white parents to boycott the public schools and establish private schools.

Shortly after midnight on September 10th, a day after 19 black children initiated desegregation of five public schools, the Hattie Cotton School in East Nashville, a previously all-white elementary school which had admitted one six-year-old black girl, was blasted by dynamite, demolishing one wing of the school. Nashville was seized with panic. The desegregated schools were surrounded by police and barricades were erected a block away from each. Attendance at the other six desegregated schools dropped to 40 percent. By the end of the week the situation had returned to normal and school attendance rose to 90 percent with 11 black children still in the desegregated schools.

On April 26, 1950, a suit had been filed by McSwain of Clinton against the County Board of Education of Anderson County, Tennessee. The case had been in litigation in the federal district court but was suspended pending the U.S. Supreme Court action on *Brown* v. *Board of Education.* In January, 1956, Federal Judge Robert L. Taylor ordered that desegregation of Clinton High School begin in the fall term of 1956. The town authorities resolved to do everything possible to ensure a smooth and peaceful transition. In Clinton the desegregation controversy was devoid of any suggestion of "nostalgic Confederate loyalty" for this section of Tennessee had stood with the Union. However, "It was this last decision which marked the beginnings of a series of riots, court actions in response to riots and riots in response to court actions which dominated the headlines through 1956 and 1957."[7]

School was scheduled to open Monday, August 27, 1956, but on Saturday, August 25th, John Kasper arrived in town and aroused hundreds and even thousands of people with his anti-Negro rhetoric. He imported segregationist organizations and the crowds who gathered to listen became rioting mobs. The final tragedy in what *Time* magazine described as "one of the most forthright Southern law-enforcement performances thus far in the desegregation struggle" was the bombing of the high school on October 5, 1958.[8]

As for the rest of Tennessee, several other major events followed. In 1960-61 blacks were admitted for the first time to desegregated schools in five of the largest cities of the South, including Memphis. Memphis, which is 10 miles from Mississippi, had continued to resist desegregation and had been considered one of the major problem cities in terms of the compliance with the *Brown* decision. In 1961 the Memphis school board, having been encouraged by the success of the desegregation operations in Dallas and Atlanta, agreed to admit blacks to previously all-white schools in the first grade only at the outset, and to the next higher grade each year thereafter. School desegregation was initiated without any preparation or previous notice to the public and 13 black children quietly entered previously all-white public schools on October 3, 1961.

Knoxville admitted 28 black first-graders to white schools in 1960 with no difficulty on the one-grade-a-year basis. However, in 1963 the federal courts ordered both Memphis and Knoxville to move faster than one grade a year and both cities began to initiate plans to comply. In 1962, Tennessee saw the last of any commotion over school openings in Chattanooga and by the fall of 1963, 18 school districts in Tennessee initiated desegregation.

By the mid-1960's about 30 percent of the state's school districts had desegregated. In the 1962 case of *Baker* v. *Carr* the U.S. Supreme Court ruled that federal courts have jurisdiction over legislative apportionment. In 1964 a federal court ordered the Tennessee legislature to correct its imbalances and in 1965 the Tennessee legislature rearranged districts to comply with the order.

THE BLACK COMMUNITY IN NASHVILLE

On September 9, 1957, 19 black children entered five white public schools and thus Nashville became the first city of any size in Tennessee to desegregate its schools. In order to understand why, one needs to know something about the black community in Nashville. About 38 percent of the people living within the corporate city limits of Nashville are black, although the total percentage for the metropolitan area is 20 percent and that for the state is 19.2 percent, with the majority residing in Shelby County. The black community in Nashville has a national reputation for being progressive and politically alert. It is considered one of the major centers for black education; historic Fisk University is located there as is one of the two black medical schools in the country, Meharry Medical College. These two institutions, as well as Tennessee A and I and several other small black colleges in Nashville, are renowned for the advancement of the black people in this country.

As of 1960 there were 2,432 black college graduates in Nashville and 6,818 high-school graduates. There were 769 black male and 1,097 black female professional workers including skilled technicians and other kindred workers. The actual breakdown for blacks by sex and occupation in the 1960 census was the following:

	Males	Females
Teachers	153	523
Nurses		158
Doctors	55	20
Librarians		59
Lawyers and judges	8	
Engineers	8	
College professors, presidents, and instructors	156	73
Craftsmen, foremen, etc.	1,541	
Operators and kindred work		1,407
Clerical	713	694
Sales workers		80
Managers, insurance, etc.	365	
Finance and real estate	396	
Educational services	1,037	
Private household workers		5,454
Cooks not in private houses		756
Hairdressers		183
Farmers and farm managers	13	

The number of blacks employed estimated by the 1965 census was 27,380; of this number 1,335 were unemployed. The median black family income was $2,794 with 259 families having no earnings. The number of black families with father and mother present in the home was 11,671 out of a total of 16,160 black families.

At the time of the initiation of school desegregation, black participation in public affairs was considered unique among Southern cities; for example, two blacks sat in the city council and one on the board of education.

In February of 1960 black college students from Fisk and Tennessee A. and I. sat in at lunch counters in downtown Nashville and were subsequently arrested. Prior to the initial sit-in the students had been schooled in the philosophy of non-violence by James Lawson, a member of NCLC, the Nashville's branch of King's SCLC, and a doctoral candidate at Vanderbilt Divinity School. The Black Community was aroused and rallied round to support the students. The NAACP, NCLC, and the Nashville Human Relations Committee elicited community support for the students. Other students from the black colleges joined in and, under the guidance of Jim Lawson, the students organized the Student Non-Violent Coordinating Committee to coordinate further civil rights activities to desegregate lunch counters, restaurants, movie theatres, and churches. Each student and every participant had to agree to the techniques of nonviolence. Events occurred rapidly. The police and the white segregationists retaliated with brutality which only reinforced the students' determination to continue their non-violent protest of segregated facilities in Nashville.

The black community organized a massive boycott of the white businesses and mass meetings were held weekly and to keep the Black Community informed. Shortly before Easter the Reverend James Lawson was arrested at First Baptist Church, which was a frequent meeting place of the students prior to sit-in demonstrations, and pastored by the Reverend Kelly Miller Smith, president of the Nashville Christian Leadership Council. The arrest was made on the grounds of inciting to riot and Jim Lawson was dragged from the church by two policemen. The next morning the *Tennesseean* carried the story written by Dave Halberstam, now foreign news correspondent for the *New York Times*, with a picture of the police violently dragging Jim Lawson, a student and believer of non-violence from the church. The picture also showed the church indicating the title of the sermon for the forthcoming Sunday—"Father Forgive Them for They Know Not What They Do."

Events within the next few months occurred rapidly. Jim Lawson was expelled from Vanderbilt and more than half of the Vanderbilt Divinity School faculty resigned. An NAACP lawyer's home was bombed and 3,000 students marched to the mayor's office for a nonviolent demonstration to protest segregated eating facilities in Nashville. The mayor made a public statement that eating places in Nashville should be desegregated and a few weeks later one by one the lunch counters and then the restaurants desegregated.

It should be noted, however, that although the first sit-in occurred in Greensboro, North Carolina, of all the student groups that formed throughout the South, the Nashville group was the most organized and best schooled in the techniques of nonviolence. At the initiative of the Nashville group under the leadership of such student leaders as Diane Nash, James Bevel, John Smith, and Bernard Lafayette a meeting of all the student movement groups throughout the South was called together in Raleigh, North Carolina. It was there that the students agreed to form a national organization, adopting the Nashville Student Group's name of the Student Non-Violence Coordinating Committee as well as "We Shall Overcome" as the song of the movement which Guy Carawan, a folk singer, sang when the Nashville students opened and closed their meetings.

Throughout the early days of SNCC the Nashville students continued to lend support and leadership to the student protest movement throughout the South.

1. Franklin, J.H. Op. cit., Vol. II, 1969, p. 10.
2. Franklin, J.H. Op. cit., 1968, p. 145.
3. Muse. Op. cit., 1964, p. 114.
4. Southern Education Report. September, 1967. p. 14.
5. Muse. Op. cit., p. 121.
6. Ibid.
7. Blaustein and Ferguson. Op. cit., 1962, p. 186.
8. Ibid., p. 213.

6

The Students and the Schools
of Nashville: Questionnaire Data

In 1957, the Nashville Public School System began to comply with the 1954 Supreme Court decision to desegregate and implemented a plan that would desegregate a grade a year. At the time of our testing, about 86 of the 141 schools had some measure of desegregation, with 33 percent of the white students and 47 percent of the black students still in 55 segregated schools.[1]

As of the school year 1966-1967, the pupil enrollment in the Nashville Metropolitan Public Schools was 91,308 with 77 percent white and 23 percent black. The amount of desegregation in Nashville as of 1968 exceeded that of most Southern cities. In 1958 the number of black students in predominantly white schools was 34 in the first two grades; by 1959 there were 41 in three grades; by 1960, 183 in four grades; 1961, 270 in five grades; 1962, 490 in six grades; and by 1963, 773 in seven grades.[2] Inasmuch as segregated housing is the most prevalent pattern, there are sections of Nashville which are all black and sections which are all white. The all-black sections are in the center city or close by and the all-white sections are in the outlying areas. Thus, schools in these sections are still segregated. However, there are changing neighborhoods where white neighborhoods are becoming predominantly black. The schools in these areas are rapidly becoming predominantly black.

The status of desegregation in the school year 1966-1967 was the following:[3] (a) 43 schools were 100 percent white representing 33 percent of the school system's white students; (b) 12 schools were 100 percent black representing 47 percent of the school system's black students; (c) 58 schools which were previously all-white had less than 10 percent black students enrolled; (d) 8 formerly segregated black schools had less than 10 percent white students; (e) 13 formerly segregated white schools had 10 percent to 50 percent black students; (f) 7 previously segregated white schools had 51 percent to 75 percent black students.

In 1968, at the time of the testing, the exact percentage per school had not been tabulated, but in the changing neighborhoods black enrollment had increased so that there were some previously segregated white schools that were close to 80 to 85 percent black.

Eight junior high schools participated in the study; three were parochial schools and five were public schools. The schools varied according to the degree of desegregation as well as the duration of desegregation. Two of the schools participating were segregated white schools, one public and one parochial. There were three desegregated schools and three schools that were predominantly black or all black. Of the 616 students who participated in the study, 317 were white and 299 were black. Among the black students, 206 were attending predominantly black or segregated black schools and 93 were attending desegregated schools. Of the white students tested 151 were attending segregated schools and 166 were attending desegregated schools.

THE SOCIOECONOMIC BACKGROUNDS OF THE PARTICIPATING STUDENTS

THE 100 PERCENT BLACK PAROCHIAL SCHOOL

This school was located in the heart of the black community very near two of the well-known black colleges. Responses to the questionnaire regarding socioeconomic status of parents, educational background, and some family data for the 67 students were as follows:

1.	Parents together	75%
	Parents not together	22%
	Father dead	1.5%
2.	Father finished high school	79%
	Father did not finish high school	21%
3.	Father had no college	32%
	Father had some college	8%
	Father had four years or more of college	60%
4.	Mother finished high school	78%
	Mother did not finish high school	22%
5.	Mother had no college	33%
	Mother had some college	15%
	Mother had four years or more college	52%
6.	Father is in profession or small business	51%
	Father is in technical trade or labor	39%
7.	Mother works	71%
	Mother does not work	29%
8.	Number of children: one to three children	59%
	four or more children	41%

Five of the sisters at this school were white and one had just recently arrived from South America. The principal of the school was white, extremely militant, and very involved in the Human Relations Council as well as other civil rights activities in the community. She had participated in the planning of the Poor People's March through Nashville, and as part of the students' course in American history, each class had spent two days at the Poor People's camp passing out food and clothing. The principal of the school had also insisted that a class in black literature be given to the students and for the more advanced students courses in black literature were taken on the black college campuses. Black history and black art were taught as part of the curriculum as well. The students at this school seemed particularly aware of the political issues confronting the community and felt free to discuss them openly with their teachers. Needless to say, the Sisters had very positive feelings about the students they were teaching. The mean IQ for the school was 110, with a range of 105 to 125 and two students below 95. All of the students were reading at grade level, many were reading above grade level, and some on the 11th to 12th grade level. Only 37 percent of the students were Catholic.

THE 100 PERCENT BLACK PUBLIC SCHOOL

This particular school was a combination elementary and junior high school. Its student body and faculty were completely black and it was located in the heart of the black community very near two famous black institutions. Black history, black literature, and black art had been taught for many years as a matter of course. On the bulletin boards and in the halls on the walls there were pictures of black politicians, scholars, and writers. The estimated mean IQ was given as 100. Very often the students participated or attended events at the neighboring black colleges. Eighty-nine students in the seventh, eighth, and ninth grades participated in the study. Their responses to the questionnaire items regarding family background, educational level of parents, and occupational status of parents were as follows:

1.	Parents together	66%
	Parents not together	25%
	Father or mother dead	3%
2.	Father finished high school	60%
	Father did not finish high school	40%
3.	Father had no college	74%
	Father had some college	9%
	Father had four years or more college	17%
4.	Mother finished high school	69%
	Mother did not finish high school	21%
5.	Mother had no college	66%
	Mother had some college	20%
	Mother had four years or more college	14%
6.	Father is in profession or own business	9%
	Father is in technical trade or labor	61%

7.	Mother works	62%
	Mother does not work	38%
8.	Number of children: one to three children	42%
	four or more children	58%

THE 80 PERCENT BLACK PUBLIC SCHOOL

At the time of the 1954 Supreme Court ruling, this school was a totally white school. During the ten years the school desegregation had been implemented in Nashville, the racial composition of the school had changed drastically. White families began to move out of the area to be replaced by black families. This process was augmented by an urban renewal process which planned a major highway through the residential area in North Nashville. At the time of the testing, the school was over 80 percent black. Although the principal was white, the majority of the faculty was black, 30 black and 23 white. The school was located in a lower socioeconomic area which abounded in dilapidated housing. Most of the white students who attended this school came from poverty homes. The black students represented middle-class but predominantly lower socioeconomic families. Twenty-nine percent of the students came from OEO designated poverty families. The major problem in the school had to do with academic achievement, which was relatively low, as well as a high percentage of drop-outs among the blacks and the whites. The mean IQ was in the 80's; 4.4 percent scored in the 90's; 6.1 percent at 104; 7.7 percent between 105 and 120; and 9.9 percent between 113 and 125. In general, the reading levels were two to four years below grade level. Fifty black students participated in the study as well as 50 white students. Responses to questionnaire items regarding family background and educational and occupational status of parents for white and black students are as follows:

		Black	White
1.	Parents together	66%	62%
	Parents not together	22%	24%
	Father or mother dead	10%	12%
2.	Father finished high school	51%	47%
	Father did not finish high school	49%	53%
3.	Father had no college	70%	80%
	Father had some college	13%	6%
	Father had four years or more college	17%	5%
4.	Mother finished high school	55%	42%
	Mother did not finish high school	45%	56%
5.	Mother had no college	56%	68%
	Mother had some college	23%	16%
	Mother had four years or more college	21%	10%
6.	Father is in profession or own business	8%	7%
	Father is in technical trade or labor	74%	82%
7.	Mother works	72%	62%
	Mother does not work	28%	38%
8.	Number of children: one to three children	42%	38%
	four or more children	58%	62%

THE 100 PERCENT WHITE PAROCHIAL SCHOOL

The school was located in a predominantly white neighborhood. It was a combination elementary and junior high school. Although there were about three or four black students in the elementary school, there were no black students in the junior high school at the time of our testing and the elementary black students had been admitted a year prior to our testing. A total of 59 students participated in the study; 33 boys and 26 girls who represented a predominantly white middle-class sampling. The median IQ was given as 100, with a range of 91 to 131, and 9 students had IQ's above 120. The Sisters who taught at the school did not feel that there were any particular outstanding problems. The response to questionnaire items regarding occupational and educational status of parents as well as family background is as follows:

1.	Parents together	94%
	Parents not together	
	Father or mother dead	6%
2.	Father finished high school	80%
	Father did not finish high school	20%
3.	Father had no college	35%
	Father had some college	25%
	Father had four years or more college	40%
4.	Mother finished high school	86%
	Mother did not finish high school	14%
5.	Mother had no college	65%
	Mother had some college	14%
	Mother had four years or more college	21%
6.	Father is in profession or own business	42%
	Father is in technical trade or labor	53%
7.	Mother works	41%
	Mother does not work	59%
8.	Number of children: one to three children	17%
	four or more children	83%

THE 100 PERCENT WHITE PUBLIC SCHOOL

This school was located in a segregated white community, very near one of the state's penitentiaries. In fact, the community grew up around the state penitentiary when families of the inmates moved into the area to be near the imprisoned family member. At least 30 percent of the students came from OEO families and were eligible for school lunches. Approximately 5 percent to 10 percent of the students had relatives who were in the state penitentiary. This estimate may be grossly inaccurate. It was the only reliable estimate available to the school personnel at the time of the testing. The school had brand new facilities, modern and up-to-date. The median IQ score of the entire student body was 90 with 34 students scoring below 70 and 31 scoring above 120. The major school problem was that of school drop-outs. A total of 88 students, 50 girls and 38 boys, participated in the study. The responses to the questionnaire items regarding family background and occupational and educational status of parents are as follows:

1.	Parents together	80%
	Parents not together	14%
	Father or mother dead	6%
2.	Father finished high school	26%
	Father did not finish high school	74%
3.	Father had no college	82%
	Father had some college	7%
	Father had four years or more of college	1%
4.	Mother finished high school	35%
	Mother did not finish high school	65%
5.	Mother had no college	98%
	Mother had some college	1%
	Mother had four years or more college	1%
6.	Father is in profession or own business	6%
	Father is in technical trade or labor	78%
7.	Mother works	46%
	Mother does not work	54%
8.	Number of children: one to three children	42%
	four or more children	59%

THE 10 PERCENT BLACK PAROCHIAL SCHOOL

Originally, this school had been a girls' parochial school. However, two years prior to the testing, boys had been admitted. Unfortunately no boys participated or were included in the 32 students tested. The school had been desegregated for about eight years at the time of the testing. In addition to black students, Oriental and Spanish-speaking children also attended this school. The predominant economic sampling at the school was middle-class, upper middle-class. The median IQ was 110. The responses to the question-naire items regarding occupational and educational status of parents as well as family background for black and white students are as follows:

		White	Black
1.	Parents together	79%	67%
	Parents not together	21%	25%
	Father or mother dead		
2.	Father finished high school	47%	58%
	Father did not finish high school	53%	42%
3.	Father had no college	79%	57%
	Father had some college	10%	10%
	Father had four years or more of college	11%	33%
4.	Mother finished high school	58%	67%
	Mother did not finish high school	42%	33%
5.	Mother had no college	95%	50%
	Mother had some college	5%	17%
	Mother had four years or more college		33%
6.	Father is in profession or own business	16%	42%
	Father is in technical trade or labor	69%	42%
7.	Mother works	58%	92%
	Mother does not work	42%	8%
8.	Number of children: one to three children	15%	41%
	four or more children	85%	59%

THE 20 PERCENT BLACK PUBLIC SCHOOL

A total of 88 students (38 black and 50 white) participated in this desegregated school with 20 percent black student enrollment. The school was located in a predominantly lower middle-class, lower-class neighborhood, with adjacent white and black communities. Two years before the testing, the school was desegregated without any turmoil. Shortly before the testing, the school had been closed for several days following the death of Martin Luther King because of the white parents' fear of violence. The school faculty was desegregated with two black faculty members in toto. There was a great deal of animosity between the white and black students and there was very little interaction between the two groups. The black boys, however, led in sports and were readily admitted to all the athletic teams. The black girls, on the other hand, found few activities within the life of the school in which they could participate. The mean IQ was in the 90's. The response to the questionnaire items regarding educational and occupational status of parents as well as family background is as follows for the white and black students:

		White	Black
1.	Parents together	65%	58%
	Parents not together	29%	35%
	Father or mother dead	6%	5%
2.	Father finished high school	17%	47%
	Father did not finish high school	83%	53%
3.	Father had no college	100%	90%
	Father had some college		10%
	Father had four years or more college		
4.	Mother finished high school	21%	41%
	Mother did not finish high school	79%	59%
5.	Mother had no college	98%	85%
	Mother had some college	2%	5%
	Mother had four years or more college		10%
6.	Father is in profession or own business		3%
	Father is in technical trade or labor	72%	63%
7.	Mother works	48%	70%
	Mother does not work	52%	30%
8.	Number of children: one to three children	51%	36%
	four or more children	48%	64%

THE 10 PERCENT BLACK PUBLIC SCHOOL

This particular school was located in a "bedroom community," i.e., a more suburban community. The school was a brand new school, having been completed five months prior to the testing and occupied by students four months prior to the testing. It was the first time in that community that black and white students of junior high school age had attended a desegregated school. The faculty was also desegregated with three black teachers who had been at previously all-black schools. Both black and white teachers agreed that the major problem in the school was discipline for both groups of students. There had been no racial strife between the two groups and no complaints from parents. The faculty was in the process of instituting a new curriculum and some innovative teaching techniques.

Most of the students were reading at grade level, 20 percent below and 20 percent above. Both teachers and pupils alike seemed to be excited about the new school and the new program. Both of the white teachers interviewed were resigned to desegregation, stating, "We would rather have our own black students than blacks from some other community," expressing their fear of the possibility of busing. Forty-three black students participated in the study and 46 white students participated. The responses to the questionnaire items regarding educational and occupational status of parents as well as family background for both white and black students are listed as follows:

		White	Black
1.	Parents together	84%	71%
	Parents not together	6%	15%
	Father or mother dead		10%
2.	Father finished high school	51%	38%
	Father did not finish high school	49%	62%
3.	Father had no college	84%	76%
	Father had some college	12%	9%
	Father had four years or more college	4%	16%
4.	Mother finished high school	57%	65%
	Mother did not finish high school	43%	35%
5.	Mother had no college	96%	55%
	Mother had some college		24%
	Mother had four years or more years of college	4%	21%
6.	Father is in profession or own business	23%	4%
	Father is in technical trade or labor	60%	54%
7.	Mother works	50%	70%
	Mother does not work	50%	30%
8.	Number of children: one to three children	54%	33%
	four or more children	46%	67%

ATTITUDES OF STUDENTS AND ASPIRATIONAL LEVELS

Tables 1 and 2 summarize the sociofamilial data of the 615 students in the eight schools tested and Table 3 tabulates the responses of the white and black students regarding self-attitudes, attitudes toward school, and aspirations. It should be noted that the educational backgrounds of the black parents, both fathers and mothers, tended to be higher than the white parents, with more black parents completing high school and college than

TABLE 1
Family Background of Nashville Students

	Percentages			
Lives With	Both Parents	Mother	Step-parents	Other Relative
White	75	13	7	6
Black	65	18	3	12
Parents	Together	Divorced	Separated	Father and/or Mother Dead
White	84	9	3	4
Black	82	10	3	5

TABLE 2
Nashville Students:
Educational Background of Parents and Occupations

	Percentages	
Fathers finished	High School	College
White	40	10
Black	55	23
Mothers finished		
White	42	5
Black	62	25
Professional	Father	Mother
White	6	5
Black	12	16
Father's work	Technician/Trade	Labor
White	54	3
Black	43	8
Mothers working	Yes	No
White	44	56
Black	71	33

white parents. This occurred even in the parochial schools. More black mothers (71 percent) were working than white mothers (44 percent), which might be related to educational background.

The aspirations of black students were more heavily weighted toward college (52 percent) and a profession (46 percent) than were those of the white students (39 percent and 25 percent respectively). Black students (61 percent) also tended to express more satisfaction with themselves than whites (56 percent). It will be interesting to see how these expressed self-

TABLE 3

Aspirations of Nashville Students

	Percentages				
	College	Marriage*	Profession	Sports*	Job
White	39	10	25	20	28
Black	52	4	46	17	10

Attitudes of Nashville Students

	Satisfied with Self-Image	Immature
White	56	15
Black	61	12

*The boys responded in terms of sports and the girls responded in terms of marriage.

attitudes correlate with self-concept scores and especially the score for self-satisfaction.

The esprit de corps in the black segregated schools was quite noticeable. Many students wore "naturals" and the familiar greeting of "Hey sister" and "Hey brother" gave the observer the feeling of a communal fraternity in which the teachers participated also. In the desegregated schools black students, especially black girls, huddled together. Very few of the black girls participated in extra-curricular activities. In some instances there were remedial classes that were predominantly black. The teachers still expressed some fear of racial conflict. The testing occurred three weeks after the death of Martin Luther King, a week after the National Guard had been withdrawn from the black community (there had been no violence), and during the time the Poor People's March was in Nashville. In spite of the tragedy of the death of Martin Luther King, who visited Nashville many times during the sit-in movement and whose strongest branch of SCLC was in Nashville, there was courage and hope expressed among the black people interviewed that his work would continue and that Black Americans would "reach the mountain top" and overcome.

In the white community there was an expressed commitment to equality, but fear of the "black militants" and the "white liberals." Most frequently the attitude was expressed that things would change with time. Paternalistic but racist attitudes were still evident. The greatest fear expressed was that of busing.

The policy in regard to assignment of pupils was based on the neighborhood school plan which was strictly enforced. All requests for transfer were reviewed and approved only if a course was not offered at the assigned school. The superintendent of schools believed that Nashville had done well in desegregating its schools, but the controlling factor in the school deseg-regation picture was housing which was causing resegregation of the schools. The school board intended to adhere to the geographical zoning plan but was moving into a standard 6-3-3 pattern that would call for larger and fewer junior and senior high schools. It was hoped that the enlarged neighborhood zones around these schools would result in further desegregation. There had also been some talk of school parks which would serve all grades and bring in students from larger sections of the city. However, many felt that unless segregated housing was solved, school desegregation would become a major issue for Nashville again.

1. Southern Education Report. Sept., 1967, p. 13.
2. Muse. Op. cit., 1962, p. 121.
3. Southern Education Report. Sept., 1967, p. 14.

7

The Self-Concept Scores of the Nashville Students

The demographic data of the black students who completed the TSCS is given in Table 1. The black girls numbered 170, with 113 in segregated schools and 57 in desegregated schools. Of those in desegregated schools, 12 were in Catholic schools and 45 were in public schools; of those in segregated schools, 77 were in public schools and 36 were in Catholic schools. In all, 48 black girls were attending Catholic schools and 122 were attending public schools.

As for the 129 black boys tested, 93 were in segregated schools and 36 were in desegregated schools. Of those 93 black boys in segregated schools, 62 were in public segregated schools and 31 were in Catholic segregated schools. As for the 36 black boys in desegregated schools, all were at a public school. In all, 31 black boys were tested from Catholic schools and 90 were tested from public schools.

The black boys ranged in age from 12 to 17 while the black girls ranged in age from 11 to 16. For the numbers of students in each age group see Table 1. Thirty-five percent of the black boys tested were in seventh grade, 39 percent were in eighth grade, and 26 percent were in ninth grade. Among the girls, 41 percent were in seventh grade, 32 percent in eighth grade, and 27 percent in ninth grade.

The Self-Concept Profile of the black students is given in Table 2. The scores are all above or equal to the normative means for TSCS except for the identity score and the moral-ethical-self score which are below the normative means.

TABLE 1

**Distribution of Black Students Tested in Nashville by Sex,
Type of School, Age, and Grade in School**

Black Girls 170				Black Boys 129			
Segregated		*Desegregated*		*Segregated*		*Desegregated*	
113		57		93		36	
Public	*Catholic*	*Catholic*	*Public*	*Public*	*Catholic*	*Catholic*	*Public*
77	36	12	45	62	31	0	36
	Total No. Catholic 48				*Total No. Catholic* 31		
Total No. Public 122				Total No. Public 98			

Age in Years of Black Students

	11	12	13	14	15	16	17
Boys	0	23	37	46	16	6	1
Girls	8	39	43	57	25	8	0

Grades in School of Black Students

	7th	8th	9th
Boys	45	50	34
Girls	70	54	46

BLACK GIRLS IN NASHVILLE

The black girls obtained a mean total positive score of 346.9 which is slightly above the normative mean of 345.57. Eleven percent scored below 300 or below the 7th percentile and 12 percent scored above 400 or the 97th percentile, but the majority of the black girls, 43 percent, scored 350 (50th percentile) or above. These scores indicate that the majority (55 percent) of the black girls have positive self-concepts.

On the self-criticism score the black girls obtained a mean score of 34, which is below the normative mean of 35.54. The girls showed an average amount of ability to criticize themselves, but with some defensiveness.

The mean variability score of 52.7 is above the normative mean of 48.53 indicating that the black girls are not always consistent in how they feel about various aspects of themselves. The mean distribution score of 128.1 is above the normative mean of 120.44 indicating that the black girls showed an average amount of certainty about themselves.

TABLE 2

Self-Concept Profile of Black Students in Nashville

Score	Mean	Standard Deviation	Standard Error	Percentile
Total Positive	348.3623	40.280	2.333	50th
Identity	118.7584	15.738	0.912	15th
Self-Satisfaction	110.7651	15.836	0.917	65th
Behavior	119.0336	15.009	0.869	65th
Physical Self	72.5302	9.663	0.560	52nd
Moral-Ethical Self	67.1208	9.629	0.558	30th
Personal Self	65.7013	11.453	0.663	50th
Family Self	75.1208	11.509	0.667	65th
Social Self	68.0369	10.125	0.587	45th
Self-Criticism	34.3087	5.961	0.345	45th
Distribution	129.7282	29.454	1.706	65th
Variability	54.2081	13.829	0.801	65th

The black girls from the various schools varied in the scores they obtained. It will be interesting to compare the TSCS scores with the family background data and aspirations and attitudes noted in Chapter 6.

At the segregated black parochial school the 36 girls obtained a TP mean of 355, the 55th percentile. Only 5 percent scored below 300 or the 7th percentile, while 12 percent scored above 400, the 97th percentile, and 60 percent scored 350 or above. Thus, 72 percent of the black girls at the segregated parochial school had high self-concepts. The mean SC score of 35 indicates average openness and defensiveness. The mean V score of 53 indicates that the girls are not always consistent in how they feel about themselves in all aspects of the self. The mean D score of 130 indicates that they feel certain how they think and feel about themselves.

At the 100 percent black school the girls obtained a TP mean of 347 with 8 percent scoring below 300, but with 46 percent scoring 350 or above, and 6 percent above 400. Thus, 52 percent of the girls at the segregated black school have high self-concepts. The mean SC score of 33 indicates some defensiveness in looking at the self, the mean V score of 53 shows relative inconsistency, and the mean D score of 128 indicates average certainty in how they feel about themselves.

The 80 percent black school has a TP mean of 354 for the 30 girls tested. Only 6 percent scored below 300, but 64 percent scored 350 or above (46 percent 350 or above and 6 percent above 400). Likewise, the majority of these girls have high self-concept. The SC mean score of 34 indicates some defensiveness in analyzing themselves, the mean V score of 56 indicates that the girls vary a great deal in how they feel about themselves in different aspects, but the mean D score of 134 would seem to indicate that they feel very certain about how they view themselves.

A low TP mean score (329) is obtained from the 19 black girls at the 20 percent black desegregated school. They score in the 30th percentile with 20 percent scoring below 300, only 20 percent scoring 350 or above, but 10 percent scoring above 400. Thus, about 30 percent of the girls have adequate self-concepts; the majority have low self-concepts. The SC mean score of 34 indicates some defensiveness, the mean V score of 47 represents consistency in how they view their total selves, and the mean D score of 115 indicates that they are very uncertain how they view or feel about themselves.

The 26 black girls in the recently desegregated 10 percent black school have a TP mean of 344 with 11 percent scoring below 300, but 40 percent scoring 350 or above, and 12 percent above 400. Thus, the majority of the girls have average to high self-concepts. The mean SC of 34 indicates some defensiveness, the mean V of 52 some inconsistency in various areas, and the mean D of 125 indicates only average certainty about their self-picture.

At the desegregated parochial school the mean TP score for the 12 girls was 339, below the normative mean of 345.5. The majority have adequate self-concepts—54 percent scored 350 or above and some above 400. Sixteen percent scored below 300, however. The mean SC score of 36 indicates openness and little defensiveness in analyzing how they feel about themselves. The mean V score of 52 indicates moderate variability, and the mean D score of 137 indicates that the girls feel very certain how they think and feel about themselves.

BLACK GIRLS IN SEGREGATED SCHOOLS

The 113 black girls in segregated or predominantly black schools seem to have high self-concepts. (See Table 3.) A closer look shows that the girls at the three segregated schools have a TP mean score of 353, above the normative mean of 345.57 and in the 55th percentile. Only 7 percent score below 300, the 7th percentile, while the majority score above the normative mean, with 53 percent scoring 350 or above, and 11 percent scoring above

TABLE 3

Black Girls, Grades 7-8-9—Nashville

Racial Composition	Type of School	TP (Mean)	Percentages	SC Score (Mean)	V Score (Mean)	D Score (Mean)
100% Black	Parochial N = 36	355	<300 = 5% >350 = 60% >400 = 12%	35	53	130
100% Black	Public N = 47	347	<300 = 8% >350 = 46% >400 = 6%	33	53	128
80% Black	Public N = 30	354	<300 = 6% >350 = 52% >400 = 13%	34	56	134
20% Black	Public N = 19	329	<300 = 20% >350 = 20% >400 = 10%	34	47	115
10% Black	Public N = 26	344	<300 = 11% >350 = 40% >400 = 12%	34	52	125
10% Black	Parochial N = 12	339	<300 = 16% >350 = 46% >400 = 8%	36	52	137
Totals	N = 170	346.9	<300 = 11% >350 = 43% >400 = 12%	34	52.7	128.1

400. The mean SC score of 34 indicates average openness, but some defensiveness, in accepting any negative statements about themselves. The mean V score of 54.2 shows that the girls change in their attitudes toward themselves in various areas, but the mean D score of 131 would seem to confirm the fact that they are very certain about how they perceive themselves (see Table 4).

BLACK GIRLS IN DESEGREGATED SCHOOLS

A closer look at the total scores for the 57 black girls in desegregated schools confirms the low mean TP scores. The group as a whole has a mean TP of 337, 35th percentile, with 16 percent scoring below 300, 34 percent obtaining 350 or above, and 10 percent scoring above 400. The mean SC score of 35 is equivalent to the normative mean, indicating moderate openness. The mean V score of 50 confirms some inconsistency, and the mean D score of 126 indicates moderate uncertainty (see Table 5).

TABLE 4

Black Students in Segregated or Predominantly Black Schools—Nashville

Sex	TP (Mean)	Percentages	SC Score (Mean)	V Score (Mean)	D Score (Mean)
Females N = 113	353 (55 percentile)	<300 = 7% >350 = 53% >400 = 11%	34.1 (45 percentile)	54.2 (70 percentile)	131 (65 percentile)
Males N = 93	353 (55 percentile)	<300 = 8% >350 = 52% >400 = 16%	35 (45 percentile)	55 (72 percentile)	129 (77 percentile)
Totals N = 206	353 (55 percentile)	<300 = 7% >350 = 52% >400 = 13%	35 (45 percentile)	55 (72 percentile)	130 (78 percentile)

TABLE 5

Black Students in Desegregated or Predominantly White Schools—Nashville

Sex	TP (Mean)	Percentages	SC Score (Mean)	V Score (Mean)	D Score (Mean)
Females N = 57	337 (35 percentile)	<300 = 16% >350 = 34% >400 = 10%	35 (45 percentile)	50 (60 percentile)	126 (60 percentile)
Males N = 36	345 (48 percentile)	<300 = 16% >350 = 52% >400 = 5%	34 (45 percentile)	57 (75 percentile)	139 (75 percentile)
Totals N = 93	341 (40 percentile)	<300 = 16% >350 = 43% >400 = 8%	34 (45 percentile)	53 (68 percentile)	132 (70 percentile)

TABLE 6

Black Boys, Grades 7-8-9—Nashville

Racial Composition	Type of School	TP (Mean)	Percentages	SC Score (Mean)	V Score (Mean)	D Score (Mean)
100% Black	Parochial N = 31	355	<300 = 16% >350 = 54% >400 = 24%	35	55	135
100% Black	Public N = 42	346	<300 = 7% >350 = 46% >400 = 8%	34	57	123
80% Black	Public N = 20	358	<300 = 0% >350 = 56% >400 = 15%	36	54	130
20% Black	Public N = 19	350	<300 = 15% >350 = 51% >400 = 10%	34	57	141 (80 percentile)
10% Black	Public N = 17	340	<300 = 17% >350 = 54% >400 = 0%	34	57	136
Totals	N = 129	350 (55 percentile)	<300 = 11% >350 = 52% >400 = 11%	34 (46 percentile)	56 (73 percentile)	133 (70 percentile)

BLACK BOYS IN NASHVILLE

The 129 black boys given the TSCS came from five schools. The mean TP score for the group was 350, above the normative mean and in the 55th percentile, with 11 percent scoring below 300, but 52 percent obtaining 350 or above, and 11 percent scoring above 400. The mean SC score of 34 represents relative defensiveness in accepting negative statements about themselves. The mean V score of 56 represents much inconsistency, but the mean D of 133 represents relative certainty about the self-picture. (See Table 6.)

The 31 black boys at the segregated parochial school obtained a TP mean of 355 with 16 percent below 300, but 54 percent scored 350 or above and 24 percent above 400. Thus, the majority of those boys had high self-concepts. The mean SC of 35, the mean V of 55, and the mean D of 135 indicate average openness, much inconsistency, and much certainty about the self-perception.

At the segregated public school, the 42 black boys obtained a TP mean of 346, just above the normative mean. The SC mean of 34, the V mean of 57, and the D mean of 135 represent some defensiveness, a great deal of inconsistency, but much certainty about the perception of the self. In general, the majority of the students have adequate to high self-concepts with 7 percent scoring below 300, 46 percent obtaining TP scores of 350 or above, and 8 percent scoring above 400.

At the 80 percent black school the 20 black boys obtained a TP mean of 358 indicating high self-concept. None of the students scored below 300, and 65 percent scored above 350, with 15 percent of those above the 97th percentile. The SC mean of 36, the V mean of 54, and the D mean of 130 represent openness about the self, some inconsistency, and a certain amount of definiteness in self-perception.

The 19 black boys at the 20 percent black desegregated school have a TP mean of 350, 55th percentile, with 15 percent scoring below 300, but 71 percent obtaining a score of 350 or above, and 15 percent of those scoring above 400. The mean SC of 34 is below the normative mean, indicating some defensiveness, but the mean V of 57 and the mean D of 141 indicate that the students are very inconsistent in the total self-perception but very definite in how they feel about themselves.

In the 10 percent black desegregated school the TP mean for the 17 black boys is 340. The SC mean of 34 is below the normative, but the mean V of 57 and the mean D of 136 represent some defensiveness, inconsistency, and great certainty in self-perception.

BLACK BOYS IN SEGREGATED SCHOOLS

The 93 black boys in three segregated or predominantly black schools have a TP mean of 353, 55th percentile, with only 8 percent scoring below 300, but 52 percent obtaining a score of 350 to 400, and 16 percent scoring above 400. The mean SC of 35, the mean V of 55, and the mean D of 129 indicate some openness in looking at the self, great variability, but some uncertainty with a high self-concept. (See Table 4.)

BLACK BOYS IN DESEGREGATED SCHOOLS

The 36 black boys in the two desegregated schools have a TP mean of 345, equivalent to the normative mean. Those obtaining a TP score of 350 to 400 are 52 percent, with 5 percent scoring above 400, and 16 percent scoring below 300. The SC mean of 34 is below the normative mean, representing some defensiveness in accepting negative concepts about the self. The group is very inconsistent about how they see themselves (V=57), but very certain about themselves and how they feel (mean D=139). (See Table 5.)

BLACK STUDENTS IN PUBLIC AND PAROCHIAL SCHOOLS

The 79 black students in parochial schools score higher (351) on the TP mean than the 220 black students in public schools (346.5), but the difference is not significant. The mean SC scores are 35.3 for parochial and 34 for public; the latter representing some defensiveness and an unwillingness to consider negative concepts about the self. The mean V scores are similar— 53.3 for parochial, 54.1 for public. However, on the mean D scores the black parochial students (134) score significantly higher than the black public students (115). The difference is significant at the 1 percent level.

The 48 black girls in the two parochial schools have a TP mean of 347 compared to the TP mean of 344.5 for the 122 black girls in public schools. However, the mean D score of 133.5 for the black parochial girls is higher than the mean D score of 124.5 for the black public school girls. The difference is significant at the 5 percent level. Although black parochial girls score higher on the SC mean score than the black public school girls, the difference is not significant.

When 122 black girls in public schools are compared to the 98 black boys in public schools, the TP mean scores are similar—344.5 and 348.5 respectively. Although the boys score higher on the SC and V means (34.5 and 56.2) than the girls (33.5 and 52), the difference is not significant.

However, the black girls in public schools have a higher mean D score (124.5) than the black boys in public schools (106); the difference is significant at the 1 percent level.

The 31 black boys in parochial schools have a higher mean D score (135) than the 98 black boys in public schools (D=106); the difference is significant at the 5 percent level. (See Table 7.)

TABLE 7

A Comparison of Black Students in Parochial and Public Schools in Nashville

Black Students in Catholic Schools—Nashville						
Sex	Type of School	No. of Students	TP (Mean)	SC Score (Mean)	V Score (Mean)	D Score (Mean)
Girls	100% Black	36	355	35	53	130
Girls	10% Black	12	339	36	52	137
Boys	100% Black	31	355	35	52	135
Total		79	351	35.3	53.3	134

Black Students in Public Schools—Nashville
Black Girls

Type of School	No. of Students	TP (Mean)	SC Score (Mean)	V Score (Mean)	D Score (Mean)
100% Black	47	347	33	53	128
80% Black	30	354	34	56	134
20% Black	19	329	34	47	115
10% Black	26	344	34	52	125
Total	122	344.5	33.5	52	124.5

Black Boys

Type of School	No. of Students	TP (Mean)	SC Score (Mean)	V Score (Mean)	D Score (Mean)
100% Black	42	346	34	57	123
80% Black	20	358	36	54	130
20% Black	19	350	34	57	141
10% Black	17	340	34	57	136
Total	98	348.5	34.5	56.2	106

Summary of Data on Black Students in Public and Parochial Schools—Nashville

Type of School	No. of Students	TP (Mean)	SC Score (Mean)	V Score (Mean)	D Score (Mean)
Parochial	79	351	35.3	53.3	134
Public	220	346.5	34	54.1	115
Total	299	348.7	34.7	53.7	124.5

WHITE STUDENTS

Of the white students who took the TSCS 183 were girls, 79 in segregated schools and 104 in desegregated schools. Among the 79 white girls in segregated schools, 50 were attending public schools and 29 were attending Catholic parochial schools. And, of the 104 white girls attending desegregated schools, 20 were attending Catholic desegregated schools and 84 were attending public desegregated schools. In all, 134 white girls were attending public schools and 49 white girls were attending Catholic parochial schools. (See Table 8.)

Of the 134 white boys participating in this study, 72 were in segregated schools and 62 were in desegregated schools. Of the 62 in desegregated schools, 62 were in public schools and there were none in Catholic parochial schools. Of the 72 boys in segregated schools, 39 were in public schools and 33 were in Catholic schools. In all, there were 101 white boys in public schools and 33 white boys in Catholic parochial schools.

The white boys ranged in age from 12 to 16 years, and the percentages for each age group is given in Table 8. Likewise, the white girls ranged in age

TABLE 8

Distribution of White Students Tested in Nashville by Sex, Type of School, and Grade in School

White Girls 183				White Boys 134			
Segregated		Desegregated		Segregated		Desegregated	
79		104		72		62	
Public	Catholic	Catholic	Public	Public	Catholic	Catholic	Public
50	29	20	84	39	33	0	62
	Total No. Catholic 49				Total No. Catholic 33		
Total No. Public 134				Total No. Public 101			

Age in Years of White Students

	12	13	14	15	16
Boys	14%	33%	27%	22%	3%
Girls	17%	37%	27%	18%	1%

Grades in School of White Students

	7th	8th	9th
Boys	38%	33%	28%
Girls	38%	29%	33%

from 12 to 16 years and their percentage per age group are given in Table 8. In the seventh grade there were 38 percent of the boys tested and 38 percent of the girls tested. In the eighth grade there were 33 percent of the boys tested and 29 percent of the girls tested. In the ninth grade 28 percent of the boys were tested and 33 percent of the girls were tested.

The self-concept profile of the white students in Nashville can be seen in Table 9. It should be noted that as a group, the white students fall below the normative mean on the total positive score, the identity score, the moral-ethical-self score, the personal-self score, and the social-self score.

WHITE GIRLS IN NASHVILLE

The 183 white girls tested obtained a TP mean score of 333 with 18 percent scoring below 300, 39 percent obtaining a score of 350 or above, and 6 percent scoring above 400. It would seem that the majority of the white girls tested have low self-concepts (56 percent). The mean SC score of 36, the mean V score of 56, and the mean D score of 124 would seem to say

TABLE 9

Self-Concept Profile of White Students in Nashville

Score	Mean	Standard Deviation	Standard Error	Percentile
Total Positive	332.5642	47.372	2.652	30th
Identity	115.3291	16.549	0.927	10th
Self-Satisfaction	104.2602	20.145	1.128	50th
Behavior	117.1881	40.661	2.277	55th
Physical Self	72.0000	45.461	2.545	52nd
Moral-Ethical Self	65.0157	10.516	0.589	20th
Personal Self	63.7555	33.257	1.862	40th
Family Self	73.8621	49.082	2.748	58th
Social Self	67.0313	12.913	0.723	40th
Self-Criticism	34.9718	6.740	0.377	45th
Distribution	124.0376	30.071	1.684	55th
Variability	53.4765	13.457	0.753	64th

that the white girls are open in analyzing themselves with average defensiveness, are very variable in how they perceive themselves in different aspects of the self, and relatively uncertain how they think and feel about themselves (see Table 10).

The 29 white girls in the segregated parochial schools obtained a TP mean score of 314 with 19 percent scoring below 300, 26 percent obtaining a score of 350 or above, and 3 percent scoring above 400. The SC mean score of 39, the V mean score of 51, and the D mean score of 112 would seem to indicate that the girls in the segregated parochial schools are critical of themselves and very open about analyzing themselves, have some degree of inconsistency in various aspects of the self, and are very uncertain about how they think and feel about themselves. The 29 white girls in the segregated parochial school also have very low self-concepts with only 29 percent scoring above the normative mean of 345.5.

In the segregated white public school the 50 white girls obtained a total mean positive score of 339. Eighteen percent of the girls scored below 300, while 46 percent obtained a score of 350 or above, and 6 percent score above 400. It would seem that on the whole the majority of the girls at this school have adequate self-concepts. The SC mean score of 34, the V mean

TABLE 10

White Girls, Grades 7-8-9 in Nashville

Racial Composition	Type of School	TP (Mean)	Percentages	SC Score (Mean)	V Score (Mean)	D Score (Mean)
100% White	Parochial N = 29	314	<300 = 19% >350 = 26% >400 = 3%	39	51	112
100% White	Public N = 50	339	<300 = 18% >350 = 46% >400 = 6%	34	55	124
10% Black	Parochial N = 20	336	<300 = 20% >350 = 35% >400 = 10%	34	55	125
10% Black	Public N = 26	330	<300 = 23% >350 = 44% >400 = 4%	36	57	127
20% Black	Public N = 26	333	<300 = 19% >350 = 46% >400 = 6%	34	55	126
80% Black	Public N = 32	346	<300 = 9% >350 = 45% >400 = 9%	36	56	129
Totals	N = 183	333	<300 = 18% >350 = 39% >400 = 6%	35	56	124

score of 55, and the D mean score of 124 would seem to indicate that these girls show some defensiveness in analyzing themselves, a great deal of inconsistency in the total self-picture, and are as certain of themselves as the normative group.

In the 10 percent black parochial school the 20 white girls obtained a TP mean score of 336 with 20 percent scoring below 300, 35 percent obtaining a score of 350 or above, and 10 percent scoring above 400. Although the group as a whole has a TP mean below the normative mean for the TSCS, it would appear that at least 45 percent of the girls have adequate or high self-concepts with 55 percent having low or inadequate self-concepts. The SC mean score of 34, the V mean score of 55, and the D mean score of 125 would seem to indicate that these girls have some defensiveness in accepting negative ideas about themselves, show variability from one area of self-perception to another, and are not very definite about how they think and feel about themselves, although the D mean is slightly above the normative mean for the scale.

In the 10 percent black public school the 26 white girls participating obtained a TP mean score of 330, with 23 percent scoring below 300, or in the 7th percentile, 44 percent obtaining a score of 350 or above, and 4 percent scoring above 400. The TP mean of 330 is below the normative mean and falls into the 30th percentile. It would appear that the majority of the students have adequate to less than adequate self-concepts while 48 percent of the students have adequate or high self-concepts. The SC mean score of 36, the V mean score of 57, and the V mean score of 127 would seem to indicate that the white girls in the 10 percent black public school are willing to be open in accepting negative aspects about themselves, show a wide range of variability in the self-picture, and have a moderate degree of certainty in how they think and feel about themselves.

The 26 white girls at the 20 percent black public school obtained a TP mean score of 333, which is below the normative mean and falls into the 30th percentile. Of the 26 white girls participating, 19 percent scored below 300, 46 percent obtained a score of 350 or above, and 6 percent scored above 400. It would seem that at least 52 percent have adequate or high self-concepts, with 48 percent having adequate to very low self-concepts. The SC mean score of 34 would seem to indicate that there is some defensiveness in accepting negative comments about themselves; the V mean score of 55 indicates some variability; and the D mean score of 126 would seem to indicate moderate certainty about the self-perception.

The 32 white girls in the 80 percent black public school obtained the highest TP mean score among the white girls from the six schools. These girls obtained a TP mean score of 346 which is just above the normative mean and within the 50th percentile. Nine percent of the girls scored below 300, but 45 percent obtained a score of 350 or above, and 9 percent scored above 400. It would seem that the majority (54 percent) have high self-concepts, with about 40 percent scoring below the normative mean. These white girls also seemed to indicate an ability to be open and less defensive about themselves (SC mean score 36), demonstrated a great deal of variability in their self picture (V mean score of 56), and demonstrated some certainty about the self (D mean score of 129).

WHITE GIRLS IN SEGREGATED SCHOOLS

There were 79 white girls in segregated or predominantly white schools. These girls obtained a TP mean score of 327 which falls into the 25th percentile. Among the 79 girls participating, 18 percent scored below 300, 36 percent obtained a score of 350 or above, and 5 percent scored above 400. Thus, it would seem that close to 58 percent of the white girls in segregated schools have adequate to very low self-concepts with only 41 percent having high self-concepts. The segregated white females obtained a SC mean score of 36 indicating openness in looking at themselves. The V mean score of 53 indicates variability from one area of self-perception to the other, and the mean D score of 118 indicates a great deal of uncertainty about the self-perception. (See Table 11).

WHITE GIRLS IN DESEGREGATED SCHOOLS

The 104 white girls in desegregated schools obtained a TP mean score of 334, the 35th percentile, with 18 percent scoring below 300, 40 percent obtaining a score of 350 or above, and 7 percent scoring above 400. At least 50 percent of the girls in desegregated schools have less than adequate self-concepts. The SC mean score of 35 is equivalent to the normative mean. The V mean score of 56 is above the normative mean and in the 73rd percentile, indicating a great deal of variability. The D mean score of 126 is above the normative mean and within the 60th percentile, indicating some certainty about the self. (See Table 12.)

WHITE BOYS IN NASHVILLE

One hundred and thirty-four white boys from five junior high schools participated in the testing (see Table 13). As a group, the white boys obtained a total positive mean score of 331 which is below the normative mean and within the 29th percentile. Among the boys tested, 23 percent scored below 300, 42 percent obtained a score of 350 or above, and 4 percent

TABLE 11

White Students in Segregated Schools in Nashville

Sex	TP (Mean)	Percentages	SC Score (Mean)	V Score (Mean)	D Score (Mean)
Females N = 79	327 (25 percentile)	<300 = 18% >350 = 36% >400 = 5%	36 (50 percentile)	53 (68 percentile)	118 (45 percentile)
Males N = 72	333 (30 percentile)	<300 = 13% >350 = 45% >400 = 5%	34 (47 percentile)	50 (60 percentile)	122 (55 percentile)
Totals N = 151	330 (28 percentile)	<300 = 15% >350 = 41% >400 = 5%	35 (48 percentile)	51 (62 percentile)	120 (50 percentile)

TABLE 12

White Students in Desegregated Schools in Nashville

Sex	TP (Mean)	Percentages	SC Score (Mean)	V Score (Mean)	D Score (Mean)
Females N = 104	334 (35 percentile)	<300 = 18% >350 = 40% >400 = 7%	35 (48 percentile)	56 (73 percentile)	126 (60 percentile)
Males N = 62	329 (28 percentile)	<300 = 26% >350 = 40% >400 = 3%	35 (48 percentile)	54 (70 percentile)	126 (60 percentile)
Totals N = 166	332 (30 percentile)	<300 = 22% >350 = 40% >400 = 5%	35 (48 percentile)	55 (72 percentile)	126 (60 percentile)

Tennessee Self-Concept Scale—Mean Scores

Total Net Positive = 345.57   Variability = 48.53
Self-Criticism = 35.54   Distribution = 120.44

TABLE 13

White Boys, Grades 7-8-9 in Nashville

Racial Composition	Type of School	TP (Mean)	Percentages	SC Score (Mean)	V Score (Mean)	D Score (Mean)
100% White	Parochial N = 33	340 (40 percentile)	<300 = 12% >350 = 42% >400 = 3%	35 (48 percentile)	45 (40 percentile)	115 (40 percentile)
100% White	Public N = 39	326 (25 percentile)	<300 = 25% >350 = 47% >400 = 6%	33	55 (72 percentile)	130 (68 percentile)
10% Black	Public N = 20	322 (20 percentile)	<300 = 30% >350 = 30% >400 = 0%	34	49	110 (30 percentile)
20% Black	Public N = 24	326 (25 percentile)	<300 = 32% >350 = 36% >400 = 4%	36	55	125 (60 percentile)
80% Black	Public N = 18	339 (40 percentile)	<300 = 16% >350 = 54% >400 = 6%	36 (50 percentile)	58 (78 percentile)	143 (80 percentile)
Totals	N = 134	331 (29 percentile)	<300 = 23% >350 = 42% >400 = 4%	35 (48 percentile)	52 (62 percentile)	125 (60 percentile)

scored above 400. It would seem that at least 50 percent of the white boys tested scored at the normative mean or below, with 46 percent having adequate or high self-concepts. The mean TP score of 331 for the group would indicate that as a whole the white boys have low self-concepts. The SC mean score is 35 which is equivalent to the normative mean. The V mean score is 52, above the normative mean and within the 62nd percentile. The D mean score is 125, in the 60th percentile, and above the normative mean.

In the 100 percent white parochial school the 33 white boys obtained a TP mean score of 340 which is below the normative mean and within the 40th percentile. Among the boys tested, 12 percent scored below 300, 42 percent scored 350 or above, and 3 percent scored above 400. The SC mean score of 35 is equivalent to the normative mean. The V mean score of 45 is below the normative mean and within the 40th percentile, indicating less inconsistency or variability about various aspects of the self. The D mean score of 115 is below the normative mean and within the 40th percentile, indicating that the boys are very uncertain how they think and feel about themselves.

There were 39 white boys from a white segregated public school who took the TSCS. These boys obtained a TP mean score of 326 which is below the normative mean and within the 25th percentile. Among the boys tested, 25 percent scored below 300 or below the 7th percentile, 47 percent obtained a score of 350 or above, and 6 percent scored above 400. It would seem that as a group the 39 white boys at the desegregated public school have a low self-concept. At least 53 percent obtained a score of 350 and above, but it is interesting to note that 25 percent scored in the 7th percentile. The SC mean score of 33 is below the normative mean, indicating defensiveness; the V mean score of 55 is above the normative mean and in the 72nd percentile; the D mean score of 130 is in the 68th percentile and indicates that these boys feel very certain how they think and feel about themselves.

In the 10 percent black public school 20 boys participated obtaining a total positive mean score of 322 which is in the 20th percentile. Among the boys tested 30 percent scored below 300, 30 percent obtained a score of 350 or above, and none scored above 400. The SC mean score is 34, the V mean score is 49, and the D mean score is 110. Only the V mean score is above the normative mean. The SC mean score and the D mean score are both below the normative means. It would seem that the 20 white boys at the 10 percent black public school have very low self-concepts, are somewhat defensive in their perception of themselves, demonstrate very little variability, and are very uncertain how they think and feel about themselves.

At the 20 percent black public school 24 white boys participated obtaining a TP mean score of 326 which is below the normative mean and within the 25th percentile. Among the boys participating, 32 percent scored below 300, or below the 7th percentile, while 36 percent obtained a score of 350 or above, and 4 percent scored above 400. The SC mean score of 36 is above the normative mean, the V mean score of 55 is above the normative mean, and the D mean score of 125 is above the normative mean. It would seem that these 24 white boys in a 20 percent black public school have very low self-concepts, but demonstrate some openness in accepting negative ideas about themselves, show variability in the self perception, and some certainty in how they think and feel about themselves.

The 18 white boys attending the 80 percent black public school obtained a TP mean score of 339 which is below the normative mean and in the 40th percentile. Among the boys participating, 16 percent scored below 300, but 54 percent obtained a score of 350 or above, and 6 percent scored above 400. Therefore, at least 60 percent of the boys at the 80 percent black public school have adequate to high self-concepts, but the total mean score is decreased to 339 by the 16 percent who score below 300. The group obtained a SC mean score of 36 which is above the normative mean and within the 50th percentile, a V mean score of 58 which is above the normative mean and within the 78th percentile, and a D mean score of 143 which is above the normative mean and within the 80th percentile. Although the group as a whole shows a low self-concept, they demonstrate a capacity for openness, much variability in the self-picture, and a high degree of certainty in how they think and feel about themselves.

WHITE BOYS IN SEGREGATED SCHOOLS

There were 72 white boys in segregated schools who obtained a TP mean score of 333 which is below the normative mean and within the 30th percentile. Among the boys participating, 13 percent scored below 300, while 45 percent obtained a score of 350 or above, and 5 percent scored above 400. The segregated white boys obtained a SC mean score of 34 which is below the normative mean and within the 47th percentile, a V mean score of 50 which is above the normative mean and within the 60th percentile, and a D mean score of 122 which is above the normative mean and within the 55th percentile. As a group, the 72 white boys in segregated schools have a low self-concept, although 50 percent of them obtained a score of 350 or above, are defensive about their self-picture, demonstrate variability in self-perception and only moderate certainty in how they think and feel about themselves. (See Table 11.)

WHITE BOYS IN DESEGREGATED SCHOOLS

Of the 62 white boys in desegregated schools, 26 percent scored below 300, 40 percent obtained a score of 350 or above, and 3 percent scored above 400. The TP mean score for the group was 329 which is below the normative mean and within the 28th percentile. The desegregated white boys obtained a SC mean score of 35 which is equivalent to the normative mean, a V mean score of 54 which is above the normative mean and within the 70th percentile, and a D mean score of 126 which is above the normative mean and within the 60th percentile. It would appear that the white boys in desegregated schools have low self-concepts. Although 43 percent of them obtained a score of 350 or above, the resulting mean score is decreased by the large number of students scoring below 300. These boys demonstrate average openness and defensiveness about themselves, a great deal of variability in self-perception, and average certainty in how they think and feel about themselves. (See Table 12.)

A COMPARISON OF WHITE STUDENTS IN CATHOLIC AND PUBLIC SCHOOLS

The 82 white students in Catholic schools obtained a total positive mean score of 330. The Catholic school students obtained a SC mean score of 36, a V mean score of 50.3, and a D mean score of 117.3. The 235 white students in public schools obtained a TP mean score of 332.7, a SC mean score of 34.9, a V mean score of 55, and a D mean score of 126.7. There is no statistical significance between any of the mean scores of the parochial or public students.

The 49 white girls in Catholic schools obtained a total positive mean score of 325 compared with that of 337.2 for the 134 white girls in public schools. The difference is not significant. There is no significant difference between the white girls in Catholic schools and the white girls in public schools on the V and D mean scores, although the white girls in public schools scored higher on both scores than those girls in Catholic schools. The white girls in Catholic schools scored somewhat higher on the SC mean score than the white girls in public schools, but the difference is not significant. (See Table 14.)

A comparison of the white boys in Catholic schools to the white boys in public schools shows the two groups scoring about the same on the SC mean score. The white boys in Catholic schools scored higher on the TP mean score than the white boys in public schools, but the white boys in public schools scored higher on the V mean score and the D mean score than the white boys in parochial schools. The differences are not significant. It is interesting to note, however, that when the 33 white boys in the 100 percent white parochial school are compared with the 39 white boys in the 100 percent white public school, some significant differences emerge. The white boys in the segregated Catholic school obtained a TP mean score of 340

TABLE 14

A Comparison of White Students in Parochial and Public Schools in Nashville

White Students in Catholic Schools—Nashville

Sex	Type of School	No. of Students	TP (Mean)	SC Score (Mean)	V Score (Mean)	D Score (Mean)
Girls	100% White	29	314	39	51	112
Girls	10% Black	20	336	34	55	125
Boys	100% White	33	340*	35	45*	115*
Totals		82	330	36	50.3	117.3

White Students in Public Schools—Nashville
White Girls

Type of School	No. of Students	TP (Mean)	SC Score (Mean)	V Score (Mean)	D Score (Mean)
100% White	50	339	34	55	124
10% Black	26	330	36	57	127
20% Black	26	333	34	55	126
80% Black	32	346	36	56	129
Total	134	337.2	35	55.7	126.5

White Boys

Type of School	No. of Students	TP (Mean)	SC Score (Mean)	V Score (Mean)	D Score (Mean)
100% White	39	326*	33	55*	130*
10% Black	20	322	34	49	110
20% Black	24	326	36	55	125
80% Black	18	339	36	58	143
Total	101	328.2	34.7	54.2	127

Summary of Data on White Students in Public and Parochial Schools—Nashville

Type of School	No. of Students	TP (Mean)	SC Score (Mane)	V Score (Mean)	D Score (Mean)
Parochial	82	330	36	50.3	117.3
Public	235	332.7	34.9	55	126.7
Total	317	331.3	35.5	52.7	122

*Significant at the 5 percent level for same score between white boys in segregated Catholic schools and white boys in segregated public schools.

compared with a TP mean score of 326 for the white boys in segregated public schools. The difference is significant at the 5 percent level. Although the white boys in the segregated Catholic school scored higher on the SC mean score (35) than the white boys in the segregated public school (33), the difference is not significant. However, the white boys in the segregated Catholic school obtained a lower V mean score than the white boys in the segregated public school (55). The difference is significant at the 5 percent level. Likewise, on the V mean scores the white boys in the segregated public school scored higher (130) than the white boys in the segregated Catholic school (115). The difference is significant at the 1 percent level (see Table 14).

CONCLUSION

The 615 students tested in Nashville obtained a total positive mean score of 340 which falls into the 40th percentile, with 16 percent scoring below 300, 45 percent obtaining a score of 350 or above, and 8 percent scoring above 400. The SC mean score for the Nashville students is 35, equivalent to the normative mean. The V mean score for the Nashville students is 54, above the normative mean and within the 70th percentile. The D mean score is 128, above the normative mean and within the 65th percentile. It would seem that the Nashville students as a group have adequate self-concepts with 53 percent scoring 350 or above. They have average openness about looking at themselves, variability in the self-perception, and some certainty in how they think and feel about themselves. (See Table 15.)

TABLE 15

Black and White Students in Nashville

Race	TP (Mean)	Percentages	SC Score (Mean)	V Score (Mean)	D Score (Mean)
White N = 317	332 (30 percentile)	<300 = 21% >350 = 41% >400 = 5%	36 (50 percentile)	54 (70 percentile)	125 (60 percentile)
Black N = 297	348 (50 percentile)	<300 = 11% >350 = 48% >400 = 12%	34 (47 percentile)	54 (70 percentile)	131 (70 percentile)
Totals N = 614	340 (40 percentile)	<300 = 16% >350 = 45% >400 = 8%	35 (48 percentile)	54 (70 percentile)	128 (65 percentile)

8

Comparison of Nashville Students in Segregated and Desegregated Schools

COMPARISON OF WHITE AND BLACK STUDENTS

When the 299 black students in Nashville are compared on the TSCS scores with the 317 white students, some significant differences can be seen (see Table 1). It is interesting to note that the black students score above the normative mean on the following: total positive, 348.3; variability, 54.2; distribution, 129.7; self-satisfaction, 110.7; behavior, 119.0; physical self, (slightly above the normative means) 72.5; personal self, (slightly above the normative means), 65.7; family self, 75.1. The black students score below the normative mean on self-criticism, 34.3 and on identity, 118.7; they score at the normative mean level on social self, 68.0. The white students score above the normative mean on the following: variability, 53.4; distribution, 124.0; self-satisfaction, 104.2 (just slightly above); behavior, 117.1; physical self, 72.0 (just slightly above); family self, 73.8. However, the white students score below the normative mean on the following: total positive, 332.5; self-criticism, 34.9; identity, 115.3; moral-ethical self, 65.0; personal self, 63.7 (just slightly below); social self, 67.0 (just slightly below). (See Table 2.)

The black students scored higher on the mean total positive score than the white students and the difference is statistically significant ($p < 0.001$). Likewise, on the mean distribution scores the black students score higher than the white students, and the difference is statistically significant ($p < 0.02$). Also, on identity and self-satisfaction, the black students score higher than the white students and the difference is statistically significant; identity, ($p < 0.009$), self-satisfaction ($p < 0.001$). On the moral-ethical

TABLE 1

Population Sample According to Sex, Race, and Type of School in Nashville

Males		261	
White 134		Black 129	
Segregated 72	Desegregated 62	Segregated 93	Desegregated 36
Number of Schools = 8 Parochial Schools = 3 Public Schools = 5			

Females		353	
White 183		Black 170	
Segregated 79	Desegregated 104	Segregated 113	Desegregated 57
Segregated White Schools = 2 Segregated Black Schools = 3 Desegregated Schools = 3			

mean score, the black students score higher than the white students and the difference is statistically significant ($p < 0.02$). There is no significant difference between the black students and white students on the mean self-criticism scores or the mean variability scores, both groups scoring similarly. Although there is no significant difference between the black students and the white students on the mean behavior scores the mean personal-self scores, the mean family-self scores, and the mean social-self scores, the black students score higher. Only on the mean physical-self scores do the black and white students score the same. (See Table 2.)

COMPARISON OF WHITE AND BLACK BOYS

When the 129 black boys in Nashville are compared on the TSCS scores with the 134 white boys in Nashville, some significant differences are seen. First of all, the black boys score above the normative mean for the scale on the following: total positive, 350.2; variability, 56.1; distribution, 131.7; self-satisfaction, 111.3; behavior, 118.8; physical self 72.6; personal self, 67.4; family self, 75.0. The black boys score below the normative mean for

TABLE 2

Comparison of White and Black Students in Nashville

TSCS Scores		*Black Students* *n = 299*	*White Students* *n = 317*	*Significance*
TP	Mean SD*	348.36 40.28	332.56 47.37	p < 0.001
SC	Mean SD	34.30 5.96	34.97 6.74	N.S.
V	Mean SD	54.20 13.82	53.47 13.45	N.S.
D	Mean SD	129.72 29.45	124.03 30.07	p < 0.02
Identity	Mean SD	118.75 15.73	115.32 16.54	p < 0.009
Self-Satisfaction	Mean SD	110.76 15.83	104.26 20.14	p < 0.001
Behavior	Mean SD	119.03 15.00	117.18 40.66	N.S.
Physical Self	Mean SD	72.53 9.66	72.00 45.46	N.S.
Moral-Ethical Self	Mean SD	67.12 9.62	65.01 10.51	p < 0.02
Personal Self	Mean SD	65.70 11.45	63.75 33.25	N.S.
Family Self	Mean SD	75.12 11.50	73.86 49.08	N.S.
Social Self	Mean SD	68.03 10.12	67.03 12.91	N.S.

*SD means standard deviation.

the scale on the following: self-criticism, 34.6; identity, 120.3; and moral-ethical self, 66.2. On the social-self the black students' score, 67.3, is equal to the normative mean for the scale. The white boys score above the normative mean for the scale on the following: variability, 51.9; distribution, 124.4; self-satisfaction, 106.3; behavior, 119.0; physical self, 76.1; personal self, 66.9; family self, 76.4. However, the white boys score below the normative mean on the following: total positive, 331.0; self-criticism, 34.6; identity, 113.7; moral-ethical self, 62.7; social self, 67.8.

The black boys score significantly higher than the white boys on the total positive mean score (p < 0.001), on the mean variability score (p < 0.02), on identity (p < 0.003), on self-satisfaction (p < 0.04), and on moral-ethical self (p < 0.008). (See Table 3.)

TABLE 3

Comparison of White and Black Boys in Nashville

TSCS Scores		Black Boys n = 129	White Boys n = 134	Significance
TP	Mean	350.20	331.03	p <0.001
	SD*	42.19	49.95	
SC	Mean	34.6250	34.60	N.S.
	SD	5.986	7.16	
V	Mean	56.15ª	51.98	p <0.02
	SD	14.15	13.79	
D	Mean	131.76	124.49	N.S.
	SD	30.87	32.85	
Identity	Mean	120.30	113.75	p <0.003
	SD	16.37	18.79	
Self-Satisfaction	Mean	111.34	106.38	p <0.04
	SD	15.04	23.36	
Behavior	Mean	118.81	119.01	N.S.
	SD	16.81	59.92	
Physical Self	Mean	72.69	76.11ᵈ	N.S.
	SD	9.43	68.76	
Moral-Ethical Self	Mean	66.21	62.77	p <0.008
	SD	9.73	11.16	
Personal Self	Mean	67.46ª	66.92	N.S.
	SD	11.60	49.11	
Family Self	Mean	75.07	76.48	N.S.
	SD	11.59	73.98	
Social Self	Mean	68.89	67.87	N.S.
	SD	10.84	16.27	

SD means standard deviation.
ªSignificance at the 5 percent level between same scores for black boys and black girls. See Table 4.
ᵈSignificance at the 1 percent level between same scores of white boys and white girls. See Table 4.

COMPARISON OF WHITE AND BLACK GIRLS

One hundred and seventy black girls and 183 white girls participated in the study. On the TSCS scores, the black girls score above the normative mean on the following: total positive score, 346.9; variability score, 52.7; distribution score, 128.1; self-satisfaction, 110.3; behavior, 119.2; physical self, 72.4; family self, 75.1. The black girls score below the normative mean on the following: self-criticism, 34.0; identity, 117.5; moral-ethical self, 67.8; social self, 67.3. On the personal-self mean score, the black girls (64.3) are equal to the normative mean.

The white girls are above the normative mean on the following TSCS scores: variability, 54.5; distribution, 123.6; family self, 71.9. However, the white girls score below the normative mean on the following: total positive, 333.6; identity, 116.4; self-satisfaction, 102.6; physical self, 68.9; moral-ethical self, 66.6; personal self, 61.3; social self, 66.4. The mean self-criticism score of 35.2 and the mean behavior score of 115.8 for the white girls are equal to the normative mean.

When the TSCS scores of the black girls are compared with those of the white girls, some significant differences emerge. The black girls score significantly higher on the total positive mean score than the white girls ($p < 0.004$). Likewise, on the mean profile scores the black girls score significantly higher than the white girls on the following items: self-satisfaction ($p < 0.001$), behavior ($p < 0.03$), physical self ($p < 0.001$), personal self ($p < 0.002$), family self ($p < 0.01$). All of these differences are statistically significant. There is no statistical significance between the scores of the black girls and white girls on self-criticism, variability, distribution, identity, moral-ethical self, or social self. (See Table 4.)

COMPARISON BY RACE AND SEX

COMPARISON OF BLACK BOYS AND BLACK GIRLS

When the 170 black girls in Nashville are compared on the TSCS scores with the 129 black boys very few differences are shown. The black boys score above the normative mean for the scale on the following: total positive, 350.2; variability, 56.1; distribution, 131.7; self-satisfaction, 111.3; behavior, 118.8; physical self, 72.6; personal self, 67.4; family self, 75.0. The black boys are below the normative mean on the self-criticism score, 34.6, and the identity score, 120.3; but their score on the social self is equal to the normative mean. On the TSCS scores, the black girls score above the normative mean on the following: total positive, 346.9; variability, 52.7; distribution, 128.1; self-satisfaction, 110.3; behavior, 119.2; physical self, 72.4; family self, 75.1. However, the black girls score below the normative mean on the following: self-criticism, 34.0; identity, 117.5; moral-ethical self, 67.8; social self, 67.3. The mean score for personal self (64.3) is equal to the normative mean. Although the black boys had a higher total positive mean score than the black girls, the difference is not significant. However, the black boys score higher on the mean variability score than the black girls and the difference is significant at the 5 percent level (see Tables 3 and 4). Although the black boys score higher on the mean distribution score than the black girls, the difference is not statistically significant. On the profile scores and subscores only one significant difference is noted. The black boys score higher than the black girls on personal self and the difference is significant at the 5 percent level (see Tables 3 and 4).

TABLE 4

Comparison of White and Black Girls in Nashville

TSCS Scores		Black Girls $n = 170$	White Girls $n = 183$	Significance
TP	Mean	346.97	333.69	p <0.004
	SD	38.86	45.48	
SC	Mean	34.07	35.24	N.S.
	SD	5.94	6.40	
V	Mean	52.74a	54.58	N.S.
	SD	13.43	13.13	
D	Mean	128.19	123.69	N.S.
	SD	28.33	27.91	
Identity	Mean	117.59	116.49	N.S.
	SD	15.18	14.60	
Self-Satisfaction	Mean	110.32	102.68	p <0.001
	SD	16.43	17.27	
Behavior	Mean	119.20	115.83	p <0.03
	SD	13.54	14.86	
Physical Self	Mean	72.40	68.93d	p <0.001
	SD	9.85	9.01	
Moral-Ethical Self	Mean	67.80	66.68	N.S.
	SD	9.51	9.70	
Personal Self	Mean	64.37a	61.39	p <0.02
	SD	11.19	11.40	
Family Self	Mean	75.15	71.91	p <0.01
	SD	11.47	11.83	
Social Self	Mean	67.38	66.40	N.S.
	SD	9.52	9.69	

*SD means standard deviation.
aSignificance at the 5 percent level between same scores for black boys and black girls. See Table 3.
dSignificance at the 1 percent level between same scores for white boys and white girls. See Table 3.

COMPARISON OF WHITE BOYS AND WHITE GIRLS

When the 183 white girls are compared with the 134 white boys on the TSCS scores very few differences can be seen. Both the white boys and girls are below the normative mean on the total positive score: 333.6 for the girls and 331.0 for the boys. Likewise, the white boys and girls score below the normative mean on identity, moral-ethical self, and social self. In addition, the white boys are below the normative mean on the self-criticism score and the white girls score below the normative mean on self-satisfaction, physical self, and personal self. The white girls are above the normative mean on the variability score, the distribution score, and the family-self score. Their mean scores for behavior and self-criticism are equal to the normative mean. The white boys are above the normative mean on the variability score, the distribution score, self-satisfaction score, the behavior score, the physical-self score, the personal-self score, and the family-self score. Although the white girls score higher on the mean variability score (54.5) than the white boys (51.9), the difference is not significant. The white girls score higher (116.4) than the white boys (113.7) on the mean identity score, but the difference is not significant. The white boys score higher (119.0) than the white girls (115.8) on the mean behavior score, but the difference is not significant. The white boys score higher (76.1) than the white girls (68.9) on the physical self mean score; the difference is significant at the 1 percent level. (See Tables 3 and 4.) However, the white girls score higher than the white boys on the moral-ethical self and the difference is significant at the 5 percent level. The white boys score higher than the white girls on personal self and family self, but the differences are not significant. (See Tables 3 and 4.)

COMPARISON BY RACIAL COMPOSITION OF
THE SCHOOL FOR BLACK STUDENTS

COMPARISON OF BLACK STUDENTS IN SEGREGATED AND DESEGREGATED SCHOOLS

When the 206 black students in segregated schools are compared with the 93 black students in desegregated schools on the TSCS scores, some interesting differences can be noted. The segregated black students score above the normative mean for the scale on the following: total positive, 351.3; variability, 54.5; distribution, 129.3; self-satisfaction, 111.2; behavior, 119.1; physical self, 72.6; personal self, 67.5; family self, 75.2. The black students in segregated schools score below the normative mean for the scale on identity, 120.6, and moral-ethical self, 66.5, and self-criticism score (34.6). However, on the mean social self score (68.4), the black segregated students are equivalent to the normative mean for the scale.

The black desegregated students score above the normative mean for the scale on the following: variability, 54.5; distribution, 130.7; self-satisfaction, 107.3; behavior, 116.6; family self, 73.2. However, the black desegregated students score below the normative mean for the scale on the following: total positive, 341.8; self-criticism, 33.8; identity, 117.8; moral-ethical self, 67.4; personal self, 63.2; social self, 67.1.

Although the black segregated students obtained a total positive mean score of 351.3, compared with a total positive mean score of 341.8 for the black desegregated students, the difference is not statistically significant. The differences between the self-criticism mean score, the variability mean score,

and the distribution mean score for the black segregated students and desegregated students is not statistically significant. On the mean profile scores,
although the black segregated students obtain a higher mean identity score
than the black desegregated students, the difference is not statistically significant. Nor is the difference between the black segregated students (119.1)
and the black desegregated students (116.6) on the mean behavior score
statistically significant, although the black segregated students score higher.
However, the black segregated students score higher on self-satisfaction
(111.2) than the black desegregated students (107.3) and this difference is
statistically significant (p < 0.03). On the sub-profile mean scores, there is
no statistical difference between the black segregated students and the black
desegregated students on the physical-self score, the moral-ethical-self score,
the family-self score, and the social-self score. However, on the personal-self
mean score the segregated black students scored higher (67.5) than the desegregated black students (63.2); the difference is statistically significant
(p < 0.02). (See Table 5.)

COMPARISON OF BLACK GIRLS IN SEGREGATED AND DESEGREGATED SCHOOLS

A comparison of the 113 black girls in segregated schools with the 57
girls in desegregated schools reveals some significant differences on the TSCS
scores. The segregated black girls are above the normative mean on the total
positive score (351.7), the variability score (54.2), distribution score (130.4),
the self-satisfaction score (111.3), the behavior score (119.4), the physical-
self score (72.6), the personal-self score (67.5), the family-self score (75.2),
and the social-self score (69.0). (See Table 6.) However, the black segregated
girls are below the normative mean on the self-criticism score (34.1), the
identity score (120.8), and the moral-ethical-self score (66.7). The desegregated black girls are above the normative mean on the variability score
(50.8), the self-satisfaction score (104.6), the behavior score (116.2), and the
family-self score (72.0). They are below the normative mean for the scale on
the total positive score (339.2), the self-criticism score (34.1), the identity
score (118.4), the physical-self score (69.9), the moral-ethical-self score
(67.6), the personal-self score (62.3), and the social-self score (67.4) (See
Table 6.)

The black segregated girls obtained a total positive mean score of 351.7
compared with a mean score of 339.2 for the black desegregated girls. The
difference is statistically significant (p < 0.001). There is no significant difference between the two groups on the self-criticism score, each obtaining a
mean score of 34.1. Although the segregated black girls score higher on the
distribution score (130.4) than the black desegregated girls (124.0), the difference is not statistically significant. Likewise, the black segregated girls
score higher on the variability score, 54.2, than the black desegregated girls,

TABLE 5

Comparison of Black Students in Segregated and Desegregated Schools in Nashville

TSCS Scores		Segregated n = 206	Desegregated n = 93	Significance
TP	Mean	351.3h	341.8e	N.S.
	SD*	39.0	43.9	
SC	Mean	34.6	33.8	N.S.
	SD	6.2	5.4	
V	Mean	54.5	54.5	N.S.
	SD	13.2	14.9	
D	Mean	129.3	130.7e	N.S.
	SD	28.5	32.5	
Identity	Mean	120.6g	117.8e	N.S.
	SD	16.2	18.5	
Self-Satisfaction	Mean	111.2h	107.3e	p <0.03
	SD	10.5	11.4	
Behavior	Mean	119.1	116.6	N.S.
	SD	36.0	9.3	
Physical Self	Mean	72.6	71.5	N.S.
	SD	4.8	4.8	
Moral-Ethical Self	Mean	66.5	67.4	N.S.
	SD	5.9	8.1	
Personal Self	Mean	67.5	63.2	p <0.02
	SD	6.1	6.3	
Family Self	Mean	75.2g	73.2	N.S.
	SD	6.4	7.7	
Social Self	Mean	68.4	67.1	N.S.
	SD	5.2	7.6	

*SD means standard deviation.
eSignificance at the 5 percent level between desegregated white and black students. See Table 10.
gSignificance at the 5 percent level between segregated white and black students. See Table 10.
hSignificance at the 1 percent level between segregated white and black students. See Table 10.

50.8, but the difference is not statistically significant. On the mean profile scores, the segregated black girls score higher than the desegregated black girls on identity, self-satisfaction, and behavior. However, the difference is only statistically significant for the mean self-satisfaction score (p < 0.01). On the mean sub-profile scores, the black segregated girls score higher than the black desegregated girls on physical self, personal self, family self, and social self. The difference in the mean physical-self scores between the black segregated girls (72.6), and the black desegregated girls (69.9), is statistically significant (p < 0.02). The difference in the mean scores for the personal-self

TABLE 6

Comparison of Black Girls in Segregated and Desegregated Schools in Nashville

TSCS Scores		Segregated $n = 113$	Desegregated[3] $n = 57$	Significance
TP	Mean	351.7m	339.2	p < 0.008
	SD*	37.1	39.9	
SC	Mean	34.1	34.1	N.S.
	SD	6.1	5.6	
V	Mean	54.2	50.8	N.S.
	SD	13.1	14.4	
D	Mean	130.4k	124.0	N.S.
	SD	25.8	32.6	
Identity	Mean	120.8k	118.4	N.S.
	SD	16.1	17.9	
Self-Satisfaction	Mean	111.3m	104.6	p < 0.01
	SD	10.9	10.4	
Behavior	Mean	119.4	116.2	N.S.
	SD	17.7	7.5	
Physical Self	Mean	72.6m	69.9	N.S.
	SD	4.6	4.6	
Moral-Ethical Self	Mean	66.7	67.6	N.S.
	SD	5.9	7.0	
Personal Self	Mean	67.5k	62.3	p < 0.03
	SD	6.3	5.8	
Family Self	Mean	75.2	72.0	N.S.
	SD	6.1	6.5	
Social Self	Mean	69.0	67.4	N.S.
	SD	5.1	6.3	

*SD means standard deviation.
kSignificance at the 5 percent level between segregated black and white girls. See Table 11.
mSignificance at the 1 percent level between segregated black and white girls. See Table 11.
[3]No significant differences on any scores between desegregated black and white girls. See Table 11.

items for the black segregated girls (67.5) compared with the black desegregated girls (62.3) is statistically significant (p < 0.03). The black desegregated girls score higher than the black segregated girls on the moral-ethical self, but the difference is not statistically significant.

COMPARISON OF BLACK BOYS IN SEGREGATED AND DESEGREGATED SCHOOLS

A comparison of the TSCS scores for black boys in segregated and desegregated schools shows no significant difference. However, the 93 black segre-

TABLE 7

Comparison of Black Boys in Segregated and Desegregated Schools in Nashville

TSCS Scores		Segregated n = 93	Desegregated n = 36	Significance
TP	Mean	350.9[o]	344.4[r]	N.S.
	SD*	40.9	48.0	
SC	Mean	35.0	33.6	N.S.
	SD	6.3	5.3	
V	Mean	54.8	57.3	N.S.
	SD	13.3	15.5	
D	Mean	128.1	137.5[r]	N.S.
	SD	30.2	32.4	
Identity	Mean	120.4[o]	117.3[p]	N.S.
	SD	16.4	19.1	
Self-Satisfaction	Mean	111.4[o]	110.1[r]	N.S.
	SD	10.2	12.4	
Behavior	Mean	118.9	117.0[p]	N.S.
	SD	19.4	11.2	
Physical Self	Mean	72.6	72.2	N.S.
	SD	5.0	5.0	
Moral-Ethical Self	Mean	66.3	66.8[p]	N.S.
	SD	6.0	9.3	
Personal Self	Mean	67.5	64.1	N.S.
	SD	6.0	6.9	
Family Self	Mean	75.2[n]	74.4[p]	N.S.
	SD	6.8	9.0	
Social Self	Mean	68.9	66.9	N.S.
	SD	5.4	8.9	

*SD means standard deviation.
[p]A significance level of 5 percent between same scores of the desegregated white and black boys. See Table 12.
[r]A significance level of 1 percent between same scores of the desegregated white and black boys. See Table 12.
[n]A significance level of 5 percent between same scores of the segregated white and black boys. See Table 12.
[o]A significance level of 1 percent between same scores of the segregated white and black boys. See Table 12.

gated boys are above the normative mean for the scale on the mean total positive score (350.9), the mean variability score (54.8), the mean distribution score (128.1), the mean self-satisfaction score (111.4), the mean behavior score (118.9), the mean physical-self score (72.6), the mean personal-self score (67.5), the mean family-self score (75.2). (See Table 7.) The segregated black boys are below the normative mean on the identity score (120.4) and the moral-ethical-self score (66.3), but are at the normative mean level on the self-criticism score (35.0) and the social-self score (68.9). The desegregated black boys are above the normative mean for the scale on the variability score (57.3), the self-satisfaction score (110.1), the behavior score (117.0), the physical-self score (72.2), the family-self score (74.4). However, the desegregated black boys are below the normative mean for the scale on the total positive score (344.4), the self-criticism score (33.6), the identity score (117.3), the moral-ethical-self score (66.8), and the social-self score (66.9).

Although the black segregated boys score higher on the total positive mean score than the black desegregated boys, the difference is not significant. Likewise, the black segregated boys score higher on the self-criticism score than the desegregated black boys, but the difference is not significant. The black desegregated boys score higher on the mean variability and the mean distribution scores than the black segregated boys, but the difference is not significant. On the three mean profile scores, the segregated black boys score higher than the desegregated black boys, but the differences are not significant. On the mean sub-profile scores, the black segregated boys score higher on personal self and social self than the desegregated black boys, but the difference is not significant.

COMPARISON OF SEGREGATED BLACK BOYS AND GIRLS

When the TSCS scores of the 113 black girls and the 93 black boys in segregated schools are compared no significant differences emerge. Both groups score above the normative mean for the scale on the following: total positive—girls (351.7), boys (350.9); variability—girls (54.2), boys (54.8), distribution—girls (130.4), boys (128.1); self-satisfaction—girls (111.3), boys (111.4); behavior—girls (119.4), boys (118.9); physical self—girls (67.5), boys (67.5); family self—girls (75.2), boys (75.2). Both the black segregated girls and boys score below the normative mean for the scale on the following: identity—girls (120.8), boys (120.4); moral-ethical self—girls (66.7), boys (66.3). The segregated black girls are below the normative mean on the self-criticism score (34.1), but above the normative mean on the social-self score (69.0). The black segregated boys are at the normative mean level on the self-criticism score (35.0), and the social-self score (68.9). (See Table 8.)

COMPARISON OF BLACK BOYS AND GIRLS IN DESEGREGATED SCHOOLS

Unlike the black boys and girls in segregated schools, when the 36 black boys and the 57 black girls in desegregated schools are compared on TSCS scores some significant differences emerge. The boys and girls score above the normative mean for the scale on the following: variability—boys (57.3),

TABLE 8
Comparison of Black Students in Segregated
Schools in Nashville

TSCS Scores		Girls n = 113	Boys n = 93	Significance
TP	Mean	351.7	350.9	N.S.
	SD*	37.1	40.9	
SC	Mean	34.1	35.0	N.S.
	SD	6.1	6.3	
V	Mean	54.2	54.8	N.S.
	SD	13.1	13.3	
D	Mean	130.4	128.1	N.S.
	SD	25.8	30.2	
Identity	Mean	120.8	120.4	N.S.
	SD	16.1	16.4	
Self-Satisfaction	Mean	111.3	111.4	N.S.
	SD	10.9	10.2	
Behavior	Mean	119.4	118.9	N.S.
	SD	17.7	19.4	
Physical Self	Mean	72.6	72.6	N.S.
	SD	4.6	5.0	
Moral-Ethical Self	Mean	66.7	66.3	N.S.
	SD	5.9	6.0	
Personal Self	Mean	67.5	67.5	N.S.
	SD	6.3	6.0	
Family Self	Mean	75.2	75.2	N.S.
	SD	6.1	6.8	
Social Self	Mean	69.0	68.9	N.S.
	SD	5.1	5.4	

*SD means standard deviation.

girls (50.8); self-satisfaction—boys (110.1), girls (104.6); behavior—boys (117.0), girls (116.2); family self—boys (74.4), girls (72.0). Also, the desegregated boys and girls score below the normative mean for the scale on the following: total positive—boys (344.4), girls (339.2); self-criticism—boys (33.6), girls, (34.1); identity—boys (117.3), girls (118.4); moral-ethical self—boys (66.8), girls (67.6); social self—boys (66.9), girls (67.4). The black desegregated boys are above the normative mean on the mean distribution score (137.5) and the mean physical and self score (72.2) but below the normative mean on the personal-self score (64.1). The black desegregated girls score below the normative mean for the scale on physical self (69.9) and personal self (62.3), but score above the normative mean for distribution (124.0). (See Table 9.)

Although the black desegregated boys score higher on the total positive mean score than the black desegregated girls, the difference is not significant.

TABLE 9

Comparison of Black Students in Desegregated
Schools in Nashville

TSCS Scores		Boys n = 36	Girls n = 57	Significance
TP	Mean	344.4	339.2	N.S.
	SD*	48.0	39.9	
SC	Mean	33.6	34.1	N.S.
	SD	5.3	5.6	
V	Mean	57.3	50.8	p <0.03
	SD	15.5	14.4	
D	Mean	137.5	124.0	p <0.002
	SD	32.4	32.6	
Identity	Mean	117.3	118.4	N.S.
	SD	19.1	17.9	
Self-Satisfaction	Mean	110.1	104.6	p <0.003
	SD	12.4	10.4	
Behavior	Mean	117.0	116.2	N.S.
	SD	11.2	7.5	
Physical Self	Mean	72.2	69.9	N.S.
	SD	5.0	4.6	
Moral-Ethical Self	Mean	66.8	67.6	N.S.
	SD	9.3	7.0	
Personal Self	Mean	64.1	62.3	N.S.
	SD	6.9	5.8	
Family Self	Mean	74.4	72.0	N.S.
	SD	9.0	6.5	
Social Self	Mean	66.9	67.4	N.S.
	SD	8.9	6.3	

*SD means standard deviation.

However, the black desegregated boys score higher on the mean variability score than the black desegregated girls and the difference is statistically significant (p < 0.03). Likewise, on the mean distribution score, the black desegregated boys score higher than the black desegregated girls and the difference is statistically significant (p < 0.002).

COMPARISON BY RACIAL COMPOSITION OF
SCHOOLS FOR WHITE STUDENTS

On the TSCS mean scores, the 151 white segregated students do not score significantly differently than the 166 white students in desegregated schools. Both groups are below the normative mean on the total positive score, identity score, behavior score, physical-self score, moral-ethical-self

TABLE 10

Comparison of White Students in Segregated and Desegregated Schools in Nashville

TSCS Scores		Segregated $n = 151$	Desegregated $n = 166$	Significance
TP	Mean	331.84[h]	332.79[e]	N.S.
	SD*	52.21	42.86	
SC	Mean	34.63	35.27	N.S.
	SD	7.19	6.31	
V	Mean	52.06	54.71	N.S.
	SD	13.69	13.15	
D	Mean	121.79	126.00[e]	N.S.
	SD	28.73	31.14	
Identity	Mean	114.83[g]	114.89[e]	N.S.
	SD	17.19	15.99	
Self-Satisfaction	Mean	103.15[h]	103.47[e]	N.S.
	SD	22.97	17.32	
Behavior	Mean	114.18	114.55	N.S.
	SD	57.09	15.52	
Physical Self	Mean	68.81	69.53	N.S.
	SD	65.70	9.72	
Moral-Ethical Self	Mean	64.01	65.01	N.S.
	SD	10.42	10.62	
Personal Self	Mean	63.85	61.91	N.S.
	SD	47.14	11.29	
Family Self	Mean	70.20[g]	70.05	N.S.
	SD	70.23	13.50	
Social Self	Mean	66.67	66.17	N.S.
	SD	15.21	10.46	

*SD means standard deviation.
[e]Significance at the 5 percent level between desegregated white and black students. See Table 5.
[g]Significance at the 5 percent level between segregated white and black students. See Table 5.
[h]Significance at the 1 percent level between segregated white and black students. See Table 5.

score, personal-self score, and social self score. (See Table 10.) Both groups are above the normative mean for the scale on the variability and distribution scores. On the mean self-satisfaction and family-self scores both groups score close to the normative mean for the scale.

WHITE GIRLS IN SEGREGATED AND DESEGREGATED SCHOOLS

When the 79 white girls in segregated schools are compared with the 104 white girls in desegregated schools on the TSCS scores, no significant differences emerge on any of the scores. Both groups score above the normative mean for the scale on self-criticism, variability, and family self. Both groups score below the normative mean for the scale on the total positive score, the identity score, the physical-self score, the moral-ethical-self score, the personal-self score, and the social-self score. Both groups score at the normative mean level for the scale on the behavior score. The segregated white girls

TABLE 11

Comparison of White Girls in Segregated and Desegregated Schools in Nashville

TSCS Scores		Segregated[1] n = 79	Desegregated[2,3] n = 104	Significance
TP	Mean	334.08m	335.61	N.S.
	SD*	50.67	41.36	
SC	Mean	35.35	35.16	N.S.
	SD	6.62	6.27	
V	Mean	53.37	55.48	N.S.
	SD	12.53	13.54	
D	Mean	119.93k	126.49	N.S.
	SD	28.08	27.58	
Identity	Mean	116.37k	116.59	N.S.
	SD	13.18	15.64	
Self-Satisfaction	Mean	101.92m	103.247	N.S.
	SD	17.84	16.90	
Behavior	Mean	115.79	115.857	N.S.
	SD	15.33	14.58	
Physical Self	Mean	67.24m	69.86	N.S.
	SD	8.91	9.01	
Moral-Ethical Self	Mean	66.35	66.67	N.S.
	SD	9.02	10.22	
Personal Self	Mean	61.12k	61.04	N.S.
	SD	11.45	11.40	
Family Self	Mean	72.13	71.49	N.S.
	SD	10.71	12.64	
Social Self	Mean	66.22	66.57	N.S.
	SD	9.13	10.12	

*SD means standard deviation.
[1]No significant difference on any scores between white segregated boys and girls. See Table 12.
[2]No significant differences on any scores between white desegregated boys and girls. See Table 12.
[3]No significant differences on any scores between desegregated black and white girls. See Table 6.
kSignificance at the 5 percent level between segregated black and white girls. See Table 6.
mSignificance at the 1 percent level between segregated black and white girls. See Table 6.

score below the normative mean on the distribution score (119.9) and the self-satisfaction score (101.9) whereas the desegregated white girls score above the normative mean on the distribution score (126.4) and at the normative mean level on the self-satisfaction score (103.2). (See Table 11.)

WHITE BOYS IN SEGREGATED AND DESEGREGATED SCHOOLS

A comparison of the 72 white boys in segregated schools with the 62 white boys in desegregated schools on the TSCS mean scores shows no significant differences on any of the mean scores (see Table 12). Both groups score below the normative mean for the scale on the total positive score, the identity score, the physical-self score, the moral-ethical-self score, the personal-self score, the family-self score, and the social-self score; and both groups score above the normative means for the scale on the variability and distribution mean scores. The desegregated and segregated white boys obtain a mean self-satisfaction score equal to the normative mean. The segregated boys obtained a mean behavior score (117.1) above the normative mean and the desegregated white boys obtained a mean behavior score (112.4) below the normative mean.

COMPARISON OF WHITE BOYS AND GIRLS IN SEGREGATED AND DESEGREGATED SCHOOLS

There are no significant differences on the TSCS mean scores between white girls and boys in segregated schools. Although the 104 white girls in desegregated schools score higher than the 62 white boys in desegregated schools on the total positive score, 335.6 and 328.2 respectively, the difference is not statistically significant. Indeed, there is no significant difference on the TSCS scores, when comparing the white desegregated boys and girls, although the white girls tend to score higher on identity (116.3), behavior (115.7), moral-ethical self (66.3), family self (72.1), and social self (66.2) than the white desegregated boys (see Tables 11 and 12).

COMPARISON BY RACE, SEX, AND RACIAL COMPOSITION OF SCHOOLS

COMPARISON OF BLACK AND WHITE STUDENTS IN DESEGREGATED SCHOOLS

A comparison of the 93 black students in desegregated schools with the 166 white students in desegregated schools reveals some significant differences on the TSCS mean scores. Both the black and white desegregated students score below the normative means on the total positive score al-

TABLE 12

Comparison of White Boys in Segregated and
Desegregated Schools in Nashville

TSCS Scores		Segregated[1] n = 72	Desegregated[2] n = 62	Significance
TP	Mean	333.60[o]	328.23[r]	N.S.
	SD*	54.17	45.14	
SC	Mean	33.83	35.44	N.S.
	SD	7.75	6.42	
V	Mean	50.61	53.47	N.S.
	SD	14.82	12.51	
D	Mean	123.83	125.21[r]	N.S.
	SD	29.49	36.38	
Identity	Mean	113.12[o]	112.15[p]	N.S.
	SD	20.81	16.30	
Self-	Mean	103.40[o]	103.84[r]	N.S.
Satisfaction	SD	27.22	18.11	
Behavior	Mean	117.13	112.46[p]	N.S.
	SD	81.17	16.82	
Physical	Mean	69.63	69.00	N.S.
Self	SD	94.46	10.82	
Moral-	Mean	63.17	62.33[p]	N.S.
Ethical Self	SD	11.55	10.79	
Personal	Mean	66.20	63.32	N.S.
Self	SD	67.21	11.05	
Family	Mean	67.49[n]	67.73[p]	N.S.
Self	SD	101.12	14.58	
Social	Mean	67.11	65.53	N.S.
Self	SD	19.74	11.03	

*SD means standard deviation.
[1]No significant differences on any scores between white segregated boys and girls.
See Table 11.
[2]No significant differences on any scores between white desegregated boys and
girls. See Table 11.
[n]A significance level of 5 percent between same scores of the segregated white
and black boys. See Table 7.
[o]A significance level of 1 percent between same scores of the segregated white and
black boys. See Table 7.
[p]A significance level of 5 percent between same scores of the desegregated white
and black boys. See Table 7.
[r]A significance level of 1 percent between same scores of the desegregated white
and black boys. See Table 7.

though the black desegregated students score higher (TP = 341.8) than the
white desegregated students (TP = 332.7); the difference is significant at the
5 percent level. There is no significant difference between the black and
white desegregated students on the mean self-criticism score, although the
white students score higher (35.2) than the black students (33.8). There is

no significant difference betwen the black and white desegregated students on the mean variability score, both scoring above the normative mean, obtaining mean scores of 54.5 and 54.7 respectively. On the mean distribution score, the black desegregated students score higher (130.7) than the white desegregated students (126.0), and the difference is significant at the 5 percent level. On the mean identity score, the black desegregated students score higher (117.8) than the white desegregated students (114.8), and the difference is significant at the 5 percent level. Likewise, on the mean self-satisfaction score, the black desegregated students score higher (107.3) than the white desegregated students (103.4), and the difference is significant at the 5 percent level. On the mean behavior score the black desegregated students score higher than the white desegregated students, but the difference is not statistically significant.

On the mean sub-profile scores, the black students score higher than do the white desegregated students on the mean physical self, mean moral-ethical self, mean personal self, mean family self, and the mean social self. However, none of the differences are statistically significant. (See Tables 5 and 10.)

COMPARISON OF BLACK AND WHITE STUDENTS IN SEGREGATED SCHOOLS

When the black students in segregated schools (206) are compared with the white students in segregated schools (151), some significant differences on the TSCS mean scores emerge. On the total positive score, the black segregated students obtained a mean score of 351.3 compared with a mean score of 333.8 for the white segregated students. The difference is significant at the 1 percent level. There is no significant difference between the black segregated and white segregated students on the self-criticism (black 34.6, white 34.6), variability (black 54.5, white 52.0), or distribution mean scores (black 129.3, white 121.7).

On the profile scores the black segregated students scored higher than the white segregated students. For example, on the identity score, the black students obtained a mean score of 120.6 compared with a mean score of 114.8 for the white segregated students. The difference is significant at the 5 percent level. On the self-satisfaction scores, the black segregated students obtained a mean scores of 111.2, compared with a mean score of 103.1 for the white segregated students. The difference is significant at the 1 percent level. On the behavior score, the black students obtained a mean score of 119.1, compared with a mean score of 114.1 for the white segregated group. The difference, however, is not statistically significant.

On each of the mean sub-profile scores the black segregated students scored higher than the white segregated students. The black segregated students obtained a mean score of 72.6 on the physical-self score, compared with a mean of 68.8 for the white segregated group, but the difference is not statistically significant. On the personal-self score, the black segregated students obtained a mean of 67.5 compared with a mean of 63.8 for the white students; the difference is not statistically significant. On the family-self score, the black segregated students obtained a mean score of 75.2, compared with a mean score of 70.2 for the white segregated group. The difference is statistically significant at the 5 percent level. (See Tables 5 and 10.)

COMPARISON OF BLACK AND WHITE GIRLS IN SEGREGATED SCHOOLS

When black girls in segregated schools (113) are compared with white girls in segregated schools (79), some significant differences on the TSCS scores emerge. (See Tables 6 and 11.) The black segregated girls obtained a total positive mean score of 351.7, compared with a mean score of 334.0 for the white segregated girls. The difference is significant at the 1 percent level. There is no significant difference between the black segregated (34.1) and white segregated (35.3) girls on the mean self-criticism and mean variability scores (54.2 and 53.3 respectively). However, on the distribution score, the black segregated girls obtained a mean score of 130.4, compared with a mean score of 119.9 for the white segregated girls. The difference is significant at the 5 percent level. On the mean profile scores, the black segregated girls scored higher on each of the three items than the white segregated girls. On the identity score, the black segregated girls obtained a mean score of 120.8, compared with a mean score of 116.3 for the white segregated girls. The difference is significant at the 5 percent level. On the self-satisfaction scale score, the black segregated girls obtained a mean score of 111.3 compared with a mean score of 101.9 for the white segregated girls, a difference which is significant at the 1 percent level. On the behavior score, the segregated black girls obtained a mean score of 119.4, compared with a mean score of 115.7 for the segregated white girls. However, the difference is not significant.

On the five sub-profile scores, the black segregated girls have a tendency to score higher than the white segregated girls on most of the items. On the physical-self score, the black segregated girls obtained a mean score of 72.6, compared with a mean score of 67.2 for the white segregated girls; the difference is significant at the 1 percent level. On the personal-self score, the black girls obtained a mean score of 67.5 compared with a mean score of 61.1 for the white segregated girls, a difference which is significant at the 5 percent level. (See Tables 6 and 11.)

COMPARISON OF BLACK AND WHITE GIRLS IN DESEGREGATED SCHOOLS

Comparison of the 57 black girls in desegregated schools with the 104 white girls in desegregated schools reveals very little difference in the TSCS mean score (see Tables 6 and 11). Although the black desegregated girls obtained a mean total positive of 339.2, compared with a mean score of 335.6 for the white desegregated girls, the difference is not significant. Neither is the difference in the self-criticism scores (34.1 for the blacks and 35.1 for the whites), the variability scores (50.8 for the blacks and 55.4 for the whites), or the distribution scores (124 for the blacks and 126 for the whites). Likewise, on the three profile scores there is no significant difference between the black desegregated girls and the white desegregated girls. On the five mean sub-profile scores, the differences in the mean scores of the black desegregated girls compared with the white desegregated girls are not significant.

COMPARISON OF BLACK AND WHITE BOYS IN DESEGREGATED SCHOOLS

When the 36 black boys in desegregated schools are compared with the 62 white boys in desegregated schools, some significant differences on the TSCS mean scores emerge (see Tables 7 and 12). The black desegregated boys obtained a total positive mean score of 344.4, compared with a mean score of 328.2 for the white desegregated boys. The difference is significant at the 1 percent level. There is no significant difference on the mean self-criticism scores (black 33.6, white 35.4), or the mean variability scores (black 57.3, white 53.4) between the black and white boys in desegregated schools, although the white boys tend to score higher on the self-criticism score and the black boys tend to score higher on the variability score. On the distribution score, the black desegregated boys obtained a mean score of 137.5, compared with a mean score of 125.2 for the white desegregated boys. The difference is significant at the 1 percent level.

The black desegregated boys scored higher than the white desegregated boys on the three profile items and significant differences are obtained. On the self-satisfaction score, the black boys obtained a mean score of 110.1, compared with a mean score of 103.8 for the white desegregated boys. The difference is significant at the 1 percent level. Likewise, on the identity scores, the black desegregated boys obtained a mean score of 117.3, compared with a mean score of 112.1 for the whites boys; and on the mean behavior scores the black desegregated boys (117.0) scored higher than the white desegregated boys (112.46). The differences for both scores are significant at the 5 percent level. On the five sub-profile items, the black desegregated boys scored higher than the white desegregated boys. On the moral-ethical-self mean scores, the black desegregated boys obtained a mean score of 66.8, compared with a mean score of 62.3 for the white desegregated boys and the difference is significant at the 5 percent level. On the family-self scores, the black desegregated boys obtained a mean score of 74.4, compared with a mean score of 67.7 for the white desegregated boys. The difference is significant at the 5 percent level.

A COMPARISON OF BLACK AND WHITE BOYS IN SEGREGATED SCHOOLS

A comparison of the 93 black boys in segregated schools with the 72 white boys in segregated schools, reveals some significant differences (see Tables 7 and 12). On the total positive score the black segregated boys have a mean score of 350.0, compared with a mean score of 333.6 for the white segregated boys. The difference is significant at the 1 percent level. There is no significant difference between the two groups on the self-criticism score (black 35.0, white 33.8), or the distribution score (black 128.1, white 123.8). On the variability score, the black segregated boys obtained a mean score of 54.8, compared with a mean score of 50.6 for the white segregated boys; the difference is not significant. On the three profile scores, the black segregated boys scored higher than the white segregated boys. On the identity score, the black segregated boys obtained a mean score of 120.4, compared with a mean score of 113.1 for the white segregated boys; the difference is significant at the 1 percent level. Likewise, on the self-satisfaction score the black boys obtained a mean score of 111.4, compared with a mean score of 103.4 for the white segregated boys; the difference is significant at the 1 percent level.

On the five sub-profile scores the black segregated boys scored higher on each item than the white segregated boys. On the family-self score the black segregated boys obtained a mean score of 75.2, compared with a mean score of 67.4 for the white segregated boys. The difference is significant at the 5 percent level.

PART THREE

New Orleans

9

New Orleans:
Its History and Its People

New Orleans is the largest city in Louisiana and one of the great ports of the world, importing bananas, coffee, sugar, and petroleum, and exporting cotton, salt, sulfur, and tobacco. The city and its suburbs have more than 900 manufacturing and processing plants that employ about 45,000 persons. Nearby sources of petroleum, natural gas, sulfur, salt, lime, and wood provide raw materials for the factories of New Orleans.

New Orleans was founded by the French in 1718 and taken over by the Spanish by 1762. In 1768 the Spanish were ousted, but by 1769 Spanish rule was reestablished. The Spanish returned Louisiana to the French in 1800 and in April, 1803, the United States purchased Louisiana from the French. Hence, New Orleans' unusual history derives from the mixed background of French and Spanish descendents or the Creoles who still follow many customs of their ancestors.

As of the 1960 census the city's population was 627, 525 with 907,123 people in the metropolitan area. The black population was 234,931 or 37 percent of the city's population. It is interesting to note that as of 1960 90.4 percent of the black population was born in Louisiana compared with 77.7 percent of the white population.

The median school year completed in New Orleans is 7.7, with 25 percent of the white population completing four years or more of college and 2 percent of the black population completing four years or more of college. As of 1960, the median income for black males was $2,421 and $5,696 for whites.

The city has been dominated politically, socially, and economically by Anglo-Saxons, who live uptown or west of Canal Street, and the French Creole, who live in the French Quarter. Since the 19th Century the area east of the French Quarter has been the section where immigrant truckgardeners of German, Italian, and non-Creole French have lived. Blacks have always lived in almost every neighborhood of the city. This phenomenon occurred as a result of the plantation system. The master's house was surrounded by slave quarters with slave houses. After the Civil War, many former slaves remained on the plantations or in the houses surrounding the master's house. This custom persisted with the resultant establishment of many mixed neighborhoods.

THE HISTORY OF BLACK PEOPLE IN LOUISIANA

Black slaves were introduced into Louisiana by the Creole planters. In 1804 an attempt was made to stop the importation of slaves into Louisiana, and on March 2, 1807, the law prohibiting slave trade was passed by the U.S. Congress. The slaves in Louisiana, as elsewhere in the country, were not a passive lot. In 1811, more than 400 slaves rebelled in Louisiana and the following year there was another uprising in New Orleans. The next decades saw other slave revolts—several in 1829 throughout Louisiana plantations and a serious revolt in New Orleans involving 2,500 slaves some years later. In the last decade before the Civil War, the price of slaves skyrocketed. By 1860 prime field hands were selling for $1,500 in New Orleans and the illicit traffic increased, with New Orleans benefitting from the profit. Bay Island, in the Gulf of Mexico, was a depot where at times as many as 16,000 Africans were shipped annually to Florida, Texas, and Louisiana. In 1859 Stephen A. Douglass stated that at that time more slaves were being brought into the United States than in any year when the trade was legal, and in Vicksburg he had seen 300 recently imported slaves.

Perhaps in no other Southern state was miscegenation more widespread than in Louisiana, and especially in New Orleans. The practice of white men maintaining young slave women in a state of concubinage was common and socially acceptable. Children born of such unions were slaves, but the reaction to the mulatto children was mixed. Often they were sold, but in many instances they were emancipated and provided for with land, money, and education. The practice of white women mixing with black men was also very common, and also helped to increase the number of mulatto children. Thus, in New Orleans, where the Creole whites predominated, a community of Creole blacks or mulatto children with a Creole parent developed. In the entire country, by 1850, there were 246,000 mulatto slaves out of a slave population of 3,200,000; by 1860, there were 411,000 mulatto slaves out of a population of 3,900,000.[1]

The number of freed slaves had started to increase since the revolution and by 1860 freed slaves were concentrated in six areas, one of which was

New Orleans where they numbered 10,600.[2] At that time the state legislature tried to enact a law of re-enslavement. In spite of the hardships imposed upon free blacks, they engaged in a variety of trades and occupations. In New Orleans they were teachers, jewelers, architects, and lithographers, as well as carpenters, barbers, shopkeepers, and clerks. The affluence of a large number of free blacks in New Orleans is well known. It is estimated that their combined wealth totaled $15,000,000 in property in 1860.[3] A large portion of this wealth was due to the large numbers of mulattos and colored Creoles.

During reconstruction, Louisiana had 133 black legislators, with 38 senators, and 95 representatives. They had virtually no power and never had control of public affairs. However, with the adoption of the first Jim Crow laws in Tennessee, disenfranchisement began to spread throughout the South. In 1898, Louisiana enacted one of the first "grandfather clauses" which required that only those males whose fathers and grandfathers were qualified to vote on January 1, 1867, were qualified to vote. Consequently, few blacks were allowed to vote.

However, the history of black people in New Orleans is incomplete without focusing on an important historical phenomenon, the desegregation of public schools in New Orleans during Reconstruction. Harlan has pointed out that the only integrated public educational institutions during Reconstruction were the University of South Carolina and the public school system of New Orleans.[4] His explanation of public school desegregation in New Orleans during the 1870's is multifaceted and based on some unique features of New Orleans itself. Desegregation of public schools in New Orleans was in effect even before the state constitution in 1867 prohibited the establishment of separate schools and declared that no student could be denied entry because of color or race. There was some resistance, but by December of 1870 the opposition had been overruled by a court decision.

> The extent of desegregation cannot be measured precisely because the official reports made no separate accounting of the races and because the population of New Orleans was so peculiarly mixed, with so many very light colored persons and swarthy white ones, that observers often found it difficult to distinguish between them. Nevertheless, there is considerable evidence of desegregation in official records and in newspapers, particularly in the reports of the annual examinations or closing exercises of schools. From such sources it is possible to identify by name twenty-one desegregated schools and some others that may have been desegregated, about one third of the city's public schools.[5]

Even six months after Reconstruction, the number was estimated to be 300, while other reports indicate that between 500 and 1,000 blacks and several thousand whites attended mixed schools. Five of the mixed schools were located in the Second and Third Districts, just below Canal Street where the descendents of the original French and Spanish settlers lived, as well as where the Irish, German, and Italian immigrants had congregated. However, the First, Fourth, Fifth, and Seventh Districts also had some deseg-regated primary schools. Two of the three public high schools were desegre-gated with a gradual increase in enrollment over the next few years. The same occurred in the Fillmore Boys' School and at the Brenville School. Most reports indicate that there were more white pupils in public schools during reconstruction than either before or after. Mixed schools had higher enrollments and high academic standing because they had more teachers and a higher salary scale, an arrangement made by the school board.

How and why did such desegregation exist? Harlan gives several explana-tions.[6] It can partially be explained on a political basis. The whites needed black votes in order to get rid of the carpetbaggers and end Reconstruction. The black population had its own elite leadership and were not responsive to white Northerners or carpetbaggers. At the time, at least 20 percent of New Orleans population was black. However, the real reason lies not in terms of black votes (Charleston, South Carolina, had a similar situation), but in the unique characteristics of New Orleans. New Orleans was probably the nation's most cosmopolitan city because of its link with "continental Europe by its Creole tradition, its large and diverse immigrant population," the more recent French immigrants, and its connections with "complex Latin Amer-ica." About half of the population was Catholic and services were desegre-gated. The city had opposed secession and had been part of the Confederacy for only two years; it underwent Reconstruction for 15 years. Many of New Orleans' merchants were more concerned with economic development than with social control and were willing to compromise on racial matters in order to change the political system which caused the city's economic plight. Last, but not least, New Orleans enjoyed a "vigorous" and "ambitious" black leadership group with "an impressive Negro solidarity on racial issues."[7]

However, with the decline of federal support and the increasing push towards states' rights and state control holding forth in the South, Lousiana, like her neighboring Southern states began to succumb to "Jim Crow" pres-sures. In 1879 the Constitution was rewritten to permit separate schools and in 1898, it was the last of the Confederate states to require separate schools.

NON-COMPLIANCE IN NEW ORLEANS

The *Bush* v. *Orleans Parish School Board* suit was filed in 1952, but was suspended pending disposition of the Brown case. The suit was then re-activated after the Supreme Court's 1955 ruling and since 1956 New Orleans had been under a school desegregation order.

No written narrative can really convey the essence of the intensity of feelings, the social and political intrigue, the personality issues involved in the backroom meetings and the secret caucasing that went on during the time that New Orleans was trying to resist and resolve the issue of school desegregation. An attempt will be made here to provide the reader with the emotional developmental history of school desegregation in order to understand the present. For such detailed information the accounts by Crain and Muse are relied upon as well as interviews with some "old timers" who were there, who saw, heard, and experienced those turbulent days.[8, 9]

In the late 1940's, the independents in New Orleans, tired of corrupt city politics, looked around for a candidate to challenge Maestri, a supporter of Long. Colonel de Lesseps Morrison was asked to run and, with the support of a group of New Orleans women who became known as the Girls, Morrison beat Maestri in 1948. The Girls then decided to reform the school board. In 1948, Mrs. Jacqueline Leonard, one of the Girls, ran for the school board and won. The reformers then persuaded two young independents, Theodore Shepard and Emile Wagner, to run and in 1952 they were elected. By 1956, the Girls had seen to it that two "young, honest, non-political businessmen" were elected, Louis Riecke and Lloyd Rittiner. Thus, by 1956, the school board consisted of Shepard, Wagner, Riecke, Rittiner, and Matthew Sutherland, who had defeated Mrs. Leonard in 1954; "Chep" Morrison was still in office pledging to give New Orleans "an honest reputation and to outstrip Miami as the gateway to Latin America." These were the people who had to deal with the issue of desegregation in 1960.

In a decision of February 15, 1956, the federal district court ordered the desegregation of public schools "with all deliberate speed." Judge J. Skelly Wright, who had the reputation of being one of "the most famous liberals in the southern district courts" in issuing the order pointed out that this did not mean that desegregation must be completed overnight or even in a year or more." He stated:

> The problem of changing a people's mores, particularly those with an emotional overlay is not to be taken lightly. It is a problem which will require the utmost patience, understanding, generosity, and forbearance from all of us of whatever race.[10]

Wright's concluding paragraph to his decision for the New Orleans schools to desegregated with all deliberate speed has been widely quoted as one of the philosophic gems of the crisis in the South.

In 1956 the Louisiana legislature adopted the following resolution:

> Until the usurpation herein complained of be settled by legal, constitutional amendment, the legislature of Louisiana does hereby solemnly declare the decision of the Supreme Court and any similar decisions that might be rendered in

connection with the public school system and public parks and recreational
facilities insofar as such decisions may affect or apply to the sovereign state of
Louisiana, to be in violation of the Constitution of the United States and of the
state of Louisiana.[11]

Thereafter resolutions of protest or interposition against the Supreme
Court ruling were adopted by the unanimous vote of the upper and lower
chambers of the Louisiana state legislature and a dozen pro-segregation bills
were passed without a single dissenting vote in either chamber.

The school board's response was that they were determined to maintain
segregation in the schools by "every legal and honorable means." In retelling
this slice of history, it is interesting to note how good men surfaced and
struggled to do what they believed to be honest and right. Many times,
history makes no note of them, but in The New Orleans Story their voices
were heard from time to time. Such a person was Sam Rosenberg, the school
board's attorney, who advised the board that the law was against them, and
if they were persistent in their intent to resist he would like to be relieved
from representing them. He was retained as the board's general attorney, but
Gerard Rault, a former assistant attorney general for the state, was hired at a
yearly salary of $25,000 of which $10,000 was paid by the state. Rault was
also attorney for a downtown savings and loan association whose president
was Emile Wagner, a school board member, a fervent segregationist, and a
close personal friend of Rault. Under Rault's legal advice the board persisted
with a series of appeals, hoping to forestall desegregation.

The course of federal court litigation was such that it was evident that
orders to end public school segregation could not be held off much longer.
However, in the city of New Orleans and all over the state of Louisiana the
level of resistance was increased and in the next four years the litigation and
a proliferation of laws designed to perpetuate public school segregation continued. On July 15, 1959, three years after the first order by Judge Wright to
desegregate, Wright instructed the board to file a desegregation plan by
March 1, 1960. Meanwhile, Wagner, a member of the school board, but also
an organizer of the New Orleans White Citizens' Council, was helping the
legislature draft laws to take over the school board and Rault continued to
work with the state attorney general. However, Sutherland, Riecke, Shepard,
and Rittiner did not want desegregation, but wanted to do "the right thing"
which did not seem to them to mean closing the schools.

Meanwhile, Morrison remained quiet hoping to run for governor in 1964.
In order to elicit Morrison's support, Rittiner, who felt that the majority of
New Orleans' parents would prefer token integration rather than no schools,
decided to conduct a poll of the parents. On April 22, 1960, the following
letter was sent to the parents to indicate their preference:[12]

1. I would like to see the schools kept open even if a small amount of integration is necessary.

or

2. I would like to see the schools close rather than be integrated even in small amounts.

The response—82 percent of the white parents voted to close the school, just eight days before the board was to present a plan to Judge Wright.

For a long time the threat of school closing to avoid racial desegregation had hung over New Orleans which had 95,000 pupils in its public schools. The Citizens Council of New Orleans was very active under the leadership of Jimmy H. Davis, a former governor who was re-elected to that office on April 19, 1960. With Davis's support and the white parents' mandate to close the schools rather than desegregate, the legislature felt free then to pass any bill presented to it that was aimed at preventing desegregation.

One of the renowned sagas in judicial annals is the struggle between Judge J. Skelly Wright, representing federal compliance on the one hand, and the governor and the state legislature, representing interposition and dogged resistance on the other hand. On May 16, 1960, when the school board had not presented a school desegregation plan, Judge Wright produced one of his own. He ordered that in September the desegregation of schools begin in accordance with the following plan:

a) All children entering the first grade may attend either the formerly all-white public school nearest their homes or the formerly all-Negro public school nearest their homes at their option.

b) Children may be transfered from one school to another provided such transfers are not based on considerations of race.[13]

At this point the school board felt confused, helpless, and indecisive, caught between the federal courts on the one hand and the governor and the state legislature on the other hand. In a desperate but foolish move at their meeting on June 20, 1960, they decided to ask Governor Davis "to interpose the sovereignty of the state to prevent integration." Needless to say, much litigation followed: on June 26, 1960, the court of appeals refused to to grant a stay of Judge Wright's order; on July 11, 1960, Supreme Court Justice Hugo Black refused to grant a stay.

A few weeks before schools were to open, Governor Davis assumed control of the school board and ordered the Superintendent "to open the schools on September 7 on a segregated basis." On that same day, 30 white parents filed for a temporary injunction to restrain the governor and other state officials "from obeying the state court injunction and state statutes with respect to segregation."[14] The *Williams* v. *Davis* case was the first action taken by white parents in the school desegregation issue.

There is strong evidence that the filing of the Williams suit, which names the school board as one of the parties defendant and seeks to enjoin the board from obeying the state court injunctions, was in fact concurred in by the four moderates on the school board and given behind-the-scenes encouragement and support. This also would mean that Sam Rosenberg and even Judge Wright may have been consulted in the drafting of the Williams brief.[15]

There may be more truth than fiction in that report, for during the tense summer months Riecke and Sutherland were discouraged and ready to resign. Rittiner convinced them not to resign; he himself had decided to keep the schools open and felt that with community support he and the other three moderate members would be able to do it. The role the Committee on Public Education played with the Williams suit will be discussed later, but the Williams suit with COPE support meant not only support to Skelly Wright to eliminate the state school-closing laws, but also an impetus to help the board to begin the desegregation process.

By the end of August, judgment was awarded for the plaintiffs in both the *Bush* and *Williams* suit. Ten days later a three-judge federal court issued an order restraining the governor and declared the seven segregation laws unconstitutional, and ordered the school board to provide a desegregation plan. Five times Governor Davis or the legislature attempted to take over the New Orleans public schools or to force members of the school board to relinquish their powers.

However, the school board under Rittiner's leadership was ready to comply with Wright's order, and met privately with Sam Rosenberg without Emile Wagner. Rosenberg advised them to go to Judge Wright and tell him they wanted to comply. They did so, and asked Judge Wright for a delay in presenting their desegregation plans until November 14 because they had no plan and with school due to open in one week, would have little time to devise one. However, there were two other unstated reasons: (1) Matthew Sutherland was up for re-election on an "open schools" platform which would provide a good test for voter support for open schools, and (2) if schools opened in September on a segregated basis, by November very few black parents would bother with transfer requests to desegregated schools in the middle of the school year.

THE LOUISIANA PUPIL PLACEMENT ACT

The school board had two months to present a plan to desegregate the New Orleans public schools. Although hindsight is always better than foresight, the plan was devised with three major principles in mind: (1) to exempt the board and the superintendent from responsibility regarding any decisions, (2) to present a plan that reflected "their reform ideology" in an "objective" and "scientific" way, (3) to limit both the number of black children involved in desegregation and the number of white schools. Thus, the Louisiana Pupil Placement Act of 1960 was conceived. The elaborate steps as outlined by Cairn are as follows:[16]

Step one: Consideration by four assistant superintendents of verification of information on application, proper age as determined by a birth certificate, nearness of school to the child's home, request or consent of parents and reasons for transfer, available room and teaching capacity of schools, availability of transportation.

Step two: Consideration by the Acting Director of Guidance and Testing, psychologists, and psychometrists of scholastic aptitude, intelligence, or ability, and results of achievement tests.

Step three: Consideration by the Assistant Superintendent for Instruction, the Director of Special Services, the Director of Kindergarten-Primary Education, psychologists, and visiting teachers of the effect of the new pupil upon the academic program, suitability of established curricula for pupil, adequacy of pupil's academic preparation or readiness for admission to school or curricula, psychological qualifications of pupil for type of teaching and associations, effect upon academic progress of other students, effect upon prevailing academic standards, psychological effect upon the pupil, home environment of the pupil, maintenance or severance of social and psychological relationships with pupils and teachers.

Step four: Consideration by an administrative review team composed of the Superintendent, the First Assistant Superintendent, the Acting Assistant Superintendent for Instruction, and the school system's Medical Director of all information previously collected on each applicant, choice and interests of pupil, possibility or threat of friction or disorder among pupils or others, possibility of breach of peace or ill will, or economic retaliation within the community.

The school board in its efforts to secure community support from elite businessmen agreed to separate the girls and the boys in the first grades and to have separate toilet facilities. The school board also told the superintendent not to inform them of the black students selected or the schools chosen. There was no screening of the white schools to be segregated. The white schools were to be those where the first-grade class median was low enough to admit black children, and if possible no more than ten black children were to be selected. All accepted applicants were to have test scores equal to or above the median for the school for which they were applying, but note again that the white schools chosen were to have the lowest achievement scores. Thus, the schools selected were the worst choices possible—William Frantz and McDonogh No. 19.

Since both schools, William Frantz Elementary and McDonogh No. 19, were in the same general neighborhood, it was easy for segregationists to concentrate their activity. Of course, the decision to limit it to two white schools—another decision by the machine—also made it easy for the segregationists to concentrate their fire. In addition, the neighborhood was generally poor, with a concentration of white working class and lower class families living in housing projects, the groups most likely to be hostile to Negro advances. But Frantz and McDonogh No. 19 were bad choices for political reasons as well, for they were both in the most neglected section of the city, the ninth ward. The ninth ward was always the last to get street lights and the last to get paved streets. . . . Though many of these people (in the ninth ward) have achieved middle-class status, their section is still politically weak. Suddenly, they discovered that two of their schools—and none in any other section of town—had been desegregated. To the residents of the ninth ward the decision seemed motivated by pure malice, and even upper middle-class moderates were furious.[17]

When one also considers that the ninth ward is adjacent to St. Bernard Parish where Leander Perez, a rabid racist, had political control, one can see that the school board operated with little wisdom and no common sense at all.

NEW ORLEANS BEGINS: NOVEMBER 14, 1960

In November the legislature went into a 12-day special session to try to block desegregation but Judge Wright, staunchly supported by the Fifth Circuit Court of Appeals, set November 14, 1960, as the date for desegregation. The legislature countered by declaring the day a school holiday and sent state police to enforce it, but the principals of the 118 schools stood firm and no school in New Orleans was closed.

However, the explosion that followed and the disgraceful performance of officials and fanatics for weeks afterward made another of those sensational post-Brown Decision episodes which engrossed the American press and radio and television and sent photos and stories to the far corners of the earth.[18]

The following excerpts from *The New Orleans School Crisis*, a report of the Louisiana State Advisory Committee to the United States Commission on Civil Rights, give a vivid picture of the struggle that ensued with the implementation of actual desegregation of the schools.[19]

On Monday, November 14, four Negro girls attended first-grade classes at two previously all-white schools (the fifth child eligible for transfer was withdrawn). The schools were William Frantz Elementary and McDonogh No. 19. . . . The Negro children were accompanied to school by federal marshals. The white parents of the neighborhood, with two exceptions, withdrew their children from the schools. The Reverend Lloyd Foreman and Mrs. Daisy Gabrielle continued to send their little girls to the Frantz school. The boycott at McDonogh No. 19 was total (it was briefly broken by the children of John Thompson in late January, 1961; the Thompsons braved the boycott for three days and then left town).

On November 15, William Rainach, Leander Perez, and others addressed a crowd of over five thousand at a White Citizens' Council meeting in New Orleans. Rainach advocated civil disobedience and a scorched-earth policy. Perez said, in part, "Don't wait for your daughters to be raped by these Congolese. Do something about it now." Some witnesses described the meeting as "a gathering straight out of Nazi Germany." The action suggested by the speakers was a march on the school board building, city hall, and Judge Wright's office by protesting citizens.

On November 16 this action was forthcoming. A crowd of teenagers and adults marched on the prescribed buildings, chanting: "Two, four, six, eight, we don't want to integrate." City police, under Superintendent Joseph Giarusso, attempted to control the mob by the use of mounted police and a few firehoses. No whites were injured, but several Negroes were hurt by flying glass as bus windows were shattered by vandals and two Negroes were severely beaten. The mob dispersed before it reached the heart of the business district.

Now the legislature abandoned its legislative committee approach and took over control of the New Orleans schools itself. The legislature urged white parents at Frantz and McDonogh No. 19 to continue their boycott of the schools . . .

A member of the Orleans Parish school staff warned that money was becoming a problem for the school board, since the state had forbidden banks to lend money to the school board and the legislature itself had refused to pay the teachers . . .

On November 23 the legislature passed a resolution authorizing the payment of the Orleans Parish school employees, with the exception of the administrative staff and the Frantz and McDonogh teachers. An anonymous citizen loaned these teachers money to cover their earned salaries. Dr. Redmond, Mr. Rosenberg, and the administrative staff went unpaid . . .

In mid-November the Whitney National Bank, which had honored payroll checks issued by the elected Orleans Parish school board, was removed as fiscal agent for the State . . .

During the last days of November the Reverend Lloyd Foreman and Mrs. James Gabrielle, who had continued to take their children to the Frantz School, were subjected to abuse and physical violence by the mob in front of the school. This, coupled with the fact that several parents in the Frantz school area had appealed to S.O.S. (Save Our Schools) for help in returning their children to school, led to the organization of a volunteer "carlift," run by parents from the uptown section of New Orleans, which transported the children to school in relative safety. The "carlift" began on December 1. The car carrying Yolanda Gabrielle was stoned and manhandled by the mob. Later in the week, it was pursued for two miles by a truck which had tried to ram it. Until Wednesday, December 7, the drivers and the women who escorted the children into the school were subjected to the vilest sort of shouted abuse from the daily assembled crowds. On December 7 the police guarding the school pushed the crowd behind barricades a full block away from the school.

The crowd then dispersed to roam the streets of the Florida Housing Project, where many of the children lived. Their parents were subjected to an organized telephone campaign of threats and abuse. Their houses and other properties were stoned, as was one of the mothers of a child at Frantz. James Gabrielle, ostracized by his fellow-workers, quit his job and took his family to Rhode Island. The volunteer drivers were threated with death, arson, disfigurement, and other unpleasantnesses in a concerted telephone campaign. The police were unable to prevent these occurrences; and, with the exception of a couple of juveniles alleged to have stoned Mrs. Marion McKinley, no one connected with the demonstrations was arrested, nor was the mob in front of the school dispersed or told to move on.

Anti-climatic, but nonetheless important, was the fact that on December 12, 1960, the United States Supreme Court gave its opinion on the federal district court's August 27 decision to prohibit implementation of segregationist legislation based on the doctrine of interposition adopted by many other Southern states. The U.S. Supreme Court stated that they found the arguments of the State of Louisiana which were based on the doctrine of interposition "without susbstance." The Supreme Court further concluded that interposition is not a constitutional doctrine and is considered an illegal defiance of constitutional authority. Following that decision, the New Orleans public schools returned to normal operation, in spite of lingering scars of interracial bitterness.

THE CATHOLIC DYNASTY DESEGREGATES

Not only did the *Brown* decision present an acute dilemma to the public school system in Louisiana, but also to the Roman Catholic hierarchy. Louisiana has ethnic characteristics that set it apart from other states of the South and other states of the Union because of its background as a French colony, a Spanish colony, and then a French colony again before its acquisition by the United States. The French influence is most apparent in the southeastern section where New Orleans is located. About two thirds of the population of New Orleans is of the Roman Catholic faith and in 1960 approximately 50,000 New Orleans children were enrolled in Catholic parochial schools. The New Orleans diocese was embarrassed by postponement of school desegregation after earlier announcements of forthcoming desegregation. It was also embarrassing that action in this area of "morality and conscience" took place only after the public school authorities had already acted. The administrators of church schools were apprehensive about the effect upon Catholic loyalties and especially the voluntary contributions on which the costly parochial school system depended.

New Orleans has the largest Catholic diocese in the South and half the total number of Catholics in the entire South live in the Archdiocese of New Orleans which had the reputation of being one of the most liberal archdioceses on race relations. As early as 1949, Archbishop Joseph Francis Rummel had canceled a service because the procession was going to be segregated. Subsequently, he had all the "white" and "colored" signs removed from the pews in the churches. Following Judge Wright's ruling on February 15, 1956, that the Orleans Parish public schools would have to desegregate, the Archbishop announced, "Racial segregation is morally wrong and sinful because it is a denial of the unity and solidarity of the human race as conceived by God in the creation of man in Adam and Eve."

He then announced that the parochial schools would begin to desegregate on a grade-per-year basis beginning in September, 1957. The opposition was overwhelming and in instances violent. The Catholic schools remained segregated and Archbishop Rummel made no other public statements from July 31, 1956, until July, 1959, when he tried again to persist that the parochial schools be desegregated. In October of 1959 the Archbishop fell and broke an arm and leg and had to retire. Consequently, the Catholic hierarchy had offered no substantial moral or political support to the desegregation crisis in New Orleans.

In 1962, Archbishop John Patrick Coty assumed the responsibility of the Archdiocese of New Orleans and racial desegregation was ordered in all the 164 schools of the Archdiocese. From the outset the desegregation of the Catholic parochial schools in New Orleans did not proceed without some widely publicized resistance, led by Leander H. Perez, a millionaire politician; Jackson G. Ricau, a Citizens' Council Director; and Mrs. B.J. Gaillot, leader of a group called Save Our Nation, Inc. These three were subsequently excommunicated from the Church, but not before increasing the tension in New Orleans.

In September, 1962, 173 black children entered 35 predominantly white parochial schools for the first time without church attendance or contributions being affected as had been anticipated. At the same time, 107 black children entered the first through the third grades of 19 predominantly white public schools, a decided increase over the 12 black pupils who had desegregated the New Orleans schools the previous year. It is interesting to note that in the midst of the turmoil regarding public school desegregation and parochial school desegregation in New Orleans, the state of Louisiana had gone farther than any other Southern state in the desegregation of institutions of higher learning. The 1960-61 term saw 634 Negroes admitted to predominantly white universities which were supported by the state and had a total enrollment of 22,565.

THE WILL AND THE WAY

In no other Southern city had school desegregation proceeded so chaotically because of the absence of constructive and responsible leadership in the white as well as in the black community. Mayor Morrison only feebly, in 1960, after the gubernatorial election, made any constructive statement. The

school board representing a reform group were too moderate, too intim-
idated, and too ambivalent to act decisively. Governor Davis was an archsegregationist and had run his campaign and won along those lines. The Save
Our Schools (SOS) group was considered too liberal and not representative
of New Orleans; they were the outsiders. The support that came from the
Jewish community was suspect and subsequently rejected. Voices from the
black community were relatively silent. In many more moderate circles it
was felt that the NAACP lawyers in the Bush case were hoping for school
closure to force more federal intervention and on the other hand unverified
sources report that Archbishop Rummel became discouraged because of the
lack of support he had received from the black community.

The Catholic hierarchy provided little consistent forceful leadership and
in fact during the major crisis in 1960 was completely silent. The news media
with the exception of WDSU-TV and radio had from the outset encouraged
noncompliance and resistance. Not until the final crunch, before November,
1960, arrived did anyone within the state of Louisiana openly and coura-
geously have the will to speak out loud and clear as did Judge Skelly Wright,
whose voice was like one crying out in the wilderness.

The story of school desegregation in Louisiana is not complete without
mention of the fact that there were significant voices heard in defense of
public education. Lloyd Rittiner, President of the Public School Board, as
well as Sam Rosenberg, had taken a firm stand to comply with the law. The
movement to prevent school closing got underway early in the summer of
1960 with the organization of two groups, Save Our Schools (SOS) and a
Committee on Public Education (COPE). These two groups published
pamphlets, held meetings, buttonholed hesitant business and professional
leaders and succeeded in stimulating a degree of public dialogue on the
question. It was COPE who organized enough white mothers to file the
Williams suit.[20] Volunteers from SOS and COPE initiated car pools to drive
children to and from school in spite of violent threats and intimidations. The
courage of those black children who braved the crowds and those two white
children of Rev. Lloyd Foreman and Mrs. Daisy Gabrielle are testimonies to
families and people who had the will to lead the way.

Support was slow in coming; it was not until January, 1961, after in-
estimable damage had been done, that a hundred business and professional
leaders signed a one-page advertisement in the two newspapers calling for law
and order. Only in August of 1960 did the local newspapers begin to express
a firm conviction that "the preservation of public education at this time
stands out as paramount." For several years the *Times Picayune* had aided
and, indeed, incited hostility and resistance to school desegregation. The
television station WDSU-TV and the radio station WDSU had been the only
media to accept early and firmly the responsibility for community leader-

ship. However, with the breaking down of resistance in Louisiana by the end of 1961 only Alabama, Mississippi, and South Carolina were totally recalcitrant to the *Brown* decision.

THE EXTENT OF SCHOOL DESEGREGATION

In the academic school year of 1960-61 there were four black students in desegregated schools. By the following school year the number had increased to 12. As of June, 1965, Louisiana had a total of 67 school districts all of which had black and white students. The estimated enrollment for whites was 472,923 and for blacks was 313,314. Three of the 67 school districts had desegregated with 3,581, or 1.14 percent, black students in desegregated schools out of a total black enrollment in those three desegregated districts of 88,677 compared with 63,591 for the white enrollment.[21]

As of the academic year 1966-67, out of Louisiana's 67 school districts, 17 had funds cut off because of noncompliance with the 1964 Civil Rights Act and four others were being considered for discontinuance of funds because of noncompliance, leaving 46 school districts in compliance.[22] The white enrollment for the 67 districts was 557,300 and the black enrollment 263,400 with 9,350, or 3.5 percent, black students in desegregated schools— 1.7 percent of the black students were in schools with 0 to 20 percent black enrollment; 0.9 percent of the black students were in schools with 20 to 80 percent black enrollment; 0.9 percent of the black students were in schools with 80 to 99 percent black enrollment; and 96.5 percent of the black students were in schools with 100 percent black enrollment.[23]

As of July, 1970, New Orleans had 132 schools and a total student enrollment of 110,854 with 68 percent of the total being black. Nine percent of the black students were in 81 desegregated schools, or 6,772 black students in white schools and 4,067 white students in black students.[24] New Orleans is one of the estimated 295 majority black school districts in the 11 Southern states. Thus, the major course of school desegregation is still to be decided.

1. Franklin, J.H. Op. cit., 1969, p. 205.
2. Ibid.
3. Ibid., p. 224.
4. Harlan, L.R. Desegregation in New Orleans public schools during Reconstruction. Meier, A. and Rudwick, E. eds. Op. cit., Vol. 1, pp. 345-358.
5. Ibid., p. 348.
6. Ibid., p. 355.
7. Ibid., p. 356.
8. Crain, R.L. The Politics of School Desegregation. Chicago, Aldine Publishing Co., 1968, pp. 223-328.
9. Muse. Op. cit., 1964.

10. Ibid., p. 218.

11. Ibid., p. 72

12. Cairn, A.L. Op. cit., 1968, p. 245.

13. Muse. Op. cit., 1964, p. 220.

14. Cairn. Op. cit., 1968, p. 256.

15. Ibid., p. 257.

16. Ibid., pp. 260-261.

17. Ibid., pp. 263-264.

18. Muse. Op. cit., p. 224.

19. United States Commission on Civil Rights, 1962. The New Orleans School Crisis, p. 34.

20. The NAACP provided no support with the *Bush* case. There was no collaboration or mutual support from those involved in the *Bush* or *Williams* cases, although the decision was handed down at the same time.

21. Southern School News. June, 1965.

22. Southern Educational Report. Jan.-Feb., 1967, pp. 31-32.

23. Ibid.

24. Race Relations Information Center, Majority-Black School Districts in the 11 Southern States. July, 1970.

10

New Orleans: The Students and The Schools

In the Orleans School Parish, 634 students in seventh, eighth, and ninth grades from eight schools participated in the study. There were three parochial schools and five public schools represented. Out of the eight schools involved in the study three are classified as predominantly white or segregated black schools.

The social and familial data regarding the students were derived from questionnaires given to the students. In many instances students did not know income, occupation, or education of parents and the information derived from the questionnaire does not coincide exactly with data obtained from interviews with teachers and principals concerning socioeconomic status of the students. We can only conclude that certain questions were too threatening to many of the students who were reluctant to reveal the nature of their family life.

Inasmuch as New Orleans is a major industrial city, we were particularly interested in knowing the migration patterns of the students being tested. Among the white students, 77 percent were born in New Orleans and 90 percent of the black students were born in New Orleans. The white students responded that 55 percent of their fathers were also born in New Orleans and 57 percent of their mothers. Among the black students, 54 percent of the fathers were born in New Orleans and 67 percent of the mothers were born in New Orleans. Less than 10 percent of the students or their parents were born outside the state of Louisiana and the majority of those students were Spanish-speaking from Central America.

In reviewing the questionnaires, the family size of New Orleans students seemed to be running very large. Actual tabulation showed the mean family size for white students was 4.6 and for black students was 5.2.

There are 20 public junior high schools in the Orleans Parish; five of these were involved in the study. There are 12 parochial elementary and high schools in the parish; three of which were involved in the study.[1] In the public junior high schools as of October, 1968, there were 15,382 black students and 7,746 white students, thus about one third of the junior high school enrollment was white.

THE 100 PERCENT BLACK SCHOOL

As of October, 1968, there were five segregated black junior high schools and two previously all-black junior high schools that had an enrollment of one white student.[2]

The segregated black school that participated in the study had a total student population of 1,656. The school building was relatively new, about five years old at the time of the testing. The school had an entirely black faculty and was located in a black low-income neighborhood. The school faculty interviewed indicated that the major problem of the school was reading, with more than 50 percent of the students reading 3 to 4 years below grade level. The median IQ for the school was 83 with approximately 20 percent with IQ's below 70, and 3 percent with IQ's above 110.

One hundred and fourteen students were tested, 63 girls and 51 boys, in response to the questionnaire.

Tabulation of the questionnaire data indicated that 50 percent of the students responded that parents were living together and 50 percent responded that they were not. The educational and occupational data revealed the following percentages:

1. Father finished high school	45%
Father did not finish high school	45%
No response	10%
2. Father had no college	82%
Father had some college	10%
Father had four years or more college	5%
No response	3%
3. Father is a professional	3%
Father is not a professional	60%
No response	36%
4. Mother finished high school	54%
5. Mother had some college	10%
Mother had four years or more college	10%
6. Mother works	48%
Mother does not work	52%
7. Number of children in family: 1 to 3 children	38%
4 to 6 children	46%
7 to 12 children	16%

THE SEGREGATED BLACK PAROCHIAL SCHOOL

Forty-one students from a segregated black parochial school participated in the study, 13 boys and 28 girls. The total student body population was 330. The majority of the students read at grade level and the median IQ score was 109. The majority of students attending were Catholic.

On the questionnaire the students' responses were as follows:

1.	Parents together	92%
	Parents not together	8%
2.	Father finished high school	61%
	Father did not finish high school	33%
3.	Father had no college	76%
	Father had four years or more college	18%
4.	Father in labor or trade	74%
	Father a professional or owns small business	11%
5.	Mother finished high school	78%
6.	Mother had some college	22%
	Mother had four years or more college	8%
7.	Mother works	46%
	Mother does not work	54%
8.	Number of children in family: 2 to 3 children	22%
	4 to 6 children	59%
	7 to 10 children	19%

THE PREDOMINANTLY WHITE OR SEGREGATED WHITE SCHOOL

The total school enrollment was 1,800 students; 8 percent of the student body was black. The school was five years old at the time of the testing and was located in a predominantly white area. Best estimates from those interviewed at the school were that at least one third of the students came from very low socioeconomic status families, and about 25 percent came from upper-middle-class families. The rest were middle class. The school population was transient because of the variety of industry surrounding the school, e.g., Boeing, Chrysler, oil industries and military, naval, and coast guard installations.

The school was desegregated three years prior to the testing and had three black teachers. The mean IQ score of the students was 103. The teachers felt that the black students who came from all-black schools were not doing as well academically as those who came from previously all-white schools. There were about 160 black students in the school at the time of the testing, but none were in any of the classes that had been selected to participate.

Seventy-eight white students participated in the study, 54 girls and 24 boys.

The responses to some of the questionnaire items are as follows:

1.	Parents together	88%
	Parents not together	10%
2.	Father finished high school	78%
	Father did not finish high school	12%
3.	Father had some college	7%
	Father had four years or more college	44%
	Father had no college	36%
4.	Father in labor, trade, technician	42%
	Father a professional or owns small business	53%
5.	Mother finished high school	80%
	Mother did not finish high school	20%
6.	Mother had some college	22%
	Mother had four years or more college	21%
	Mother had no college	55%
7.	Mother works	31%
	Mother does not work	69%
8.	Number of children in the family: 1 to 3 children	47%
	4 to 6 children	47%

The teachers interviewed indicated that there was very little socialization between the white and black students. White students had the same attitudes as their parents and were against desegregated schools. Most of the black students were in remedial classes and used public transportation to come to the school.

THE 59 PERCENT BLACK PUBLIC SCHOOL

The student population was 749—437 black students and 312 white. There were a large number of Spanish-speaking students from Cuba and Central America, close to 100. Some of the students were so poor that they could not come to school when it rained. Close to 40 percent of the student body received free lunches from federal subsidy. One of the major problems was truancy, especially among the white students.

Eighty-four students participated in the study, 31 white students and 53 black students. Responses to questionnaire items relating to educational and occupational status of parents, and certain items concerning family composition, were as follows:

		White	Black
1.	Parents together	46%	46%
	Parents not together	54%	54%
2.	Father finished high school	42%	35%
	Father did not finish high school	47%	60%
3.	Father had no college	90%	97%
	Father had some college	6%	–
	Father had four years or more college	none	–
4.	Father in labor, trade, technician	65%	53%
	Father a professional or owns small business	23%	7%
5.	Mother finished high school	50%	52%
	Mother did not finish high school	50%	39%
6.	Mother had no college	94%	98%

Mother had some college	3%	2%
Mother had four years or more college	2%	–
7. Mother works	55%	36%
Mother does not work	45%	64%
8. Number of children in family: 1 to 3 children	35%	15%
4 to 6 children	53%	58%
7 to 10 children	13%	27%

This school was formerly all white and was desegregated two years prior to the testing. The mean IQ score was 90.

THE 58 PERCENT BLACK PUBLIC SCHOOL

The school was formerly an all-white school which was desegregated two years prior to the testing. The 731 students came from middle-class and upper-lower-class families. The occupations among black parents consisted of domestics, longshoremen, a few teachers, and one black parent was principal of a black school. The neighborhood itself had been mixed for many years so that the desegregation process was not as difficult as in other schools. Although there were many remedial problems with white students, the problem was far greater among the black students. The IQ average for the student body was about 93. The most outstanding student in the school was a black boy with an IQ of 120. He was editor of the school paper and the son of a policeman.

Since desegregation, profanity, obscenity, and many other discipline problems had increased. Discipline at home was quite severe and several cases of battered children had been reported by school personnel to the authorities.

There was really no socialization among the students, although a week prior to this interview the school had had a dance and black and white students attended. The sweetheart of the dance was a black girl, second place was held by a white girl, third place by a Spanish-speaking girl, and fourth place by a black girl.

There were eight black faculty members out of a total of 48; the year before the study, there had been only one. One of the vice-principals was black and there were two black male teachers.

Seventy-four students were tested, 43 black students and 31 white students. The responses to questionnaire items by the students were as follows:

	White	Black
1. Parents are together	71%	56%
Parents are not together	29%	44%
2. Father finished high school	47%	44%
Father did not finish high school	48%	47%
3. Father had no college	82%	91%
Father had some college	3%	5%

Father had four years or more college	9%	4%
4. Mother finished high school	66%	42%
Mother did not finish high school	34%	51%
5. Mother had no college	77%	90%
Mother had some college	12%	5%
Mother had four years or more college	8%	3%
6. Mother works	46%	46%
Mother does not work	54%	55%
7. Number of children in family: 1 to 3 children	27%	19%
4 to 6 children	51%	43%
7 to 9 children	12%	32%
10 or more children	–	–
8. Father in trade, labor, technician	68%	75%
Father is a professional or owns small business	15%	5%

THE 18 PERCENT BLACK PUBLIC SCHOOL

The student population at this school was approximately 1,400 with close to 18 percent black enrollment. The school was desegregated three years prior to the testing on a grade-a-year basis.

According to information obtained from staff of the school most of the students came from lower socioeconomic backgrounds with many broken homes. The IQ range was given as 70 to 110 with a mean of 93. Achievement was reported as being very low, especially among the black students, and many students dropped out because they were over 17 years of age.

The students, black and white, came from the same neighborhood, but did not socialize and especially not with the opposite sex of a different race. It was reported that the militant black children hated the white children and teachers, and many of the white students disliked being in a desegregated school and had asked for transfer permits.

The educational, occupational, and family data obtained from the questionnaires of the 68 white students and 23 black students were as follows:

	White	Black
1. Parents together	74%	76%
Parents not together	26%	24%
2. Father finished high school	35%	52%
Father did not finish high school	56%	48%
3. Father had no college	95%	100%
Father had some college	42%	--
Father had four years or more college	1%	--
4. Father in trade, labor, technician	80%	76%
Father a professional or owns small business	7%	12%
5. Mother finished high school	45%	53%
Mother did not finish high school	49%	42%
6. Mother had no college	93%	100%
Mother had some college	4%	--
Mother had four years or more college	1%	--
7. Mother works	35%	28%
Mother does not work	65%	72%
8. Number of children in family: 1 to 3 children	53%	23%
4 to 6 children	37%	16%
7 to 10 children	17%	55%

THE 50 PERCENT BLACK PAROCHIAL SCHOOL

Thirty black students and 34 white students responded to the questionnaire items regarding educational and occupational status of parents and family. The responses were as follows:

		Black	White
1.	Parents together	74%	63%
	Parents not together	14%	37%
2.	Father finished high school	50%	65%
	Father did not finish high school	30%	32%
3.	Father had no college	75%	73%
	Father had some college	--	11%
	Father had four years or more college	21%	16%
4.	Father in trade, labor, technician	45%	65%
	Father professional or owns small business	21%	26%
5.	Mother finished high school	64%	68%
	Mother did not finish high school	7%	22%
6.	Mother had no college	73%	75%
	Mother had some college	7%	9%
	Mother had four years or more college	14%	10%
7.	Mother works	67%	33%
	Mother does not work	33%	67%
8.	Number of children in family: 1 to 3 children	49%	55%
	4 to 6 children	37%	35%
	7 to 9 children	10%	15%

THE LESS THAN 10 PERCENT BLACK PAROCHIAL SCHOOL

This particular Catholic school began at kindergarten and continued up to ninth grade. The total school enrollment was approximately 300, with a total of 33 black students in all the grades. The enrollment of black students in seventh, eighth, and ninth grades was less than 10 percent. The school began to desegregate in 1961 on a grade-a-year basis. At the time desegregation was started many white parents took their children out, but some white parents wanted their children in a desegregated school. The parents of both races are decidedly middle class. According to one staff member interviewed, there were no academic differences between white and black students because "they come early." The mean IQ is about 100 to 105. The only problem that they have with the "colored" is their speech, but the staff must "help them with the niceties they never had before and there is a special program." The children socialized in school but not outside.

The 59 white students made the following responses on the questionnaire:

1.	Parents are together	76%
	Parents are not together	24%
2.	Father finished high school	81%
	Father did not finish high school	14%
3.	Father had no college	78%
	Father had some college	7%
	Father had four years or more college	12%

4.	Father in labor or trade	65%
	Father professional or owns small business	20%
5.	Mother finished high school	71%
	Mother did not finish high school	18%
6.	Mother had no college	81%
	Mother had some college	7%
	Mother had four years or more college	6%
7.	Mother works	46%
	Mother does not work	54%
8.	Number of children in family: 1 to 3 children	51%
	4 to 6 children	38%
	7 to 9 children	10%

FAMILY BACKGROUND AND ASPIRATIONS OF STUDENTS

Among the black students 63 percent reported that their parents were living together and 37 percent indicated that their parents were separated or divorced (see Table 1). The majority of black students (42 percent) came from families that had four to six children, but a substantial percentage of them (27 percent) were part of families that had seven children or more. Twenty-nine percent of the black students came from families with one to three children. It is interesting to note, however, that at the black segregated parochial school 92 percent of the parents were together, at the 18 percent black public school 76 percent of the black parents were together, and at the desegregated black parochial school 74 percent of the black parents were living together. The group of black students having the largest families were those at the 18 percent black public school where 55 percent of the students came from families that had seven to fifteen children. Compared with white students, however, there were more black students coming from families with more than seven children.

Among the white students 69 percent reported that their parents were living together and 31 percent indicated that their parents were separated or divorced. Forty-four percent of the students came from families with one to three children and 41 percent came from families with four to six children with only 11 percent coming from families with more than seven children. It is interesting to note that the white students at the 59 percent black school reported that only 46 percent of their parents were living together. This school was a central city school where the incidence of poverty was high, migration of Spanish-speaking students was high, and discipline and school drop-out problems were prevalent. It will be interesting to see how the TSCS scores of these students correlate with their family backgrounds (Chapter 11).

The educational background of the white parents tended to be higher than that of the black parents, but not especially so. For instance, 58 percent of white students reported that their fathers had finished high school, whereas

50 percent of the black students responded in such a way. Among white fathers, 13 percent finished college and 12 percent had some college, compared with 7 percent and 5 percent respectively for black fathers. The educational attainment of white mothers is higher than black mothers, but not strikingly so; 63 percent of white mothers finished high school and 58 percent of black mothers finished. Among white mothers, 8 percent finished college and 10 percent had some college, while 5 percent of black mothers had finished college and 8 percent had some college. The percent of white and black mothers working is quite similar, 41 percent and 39 percent respectively.

It would seem that twice as many white fathers as black fathers are in professions or own their own businesses, 24 percent and 11 percent respectively. The percentage in the technician-trade category runs 40 percent for the whites and 50 percent for the blacks, with 23 percent black fathers and 28 percent of the white fathers employed as laborers. Most of the students (75 percent) were uncertain of family income and many were uncertain (85 percent) as to occupation of their parents. However, those students whose parents were teachers, lawyers, doctors, engineers, successful business people, and in the professional categories, knew what their parents did and could approximate their salaries. (See Table 1.)

TABLE 1

**Occupational and Educational Background of
Parents in New Orleans**

Percentages

	Father High School		Father College		
	Yes	No	Yes	No	Some
Black	50	44	7	72	5
White	58	35	13	75	12

	Father's Occupation			
	Profession/Own Business	Technician/Trade	Labor	N.D.
White	24	40	28	8
Black	11	50	23	9

	Mother Works		Mother High School		Mother College		
	Yes	No	Yes	No	Yes	No	Some
Black	39	61	58	37	5	69	8
White	41	59	63	32	8	79	10

	Family Background				
	Parents		Number of Children		
	Together	Separated or Divorced	1 to 3	4 to 6	7 plus
Black	63	37	29	42	27
White	69	31	44	41	11

The questionnaire was devised in such a way that aspiration, goals, and attitudes could be assessed from a variety of questions or open-ended statements (see Appendix 2).

The white and black students aspiring to college and a profession were quite similar, with 40 percent of white students and 38 percent of the black students expressing such a desire; 29 percent of the white students desired to enter some profession, compared with 22 percent of the black students. Both groups had aspirational levels above the educational and occupational attainments of their parents. Among the white students 40 percent were interested in getting a job when they finished school, compared with 24 percent of the black students. The other definite goals were expressed in terms of wanting money or success, to be an entertainer, or to emulate some hero.

Both black and white students, 45 percent and 50 percent respectively, indicated that they were satisfied with themselves in general; but 22 percent of the black students indicated that there were certain attitudes they wanted to change or they had attitudes that went beyond expressing satisfaction or dissatisfaction with themselves. (See Table 2.)

TABLE 2

Aspirations of Students in New Orleans

Percentages

	College	Marriage*	Profession	Sports*	Job	Other Definite Goals	N.D.†
White	40	7	29	17	40	15	9
Black	38	4	22	7	24	16	14

Attitudes

	Satisfied with Self-Image	Immature	N.D.†	Other Definite Attitudes
White	50	18	7	12
Black	49	9	18	22

*The boys responded in terms of sports and the girls responded in terms of marriage.
†No data given.

THE SOCIOPOLITICAL CLIMATE AT THE TIME OF THE TESTING

It should be noted that in those schools that had at least 50 percent black enrollment the black students were included more in the extra-curricular activities at the school. Although the prevailing attitude among white students and white parents was unfavorable toward desegregation in these schools, it was a *fait accompli*, and most whites were trying to make the best of it. However, in those schools that were all white or predominantly white or where school desegregation was less than 20 percent black, anti-black, anti-desegregation feelings were high.

Several weeks prior to the testing three significant community events had occurred that had aroused controversy in many sectors of the community. First of all, for the first time in the history of New Orleans, a black man had been elected to the school board. His candidacy had been supported by the *Times Picayune* and his qualifications were outstanding. He was dean of students at Dillard University where he had taught for many years, had a doctorate degree, and was well known and respected in the white and black communities. However, there were some factions in the black community that believed he was "colored" and not "black" and was not in touch with the new black mood in spite of his reputation in civil rights activities. He was an integrationist and many blacks felt that he would be too ready to compromise.

Shortly after the school board election, a group of black students at a newly desegregated high school had a strike. They wanted more black studies courses and a black student union for black students. Some violence occurred, the black students were arrested, and then subsequently released. Their demands were never met.

The newly elected black school board member was called upon to comment on the incident. According to reports, he criticized the black students and their demands for a black studies program and a black student union. He was reported to have said that the days of segregation must end and that the actions of the black students would only further the cause of segregation. He was severely criticized by the more militant blacks who felt that he should have personally listened to the side of the black students, that he represented "the old guard" and did not understand the real meaning underlying the black students' protest.

On the other hand, the newly elected black school board member could not understand why the black students would want special courses for themselves. He felt that segregating themselves in a newly desegregated school would only defeat the purposes of integration. "All my life I've fought for integration and now the young Negroes cry for separation. I don't understand." Clearly, there was a generation gap and not enough black leadership or unity to help the black community deal with the issues concisely. Clearly, the black students in the newly desegregated high school felt threatened and alienated and set apart. Their demand for separate black studies programs and a black student union was a cry for help to assist them in finding a socially relevant and less degrading educational experience than the one that had been thrust upon them.

A six-million-dollar housing project for poor people was to be built near the center city but close to a white neighborhood. The purpose of the project was to remodel a ghetto section of the central city which would displace the people who lived there but would provide townhouses with comparable rent for the people who would be displaced. The project was also to be integrated. A community meeting was called to discuss the project and a group of angry whites appeared who threatened to lynch any "nigger" or "nigger lover" who dared to move into the townhouses.

Finally, although some civil rights activity occurred in the 1960's during the sit-ins, New Orleans blacks never participated to the extent that other Southern black communities had. The New Orleans black community is divided along economic and racial lines. There has always been a distinction made between blacks of pure African ancestry and the Creole black, many of whom for years denied that they were Negroes. Thus, the dynamics of race relations in New Orleans proceeds along many lines.

1. Facts and Finances: New Orleans Public Schools. 1968-1969, p. 4.
2. Ibid., pp. 19-22.

11

New Orleans Self-Concept Data

Eight schools participated in the study, three parochial and five public schools. Of the eight schools participating, two were segregated or predominantly white schools, four were desegregated schools, and two were segregated black schools. Six hundred and forty students were tested, 381 females and 259 males. The sampling included 316 black students and 324 white students. On the self-concept scale the New Orleans students achieved a total positive mean score of 340.3 which falls into the 40th percentile for the TSCS and below the normative mean. Sixteen percent of the New Orleans students scored below 300, 43 percent achieved a score of 350 or above, and 6 percent scored above 400. The mean self-criticism score achieved by the New Orleans students was 36, which is above the normative mean for the self-concept score; their mean variability score was 56, above the normative mean; and their mean distribution score was 131, also above the normative. Thus, as a whole, the majority of the participating students from New Orleans have an adequate self-concept, capacity for openness, variability, and certainty about their self-perception. (See Table 1.)

In the three major profile scores the New Orleans students obtained a mean identity score of 115 which is below the normative mean, a mean self-satisfaction score of 110.3 which is above the normative mean, and a mean behavior score of 115.5 which is equal to the normative mean. On the sub-profile scores, the New Orleans students were below the normative means on the following scores: moral-ethical self, personal self, and social self. The group scored above the normative mean on physical self and family self.

BLACK STUDENTS IN NEW ORLEANS

Of the 316 black students tested in New Orleans, 182 were girls and 134 were boys attending parochial and public schools. Ninety-two of the black girls were attending segregated schools and 90 were attending desegregated schools. Among the black boys, 63 were attending segregated schools and 71 were attending desegregated schools. Of the 316 black students in the sample, 245 were attending public schools and 71 were attending parochial schools. (See Table 2.) The black boys ranged in age from 12 to 18 years, and the black girls ranged in age from 11 to 18 years. The distribution of boys and girls according to age is given in Table 2. Among the boys, 45 were in the seventh grade, 54 were in the eighth grade, and 35 were in the ninth grade. The distribution of the girls according to grades is similar to that of the boys, with 54 in the seventh grade, 75 in the eighth grade, and 53 in the ninth grade.

The black students in New Orleans achieved a mean total positive score of 348, with 9 percent scoring below 300, 8 percent scoring above 400, and 50 percent scoring 350 or above. The total positive mean score is above the normative mean score for the TSCS. On the other three major self-concept scores—self-criticism, variability, and distribution—the black New Orleans students achieved mean scores of 36.1, 58, and 140.1 respectively, all above the normative mean scores. (See Tables 1 and 3.)

On the three major profile scores, identity, self-satisfaction, and behavior, the mean scores were 117.5, 113.9, and 117.5 respectively. The mean identity score (117.5) was below the normative mean. The sub-profile mean scores of physical self (74.7) and family self (74.8) were above the normative mean. However, the sub-profile mean scores of moral-ethical self (69.4), personal self (62.7), and social self (66.3) were below the normative means.

TABLE 1

Black and White Students in New Orleans

Race	TP (Mean)	Percentages	SC Score (Mean)	V Score (Mean)	D Score (Mean)
White N = 324	332.9	<300 = 22% >350 = 35% >400 = 5%	36.2	53.9	124.3
Black N = 316	348.8	<300 = 9% >350 = 50% >400 = 8%	36.1	58.3	140.1
Totals N = 640	340.3	<300 = 16% >350 = 43% >400 = 6%	36	56	131

TABLE 2

Distribution of Black Students Tested in New Orleans by Sex, Type of School, Age, and Grade in School

Black Students 316							
Black Girls 182				Black Boys 134			
Segregated		Desegregated		Segregated		Desegregated	
Public	Parochial	Parochial	Public	Public	Parochial	Parochial	Public
64	28	14	76	50	13	16	55
Total No. Parochial 42				Total No. Parochial 29			
Total No. Public 140				Total No. Public 105			

Age in Years of Black Students

	11	12	13	14	15	16	17	18
Boys	0	15	29	29	26	19	8	2
Girls	1	26	51	59	20	16	5	1

Grades in School of Black Students

	7th	8th	9th
Boys	45	54	35
Girls	54	75	53

TABLE 3

Self-Concept Profile of Black Students in New Orleans

Score	Mean	Standard Deviation	Standard Error	Percentile
Total Positive	348.8	3.836	0.215	50th
Identity	117.5	1.437	0.081	15th
Self-Satisfaction	113.9	1.714	0.096	72nd
Behavior	117.5	1.591	0.089	60th
Physical Self	74.7	0.890	0.050	65th
Moral-Ethical Self	69.4	1.019	0.057	45th
Personal Self	63.7	1.148	0.064	45th
Family Self	74.8	1.177	0.066	65th
Social Self	66.3	1.055	0.059	35th
Self-Criticism	36.1	0.658	0.037	50th
Distribution	140.1	2.681	0.150	75th
Variability	58.3	1.405	0.079	75th

BLACK GIRLS IN NEW ORLEANS

There were 182 black girls with 42 in parochial schools and 140 in public schools. Of the 42 black girls in parochial school, 28 were in a segregated school and 14 were attending a desegregated school. Those black girls in public schools represented 64 from one black segregated school and 76 from three public desegregated schools (see Table 4). The black girls obtained a total positive mean score of 352.9 with 9 percent scoring below 300, 12 percent scoring above 400, and 51 percent obtaining a score of 350 or above. The total positive mean score is above the normative mean as is the self-criticism mean score of 36, the variability mean score of 58, and the distribution mean score of 136. Thus, the black girls in New Orleans have a very positive self-concept and certainty about their self-perception; they are critical of themselves, but show a degree of variability from one area of self-perception to another. (See Table 4.)

BLACK GIRLS IN PAROCHIAL SCHOOLS

The 28 black girls in the segregated black parochial school obtained a total positive mean score of 359.1, which is above the normative mean and falls in the 65th percentile for the scale. Among the black girls in the segregated parochial schools, 8 percent scored below 300, 60 percent obtained a score of 350 or above, and 24 percent scored above 400. The self-criticism mean score achieved by the black segregated parochial girls is 32 which is below the normative mean. The variability mean score is 56, above the normative mean, and the distribution mean score is 132, above the normative mean. Thus, black girls in the segregated parochial schools who participated in the study have a very positive self-concept and express certainty about their self-picture. The low self-criticism score indicates some defensiveness and the high variability score would indicate some inconsistency from one area of the self-picture to another. (See Table 4.)

Fourteen black girls from a desegregated parochial school (50 percent black) achieved a total positive mean score of 339.5 which is below the normative mean. Among the desegregated parochial group, 7 percent scored below 300, 28 percent scored 350 or above, and there were no students who scored above 400. The girls achieved a self-criticism mean score of 36 and a variability mean score of 55, both above the normative mean. The distribution mean score for the group is 123, just slightly above the normative mean. Thus, the black girls in the desegregated parochial school have a less positive self-concept than those in the segregated parochial school and show less certainty about their self-picture. However, their mean self-criticism score would indicate less defensiveness and more ability to accept derogatory

TABLE 4

Black Girls Grades 7-8-9 New Orleans

Racial Composition	Type of School	TP (Mean)	Percentages TP Scores	SC Score (Mean)	V Score (Mean)	D Score (Mean)
100% Black	Parochial N = 28	359.1	<300 = 8% >350 = 60% >400 = 24%	32	56	132.7
59% Black	Public N = 36	360.6	<300 = 13% >350 = 77% >400 = 21%	36	58	151.3
50% Black	Parochial N = 14	339.5	<300 = 7% >350 = 28% >400 = 0%	36	55	123.8
58% Black	Public N = 28	344.8	<300 = 14% >350 = 43% >400 = 4%	38	62	132.9
18% Black	Public N = 12	354.6	<300 = 8% >350 = 32% >400 = 8%	38	58	138.7
100% Black	Public N = 64	357.1	<300 = 9% >350 = 68% >400 = 16%	38	59	142.6
Totals	N = 182	352.9	<300 = 9% >350 = 51% >400 = 12%	36.5	58.3	139.9

statements about the self. The variability mean score is similar to that of the black girls in the segregated parochial schools, indicating some variability from one area of self-perception to another.

For the 42 black girls attending parochial schools, the total positive mean score is 344.3, the self-criticism mean score is 34, the variability mean score is 55.5, and the distribution mean score is 127.5. The mean V and mean D scores fall above the normative means for the scale, but the mean TP and mean SC are just below the normative mean. (See Table 5.)

BLACK GIRLS IN PUBLIC SCHOOLS

There were 140 black girls tested in public schools in New Orleans. The black girls in public schools achieved a total positive mean score of 354.4, a self-criticism mean score of 37, a variability mean score of 59, and a distribution mean score of 141. The self-concept scores for the black girls in public schools would indicate that they feel very positive about their self-concept, are very open to criticism with little defensiveness, feel very definite about themselves, but have many variations in different areas of self-perception. (See Table 5.)

TABLE 5

A Comparison of Black Students in Parochial and
Public Schools in New Orleans

Black Students in Parochial Schools in New Orleans

Sex	Racial Composition	No. of Students	TP (Mean)	SC Score (Mean)	V Score (Mean)	D Score (Mean)
Girls	100% Black	28	359.1	32	56	132
Girls	50% Black	14	339.5	36	55	123
Boys	100% Black	13	346.8	36	58	132
Boys	50% Black	16	347	35	57	157
	Totals/Means	71	348.1	34	57	136

Black Students in Public Schools in New Orleans

Black Girls

Racial Composition	No. of Students	TP (Mean)	SC Score (Mean)	V Score (Mean)	D Score (Mean)
100% Black	64	357.1	38	59	142
59% Black	36	360.6	36	58	151
58% Black	28	344.8	38	62	132
18% Black	12	354.6	38	58	138
Totals/Means	140	354.4	37	59	141

Black Boys

Racial Composition	No. of Students	TP (Mean)	SC Score (Mean)	V Score (Mean)	D Score (Mean)
100% Black	50	348	35	59	144
59% Black	17	329	32	57	124
58% Black	27	338.9	38	62	143
18% Black	11	356	38	51	140
Totals/Means	105	343.2	36	58	138

Summary of Data on Black Students in Public and
Parochial Schools in New Orleans

Type of School	No. of Students	TP (Mean)	SC Score (Mean)	V Score (Mean)	D Score (Mean)
Parochial	71	348.1	34	57	136
Public	245	348.8	36	58	140
Total/Mean	316	348.5	35	57.5	138

Of the 140 black girls tested in public schools, 64 were in a black segregated school. These girls obtained a total positive mean score of 357.1, with 9 percent scoring below 300, 68 percent obtaining a score of 350 or above, and 16 percent scoring above 400. The mean self-criticism score is 38, the mean variability score is 59, and the mean distribution score is 142; all of these means are above the normative mean for the scale. (See Table 4.) Thus, the 64 black girls at the segregated public school have high self-concepts, are very open and not defensive about criticizing themselves, are very certain about how they perceive themselves, but vary in how they think about different aspects of themselves.

Three desegregated public schools participated in the study with a total of 76 black girls participating. It is interesting to note the differences in TSCS scores among the three desegregated schools. The 59 percent black public school with 36 black girls participating achieved a total positive mean score of 360.6, well above the normative mean and within the 65th percentile for the TSCS. Fourteen percent of the girls scored below 300, but 77 percent of the girls scored 350 or above, and 21 percent scored above 400. The mean self-criticism score of 36, the mean variability score of 58, and the mean distribution score of 151 are all above the normative means for the scale (see Table 4).

However, the 28 girls at the 58 percent black school achieved a total positive mean score of 344.8, just below the normative mean for the scale, with 14 percent scoring below 300, 43 percent scoring 350 or above, and 4 percent scoring above 400. The mean self-criticism score of 38, the mean variability score of 62, and the mean distribution score of 132 are all above the normative means for the scale. Thus, the 28 black girls at the 58 percent black desegregated school have adequate self-concepts, are very open to criticism about themselves, are very certain about how they perceive themselves, and have extremely high variability in different areas of self-perception (this would indicate that on the profile items there would be great variability in how negative or positive they felt about themselves on various items.) (See Table 4.)

In the 18 percent black desegregated school, the 12 black girls participating achieved a total positive mean score of 354.6, which is above the normative mean for the scale. Eight percent of the girls scored below 300, 32 percent scored 350 or above, and 8 percent scored above 400. The mean self-criticism score for this group is 38, the mean variability score is 58, and the mean distribution score is 138. All are above the normative means for the scale, indicating that these girls have a high self-concept, are very open to accepting negative statements about themselves, and are very inconsistent in their self-perception.

The TSCS mean scores for the 76 black girls in desegregated public schools are the following:

1. Total positive mean score, 353.3
2. Self-criticism mean score, 37.3
3. Variability mean score, 59.3
4. Distribution mean score, 140

All of these mean scores are above the normative mean for the self-concept scale (see Table 5).

BLACK GIRLS IN SEGREGATED SCHOOLS

The TSCS scores of the 64 black girls in segregated public schools have already been mentioned in the paragraph above. Likewise, the TSCS scores of the 28 black girls in segregated parochial schools have been discussed in the section on parochial schools.

Of the total 92 black girls in segregated black public and parochial schools in New Orleans, the total positive mean score is 358.1, with eight percent of the girls scoring below 300, 64 percent scoring 350 or above, and 20 percent scoring above 400. The total positive mean score is above the normative mean for the self-concept scale (see Table 6). The mean self-criticism score for the black segregated girls is 36.4, the mean variability score is 57.7, and the mean distribution score is 138.8.

TABLE 6

Black Students in Segregated Black Schools in New Orleans

Sex	TP (Mean)	Percentages TP Scores	SC Score (Mean)	V Score (Mean)	D Score (Mean)
Boys N = 63	343.3	<300 = 8% >350 = 49% >400 = 1%	35.2	58.9	141.6
Girls N = 92	358.1	<300 = 8% >350 = 64% >400 = 20%	36.4	57.7	138.8
Totals N = 155	348.8	<300 = 8% >350 = 57% >400 = 10%	35.9	58.2	139.9

BLACK GIRLS IN DESEGREGATED SCHOOLS

There were 90 black girls tested from desegregated schools in New Orleans, 14 from parochial schools and 76 from public schools. The TSCS mean scores for the 76 black girls in desegregated public schools have been discussed in the section on public schools and the scores for the 42 black girls in parochial schools have been discussed in the section on parochial schools.

The 90 black girls in desegregated schools in New Orleans achieved a total positive mean score of 347.3, which is above the normative mean for the scale. The distribution of the total positive scores were such that 8 percent of the girls scored less than 300, 45 percent scored 350 or above, and 8 percent scored above 400. (See Table 7.) The black girls in desegregated schools achieved a mean self-criticism score of 36.6, a mean variability score of 58.8, and a mean distribution score of 139.4, all above the normative means for the scale.

TABLE 7

Black Students in Desegregated Schools in New Orleans

Sex	TP (Mean)	Percentages TP Scores	SC Score (Mean)	V Score (Mean)	D Score (Mean)
Boys N = 71	340	<300 = 12% >350 = 42% >400 = 6%	35.8	57.8	141.6
Girls N = 90	347.3	<300 = 8% >350 = 45% >400 = 8%	36.6	58.9	139.4
Totals N = 161	344	<300 = 10% >350 = 44% >400 = 7%	36	57.5	138.5

BLACK BOYS IN NEW ORLEANS

The number of black boys tested in New Orleans was 134 with 63 from segregated schools and 71 from desegregated schools, 105 from public schools and 29 from parochial schools. The 134 black boys tested obtained a total mean positive score of 343.3, with 11 percent scoring below 300, 44 percent scoring 350 or above, and 5 percent scoring above 400. The self-criticism mean score of 35.5 is equal to the normative mean, the variability mean score of 58.3, and the distribution mean score of 131.6 are above the normative mean for the scale. The mean total positive score of 343.3 is below the normative mean score and falls into the 45th percentile of the scale (see Table 8).

BLACK BOYS IN PAROCHIAL SCHOOLS

Thirteen black boys in a segregated parochial school participated in the study. They achieved a total positive mean score of 346.8, which falls into the 45th percentile and below the normative mean. Eight percent of the boys scored below 300, 48 percent scored 350 or above, and none of the boys

TABLE 8

Black Boys Grades 7-8-9—New Orleans

Racial Composition	Type of School	TP (Mean)	Percentages TP Scores	SC Score (Mean)	V Score (Mean)	D Score (Mean)
59% Black	Public N = 17	329	<300 = 12% >350 = 30% >400 = 0%	32	57	124
18% Black	Public N = 11	356	<300 = 9% >350 = 54% >400 = 9%	38	51	140
58% Black	Public N = 27	338.9	<300 = 22% >350 = 44% >400 = 4%	38	62	143
100% Black	Public N = 50	348	<300 = 8% >350 = 50% >400 = 2%	35	59	144
100% Black	Parochial N = 13	346.8	<300 = 8% >350 = 48% >400 = 0%	36	58	132
50% Black	Parochial N = 16	347	<300 = 6% >350 = 38% >400 = 12%	35	57	157
Totals	N = 134	343.3	<300 = 11% >350 = 44% >400 = 5%	35.5	58.3	141.6

scored above 400. The mean self-criticism score of 36 is above the normative mean, as is the mean variability score of 58, and the mean distribution score of 132. Of the 48 boys in parochial schools, 16 were attending a desegregated parochial school (50 percent black). These boys obtained a total positive mean score of 347, which is above the normative mean, with 6 percent scoring below 300, 38 percent scoring 350 or above, and 12 percent scoring above 400. The self-criticism mean score of 35 is equivalent to the normative mean, but the mean variability score of 57, and the mean distribution score of 157 are all above the normative means for the scale. (See Table 5.)

BLACK BOYS IN PUBLIC SCHOOLS

One hundred and five black boys from four public schools participated in the study. Three of the schools were desegregated, 59 percent black, 58 percent black and 18 percent black; one of the schools was segregated (10 percent black). (See Table 5.)

The 50 boys at the segregated public school achieved a total positive mean score of 348 which is above the normative mean for the scale, with 8 percent scoring below 300, 50 percent scoring 350 or above, and 2 percent scoring above 400. The mean self-criticism score of 36, the mean variability score of 58, and the mean distribution score of 132 are all above the normative mean for the scale. The black boys at the segregated black schools have an adequate self-concept, are open to criticism, are very variable, but very definite about their self-concept.

At the 18 percent black desegregated school 11 boys participated in the study. They obtained a total positive mean score of 356, which is above the normative mean for the scale, with 9 percent scoring below 300, 54 percent scoring above 350, and 9 percent scoring above 400. The mean self-criticism score of 38, the mean variability score of 51, and the mean distribution score of 140 are all above the normative means. Hence, it could be said that the boys at the 18 percent black desegregated school have a high self-concept, felt very definite and certain about themselves, are very critical in evaluating themselves, and perceive themselves differently in various aspects of the self.

The 27 boys at the 59 percent black desegregated school achieved a total positive mean score of 338.9, which is below the normative mean and falls into the 38th percentile for the scale. Twenty-two percent of the students scored below 300, 44 percent of the students scored 350 or above, and 4 percent of the students scored above 400. The mean self-criticism score of 38 and the mean distribution score of 143 are both above the normative means. However, the mean variability score of 62 is exceedingly high, representing a great deal of inconsistency in various areas of self-perception.

At the 59 percent black desegregated school 17 black boys participated achieving a total positive mean score of 329 which is below the normative mean and falls into the 28th percentile. Twelve percent of the boys scored below 300, 30 percent scored 350 or above, and none scored above 400. The mean variability score of 57 and the mean distribution score of 124 are above the normative means for the scale. However, the mean self-criticism score of 32 is below the normative mean for the scale. Thus, for the TSCS scores, these boys seem to have low self-concepts, little certainty about the self, relative inconsistency about the self-picture, and defensiveness in evaluating the self.

BLACK BOYS IN SEGREGATED SCHOOLS

There were 63 black boys in segregated public and parochial schools who participated in the study in New Orleans. The self-concept scores for the 50 boys in segregated public schools have been discussed under the heading of public schools and the 13 black boys in segregated parochial schools have been discussed under the heading of parochial schools.

The 63 black boys in segregated schools in New Orleans achieved a total positive mean score of 343.3 which is just below the normative mean. Eight percent of the boys scored below 300 and 1 percent above 400. The mean self-criticism score of 35.2 is equal to the normative mean, the mean variability score of 58.9, and the mean distribution score of 141.6 are both above the normative means for the scale. Thus, it could be said that the black segregated boys in New Orleans have adequate self-concepts, a moderate degree of openness, a high degree of variability in how they perceive themselves, and are very certain how they feel about themselves. (See Table 6.)

BLACK BOYS IN DESEGREGATED SCHOOLS

There were 71 black boys in desegregated public and parochial schools in New Orleans who participated in the study, 16 came from parochial schools and 55 came from public schools. The self-concept scores of the 55 black boys in desegregated public schools have been discussed in the section on public schools, and the self-concept scores of the 16 black boys in a desegregated parochial school have been discussed on the section on parochial schools.

The black boys in desegregated public and parochial schools in New Orleans achieved a total positive mean score of 340, with 12 percent scoring below 300, 42 percent scoring 350 or above, and 6 percent scoring above 400. The total positive mean score of 340 is below the normative mean for the scale. The self-criticism mean score of 35.8, the variability mean score of 57.8, and the distribution mean score of 141.6 are all above the normative means for the scale. The desegregated black boys seem to score below the norm on self-concept, but have an adequate degree of openness and honesty, a great deal of variability in what they think about different aspects of themselves, and are very certain how they feel about themselves. (See Table 7.)

COMPARISON OF BLACK STUDENTS
IN PUBLIC AND PAROCHIAL SCHOOLS

The TSCS mean scores of students in segregated and desegregated public and parochial schools have been discussed in previous paragraphs in this chapter.

It would appear that the 42 black girls in parochial schools (TP mean = 349.3, SC mean = 34, V mean = 35.6, D mean = 127.5) score lower on all scores than the 140 black public school girls; but the 29 black boys in parochial schools (TP mean = 346.9, SC mean = 35.5, V mean = 57.5, D mean = 144.5) score quite similarly to the 105 black boys in public schools. None of the differences are statistically significant.

The black parochial boys have a tendency to score higher on the four TSCS scores than the black parochial girls, but the black public school girls have a tendency to score higher than the black public school boys. There are no significant differences. (See Table 5.)

WHITE STUDENTS IN NEW ORLEANS

The 318 white students who participated in the study in New Orleans came from segregated and desegregated public and parochial schools. There were 193 white girls who participated, 88 from segregated schools, and 105 from desegregated schools. One hundred and twenty-five white boys participated with 49 coming from segregated schools and 76 coming from desegregated schools. Two hundred and twenty-five of the students came from public schools and 93 came from parochial schools (see Table 9). The white boys ranged in age from 14 to 17 years, and the white girls ranged in age from 11 to 17 years. Fifty-eight of the white boys were in seventh grade, 57 were in eighth grade, and 7 were in ninth grade. Among the girls, 60 were in seventh grade, 71 were in eighth grade, and 56 were in ninth grade. The 318 white students in New Orleans achieved a total positive mean score of 332.9 which is below the normative mean and falls into the 30th percentile for the scale. The mean self-criticism score of 36.2, the mean distribution score of 124.3, and the mean variability score of 53.9 are all above the normative means for the scale. (See Table 1.) On the profile and sub-profile mean scores, the white students scored below the normative means on identity, behavior, physical self, moral-ethical self, personal self, and social self. They scored above the normative means on self-satisfaction and family self. (See Tables 9 and 10.)

THE WHITE GIRLS

The 193 white girls tested represented 54 from parochial schools and 139 from public schools. Eighty-eight of the white girls were attending segregated schools and 105 were attending desegregated schools. The white girls in New Orleans achieved a total positive mean score of 335.3, which falls below the normative mean for the scale, with 18 percent scoring below 300, 40 percent scoring 350 or above, and 5 percent scoring above 400. The mean self-criticism score of 36.5, the mean variability score of 53.5, and the mean distribution score of 121.1 are all above the normative mean. (See Table 11.)

WHITE GIRLS IN PAROCHIAL SCHOOLS

There were 54 white girls in parochial schools, 34 in a segregated school and 20 in a desegregated or 50 percent black parochial school. The 34 girls in the segregated parochial school obtained a total positive mean score of

TABLE 9

Distribution of White Students Tested in New Orleans by Sex, Type of School, Age, and Grade in School

White Students 318							
White Girls 193				White Boys 125			
Segregated		Desegregated		Segregated		Desegregated	
Public	Parochial	Parochial	Public	Public	Parochial	Parochial	Public
53	34	20	85	24	25	14	62
	Total No. Parochial				Total No. Parochial		
	54				39		
	Total No. Public 139				Total No. Public 86		

Age in Years of White Students

	11	12	13	14	15	16	17
Boys	0	14	49	32	21	3	2
Girls	0	31	61	60	32	2	1

Grades in School of White Students

	7th	8th	9th
Boys	58	57	7
Girls	60	71	56

TABLE 10

Self-Concept Profile of White Students in New Orleans

Score	Mean	Standard Deviation	Standard Error	Percentile
Total Positive	332.9	4.106	0.230	30th
Identity	112.6	1.457	0.082	7th
Self-Satisfaction	106.8	1.809	0.101	55th
Behavior	113.5	1.459	0.082	45th
Physical Self	69.5	0.995	0.056	35th
Moral-Ethical Self	66.4	1.095	0.061	55th
Personal Self	60.5	1.145	0.064	25th
Family Self	70.3	1.263	0.071	47th
Social Self	65.8	0.942	0.053	35th
Self-Criticism	36.2	0.689	0.039	50th
Distribution	124.3	2.731	0.153	60th
Variability	53.9	1.317	0.074	65th

TABLE 11

White Girls Grades 7-8-9—New Orleans

Racial Composition	Type of School	TP (Mean)	Percentages TP Scores	SC Score (Mean)	V Score (Mean)	D Score (Mean)
58% Black	Public N = 29	345	<300 = 9% >350 = 48% >400 = 9%	40	59	136
18% Black	Public N = 43	331	<300 = 18% >350 = 26% >400 = 2%	35	55	121
50% Black	Parochial N = 20	336.6	<300 = 20% >350 = 35% >400 = 10%	35	52	121
59% Black	Public N = 13	341	<300 = 15% >350 = 63% >400 = 0%	32	47	115
<10% Black	Parochial N = 34	330.6	<300 = 27% >350 = 39% >400 = 3%	36	52	113
<10% Black	Public N = 54	334	<300 = 20% >350 = 32% >400 = 8%	38	53	120
Totals	N = 193	335.3	<300 = 18% >350 = 40% >400 = 5%	36.5	53.5	121.1

330.6, with 27 percent scoring below 300, 39 percent scoring above 350, and three percent scoring above 400. The mean self-criticism score of 36 and the mean variability score of 52 were above the normative means. However, the mean distribution score of 113 was below the normative mean. The 20 girls in the 50 percent black desegregated school obtained a total positive mean score of 336.6, with 20 percent scoring below 300, 35 percent scoring 350 or above, and 10 percent scoring above 400. The mean self-criticism score of 35 was equal to the normative mean, but the mean variability score of 52 was above the normative mean for the scale. (See Table 12.) The mean distribution score of 121 was just barely above the normative mean for the scale.

WHITE GIRLS IN PUBLIC SCHOOLS

There were 139 white girls from four public schools who participated in the study. Eighty-five of the students were from three desegregated public schools: a 58 percent black, a 59 percent black, and an 18 percent black

TABLE 12

A Comparison of White Students in Parochial and
Public Schools in New Orleans

White Students in Parochial Schools in New Orleans

Sex	Racial Composition	No. of Students	TP (Mean)	SC Score (Mean)	V Score (Mean)	D Score (Mean)
Girls	50% Black	20	336.6	35	52	121
Boys	50% Black	14	333	40	60	134
Girls	<10% Black	34	330.6	36	52	113
Boys	<10% Black	25	326.1	33	53	131
	Totals/Means	93	331.5	36	54	125

White Students in Public Schools in New Orleans

White Girls

Racial Composition	No. of Students	TP (Mean)	SC Score (Mean)	V Score (Mean)	D Score (Mean)
58% Black	29	345	40	59	136
18% Black	43	331	35	55	121
59% Black	13	341	32	47	115
<10% Black	54	334	38	53	120
Totals/Means	139	338	36	54	123

White Boys

Racial Composition	No. of Students	TP (Mean)	SC Score (Mean)	V Score (Mean)	D Score (Mean)
<10% Black	24	297	36	49	105
18% Black	25	319	37	56	129
58% Black	19	349	35	57	138
59% Black	18	346	36	56	146
Totals/Means	86	327.7	36	55	130

Summary of Data on White Students
in Public and Parochial Schools in New Orleans

Type of School	No. of Students	TP (Mean)	SC Score (Mean)	V Score (Mean)	D Score (Mean)
Public	225	332.8	36	55	127
Parochial	93	331.5	36	54	125
Total/Mean	318	332.1	36	54	126

school. Fifty-four of the white girls were attending a segregated or predominantly white school (less than 10 percent black enrollment).

The 54 white girls at the public segregated school obtained a total positive mean score of 334, with 20 percent scoring below 300, 32 percent scoring 350 or above, and 8 percent scoring above 400. The mean self-criticism score of 38 and the mean variability score of 53 are above the normative means for the scale. The mean distribution score of 120 is equal to the normative mean for the scale.

The 29 white girls from the 58 percent black desegregated school obtained a total positive mean score of 345, with 9 percent scoring below 300, 48 percent scoring 350 or above, and 9 percent scoring above 400. The mean self-criticism score of 40 is especially high, the mean distribution score of 136 is very high, and the mean variability score of 59 is high, all considerably above the normative means for the scale.

The 13 white girls at the 59 percent black desegregated public school obtained a total positive mean score of 341, with 15 percent scoring below 300, 63 percent scoring 350 or above, and none scoring over 400. The mean self-criticism score of 32, the mean variability score of 47, and the mean distribution score of 115 are all well below the normative means for the scale.

The 43 white girls at the 18 percent black desegregated public school, obtained a total positive mean score of 331, with 18 percent scoring below 300, 26 percent scoring 350 or above, and 2 percent scoring above 400. The mean variability score of 55 and the mean distribution score of 121 fall above the normative means for the scale. However, the mean self-criticism score of 35 is equivalent to the normative mean. (See Table 12.)

WHITE GIRLS IN SEGREGATED SCHOOLS AND DESEGREGATED SCHOOLS

The 88 white girls in segregated or predominantly white schools in New Orleans achieved a total positive mean score of 334, with 23 percent scoring below 300, 35 percent scoring 350 or above, and 5 percent scoring above 400. Both the self-criticism mean score of 37.9 and the mean variability score of 52.5 are above the normative means for the scale, but the mean distribution score of 119.6 is below the normative mean for the scale. It would seem that segregated white girls have low self-concepts, are very open and honest in evaluating themselves, and vary greatly in what they think about different aspects of themselves. It would also seem that they are not certain how they think and feel about themselves.

The 105 white girls in desegregated schools achieved a total positive mean score of 335.8, with 16 percent scoring below 300, 43 percent scoring 350 or above, and 5 percent scoring above 400. The mean self-criticism score

of 35.9 and the mean distribution score of 121.7 are just above the normative means for the scale. The mean variability score of 53.9 is well above that
for the normative mean. The desegregated white girls as a group have a low
self-concept, average honesty and defensiveness, a great amount of variability
in the self-picture, and moderate certainty in how they feel about themselves. (See Tables 13 and 14.)

TABLE 13

**White Students in Segregated or Predominantly White Schools
in New Orleans**

Sex	TP (Mean)	Percentages TP Scores	SC Score (Mean)	V Score (Mean)	D Score (Mean)
Boys N = 49	311.6	<300 = 33% >350 = 26% >400 = 4%	34.5	51.5	118.5
Girls N = 88	334	<300 = 23% >350 = 35% >400 = 5%	37.9	52.4	119.6
Totals N = 137	322.8	<300 = 28% >350 = 31% >400 = 4%	36.7	51.4	119.05

TABLE 14

White Students in Desegregated Schools in New Orleans

Sex	TP (Mean)	Percentages TP Scores	SC Score (Mean)	V Score (Mean)	D Score (Mean)
Boys N = 76	336.9	<300 = 15% >350 = 37% >400 = 9%	35.7	56	135.1
Girls N = 105	335.8	<300 = 16% >350 = 43% >400 = 5%	36.9	53.9	121.7
Totals N = 187	336.3	<300 = 16% >350 = 40% >400 = 7%	35.8	54.8	127.4

WHITE BOYS IN NEW ORLEANS

Among the 125 white boys who participated in the study in New Orleans
49 attended segregated schools and 76 attended desegregated schools. There
were 49 boys tested from parochial schools and 86 boys tested from public
schools. (See Table 15.)

The 125 white boys obtained a mean total positive score of 329.3, below
the normative mean, with 21 percent scoring below 300, 33 percent scoring

TABLE 15
White Boys Grades 7-8-9 New Orleans

Racial Composition	Type of School	TP (Mean)	Percentages TP Scores	SC Score (Mean)	V Score (Mean)	D Score (Mean)
<10% Black	Public N = 24	297	<300 = 50% >350 = 12% >400 = 0%	36	49	105
18% Black	Public N = 25	319	<300 = 24% >350 = 24% >400 = 0%	37	56	129
58% Black	Public N = 19	349	<300 = 10% >350 = 45% >400 = 10%	35	57	138
50% Black	Parochial N = 14	333.7	<300 = 7% >350 = 28% >400 = 7%	40	60	134
59% Black	Public N = 18	346	<300 = 18% >350 = 48% >400 = 18%	36	56	146
<10% Black	Parochial N = 25	326.1	<300 = 16% >350 = 25% >400 = 8%	33	53	131
Totals	125	329.3	<300 = 21% >350 = 33% >400 = 7%	35.7	54.6	129.2

350 or above, and 7 percent scoring above 400. The mean self-criticism score of 35.7, the mean variability score of 54.6, and the mean distribution score of 129.2 are all above the normative means. (See Table 12). It would appear that the white boys have low self-concepts and experience only moderate certainty about themselves. They are open, but vary in how they feel about various aspects of themselves.

WHITE BOYS IN PAROCHIAL SCHOOLS

There were 39 white boys in parochial schools; 25 were in a segregated or predominantly white parochial school, and 14 were in a desegregated parochial school (50 percent black). The 25 white boys in the segregated white parochial school (less than 10 percent black) obtained a total positive mean score of 326.1, which is below the normative mean, with 16 percent scoring below 300, 25 percent scoring 350 or above, and 8 percent scoring above 400. The mean self-criticism score of 33 is below the normative mean, but the mean variability score of 53 and the mean distribution score of 131 are both above the normative means. It would seem that the white boys in the segregated parochial school have a low self-concept, little ability to criticize the self, great variability, and much certainty about the self-picture.

The 14 white boys attending the desegregated parochial school (50 percent black) obtained a total positive mean score of 333.7, which is below the normative mean, with 7 percent scoring below 300, 28 percent scoring 350 or above, and 7 percent scoring above 400. The mean self-criticism score of 40, the mean variability score of 60, and the mean distribution score of 134 are all well above the normative mean for the scale. The desegregated white boys in parochial schools have low self-concepts, are looking at the self in a very critical fashion, have great variability, and have much certainty about the self-picture (see Table 12).

The 39 boys in segregated and desegregated parochial schools together achieved a total positive mean score of 328.6, which is below the normative mean, and a mean self-criticism score of 36.5, a mean variability score of 56.5, and a mean distribution score of 132.5, all above the normative means for the scale. (See Table 12.)

WHITE BOYS IN PUBLIC SCHOOLS

There were 86 white boys from segregated and desegregated public schools. The 24 white boys attending the segregated or predominantly white public school (less than 10 percent black) obtained a total positive mean score of 297, with 50 percent scoring below 300, 12 percent scoring 350 or above, and none scoring above 400. The mean self-criticism score of 36 and the mean variability score of 49 are above the normative means for the scale, but the mean distribution score of 105 is below the normative mean for the scale. The white boys in the segregated public school have very, very low self-concepts and are very uncertain about how they perceive themselves.

The remaining 62 boys in public schools who participated in the study came from three desegregated schools, an 18 percent black school, a 58 percent black school, and a 59 percent black school. The 25 white boys attending the 18 percent black desegregated public school obtained a total positive mean score of 319, which is below the normative mean, with 24 percent scoring below 300, 24 percent scoring 350 or above, and none scoring above 400. The mean self-criticism score of 37, the mean variability score of 56, and the mean distribution score of 129 are above the normative means for the scale.

The 19 white boys in the 58 percent black desegregated public school, obtained a total positive mean score of 349, with 10 percent scoring below 300, 45 percent scoring 350 or above, and 10 percent scoring above 400. The total positive mean score as well as the mean self-criticism score of 35, the mean variability score of 57, and the mean distribution score of 138 are above the normative means for the scale.

The 18 white boys attending the 59 percent black desegregated public school obtained a total positive mean score of 346, slightly below the normative mean for the scale, with 18 percent scoring below 300, 48 percent scoring 350 or above, and 18 percent scoring above 400. The mean self-criticism score of 36, the mean variability score of 56, and the mean distribution score of 146, are above the normative means for the scale (see Table 12).

WHITE BOYS IN SEGREGATED SCHOOLS AND DESEGREGATED SCHOOLS

(See Tables 13 and 14.) The 49 white boys in segregated schools in New Orleans obtained a total positive mean score of 311.6, below the normative mean, with 43 percent scoring below 300, 26 percent scoring 350 or above, and 4 percent scoring above 400. Although the mean variability score of 51 is above the normative mean for the scale, the mean self-criticism score of 34.5, and the mean distribution score of 118.5 fall below the normative means for the scale.

The TSCS scores for the 25 white boys attending segregated parochial schools and the 24 white boys attending segregated public school has been discussed in the section above on public and parochial schools for white boys. In general, the white boys in segregated schools have very low self-concepts, and feel uncertain about how they perceive themselves.

The 76 white boys in desegregated school in New Orleans obtained a total positive mean score of 336.9, which is below the normative mean, with 15 percent scoring below 300, 87 percent scoring 350 or above, and 9 percent scoring above 400. The mean variability score of 56, and the mean distribution score of 135.1, are above the normative means for the scale.

The TSCS scores for the 62 white boys in desegregated public schools and the 14 white boys in the desegregated parochial schools have been discussed in the section on white boys in parochial schools and public schools. The desegregated white boys have a low self-concept as a group with much inconsistency, but much certainty about their self-perception.

A COMPARISON OF WHITE STUDENTS IN PAROCHIAL AND PUBLIC SCHOOLS

The scores of the white girls and boys in segregated and desegregated public and parochial schools have been discussed in previous paragraphs in this chapter. Table 12 gives a summary of that comparison.

The TSCS mean scores of the 54 white girls in parochial schools (TP mean = 333.6, SC mean = 35.5, V mean = 52, D mean = 117) do not differ significantly from those of the public school girls. Nor do the TSCS mean scores of the 39 white boys in parochial school (TP mean = 329.5, SC mean = 36.5, V mean = 56.5, D mean = 132.5) differ significantly from those of the public school white boys.

In general, parochial school girls and public school girls score higher on the TP mean score than the boys. However, the parochial school boys tend to score higher on the other three scores than the parochial school girls; the differences are not significant. The public school girls and boys score about the same on the mean SC and mean V scores, but the boys score higher than the girls on the mean D scores.

12
Comparison of New Orleans Students in Segregated and Desegregated Schools

The total number of students from seventh, eight, and ninth grades who participated in the study in New Orleans was 634—316 black students and 318 white students. The female sampling numbered 375, with 193 white girls and 182 black girls. Among the 259 males tested, 125 were white and 134 were black. The total number of white students in segregated or predominantly white schools was 137 and the total number of black students in segregated or predominantly black schools was 155. A total of 342 white and black students were tested from four desegregated schools, 181 white students and 161 black students. (See Table 1.)

COMPARISON BY RACIAL COMPOSITION OF
SCHOOL FOR BLACK STUDENTS

The 155 black students in segregated schools obtained a total positive mean score of 353.7, which is above the normative mean. The 161 black students in desegregated schools obtained a total positive mean score of 344.0, which is below the normative mean. Thus, black students in segregated schools have a higher self-concept than those in desegregated schools, a difference that is statistically significant ($p < 0.02$). The mean self-criticism score for the black students in segregated schools is 35.9, compared with one of 36.3 for black students in desegregated schools. Thus, there is a tendency for the black students in desegregated schools to be more critical of themselves and less defensive. However, the difference between the two groups is not statistically significant. The mean variability score for the segregated

TABLE 1

Population Sample According to Sex, Race, and Type of School in New Orleans

Males 259				Females 375			
White 125		Black 134		White 193		Black 182	
Segregated (Predominantly White)	Desegregated	Segregated	Desegregated	Segregated (Predominantly White)	Desegregated	Segregated	Desegregated
49	76	63	71	88	105	92	90

Number of Schools = 8
Parochial Schools = 3
Public Schools = 5

Segregated or Predominantly White Schools = 2
Desegregated Schools = 4
Segregated Black Schools = 2

black students and the desegregated black students is about the same, 58.2 and 58.4 respectively. There is little difference between the mean distribution scores of the segregated group (139.9) and the desegregated group (140.4).

It is interesting to note that the segregated and desegregated students both score below the normative mean on identity, 118.3 and 116.7 respectively. The difference is not statistically significant. On self-satisfaction the black segregated group obtained a higher mean score (115.0) than the desegregated group (112.8), but the difference is not statistically significant. However, on behavior the segregated group obtained a mean score of 119.4 compared with a mean score for the desegregated group of 115.6; the difference is statistically significant (p < 0.03).

On the sub-profile scores, the segregated black students achieved a physical-self mean score of 75.3 compared with the mean score of 74.1 for the desegregated black students; the difference is not statistically significant. However, on moral-ethical self, the segregated black students achieved a mean of 71.0 compared with a mean for the desegregated black group of 67.8, which is below the normative mean for the scale. The difference is statistically significant (p < 0.005). The mean scores on the personal-self items for the two groups are not statistically significant, although the segregated black students obtained a mean of 64.2 which is equal to the normative mean for the scale, while the desegregated black students obtained a mean of 63.3, which is below the normative mean for the scale. On family self, both groups obtained mean scores above the normative mean for the test, with the black segregated students scoring higher (75.7) than the black desegregated group (73.9). However, the difference is not statistically significant. On the social-self items, the segregated black students and the desegregated black students scored below the normative mean, 66.7 and 65.8 respectively. The difference is not statistically significant. (See Table 2.)

COMPARISON OF BLACK GIRLS IN SEGREGATED AND DESEGREGATED SCHOOLS

In comparing the TSCS scores of the 92 black girls in segregated schools with the 90 black girls in desegregated schools, the total positive mean score for the segregated black girls was 358.1 compared to 347.3 for the desegregated black girls. The difference is statistically significant (p < 0.05). The mean self-criticism scores for the segregated black girls and the desegregated black girls are very similar, 36.4 and 36.6 respectively; there is not a statistical significance. Likewise, the mean variability scores and the mean distribution scores for the segregated black girls and the desegregated black girls are quite similar, 57.7 and 138.8 compared with 58.9 and 139.4 respectively. The differences are not statistically significant.

On the profile scores it is interesting to note that on the identity scores both groups scored below the normative mean for the scale, 118.8 for segre-

TABLE 2

Comparison of Black Students in Segregated and Desegregated Schools in New Orleans

TSCS Scores		Segregated $n = 137$	Desegregated $n = 155$	Significance
TP	Mean	353.74[b]	344.08[c]	$p < 0.02$
	SD*	36.59	39.47	
SC	Mean	35.94	36.31	N.S.
	SD	6.72	6.46	
V	Mean	58.20[b]	58.46[c]	N.S.
	SD	13.73	14.39	
D	Mean	139.96[b]	140.43[d]	N.S.
	SD	26.49	27.20	
Identity	Mean	118.36[a]	116.70[c]	N.S.
	SD	14.02	14.71	
Self-Satisfaction	Mean	115.07[a]	112.88[c]	N.S.
	SD	16.58	17.67	
Behavior	Mean	119.48[b]	115.62	$p < 0.03$
	SD	16.35	15.26	
Physical Self	Mean	75.33[b]	74.14[c]	N.S.
	SD	8.75	9.04	
Moral-Ethical Self	Mean	71.03[b]	67.80	$p < 0.005$
	SD	9.70	10.44	
Personal Self	Mean	64.25[b]	63.33	N.S.
	SD	10.34	12.53	
Family Self	Mean	75.74[b]	73.99	N.S.
	SD	11.19	12.29	
Social Self	Mean	66.77	65.84	N.S.
	SD	11.03	10.07	

*SD means standard deviation.
[a]Significance at the 5 percent level between same scores of the segregated white and black students. See Table 5.
[b]Significance at the 1 percent level between same scores of the segregated white and black students. See Table 5.
[c]Significance at the 5 percent level between same scores of the desegregated white and black students. See Table 5.
[d]Significance at the 1 percent level between same scores of the desegregated white and black students. See Table 5.

gated black girls and 117 for the desegregated black girls. The difference is not statistically significant. On the self-satisfaction items, the black segregated girls obtained a higher mean score (117.8) than the desegregated black girls (114.2); the difference is not statistically significant. Likewise, on the behavior items, the segregated black girls scored higher, obtaining a mean of 120 compared with a mean of 116.3 for the black desegregated girls; the difference is not statistically significant. Again, on the physical-self items, the black segregated girls obtained a higher mean score (75.3) than the desegregated black girls (74.4). However, the difference is not statistically significant. The segregated black girls achieved a mean score on the moral-ethical self items of 72.6 which is above the normative mean. The desegregated black girls, however, obtained a mean score of 69.6 on the moral-ethical-self items, which falls below the normative mean for the scale. The difference between the two groups is statistically significant ($p < 0.03$). On the personal-self items, the black segregated girls have a mean score of 65.8, which is above the normative mean for the scale, while the black desegregated girls have a mean score of 63, which is below the normative mean for the scale. The difference, however, is not significant. On the family-self items, both the black segregated and desegregated girls scored above the normative mean, 76.5 and 74.5 respectively, but the difference is not significant. Both the black segregated girls and black desegregated girls scored below the normative mean on the social self items, the segregated group having a mean of 66.7 and the desegregated group having a mean of 65.7. The difference is not significant. (See Table 3.)

COMPARISON OF BLACK BOYS IN SEGREGATED AND DESEGREGATED SCHOOLS

A comparison of the 63 black boys in segregated schools with the 71 black boys in desegregated schools shows the segregated black boys achieving a total positive mean score of 347.1, which is above the normative mean, compared with a mean score of 340 for the desegregated black boys. The difference is not statistically significant. On the mean self-criticism score, the segregated and desegregated black boys score similarly, 35.2 and 35.8 respectively, both above the normative mean. Likewise, on the mean variability score the segregated black boys (58.9) scored about the same as the desegregated black boys (57.8), and the difference is not statistically significant. The segregated black boys score the same as the desegregated black boys on the mean distribution score, both achieving a mean score of 141.6.

In comparing the mean profile scores of the segregated black boys with those of the desegregated black boys, it should be noted that both groups score below the normative mean on identity, and above the normative mean on self-satisfaction and behavior. There is no statistical significance between the two groups on the mean profile scores (see Table 4).

On the sub-profile mean scores, the segregated black boys and the desegregated black boys score above the normative means on physical self and family self. The segregated black boys obtained a mean score of 75.3 on physical self compared with a mean score of 73.1 for the desegregated black group. On the family-self items, segregated black boys obtained a mean score of 74.6 compared with a mean score of 73.3 for the desegregated black group. However, there is no statistical significance between the two groups on either the physical-self mean score or the family-self mean score. It is

TABLE 3

**Comparison of Black Girls in Segregated and Desegregated
Schools in New Orleans**

TSCS Scores		Segregated $n = 92$	Desegregated $n = 90$	Significance
TP	Mean	358.11[f]	347.38[g]	$p < 0.05$
	SD*	37.41	38.97	
SC	Mean	36.43	36.67	N.S.
	SD	6.98	6.31	
V	Mean	57.71[e]	58.96[g]	N.S.
	SD	13.53	14.14	
D	Mean	138.87[f]	139.46[h]	N.S.
	SD	26.67	26.94	
Identity	Mean	118.87	117.04	N.S.
	SD	13.75	14.85	
Self-Satisfaction	Mean	117.85[f,1]	114.24[h]	N.S.
	SD	15.75	17.78	
Behavior	Mean	120.08[e]	116.31	N.S.
	SD	18.75	13.93	
Physical Self	Mean	75.33[f]	74.48[h]	N.S.
	SD	8.65	8.82	
Moral-Ethical Self	Mean	72.69[e]	69.61	$p < 0.03$
	SD	9.01	10.51	
Personal Self	Mean	65.88[f]	63.09	N.S.
	SD	10.12	12.04	
Family Self	Mean	76.50[f]	74.52	N.S.
	SD	11.39	13.04	
Social Self	Mean	66.78	65.72	N.S.
	SD	12.47	9.97	

*SD means standard deviation.
[1]Significance at the 5 percent level between same scores of the segregated black
girls and boys. See Table 4.
[e]Significance at the 5 percent level between same scores of the segregated white
and black girls. See Table 6.
[f]Significance at the 1 percent level between same scores of the segregated white
and black girls. See Table 6.
[g]Significance at the 5 percent level between same scores of the desegregated white
and black girls. See Table 6.
[h]Significance at the 1 percent level between same scores of the desegregated white
and black girls. See Table 6.

interesting to note that both the segregated black boys and the desegregated
black boys scored below the normative mean on sub-profile items such as
moral-ethical self, personal self, and social self. The segregated black boys
obtained a mean score of 68.5 on the moral-ethical self compared with a
mean of 65.5 for the desegregated black group. There is no statistical signif-

TABLE 4

Comparison of Black Boys in Segregated and Desegregated Schools in New Orleans

TSCS Scores		Segregated n = 63	Desegregated n = 71	Significance
TP	Mean	347.17q	340.06	N.S.
	SD*	34.46	39.91	
SC	Mean	35.20	35.87	N.S.
	SD	6.27	6.65	
V	Mean	58.93q	57.84	N.S.
	SD	14.11	14.78	
D	Mean	141.60q	141.62	N.S.
	SD	26.34	27.64	
Identity	Mean	117.58q	116.29	N.S.
	SD	14.48	14.63	
Self-Satisfaction	Mean	110.88q,1	111.22	N.S.
	SD	17.04	17.51	
Behavior	Mean	118.57q	114.77	N.S.
	SD	11.94	16.80	
Physical Self	Mean	75.33q	73.72p	N.S.
	SD	8.97	9.36	
Moral-Ethical Self	Mean	68.53q	65.59	N.S.
	SD	10.24	10.00	
Personal Self	Mean	61.80q	63.62	N.S.
	SD	10.28	13.17	
Family Self	Mean	74.60q	73.36	N.S.
	SD	10.87	11.36	
Social Self	Mean	66.76	66.00	N.S.
	SD	8.50	1.02	

*SD means standard deviation.
[1]Significance at the 5 percent level between same scores of the segregated black girls and boys. See Table 3.
pSignificance at the 5 percent level between same scores of the desegregated white and black boys. See Table 7.
qSignificance at the 1 percent level between same scores of the segregated white and black boys. See Table 7.

icance between the means. On the personal-self items, the segregated black boys obtained a mean of 61.8 compared with a mean of 63.6 for the desegregated black boys. The difference is not significant. On the social-self items, both the segregated black boys and the desegregated black boys obtained a mean score of 66. (See Table 4.)

COMPARISON OF BLACK GIRLS AND BLACK BOYS IN SEGREGATED SCHOOLS

(See Tables 3 and 4.) When the 63 black boys in segregated schools are compared with the 92 black girls in segregated schools, the black girls score higher on the total positive mean score (358.1) than the black boys (347.1). Likewise, on the mean self-criticism score the black girls score higher (36.4) than the black boys (35.2). However, there is no significant difference between the black girls and the black boys on either mean scores. On the mean variability score and mean distribution score, the black boys score slightly higher than the black girls, with a variability mean score of 58.9 and a distribution mean score of 141.6 for the black boys, compared with a variability mean score of 57.7 and a distribution mean score of 138.8 for the black girls. There is no significant difference between the black girls and the black boys on these two scores. It is interesting to note, however, that both the black girls in segregated schools and the black boys in segregated schools score below the normative mean on identity and social self. The difference between the segregated black boys and girls on these two scores is not statistically significant. The mean score on the self-satisfaction items for the black segregated girls is 117.8, compared with the mean score of 110.8 for the black boys. The difference is significant at the 5 percent level. Both the segregated black girls and boys score about the same and above the normative means on behavior, physical self, and family self, with no significant differences between the two groups on the mean scores. The mean scores for the social-self items are the same for both the segregated black boys and girls, both scoring below the normative means for the scale. The black girls in segregated schools score higher on the moral-ethical self (72.6) and the personal self (65.8) than do the black boys in segregated schools with a mean score of 68.5 on the moral-ethical self items and a mean score of 61.8 on the personal self items, both of which are below the normative means for the scale. The difference between the two groups on these two items, however, is not statistically significant (see Tables 3 and 4).

COMPARISON OF BLACK BOYS AND BLACK GIRLS IN DESEGREGATED SCHOOLS

(See Tables 3 and 4.) When the 90 black girls in desegregated schools are compared with the 71 black boys in desegregated schools, the black girls have higher means for total positive, self-criticism, and variability scores (347.3, 36.6, 59.9 respectively) than the black boys (340, 35.8, 57.8). The difference between the two groups for each of the mean scores is not significant. The mean distribution score (141.6) for the black boys in desegregated schools is higher than that for the black girls in desegregated schools (139.4); the difference is not significant. The mean profile scores and the mean sub-profile scores are higher for the desegregated black girls than the desegregated black boys on the following items: identity, self-satisfaction, behavior, physical self, moral-ethical self, and family self. The difference between the two groups on these mean scores is not significant. The mean score for the personal-self items for the desegregated black boys and girls is about the same, 63.6 and 63.0 respectively. However, the mean score for the social-self items is higher for the black desegregated boys than for the black desegregated girls, 66 and 65.7 respectively. The differences in the personal-self mean scores and the social-self mean scores between the two groups are not significant.

COMPARISON BY RACIAL COMPOSITION OF SCHOOL FOR WHITE STUDENTS

Of the 318 white students who participated in the study, 137 were in segregated schools, and 181 were in desegregated schools. The white desegregated group obtained a total positive mean score of 336.3 compared with a mean score of 322.8 for the segregated white. The difference is statistically significant ($p < 0.01$). The difference in the mean self-criticism scores between the white desegregated and white segregated group is not significant, 35.8 and 36.7 respectively. However, when the mean variability score of the white desegregated group (54.8) is compared with that of the white segregated group (51.3), the difference is statistically significant ($p < 0.04$). Likewise, on the mean distribution scores, the white desegregated group scores higher (127.4) than the white segregated group (119.0). The difference is statistically significant ($p < 0.001$) (see Table 5).

On the mean profile scores and the mean sub-profile scores, the white desegregated group is higher than the white segregated group on every item. The difference between the mean scores for the white desegregated group compared with the white segregated group is statistically significant, for the mean self-satisfaction score ($p < 0.002$), for the mean behavior score ($p < 0.02$), for the mean personal-self score ($p < 0.003$), for the mean family-self score ($p < 0.01$). There is no significant difference between the desegregated white and segregated white students on the mean identity scores (113.1 and 111.0), the mean moral-ethical self scores (66.7 and 65.3), or the mean social self scores (66.1 and 64.8).

COMPARISON OF WHITE GIRLS IN SEGREGATED AND DESEGREGATED SCHOOLS

(See Table 6.) When the 88 white girls in segregated schools are compared with the 105 white girls in desegregated schools, there is no significant difference between the two groups on the TSCS scores. Both are below the normative mean on the total positive mean scores with the segregated group obtaining a total positive mean score of 334 and the desegregated group obtaining a total positive mean score of 335.8. These scores fall into the 35th percentile for the self-concept scale. The segregated whites and the

TABLE 5

Comparison of White Students in Segregated and Desegregated Schools in New Orleans

TSCS Scores		Segregated n = 137	Desegregated n = 181	Significance
TP	Mean	322.82[b]	336.31[c]	p < 0.01
	SD*	42.57	40.05	
SC	Mean	36.70	35.88	N.S.
	SD	6.45	7.01	
V	Mean	51.32[b]	54.82[c]	p < 0.04
	SD	13.46	12.98	
D	Mean	115.08[b]	127.40[d]	p < 0.001
	SD	24.49	27.55	
Identity	Mean	111.06[a]	113.11[c]	N.S.
	SD	15.48	14.25	
Self-Satisfaction	Mean	101.40[a]	108.64[c]	p < 0.002
	SD	18.66	17.56	
Behavior	Mean	110.40[b]	114.58	p < 0.02
	SD	15.07	14.31	
Physical Self	Mean	67.70[b]	70.10[c]	N.S.
	SD	10.24	9.81	
Moral-Ethical Self	Mean	65.31[b]	66.79	N.S.
	SD	11.16	10.88	
Personal Self	Mean	57.24[b]	61.63	p < 0.003
	SD	11.63	11.20	
Family Self	Mean	67.56[b]	71.26	p < 0.01
	SD	11.50	12.88	
Social Self	Mean	64.83	66.13	N.S.
	SD	8.74	9.62	

*SD means standard deviation.
[a]Significance at the 5 percent level between same scores of the segregated white and black students. See Table 2.
[b]Significance at the 1 percent level between same scores of the segregated white and black students. See Table 2.
[c]Significance at the 5 percent level between same scores of the desegregated white and black students. See Table 2.
[d]Significance at the 1 percent level between same scores of the desegregated white and black students. See Table 2.

desegregated white girls score above the normative mean on the self-criticism mean scores, 37.9 and 35.9 respectively, and above the normative mean on the variability score, 52.5 and 53.9 respectively. On the mean distribution scores the white segregated girls score below the normative mean, with a distribution mean of 119.67, and the white desegregated girls score just above the normative mean, with a distribution mean of 121.7. There is no significant difference on any of the mean scores between the two groups.

TABLE 6

Comparison of White Girls in Segregated and Desegregated Schools in New Orleans

TSCS Scores		Segregated n = 88	Desegregated n = 105	Significance
TP	Mean	334.01[f,2]	335.87[g]	N.S.
	SD*	37.62	38.22	
SC	Mean	37.90	35.97	N.S.
	SD	6.46	6.64	
V	Mean	52.54[e]	53.91[g]	N.S.
	SD	13.22	11.67	
D	Mean	119.67[f]	121.73[h,3]	N.S.
	SD	23.01	25.04	
Identity	Mean	115.59[2]	113.45	N.S.
	SD	13.04	12.90	
Self-Satisfaction	Mean	103.94[f,2]	107.55[h]	N.S.
	SD	18.63	17.21	
Behavior	Mean	114.47[e,1]	114.89	N.S.
	SD	12.20	14.19	
Physical Self	Mean	69.54[f]	69.81[h]	N.S.
	SD	9.19	9.16	
Moral-Ethical Self	Mean	68.65[e,2]	67.82	N.S.
	SD	8.54	10.01	
Personal Self	Mean	59.27[f]	60.31	N.S.
	SD	11.56	10.73	
Family Self	Mean	69.30[f]	72.55	N.S.
	SD	11.14	11.70	
Social Self	Mean	67.23[1]	65.42	N.S.
	SD	8.48	9.69	

*SD means standard deviation.
[1]Significance at the 5 percent level between same scores of the segregated white girls and boys. See Table 7.
[2]Significance at the 1 percent level between same scores of the segregated white girls and boys. See Table 7.
[3]Significance at the 1 percent level between same scores of the desegregated white girls and boys. See Table 7.
[e]Significance at the 5 percent level between same scores of the segregated white and black girls. See Table 3.
[f]Significance at the 1 percent level between same scores of the segregated white and black girls. See Table 3.
[g]Significance at the 5 percent level between same scores of the desegregated white and black girls. See Table 3.
[h]Significance at the 1 percent level between same scores of the desegregated white and black girls. See Table 3.

Both groups score very similarly on the profile and sub-profile items. However, it is interesting to note that both groups also score below the normative means on such items as identity, behavior, physical self, moral-ethical self, personal self, and social self. The desegregated white girls score above the normative mean on the self-satisfaction items, obtaining a mean of 107.5, compared with the segregated white girls who obtained a mean of 103.9, equal to the normative mean for the scale. On the family-self mean score, the desegregated white girls score above the normative mean achieving a mean of 72.5 compared with the segregated white girls who scored below the normative mean with a mean of 69.3.

COMPARISON OF WHITE BOYS IN SEGREGATED AND DESEGREGATED SCHOOLS

(See Table 7.) A comparison of TSCS scores of white boys in segregated and desegregated schools in New Orleans, reveals some significant differences. The 76 white boys in desegregated schools obtained a total positive mean score of 336.9, compared with the mean score of 311.6 for the segregated white boys. The difference is statistically significant ($p < 0.001$). There is no significant difference between the two groups on the self-criticism mean score, both achieving the normative mean for the scale (segregated white boys, 35.5 and desegregated white boys, 35.7). However, on all the other TSCS scores, the desegregated white boys scored statistically significantly higher than the segregated white boys. The desegregated white boys obtained a mean variability score of 56, compared with a mean of 51.5 for the segregated white boys. The difference is significant ($p < 0.03$). On the mean distribution score, the desegregated white boys had a mean score of 135.1 compared with a mean score of 118.5 for the segregated white boys; the difference is statistically significant ($p < 0.008$). The 49 white boys in segregated schools scored below the normative means on identity (105.3), self-satisfaction (100.3), behavior (105.8), physical self (66.3), moral-ethical self (60.5), personal self (55.4), family self (66.4), and social self (62.1). The 76 white boys in desegregated schools scored below the normative mean on identity (112.6), behavior (114.1), physical self (70.4), moral-ethical self (65.3), personal self (63.4), family self (69.5), social self (67.1); they scored above the normative mean on self-satisfaction (110.1). When the 76 white boys in desegregated schools are compared with the 49 white boys in segregated schools, the differences between the two groups on the mean profile and sub-profile scores are all statistically significant, with the exception of the family-self mean scores.

COMPARISON OF WHITE BOYS AND WHITE GIRLS IN SEGREGATED SCHOOLS

When the 49 white boys in segregated schools are compared with the 88 white girls in segregated schools, some significant differences in TSCS scores are noted (see Tables 6 and 7). The segregated white girls obtained a total positive mean score of 334, compared with a total positive mean score of 311.6 for the segregated white boys; the difference is significant at the 1 percent level. Although the white segregated girls score higher on the mean self-criticism score than the white segregated boys, the difference is not

TABLE 7

Comparison of White Boys in Segregated and Desegregated Schools in New Orleans

TSCS Scores		Segregated n = 49	Desegregated n = 76	Significance
TP	Mean	311.16[q,2]	336.94	p < 0.004
	SD*	42.85	42.50	
SC	Mean	35.58	35.77	N.S.
	SD	6.27	7.52	
V	Mean	51.54[q]	56.06	p < 0.04
	SD	13.87	14.56	
D	Mean	118.58[q]	135.14[3]	p < 0.008
	SD	25.02	29.0	
Identity	Mean	105.39[q,2]	112.64	p < 0.007
	SD	15.87	15.97	
Self-Satisfaction	Mean	100.31[q]	110.13	p < 0.008
	SD	17.76	18.01	
Behavior	Mean	105.81[q,1]	114.15	p < 0.009
	SD	17.05	14.53	
Physical Self	Mean	66.36[q,2]	70.49[p]	p < 0.002
	SD	11.42	10.66	
Moral-Ethical Self	Mean	60.52[q,2]	65.39	p < 0.02
	SD	12.78	11.88	
Personal Self	Mean	55.44[q]	63.43	p < 0.006
	SD	10.57	11.63	
Family Self	Mean	66.44[q]	69.50	N.S.
	SD	11.54	14.21	
Social Self	Mean	62.19[1]	67.10	p < 0.04
	SD	6.69	9.49	

*SD means standard deviation.
[1]Significance at the 5 percent level between same scores of the segregated white girls and boys. See Table 6.
[2]Significance at the 1 percent level between same scores of the segregated white boys and girls. See Table 6.
[3]Significance at the 1 percent level between same scores of the desegregated white girls and boys. See Table 6.
[p]Significance at the 5 percent level between same scores of the desegregated white and black boys. See Table 4.
[q]Significance at the 1 percent level between same scores of the segregated white and black boys. See Table 4.

statistically significant. Nor is there any significant difference between the two groups on the mean variability scores or the mean distribution scores, both scoring about the same (see Tables 6 and 7). On the mean score for the identity items, the segregated white girls score higher (115.5) than the segregated white boys (105.3), and the difference is significant at the 1 percent level. Although the segregated white girls score higher (103.9) on the mean self-satisfaction score, than do the segregated white boys (100.3), the difference is not significant. The difference is significant, however, between the mean behavior score of the segregated white girls (114.4) and the white segregated boys (105.8); the significance is at the 5 percent level.

On the mean sub-profile scores, there is no significant difference between the segregated white girls and the white boys, although the segregated white girls score higher. Especially on the personal-self and family-self mean scores, the segregated white girls score higher (59.2 and 69.3 respectively) than the segregated white boys (55.4 and 66.4 respectively), but the difference is not significant. The mean score for the social-self items for the segregated white girls is 67.2 compared with the mean score of 62.1 for the segregated white boys; the difference is significant at the 5 percent level (see Tables 6 and 7).

COMPARISON OF WHITE BOYS AND GIRLS IN DESEGREGATED SCHOOLS

When the 105 white girls in desegregated schools are compared with the 76 white boys in desegregated schools, the total positive mean scores are quite similar, 335.8 and 336.9 respectively. There is no significant difference between the desegregated white boys and girls on the mean self-criticism scores, 35.7 and 35.9 respectively, or on the mean variability scores, 56.0 and 53.9 respectively, although the desegregated white boys tend to score higher. However, there is a significant difference between the mean distribution score of the desegregated white girls (121.7), and the desegregated white boys (135.1), and the difference is significant at the 1 percent level.

There is no significant difference between the desegregated white girls and boys on the mean profile scores or the mean sub-profile scores. It should be noted that both groups scored below the normative mean on identity, behavior, physical self, moral-ethical self, personal self, and social self. Both groups scored above the normative mean on self-satisfaction and the desegregated white girls scored above the normative mean on family self (see Tables 6 and 7).

COMPARISON OF NEW ORLEANS STUDENTS BY RACE AND SEX

When the 316 black students who participated in the study in New Orleans are compared on the TSCS scores with the 318 white students, the black students are above the normative mean on the total positive score, the self-criticism score, the variability score, the distribution score, the self-satisfaction score, the behavior score, the physical-self score, and the family-self score. The white students are above the normative mean on the self-criticism score, the variability score, the distribution score, and the self-satisfaction score. The black students are below the normative mean on the identity score, the moral-ethical self-score, the personal-self score, and the social-self score. The white students are below the normative means on the total positive score, the identity score, the behavior score, the physical-self score, the moral-ethical-self score, the personal-self score, and the social-self score; the family-self score is equal to the normative mean. The black students have a higher total positive mean score (348.8) than the white students (332.9), and the difference is statistically significant (p < 0.001). The black and white students have similar self-criticism mean scores, 36.1 and 36.2 respectively. However, there is significant difference between the two groups on the mean variability scores and the mean distribution scores. The black students have a mean variability score of 58.3 compared with a mean variability score of 53.9 for the white students; the difference is statistically significant (p < 0.001). On the mean distribution scores, the black students score 140.0 compared with the white students' 124.3; the difference is statistically significant (p < 0.001).

The black students score higher on all of the profile and sub-profile scores than the white students, with some significant differences noted. The difference between the black students' mean identity score of 117.5 and the white students' mean identity score of 112.6 is statistically significant (p < 0.001). Likewise, on the mean scores for self-satisfaction, behavior, physical self, moral-ethical self, personal self, and family self, the black students score significantly higher than the white students (p < 0.001 for each score). Although the black students score higher on the mean score for the social-self items (66.3) than the white students (65.8), the difference is not statistically significant (see Table 8).

COMPARISON OF WHITE AND BLACK GIRLS

(See Table 9.) When the 182 black girls in New Orleans who participated in the study are compared with the 193 white girls who participated, some significant differences in the TSCS scores of the two groups can be seen. The black girls score above the normative mean on the total positive score (352.9), the self-criticism score (36.5), the variability score (58.3), and the distribution score (139.9). Likewise, on the profile and sub-profile scores, the black girls score above the normative means on self-satisfaction, behavior, physical self, moral-ethical self, and family self. On the personal-self score of 64.5 the black girls are at the normative mean for the scale, but on the social-self score of 66.2 and on the identity score of 117.9 they are below the normative mean.

The white girls are above the normative means for the scale on the self-criticism score (36.5), the variability score (53.5), and slightly above the normative mean on the distribution score (121.14). On the profile and sub-profile scores the white girls are above the normative mean on self-satisfaction (106.5) and family self (71.6). All other scores, such as the total

TABLE 8

Comparison of Black and White Students in New Orleans

TSCS Scores		Black Students n = 316	White Students n = 318	Significance
TP	Mean	348.88	332.96	p < 0.001
	SD*	38.36	41.06	
SC	Mean	36.12	36.21	N.S.
	SD	6.58	6.89	
V	Mean	58.33	53.95	p < 0.001
	SD	14.05	13.17	
D	Mean	140.19	124.34	p < 0.001
	SD	26.81	27.31	
Identity	Mean	117.52	112.60	p < 0.001
	SD	14.37	14.57	
Self-Satisfaction	Mean	113.97	106.84	p < 0.001
	SD	17.14	18.09	
Behavior	Mean	117.54	113.54	p < 0.001
	SD	15.91	14.59	
Physical Self	Mean	74.73	69.50	p < 0.001
	SD	8.90	9.95	
Moral-Ethical Self	Mean	69.41	66.43	p < 0.001
	SD	10.19	10.95	
Personal Self	Mean	63.79	60.54	p < 0.001
	SD	11.48	11.45	
Family Self	Mean	74.86	70.34	p < 0.001
	SD	11.77	12.63	
Social Self	Mean	66.31	65.81	N.S.
	SD	10.55	9.42	

*SD means standard deviation.

positive score of 335.3, the identity score of 114.4, the behavior score of 114.7, the physical-self score of 69.7, the moral-ethical-self score of 68.0, the personal-self score of 60.0, and the social-self scores of 65.9, are below the normative mean for the scale.

When the black and white girls are compared on the total positive mean score the black girls score higher and the difference is statistically significant (p < 0.001). Likewise, when the black girls are compared with the white girls on the mean variability scores and the mean distribution scores, the black girls score higher than the white girls and the difference for each mean score is statistically significant (p < 0.001 for variability and distribution). Black girls score significantly higher on the identity score than the white girls (p < 0.05), on the self-satisfaction score (p < 0.001), and on the behavior score (p < 0.03). Likewise, the black girls score significantly higher than the

TABLE 9
Comparison of Black and White Girls in New Orleans

TSCS Scores		Black Girls n = 182	White Girls n = 193	Significance
TP	Mean	352.94[5]	335.34	p < 0.001
	SD*	38.49	38.00	
SC	Mean	36.54	36.52	N.S.
	SD	6.65	6.63	
V	Mean	58.31	53.52	p < 0.001
	SD	13.80	12.11	
D	Mean	139.91	121.14[8]	p < 0.001
	SD	26.73	24.44	
Identity	Mean	117.99	114.40[7]	p < 0.005
	SD	14.20	12.93	
Self-Satisfaction	Mean	116.11[6]	106.52	p < 0.001
	SD	16.81	17.65	
Behavior	Mean	118.27	114.71	p < 0.03
	SD	16.67	13.62	
Physical Self	Mean	74.92	69.74	p < 0.001
	SD	8.71	9.15	
Moral-Ethical Self	Mean	71.21[6]	68.06[8]	p < 0.002
	SD	9.85	9.60	
Personal Self	Mean	64.54	60.02	p < 0.002
	SD	11.14	10.95	
Family Self	Mean	75.55	71.62[7]	p < 0.002
	SD	12.22	11.61	
Social Self	Mean	66.27	65.94	N.S.
	SD	11.32	9.38	

*SD means standard deviation.
[5] Significance at the 5 percent level between same scores of the black boys and girls. See Table 10.
[6] Significance at the 1 percent level between same scores of the black boys and girls. See Table 10.
[7] Significance at the 5 percent level between same scores of the white boys and girls. See Table 10.
[8] Significance at the 1 percent level between same scores of the white boys and girls. See Table 10.

white girls on identity (p < 0.001), moral-ethical self (p < 0.002), personal self (p < 0.002), family self (p < 0.002). Although the black girls score higher (66.2) than the white girls (65.9), on the social-self scale, the difference is not statistically significant.

COMPARISON OF WHITE AND BLACK BOYS

(See Table 10.) A comparison of the 134 black boys in New Orleans with the 125 white boys who participated in the study, shows that the black boys

TABLE 10

Comparison of Black and White Boys in New Orleans

TSCS Scores		Black Boys n = 134	White Boys n = 125	Significance
TP	Mean	343.38[5]	329.30	p < 0.007
	SD*	37.50	45.21	
SC	Mean	35.56	35.73	N.S.
	SD	6.46	7.27	
V	Mean	58.35	54.62	p < 0.04
	SD	14.43	14.68	
D	Mean	141.61	129.27[8]	p < 0.001
	SD	26.94	30.69	
Identity	Mean	116.89	110.34[7]	p < 0.001
	SD	14.52	16.57	
Self-	Mean	111.06[6]	107.34	N.S.
Satisfaction	SD	17.23	18.79	
Behavior	Mean	116.54	111.64	p < 0.01
	SD	14.80	15.84	
Physical	Mean	74.47	69.15	p < 0.001
Self	SD	9.18	11.12	
Moral-	Mean	66.97[6]	63.91[8]	p < 0.03
Ethical Self	SD	10.18	12.39	
Personal	Mean	62.77	61.35	N.S.
Self	SD	11.90	12.17	
Family	Mean	73.94	68.36[7]	p < 0.001
Self	SD	11.11	13.90	
Social	Mean	66.35	65.61	N.S.
Self	SD	9.46	9.51	

*SD means standard deviation.
[5] Significance at the 5 percent level between same scores of the black boys and girls. See Table 9.
[6] Significance at the 1 percent level between same scores of the black boys and girls. See Table 9.
[7] Significance at the 5 percent level between same scores of the white boys and girls. See Table 9.
[8] Significance at the 1 percent level between same scores of the white boys and girls. See Table 9.

and white boys are below the normative means for the scale on the total positive score, 343.3 for blacks, 329.3 for whites; on the identity score, 116.8 for blacks, 110.3 for whites; on the personal-self score, 62.7 for blacks, 61.3 for whites; and the social-self scale, 66.3 for blacks, and 65.6 for whites. The black boys are above the normative mean on the self-satisfaction score (111.0), the behavior score (116.5), the physical-self score (74.4), the moral-ethical-self score (66.9), and the family-self score (73.9). The black boys are also above the normative mean on the variability score (58.3) and the distribution score (141.6), but at the normative mean level on the self-criticism score (35.5). The white boys are at the normative mean level on the self-criticism score (35.7), but above the normative mean on variability (54.6), distribution (129.2), and self-satisfaction (107.3). However, the white boys score below the normative mean on behavior, physical self, moral-ethical self, personal self, family self, social self, and identity.

On the mean variability score, the black boys score significantly higher than the white boys ($p < 0.04$), and also significantly higher than the white boys on the distribution score ($p < 0.001$).

On the profile scores the black boys score significantly higher than the white boys on identity ($p < 0.001$), as well as on behavior ($p < 0.01$). On the sub-profile scores the black boys score statistically higher than the white boys on physical self ($p < 0.001$), moral-ethical self ($p < 0.03$), and family self ($p < 0.001$). There is no significant difference between the black boys and the white boys on the self-criticism score, the self-satisfaction score, personal-self score, or the social-self score.

COMPARISON OF BLACK BOYS AND BLACK GIRLS

(See Tables 9 and 10.) When the TSCS scores of 182 black girls are compared with the scores of 134 black boys, some significant differences emerge. The black girls have a total positive mean score of 352.9 compared with a total positive mean score for the black boys of 343.3; the difference is significant at the 5 percent level. Although the black girls score higher on the self-criticism score (36.5) compared with the black boys (35.5), the difference is not significant. The black boys and the black girls obtain the same mean variability scores of 58.3, and although the black boys score higher on the mean distribution score (141.6) than the black girls (139.9), the difference is not significant. There is no significant difference between the black boys and black girls on identity scores, behavior scores, physical-self scores, personal-self scores, family-self scores, or social-self scores. The black girls have a tendency to score higher on each of these scores, with the exception of physical self and social self, on which both groups have the same score. However, the black girls score higher on the self-satisfaction score (116.1) than do the black boys (111.2), with a significance at the 1 percent level. Likewise, the black girls (71.2) score higher than the black boys (66.9) on the moral-ethical-self scores, and the difference is significant at the 1 percent level.

COMPARISON OF WHITE GIRLS AND BOYS

When the TSCS scores of 193 white girls are compared with the scores of 125 white boys in New Orleans, some significant differences emerge (see Tables 9 and 10). Although the white girls obtained a total positive mean score of 335.3 compared with 329.3 for the white boys, the difference is not statistically significant; nor is there any significant difference in the self-criticism score or the variability score for the white boys and girls. However, the white boys obtained a mean distribution score of 129.2 compared with that of 121.1 for the white girls and the difference is significant at the 1 percent level.

The white girls score higher on the identity score, 114.4, compared with the white boys, 110.3, and the significance is at the 5 percent level. There is no significant difference between the white boys and girls on the profile scores of self-satisfaction and behavior. However, on the sub-profile scores, the white girls show a significant difference in the moral-ethical mean score compared with the boys, 68.0 for the white girls, and 63.9 for the white boys. The difference is significant at the 1 percent level. Likewise, the white girls score higher on the family-self items than the white boys, and the difference is significant at the 5 percent level.

COMPARISON OF NEW ORLEANS STUDENTS BY RACE, SEX, AND RACIAL COMPOSITION OF SCHOOL

COMPARISON OF WHITE AND BLACK STUDENTS IN SEGREGATED SCHOOLS

When the 137 white students in segregated schools are compared with the 155 black students in segregated schools, some significant differences emerge. (See Tables 2 and 5.) The black segregated students achieved a total positive mean score of 353.7 compared with that of the white segregated students of 322.8. The difference is significant at the 1 percent level. There is no significant difference between the white and black segregated students on the mean self-criticism scores, 36.7 and 35.9 respectively. However, the black students scored higher on the mean distribution score, 139.9, compared with a mean score for the white students of 119.0; the difference is significant at the 1 percent level. Likewise, on the mean variability score, the black students scored higher (58.2) than the white students (51.3), and the difference is significant at the 1 percent level. On the profile and sub-profile mean scores, the black students scored higher than the white students on every item: (1) for identity the difference is significant at the 1 percent level; (2) for self-satisfaction the difference is significant at the 1 percent level; (3) for behavior the difference is significant at the 1 percent level; (4) for physical self the difference is significant at the 1 percent level; (5) for moral-ethical self the difference is significant at the 1 percent percent level; (6) for personal self the difference is significant at the 1 percent level; (7) for family self the difference is significant at the 1 percent level. Although the black students scored higher on the social-self score (66.7) than did the white students (64.8), the difference is not significant.

COMPARISON OF WHITE AND BLACK STUDENTS IN DESEGREGATED SCHOOLS

When the 161 black students in desegregated schools are compared with the 181 white students in desegregated schools some significant differences emerge. (See Tables 2 and 5.) The black desegregated students obtained a total positive mean score of 344.0 compared with a total positive mean score for the white desegregated students of 336.3; the difference is significant at the 5 percent level. There is no significant difference between the black desegregated and the white desegregated students on the self-criticism mean scores, 36.3 and 35.8 respectively. However, on the mean variability score, the black students scored higher (58.4) than the white students (54.8), and the difference is significant at the 5 percent level. Likewise, on the mean distribution scores the black desegregated students scored higher (140.4) than the white desegregated students (127.4), and the difference is significant at the 1 percent level. On the mean profile scores, there are some significant differences between the scores of the desegregated black students and the desegregated white students. On identity, the black desegregated students achieved a mean score of 116.7 compared with a mean score of 113.1 for the desegregated white students; the difference is significant at the 5 percent level. Also, on the self-satisfaction score, the desegregated black students achieved a mean of 112.8 compared with a mean of 108.6 for the desegregated white group; the difference is significant at the 5 percent level. However, there is no significant difference between the mean scores of the desegregated black students and the desegregated white students on behavior, moral-ethical self, personal self, family self, or social self. On the physical-self mean score the desegregated black students have a higher mean score (74.1) than the desegregated white students (70.1), and the difference is significant at the 5 percent level.

COMPARISON OF BLACK AND WHITE GIRLS IN SEGREGATED SCHOOLS

When the 92 black girls in segregated schools are compared with the 88 white girls in segregated schools, some significant differences can be seen. (See Tables 3 and 6.) The black segregated girls obtained a higher total positive mean score (358.1) than the white segregated girls (334.0), and the difference is significant at the 1 percent level. Likewise, on the mean variability score, the black segregated girls have a mean of 57.7 compared with a mean of 52.4 for the white segregated girls; the difference is significant at the 5 percent level. On the mean distribution score, the black segregated girls scored higher (138.8) than the white segregated girls (119.6), and the difference is significant at the 1 percent level. On the self-satisfaction score the black segregated girls again scored higher (117.8) than the white segregated girls (103.9), and the difference is significant at the 1 percent level. The black girls scored higher than the white girls on physical self (black 75.3, white 69.5), personal self (black 65.8, white 59.2), and family self (black

76.5, white 69.3). The difference for each mean score is significant at the 1 percent level. The black segregated girls scored higher than the white segregated girls on behavior (black 120, white 114.4) and moral-ethical self (black 72.6, white 68.6); and the difference for both mean scores is significant at the 5 percent level. There is no significant difference between the black segregated girls and the white segregated girls on the self-criticism score, identity score, or the social-self score.

COMPARISON OF BLACK AND WHITE GIRLS IN DESEGREGATED SCHOOLS

(See Tables 3 and 5.) When the 90 black girls in desegregated schools are compared with the 105 white girls in desegregated schools, there are some significant differences on the TSCS scores. For instance, the black desegregated girls obtained a total positive mean score of 347.3 compared with a total positive mean score for the white desegregated girls of 335.8. The difference is significant at the 5 percent level. There is a significant difference between the mean variability scores of the black desegregated girls (58.9) and the desegregated white girls (53.9); that difference is significant at the 5 percent level. On the mean distribution score, the black desegregated girls obtained a score of 139.4 compared with a score of 121.7 for the desegregated white group; this difference is significant at the 1 percent level. On the mean scores for self-satisfaction (black 114.2, white 107.5), and physical self (black 75.3, white 69.8), the black desegregated girls scored higher than the white desegregated girls. The difference for both mean scores is significant at the 1 percent level. There is no significant difference between the black desegregated girls and the white desegregated girls on the mean self-criticism score, the mean identity score, the mean behavior score, the mean moral-ethical score, the mean personal-self score, the mean family-self score, and the mean social-self score. However, the black desegregated girls have a tendency to score slightly higher on each score than the white desegregated girls.

COMPARISON OF BLACK AND WHITE BOYS IN SEGREGATED SCHOOLS

When the 63 black boys in segregated schools are compared on the TSCS scores with the 49 white boys in segregated schools, many significant differences can be seen. (See Tables 4 and 7.) The black segregated boys obtained a total positive mean score of 347.1 compared with that of the white segregated boys of 311.6; the difference is signficant at the 1 percent level. Likewise, on the mean variability score (black 58.9, white 51.5), mean distribution score (black 141.6, white 118.5), mean identity score (black 117.5, white 105.3), mean self-satisfaction score (black 110.8, white 100.3), mean behavior score (black 118.5, white 105.8), mean physical-self score (black 75.3, white 66.3), mean moral-ethical score (black 68.5, white 60.5), mean personal-self score (black 61.8, white 55.4), and mean family-self score (black 74.6, white 66.4), the black segregated boys scored significantly higher than the white segregated boys, and the difference for each mean score is significant at the 1 percent level. There is no significant difference between the black segregated boys and the white segregated boys on mean self-criticism scores (black 35.2, white 35.5) and mean social-self scores (black 66.7, white 62.1).

COMPARISON OF BLACK AND WHITE BOYS IN DESEGREGATED SCHOOLS

A comparison of the 71 black boys in desegregated schools with the 76 white boys in desegregated schools on the TSCS scores, shows that the desegregated black boys score higher on physical self (73.7) than the desegregated white boys (70.4), and the difference is significant at the 5 percent level. However, on all the other TSCS scores, there is no significant difference in the mean scores between the desegregated black boys and the desegregated white boys (see Tables 4 and 7). However, the desegregated black boys have a higher total positive mean score (340.0) than the desegregated white boys (336.9), and a higher mean distribution score (141.6) than the desegregated white boys (135.1). It should also be noted that both the desegregated black boys and the desegregated white boys score below the normative means on identity and behavior, but above the normative mean of self-satisfaction.

TSCS SCORES OF THE NEW ORLEANS STUDENTS

Among the 634 students tested in New Orleans the mean total positive score was 340.3, below the normative mean. The mean SC score was 36.1, above the normative mean. The mean variability score of 51.1 and the mean distribution score of 132.3 are above the normative means. However, the mean identity score (115.0), the moral-ethical mean score (67.9), the personal-self mean score (62.1), and the social-self mean score (66.0) are all below the normative means. The self-satisfaction mean score (110.3), the physical-self mean score (72.1), and the family-self mean score (72.6) are above the normative means and the mean behavior score (115.5) is equivalent to the normative mean.

In the distribution of the TSCS scores among boys and girls, blacks and whites, segregated and desegregated students, it has been noted how the groups compare with each other as well as with the normative scores. It is hoped that the reader will be able to discern certain differences among groups in how they think and feel about themselves. In Part 5 an attempt will be made to explain why.

PART FOUR

Greensboro

13

Greensboro, North Carolina: Past and Present

Chartered in 1808, Greensboro was named for Major General Nathanael Greene who was the commander of the Continental Army at the Battle of Guilford Courthouse in March, 1781. With Winston-Salem and Highpoint, Greensboro forms a metropolitan area with a population of 520,249, although the population of Greensboro itself is 119,574. As the seat of Guilford County, which is a large industrial and insurance center, Greensboro is an industrial and educational center, 85 miles northwest of the capital city, Raleigh. Greensboro is the home of a campus of the University of North Carolina, Bennett College, Greensboro College, Guilford College, and North Carolina Agricultural and Technical State University.

THE PAST

The first permanent white settlers in Carolina came from Virginia and settled in the Albemarle Sound region around 1650. In 1663 Carolina was divided into three countries—Albermarle in the north, Clarendon in the Cape Fear Region, and Craven in what is now South Carolina. In 1664 a governor was appointed for Albemarle County, in 1667 Clarendon County was abolished, and until 1689 Albemarle County had the only government in the North Carolina Region. In 1712 North Carolina became a separate colony and in 1789 North Carolina became the 12th state in the Union, having delayed approving the U.S. Constitution because of opposition to a strong federal government. From about 1800 to 1835 North Carolina was called the

Rip Van Winkle State because it was so backward that it seemed to be asleep, with few seaports and transportation facilities and backward farming. An age of progress began in 1835 with the building of railroads and roads and increased agricultural production, all initiated by a revision in the state's constitution giving most taxpayers the right to vote and granting equal representation to the people of the western region. It is interesting to note that three presidents came from North Carolina—Andrew Jackson, James K. Polk, and Andrew Johnson.

The state seceded from the Union on May 20, 1861, and Union forces captured most of eastern North Carolina early in the war. In 1865 Union forces under General William T. Sherman defeated the Confederate troops of General Joseph E. Johnston who surrendered near Durham on April 26, 1865. About one fourth of all the Confederate soldiers killed came from North Carolina. During the Reconstruction period from 1867 to 1877, the Republican party, which consisted of freed slaves, Union sympathizers, and carpetbaggers, was in control of the state government. It abolished slavery, gave Freedmen the right to vote, and re-entered the Union in 1868. By 1870 the Democrats and white supremists gained control of the state legislature and by 1875 the Democratic legislature added 30 amendments to the constitution which ensured white, Democratic, segregationist control of the state.

By the late 1800's the people of North Carolina began to rebuild their state rapidly. The state's industries developed at a tremendous rate during the early 1900's and by the late 1920's North Carolina led the nation in the production of cotton textiles, tobacco products, and wooden furniture.

THE PRESENT

Today North Carolina is enjoying a period of social and economic progress. During the 1940's and 1950's new industries were attracted to North Carolina by the improved electric power, roads, and schools. In 1956 alone nearly 150 new industries moved into the state and in 1962 about 200 new industries started to operate. As a matter of fact, North Carolina is the leading tobacco state of the United States, with more tobacco grown and more tobacco products manufactured there than in any other state. The state also leads the nation in the manufacturing of cloth and wooden furniture. Indeed, manufacturing earns more money and provides more jobs than any other industry in North Carolina. Annual gross national product is $5,695,572,000 with manufactured products contributing 75 percent and agricultural products, 24 percent. In 1967, 130 new industrial plants began to operate and 338 other industries expanded their facilities creating 24,774 new jobs.

In North Carolina there are 70 senior and junior colleges and universities with more than 120,000 students. Twenty-eight of these are state supported with an enrollment over 73,000.

About 40 percent of North Carolina's people live in urban areas and 60 percent in rural areas. More than one fourth of the people live in one of he state's seven metropolitan areas, with Greensboro being the state's second largest city. Seventy-five percent of the total population resides in the state of their birth.

Greensboro reflects the economic progress of the state. In addition to textile factories located there which manufacture denim, flannel, khaki, and rayon, there are other major industries producing chemicals, medicines, cosmetics, electrical equipment, iron, steel, tobacco, and wood products. The median family income is $5,845 with 16 percent of family incomes being $10,000 or more and 19 percent under $3,000. Fifty-eight percent of the people are working 50 to 52 weeks a year and labor has the highest hourly rate in the state. The educational level is high compared to other Southern cities; the median school years completed are 11.7 and 48 percent of the population has completed high school or more. Among the five universities and colleges located in Greensboro, the 1967 college fall enrollment was 7,799.

In the non-white population of 51,376 the median number of years in school is 8.2 with 2,342 completing eight years and 1,682 completing high school. The family median income is $3,121 with 235 families with an income of $10,000 or more. The number of employed non-white males 14 and over is 16,139 and females 17,811. Those blacks working in the professional category are 495 males and 790 females; private household workers, 3,687 females, 72 males; craftsmen (males), 1,301; operative and kindred workers, 3,017; service, 1,785; laborers, 2,532. Large numbers of blacks have migrated to industrialized areas of North Carolina in more recent years because more jobs in industry are opening up. In the total population 3,823 males and 3,591 females are listed as professionals, and 17,000 males and 10,405 females are in the manufacturing industries.

In 1960 the U.S. Census reported that North Carolina had a population of 4,556,155 and in 1965 it was estimated to be about 4,800,000 with about one of every four North Carolinians being black. In 1960 the population of Greensboro was 119,574 with 88,444 whites, 30,817 blacks, and 313 classified as other races. As of 1966, the population of Greensboro was 131,711.

THE REPERCUSSIONS OF THE BROWN DECISION

During the very early years of North Carolina's statehood, churches and religious leaders controlled most of the education in the state. In 1705

Charles Griffin, a school teacher and member of the Anglican church, established the first school in the state. Early attempts at public education were opposed by the churches who felt that education belonged in the hands of the church. In 1776 the state constitution provided for the establishment of a public school system, but the state did not build the first public school until 1840. The Charter for the University of North Carolina was drawn up in 1776 and in 1795 the University became the first state university in the country. In 1901 Governor Charles B. Aycock started a vast long-reaching program to improve North Carolina's public education system. The involvement of the Freedman's Bureau as well as private philanthropists in the establishment of schools for blacks has been reviewed in a previous chapter.

At the time of the *Brown* decision in 1954 the North Carolina constitution did not permit white and black children to attend school together and, like other Southern states after Reconstruction, Jim Crow laws were enacted which extended to include public education. However, in 1954 in the Raleigh diocese the few Catholic schools were desegregated.

When the story broke on "that Monday" virtually all major newspapers in North Carolina urged a calm, constructive approach to the problem. However, with the pronouncement of the end of school desegregation, interracial relations began to deteriorate and a racial estrangement could be felt which did not really begin to relax for many years. North Carolina was afflicted with considerable Klan activity. In March, 1958, a group of Klansmen tried to terrorize 30,000 Lumbee Indians in Robeson County, but the Lumbees surrounded the Klansmen and fired their rifles in the air. The Klansmen fled in terror and "their rebuff and defeat by the Indians resounded around the nation as one of the few genuinely humorous incidents in the desegregation crisis."[1] The movement of resistance to desegregation in North Carolina sprang up in the founding of the North Carolina Defenders of States' Rights. The Ku Klux Klan was not an affiliate, but the organization allied themselves with the Citizens Councils of America, Incorporated. Neither was North Carolina without incidents of violence; there were two bombing attempts on schools in Charlotte, and a bombing was attempted on Jewish buildings in Gastonia and Charlotte.

Resolutions of protest or "interposition" against the Supreme Court ruling were adopted unanimously by the North Carolina Senate and only two opposed in the lower chamber. By September of 1955 North Carolina had not initiated any plan for compliance and not one school district or school had been desegregated as a result of the 1954 Supreme Court ruling. The idea of resorting to segregated private schools as a strategy to avoid federal court desegregation orders had been considered and the state had laws that could be used to close public schools in which racial desegregation might be imminent.

In March of 1956 Senator Byrd was circulating his "Southern Manifesto" as a part of a plan to organize the South for massive resistance. Under pressure from Manifesto promoters who reminded Southerners of the "feelings back home" and the possibility of being labeled "betrayers of the South" or worse still "nigger lovers," the North Carolina Senators signed, but three North Carolina members of the House of Representatives refused to sign—Thurman Chatham, C.B. Deane, and Harold D. Cooley. Chatham, in addition to refusing to sign, stated: "I personally will not sign anything that will tear down the power and prestige of the Court as the final arbiter of Justice."[2] Only Cooley succeeded in being re-elected two months later; Deane and Chatham were defeated.

By September, 1955, fourteen formal applications by black children for admission to white schools had been made. Before the end of 1955, desegregation litigation had been initiated in two North Carolina counties and in one county, McDowell, an old equalization suit was revised to one requesting desegregation.

North Carolina's Governor, Luther Hodges, tried to resist segregation hysteria. Hodges' objectives had been to maintain, if possible, a system of public education for all children of the state and to maintain law and order. By early 1955 he recommended to the General Assembly the repeal of all statutes that required that white and black children be assigned to separate schools. This recommendation was passed as well as a pupil-assignment law which placed full authority and responsibility for assignment of pupils to public schools to local boards of education "in accordance with valid and reasonable standards."[3] Governor Hodges also recommended that voluntary separation of the races in public schools be observed "in the interest of maintaining peace and for the maintenance of the public school education."[4] The North Carolina blacks were opposed to such practice, but in spite of their opposition the legislature was called in special session in July, 1965, to add amendments to the state constitution as "safety valves." These amendments authorized tuition grants for private schooling to be paid to the parents of any child assigned against his wishes to a school in which the races were mixed. They also permitted the people in any locality to discontinue operation of public schools in that community by majority vote.

On September 4, 1957, black children were admitted for the first time to previously all-white public schools in three cities in North Carolina: Charlotte, Winston-Salem, and Greensboro. The previous June, 31 black children in Charlotte, nine in Greensboro, seven in Winston-Salem, and one in Raleigh, a total of 48, had filed applications for admission to white schools. All but twelve of the applications were rejected. The Charlotte, Greensboro, and Winston-Salem school boards consulted each other and decided to adopt the same schedules for implementation of the desegregation plan. Consequently five black students were assigned to white schools in Charlotte, six in Greensboro, and one in Winston-Salem. The assignments were announced in simultaneous meetings on July 23rd. The North Carolina Patriots, Inc., presented a petition with 16,000 signatures to the school board in Charlotte to the applause of visitors and sympathizers who were present at the meeting. The North Carolina Patriots gave an impassioned speech in Greensboro and a more restrained one in Winston-Salem. John Kasper visited each of the three cities a few days before the opening of schools, but the press hailed his coming as "unwelcomed." Ku Klux Klansmen appeared in Charlotte but fled when police broke up their picket lines.

On September 3, 1957, the governor warned against any disruption to the opening of the schools and indicated that he was not opposed to using the National Guard to preserve order. On September 4th schools opened without any incidents in Winston-Salem and Greensboro except for some heckling. Negro students entered three white high schools in Charlotte without trouble but the admission of 15-year-old Dorothy Counts at Harding High School was met with marked disturbance. Dorothy Counts was the daughter of a minister who was an instructor at Johnson C. Smith University. A mob followed her to and from school. After one week, seeing no hope of enjoying tolerable relations with her white schoolmates, she withdrew and attended a biracial school in suburban Philadelphia. "Dorothy's walk" was watched all over the United States and around the world. One of the photos won the World Press Award. In spite of the Counts incident the news from North Carolina was that "white schools in three cities had admitted Negro pupils without serious public disorder."[5] By 1960 North Carolina had achieved integration in only nine of the 173 school districts, but had avoided radical resistance efforts or serious public disorder. William T. Jagner, vice-chairman of the committee that drafted the Pearsall Plan as the pupil-assignment plan of North Carolina, was heard to state:

> I do not hesitate to advance my personal opinion, and it is that the admission of less than 1 percent—for example one tenth of 1 percent—of Negro children to the schools heretofore attended only by white children is a small price to pay for the ability to keep the mixing within bounds of reasonable control.[6]

In evaluating North Carolina's attitude and approaches to the desegregation issue, it becomes clear that "the plan" was largely one of opposition or resistance to interposition resolutions and one to support local option. Meanwhile North Carolina's neighbor, Virginia, which enjoyed a unique prestige in the South, mounted a plan of massive resistance, and anathema to the North Carolina plan of peace and compliance. In comparison, the end economic result in the two states as a result of their approach to the *Brown* decision was that the confusion and uncertainty frightened new industry away from Virginia. Meanwhile in North Carolina where schools were operating normally, even if with token desegregation, the state was enjoying an unprecedented industrial boom.

From August, 1956, to September, 1957, disorders in connection with public school desegregation across the South reached a peak. Although hostility to school desegregation had been expressed in North Carolina, no serious violence occurred in North Carolina cities. Muse attributes the lack of agitation to some sobering influences at work in North Carolina and enumerates the influences counteracting resistance:[7]

1. Dr. Frank P. Graham, who had been president of the University of North Carolina, governor of the state, U.S. Senator, and then mediator for the United Nations, supported the *Brown* decision vigorously.

2. Irving Carlyle of Winston-Salem, who had been a former state senator, not only accepted the desegregation ruling but became a crusader for compliance with it.

3. Two literary celebrities, the writer Harry Golden of Charlotte and playwright Paul Green of Chapel Hill, were outspoken foes of discrimination.

4. Two important daily newspapers in North Carolina presented inflammatory opposition to the *Brown* decision but later advised orderly adjustment. Charlotte (*Charlotte Observer*), Winston-Salem (*Winston-Salem Journal*), and Greensboro (*Greensboro Daily News*) had from the outset prepared the public for change.

From 1956 to 1962 North Carolina went from 11 black students in desegregated schools to 203 and from 1.7 percent of the 170 school districts desegregated to 6.4 percent.[8] In 1965, North Carolina's 170 school districts had a total white enrollment of 828,638 and a total black enrollment of 349,382. There were 86 desegregated school districts with 555,997 white students enrolled and 207,551 black students enrolled in those districts.[9] However, only 4,963 black students or 1.42 percent of North Carolina's black students were in desegregated schools.

As of the school year 1966-67, of the 169 school districts in North Carolina 159 were considered in compliance with the Civil Rights Act of 1964 and 10 districts were having funds deferred because of HEW's request for cutoffs because of noncompliance.[10] In the state the total white student enrollment was 321,800 and the black student enrollment was 263,200, with 8,500 black students (3.2 percent) in desegregated schools.[11] Of the black students, 9.5 percent were in schools with less than 20 percent black enrollment; 3.1 percent were in schools with 20 to 80 percent black enrollment; 3 percent were in schools with 80 to 99 percent black enrollment; and 84.4 percent were in schools with 100 percent black enrollment.[12] Clearly, North Carolina had been dragging its desegregating feet.

THE BLACK COMMUNITY IN NORTH CAROLINA

Before the Civil War, North Carolina had a substantial number of free blacks who were laborers, tenants, farmers, and landowners. North Carolina was never one of the chief slaveholding states. According to Franklin, North Carolina had fewer slaves than her neighbor states of Virginia, South Carolina, and Georgia.

> As a matter of fact, 67 percent of the slaveholding families held fewer than ten slaves in 1860, while 72 percent of North Carolina's families held no slaves at all. (Guion G. Johnson, *Antebellum North Carolina*, p. 468 ff.) This suggests that in a state where the plantation system was only fairly well entrenched, the supply of slave labor was definitely limited. The farm labor in North Carolina was done not only by the slave but, in some areas, by the members of the white farming family, by white farm laborers, and by free Negro farm laborers.[13]

The free Negro would obtain work on the farms that had no slaves at all. There were more free Negro farm laborers in counties where the free Negro population was large; those counties also had large slave populations. Of the 1,746 free Negro farm laborers in North Carolina in 1860, more than 1,000 were located in the seven eastern counties with the highest numbers of slaves. The most interesting group of free Negroes were the free Negro yeomanry and a considerable number of them owned their own farms. Their major crops were tobacco and cotton. In fact, the free Negro farmer was generally in better circumstances than free Negroes in other areas of economic activity. According to Franklin, the free Negroes who made their living from the soil were about 3,000 and about 50 percent owned their own land.[14]

> But the poverty of the free Negro group can be seen clearly through a study of the value of the property of the group. They possessed an aggregate wealth of $1,645,643. When one considers that more than 30,000 people had to share in this wealth of slightly more than one million dollars, the realization of their plight is inescapable. The per capita wealth of the free Negroes of North Carolina was only $34 in 1860.[15]

In the early 1900's blacks began to migrate to more industrialized areas of the North in the hope of finding jobs, for as industries opened up in North Carolina more Jim Crow laws were enacted. By 1900 North Carolina passed laws segregating blacks and whites on railroads and buses. By 1907 a law requiring the separation of the races on streetcars was enacted. In 1915 North Carolina had stringent rules covering fumigation of textbooks and providing separate maintenance of textbooks used by black children and white children. By the middle of the 20th century the pattern of segregation in North Carolina, as in other Southern states, was very complex.

Although Jim Crow laws had been enacted in public school education as early as 1868, in North Carolina greater attention was given to the education of blacks than in most Southern states. In 1910 Dr. James E. Shepard founded the National Religious Training School of Durham. In 1923 the state of North Carolina assumed support of the school and the name was changed to the North Carolina College for Negroes and became the only state-supported liberal arts college for blacks in the country. By 1944, 22 of the 231 high schools for blacks in North Carolina had been accredited by the Southern Association of Colleges and Secondary Schools.[16]

In the 1938 Supreme Court decision of *Gaines* v. *Canada* Chief Justice Hughes said that it was the duty of the state to provide education for all its citizens and that provision must be made within the state. North Carolina had already made some moves to provide graduate training for blacks and increased its program.

In 1944 North Carolina had reduced its differential between salaries of black and white teachers. The state established a Negro library in Charlotte and one of the first state-supported black schools of library science, at North Carolina College. As early as 1900 there were 10 black newspapers in North Carolina and by the late 1930's there were separate Negro-white CIO labor unions in Virginia and North Carolina, the only CIO unions where such arrangements existed. In 1898 one of the largest black insurance companies was founded in Durham by John Mernick, Dr. A.M. Moore, James E. Shepard, W.G. Pearson, and others. In 1899 C.C. Spaulding was added to the board and the company was reorganized.

Meanwhile, in Greensboro itself North Carolina Agriculture and Technical State University was founded in 1891 and Bennett College for girls was found in 1873 with current approximate enrollments of 3,930 and 669 respectively.

In February of 1960 a group of students from North Carolina A and T, under the leadership of CORE, sat-in at a drugstore. The demonstration became the catalyst for the massive black student sit-in movement in the 1960's.

GREENSBORO, APRIL 30, 1969

At the time of the arrival of the research team in Greensboro, the community was confronted with three issues. First of all, the reviewers from

HEW had just departed, having declared the Greensboro City Board of Education in noncompliance with the Civil Rights Act of 1964. Dr. W.J. House, superintendent of the city's schools, had recommended to the Board of Education that an appeal be carried to HEW's reviewing authority in an effort to save more than $1,000,000 in federal funds being used annually in the school system to pay for a variety of academic programs. The HEW hearing examiners ruled that "the board be denied this money because a dual system was being perpetuated along racial lines in defiance of the Civil Rights Act of 1964."[17]

Superintendent House's response to the HEW reviewer's ruling was:

> Our position is that we have complied with the Civil Rights Act. The school board has acted in good faith and significant progress has been made.
>
> The only way to eliminate all-Negro schools, other than freedom of choice, would be forced attendance by white students at what HEW refers to as all-Negro schools.
>
> The unfavorable ruling relies upon the continued existence of schools currently attended exclusively by Negro students.[18]

The examiners from HEW based their decisions on the fact that in 1965 there were 11 all-black schools and there was no evidence that there would be fewer than 11 all-black schools in the next school year. Ninety-one percent of the black population of Greensboro lives in the southeast quadrant and "racial imbalance in the school population resulted from that private housing pattern."[19] However, HEW's reviewing authority ruled that segregated housing does not justify segregated schools. According to the *Greensboro Daily News*, the three-man panel made the decision while considering an integration plan submitted by the Raleigh Board of Education. The plan had already been reviewed and approved by a hearing examiner, who said that continuing segregation was caused by Raleigh's housing pattern, not by the school system's plan. The reviewing authority rejected this reasoning and adopted the same attitude that the Supreme Court took on "freedom of choice," that is, desegregation plans are acceptable only if they work. This was the first time the reviewing authority applied the Supreme Court doctrine to attendance zoning.

> During the 1964-65 and 1965-66 school years, of 40 regular schools, there were 13 all-white, 11 all-Negro, and 16 integrated schools.
>
> What the hearing examiner appears to be saying is that, in spite of the board's good faith and significant progress in desegregation of pupils and staff, we still have the obligation to eliminate the so-called dual structure in spite of local residential patterns resulting from the attitudes and actions of private individuals in years past, and over which the board has no control.[20]

However, the *Carolina Peacemaker*, a black newspaper, had the following statement regarding school desegregation:[21]

A potential candidate for the City Council should be aware of the fact that the Council needs to take steps to see to it that the Greensboro School Board begins to act positively on the matter of school integration which has bedogged and bedeviled our community for the past fifteen years since the Supreme Court's decision. It seems to us that either the School Board needs some new leadership and a change of representatives or that those presently serving need to become more aware and sensitive to the growing feelings of despair on the part of black parents of school children who are forced to brave the rigors of venturing across the tracks to get an integrated education.

It is indeed true that no court can legislate love, but it can legislate laws regarding human conduct, and that is all that black people are concerned about. We are concerned about the "human use of human beings" and we are determined that white people know through our spokesmen, who are unafraid to speak out on matters, that we are indeed tired of singing the Lord's song in a strange land—that our melody grows weaker along with our patience and that it is time for some modern day Joshua to come forth and help us blow down the walls of segregation and discrimination and indifference and second class services in the ghetto.

The second major event occurring at the time of the research was the primary election for city council in which seven black candidates and 24 white candidates presented themselves to the electorate for the seven-man city council. The seven black candidates were J. LaFayette Morgan, local contractor; Mrs. Pearlene Harris, proprietor of a boarding home for the elderly; O.C. Stafford, electrical engineer at Western Electric; Vance Chavis, principal of Lincoln Junior High School; Jimmie I. Barber, Director of Off-Campus Housing at A and T State University; Herman L. Matherson, insurance agent; and Dr. John Marshall Stevenson, professor of English at A and T and publisher of the *Carolina Peacemaker*.

The black organizations had made no attempt to support any candidate and many black people interviewed were disgusted and dismayed by the general apathy of the black community. However, two black candidates were in the top 14 to be considered for the final run-off—Barber, 8th, and Chavis, 10th.

A third event in the public eye was the Poor People's March which had convened in Winston-Salem. Many of the marchers were students who were anxious to tell Governor Scott of their dissatisfaction at closing all black schools and desegregating the white ones. Eight hundred high school students were out of school to register their protest and 75 were on the March. Rev. J.T. McMillian, pastor of the Saint James A.M.E. Zion Church on Patterson Avenue in Winston-Salem where the mass meeting was held, stated the purpose of the March: "The purpose of the March can be summed up in two words: Humanity and Respect. They killed the dreamer [Martin Luther King], but not the dream. There will be turmoil, marching, some burning, some tearing down until we get our freedom."[22]

Mr. Milton Fitch, state coordinator of SCLC and the March, stated another purpose: the concern of poverty and education in Hyde County where desegregation involved "scooping up black children and putting them in trailers in back of the white school."[23] The average income per family in Hyde County is $1,129 and the average for black families is $770.

The marchers were to leave Winston-Salem two days later for Greensboro and, indeed, arrived shortly after the researchers left.

1. Muse. Op. cit., 1962, p. 50.
2. Ibid., p. 63.
3. Ibid., p. 66.
4. Ibid.
5. Ibid., p. 68.
6. Ibid., p. 69.
7. Ibid., p. 113.
8. Southern School News. June, 1965.
9. Ibid.
10. Southern Education Report. Jan.-Feb., 1967, p. 31.
11. Ibid., p. 32.
12. Ibid.
13. Franklin, J.H. The free Negro in economic life of ante-bellum North Carolina. *In* The Making of Black America, Vol. 1. Meier, A., and Rudwick, E., eds. New York: Atheneum, 1969, p. 217.
14. Ibid., p. 219.
15. Ibid., p. 227.
16. Franklin, J.H. From Slavery to Freedom, 3rd ed. New York, Vintage Books, 1967, p. 552.
17. City school chief favors appealing HEW's decision. Greensboro Daily News. Wed., April 30, 1969, p. B1.
18. Ibid., p. B5.
19. Ibid.
20. Ibid.
21. Marshall, J. The other side of the tracks. The Carolina Peacemaker. Sat., April 26, 1969, p. 4.
22. Poor people's marchers hold mass meeting. Ibid., p. 1.
23. Ibid.

14

Greensboro: The Students and the Schools

As of the 1967-68 school year, the Greensboro Public School System had a student enrollment of 31,249 students with an expected increase to 34,000 by 1972. During the 1968-69 school year, there were 32,094 pupils of whom 10,025 were black and 21,998 were white. Of the black children, 1,897 (19 percent) were attending schools with white children.[1] Five public junior high schools of the ten in the system participated in the study—one all-black, one with less than 10 percent black enrollment, and three with 10 percent black enrollment. Of the 160 black students tested 35.6 percent were in the seventh grade, 34.4 percent were in the eighth grade, and 30 percent were in the ninth grade. Of the 310 white students, 30.3 percent were in the seventh grade, 31.5 percent were in the eighth grade, and 38.2 percent were in the ninth grade. The ages of the black students ranged in years from 11 to 16, seven being 11 years old, 74 being 12 years old, 65 being 13 years old, 68 being 14 years old, 21 being 15 years old, and 5 being 16 years old. The white students' were the following: 2 were 11 years old, 34 were 12 years old, 68 were 13 years old, 54 were 14 years old, 51 were 15 years old, and 12 were 16 years old. (See Tables 1 and 2.) The data regarding family and educational and occupational status of parents, as well as aspirations of students, were assessed by questionnaire.

FAMILY BACKGROUND OF STUDENTS

THE SEGREGATED BLACK SCHOOL

The student enrollment was 1,295; 46 boys and 48 girls participated. The average IQ was 95. Sixty-four percent of the students responded that

210

TABLE 1

Grades of Students in Greensboro

	Girls			Boys		
	7th	8th	9th	7th	8th	9th
Black	29 (17.8%)	27 (16.6%)	26 (15.5%)	29 (17.8%)	29 (17.8%)	23 (14.5%)
White	50 (16.2%)	42 (13.5%)	58 (18.6%)	44 (14.1%)	56 (18%)	61 (19.6%)

TABLE 2

Age in Years of Students in Greensboro

	11 years	12 years	13 years	14 years	15 years	16 years
White Girls	5	48	35	37	17	5
Black Girls	2	26	30	31	4	—
White Boys	2	28	46	30	36	11
Black Boys	—	6	22	24	15	1

their parents were living together and 36 percent indicated that their parents were separated or divorced. Sixty percent of the students came from families with four or more children. In terms of educational and occupational status of parents, the following information was obtained:

1.	Father finished high school	63%
	Father did not finish high school	31%
2.	Father had no college	69%
	Father had some college	18%
	Father had four years or more college	12%
3.	Father in a profession or own business	8%
	Father in trade or labor	67%
4.	Mother finished high school	72%
	Mother did not finish high school	26%
5.	Mother had no college	64%
	Mother had some college	18%
	Mother had four years or more college	17%
6.	Mother works	74%
	Mother does not work	25%
7.	Number of children in family: 1 to 3 children	45%
	4 to 10 children	51%

THE LESS THAN 10 PERCENT BLACK SCHOOL

The student enrollment at the time of the testing was 1,549. Most of the black students attending had professional parents who provided their own transportation to and from school for their children. Only one black family lived within walking distance of the school. The enrollment of black students was decidedly less than 10 percent, although no staff person was ready to state a definite percentage. The staff included five black teachers. The average IQ was 105 and there were some remedial classes. The socioeconomic status of the students' families was estimated by staff to be middle and upper class.

The 88 students tested included six black students, three girls and three boys. The black students' questionnaire responses indicated that 100 percent of their parents were together. Eighty-three percent indicated that their fathers had completed high school, and 50 percent of the fathers had four years or more of college with one third in professions or owning their own businesses, and two thirds in labor, trade or other occupations. All of the mothers had finished high school and one third had had four years or more of college; one third of the mothers worked and two thirds did not. Two thirds of the children had at least two siblings and one third had three or more.

Of the 82 white students tested, 96 percent indicated that their parents were together and 3 percent indicated that their parents were separated or divorced.

The educational and occupational status of white parents were indicated as follows:

1. Father finished high school   91%
   Father did not finish high school   7%
2. Father had no college   16%
   Father had some college   12%
   Father had four years or more college   72%
3. Father in profession or own business   76%
   Father in trade, labor, technician   24%
4. Mother finished high school   100%
5. Mother had no college   30%
   Mother had some college   23%
   Mother had four years or more college   45%
6. Mother works   41%
   Mother does not work   59%

THE 10 PERCENT BLACK SCHOOL (FOUR YEARS)

The school enrollment was 501; 10 percent of the students were black and there was one black teacher. The school was desegregated "all at once" four years prior to the testing. The staff interviewed felt that there were marked differences in academic performance between the white and black students, and remedial classes in reading were started primarily for the black students. Many of the black students, about 25 percent were bused to the school because there was no other way for them to get there. The economic status of the students' families ranged from welfare status to professional. Mean IQ for the school was 100.

Ninety-nine students participated in the study, 45 black students and 54 white students. The responses on the questionnaire concerning family and educational and occupational status of parents for each group were as follows:

		White	Black
1.	Parents together	75%	62%
	Parents not together	25%	38%
2.	Father finished high school	70%	41%
	Father did not finish high school	25%	59%
3.	Father had no college	60%	81%
	Father had some college	8%	9%
	Father had four years or more college	31%	10%
4.	Father in profession or own business	23%	21%
	Father in trade, labor, other	67%	75%
5.	Mother finished high school	75%	39%
	Mother did not finish high school	23%	56%
6.	Mother had no college	71%	93%
	Mother had some college	16%	4%
	Mother had four years college or more	13%	3%
7.	Mother works	51%	75%
	Mother does not work	49%	25%
8.	Number of children in family: 1 to 3 children	32%	27%
	4 or more children	43%	73%

THE 10 PERCENT BLACK SCHOOL (SIX YEARS)

The school enrollment was 1,269 with black students making up 10 percent of the student population. The school had been desegregated for six years at the time of the study, but desegregation had been slow partly because of housing patterns. Very few blacks lived near the school so many who did attend were bused. In spite of the 10 percent black student population, of the 99 students tested only four were black. The parents of all of the black students were living together. Three fathers had finished high school and one father had had four years of college or more. One father was in a profession, the others were engaged in labor or trade. Three of the mothers had finished high school, but none had finished college. Two of the mothers were working. Only one of the students had more than three siblings.

The 95 white students who participated in the study made the following responses to questionnaire items related to family and educational and occupational status of parents:

1.	Parents are together	89%
	Parents are not together	11%
2.	Father finished high school	58%
	Father did not finish high school	38%
3.	Father had no college	78%
	Father had some college	8%
	Father had four years or more college	12%

4. Father in profession or own business   25%
    Father in trade, labor, or other   66%
5. Mother finished high school   68%
    Mother did not finish high school   32%
6. Mother had no college   85%
    Mother had some college   5%
    Mother had four years or more college   8%
7. Mother works   63%
    Mother does not work   35%
8. Number of children in family: 1 to 3 children   31%
                                 4 or more children   37%

THE 10 PERCENT BLACK SCHOOL (EIGHT YEARS)

The student population was about 500 with about 50 black students. The school began to desegregate eight years prior to the study and the first black teacher was added to the faculty three years before the study; the new assistant principal was black.

Among the 90 students tested, 11 were black. The responses of the students to questionnaire items were as follows:

		White	Black
1.	Parents are together	72%	72%
	Parents not together	28%	28%
2.	Father finished high school	41%	45%
	Father did not finish high school	54%	55%
3.	Father had no college	85%	82%
	Father had some college	7%	17%
	Father had four years or more college	4%	
4.	Father in profession or own business	18%	19%
	Father in trade, labor, or other	69%	91%
5.	Mother finished high school	49%	65%
	Mother did not finish high school	46%	35%
6.	Mother had no college	83%	82%
	Mother had some college	9%	9%
	Mother had four years or more college	4%	9%
7.	Mother works	66%	82%
	Mother does not work	34%	18%
8.	Number of children in family: 1 to 3 children	50%	36%
	4 or more children	43%	64%

A summary of the educational and occupational status of white and black students is outlined in Table 3. Among the white students, 65 percent of the fathers completed high school compared with 62 percent of the black fathers, and 27 percent of white fathers finished college compared with 20 percent of black fathers. As far as occupations of fathers, 70 percent of black fathers are in the technician-trade category compared to 47 percent for

TABLE 3
Educational and Occupational Background of Parents in Greensboro

Father Finished High School

	Yes	No
White	65%	31%
Black	62%	37%

Father Finished College

	No	Some	Yes
White	60%	9%	27%
Black	66%	14%	20%

Father's Occupation

	Profession/ Business	Technician/ Trade	Labor
White	36%	47%	10%
Black	21%	70%	5%

Mother Finished High School

	Yes	No
White	73%	20%
Black	70%	28%

Mother Finished College

	No	Some	Yes
White	67%	13%	18%
Black	48%	6%	13%

Mother Works

	Yes	No
White	55%	42%
Black	63%	37%

Mother's Occupation

	Professional	Secretary	Factory	Service	Other
White	5%	23%	12%	7%	3%
Black	10%	11%	8%	24%	26%

the white fathers. High school education of white and black mothers, 73 percent and 70 percent respectively, is about the same, as is college education, 18 percent and 13 percent respectively. The degree of family stability is about the same for both groups, although black families tend to be larger. (See Table 4.)

TABLE 4

Family Background

	Parents Together	*Parents Separated or Divorced*
White	83%	17%
Black	80%	21%

	One to Three Children in Family	*Four or More Children in Family*
White	45%	39%
Black	49%	51%

ASPIRATIONS AND ATTITUDES OF STUDENTS

Table 5 gives a summary of the aspirational levels of students. There is no marked difference between white and black students in what they want for the future in terms of occupational goals. However, 71 percent of the black students report being satisfied with self, compared with 56 percent of the white students. It will be interesting to see how these attitudes correlate with self-satisfaction scores.

In the "desegregated schools" black students were having social, personal, and academic difficulties in adjustment. In many instances the problems overlapped and it would be difficult to say which was the primary cause of the difficulty. In many instances remedial classes had been set up which were all black, or predominantly black, which made the black students feel inferior. One teacher related several incidents over the past several years in which black students would refuse to participate orally in class because of the fear that their white classmates would make fun of them if they did not answer correctly. White students frequently made disparaging remarks about black students being "dumb" or "stupid" and laughed at "the way they talk." Other teachers related incidents in which black students felt too uncomfortable to do problems at the board because they felt that white students would make fun of their clothes, a fear that was not unrealistic.

Among the girls especially, there were cliques from which the black girls were excluded. One teacher related an incident in which a class party was planned. The girls were in charge of the food and were divided into committees. The two black girls in the class were selected for committees also, but their committees met without them because the white girls met at each

TABLE 5

Aspirations of Students in Greensboro

	College	Marriage*	Profession	Sports*	Job
	Percentages				
White	50	9	25	10	16
Black	44	4	33	8	8

Attitudes		
	Satisfied with Self-Image	Immature
White	56	15
Black	71	10

*The boys responded in terms of sports and the girls responded in terms of marriage.

other's houses and none of the white parents would allow their children to invite the black girls home. Similar incidents occurred for other class social events; black students were not allowed to participate unless the activity was on the school premises.

The following account of an actual incident demonstrates the conflict and dilemma in which both white and black students find themselves in a desegregated school:

Pam, a black student in seventh grade, was shy but very bright. As a matter of fact she was the most outstanding student in her class. Her father was a dentist and her mother taught at a desegregated school in town. Unlike many of the other black students, it was very apparent from the way Pam talked, acted, and dressed that she came from an "elite" family by anyone's standards. Pam, however, was never ostentatious and was friendly in her own shy way with everyone. She soon became the favorite of all her white teachers and, in spite of this, very popular with white and black students alike.

In the seventh grade debates Pam won first place and the seventh grade class voted to run her for class vice-president, the first time any black girl had been considered for such an office.

Susanne, a white classmate of Pam's, who had pushed for her nomination was elated, and the two girls talked about Pam's campaign with the black seventh-grade history teacher who had helped Pam during the debate.

It was decided that Pam needed a campaign manager and inasmuch as Susanne was very popular and an astute politician, she decided to organize the campaign for Pam—to be her campaign manager. The usual custom was to put up posters, have cheerleaders give demonstrations for the candidates at lunch time and after school on the athletic field, and even give parties. Susanne was very excited and had many ideas.

Inasmuch as Pam lived across town, it was decided that the two girls would meet after school at Susanne's house to plan the campaign and get the kids organized who wanted to work for Pam. Pam had transportation problems and usually waited for her mother until 4 p.m. each day inside the school, because her mother worked and then had to pick up two younger siblings who went to another desegregated school in another section of town. The two girls were to meet after school the next day and Susanne was to take Pam home to meet the group of kids who were going to plan the campaign. On that day Pam waited after school for Susanne, who never showed up. The next day Susanne gave some excuse and the meeting was scheduled for Saturday. Susanne would call Friday night and let Pam know what time. Susanne never called. During the next week appointments were made by Susanne and never kept. Meanwhile the other vice-presidential candidate had his posters up, had started giving after-school parties, and had lined up a group of girls to be cheerleaders.

Pam realizing the crux of the difficulty began to try to organize her own campaign with the help of some of her black friends in her neighborhood and at school. In the course of the campaign, Pam became very depressed for she could not compete with the after-school parties and other outside school events that her opponent could provide.

Susanne felt guilty and tried to avoid Pam. The situation grew very tense between the two girls. The other black students began to feel resentful and several fights started. One day in history class the two girls started to argue. The black history teacher who had been watching the development of events had the two girls stay after school. In the discussion that followed Susanne started to cry. Her parents, who had said they were pleased that Susanne was attending a desegregated school, had been very pleased to have Susanne be campaign manager and organize parties at their home, etc. Susanne never told her parents that Pam was black and on the day that Pam was to come to Susanne's house, Susanne's mother came to the school to pick up the girls and take them shopping for posters and paints. Susanne got out of school first and ran to the car and got in. When Pam came out of school and stood at the designated meeting place, Susanne pointed her out and was climbing out of the car to get her when her mother ordered her into the car and drove her home.

Susanne's mother was very angry that her daughter would consider having "one of them" in her house. "It's all right to go to school with them, but you never bring them home. What would our neighbors think and what about your father's job?" Susanne tried to explain that she had promised to be Pam's manager and how much fun it would be to have campaign parties at her house. Her parents refused. Susanne was too ashamed and too bewildered to tell Pam. She was afraid Pam would hate her and retaliate in some way.

The girls talked about school desegregation and the problems that had occurred. Susanne shared with Pam the attitudes of some of the white students toward the black students, some negative, some fearful. Pam shared her feelings with Susanne, describing how unwelcomed many of the black students felt. The black history teacher arranged for the campaign meetings to occur after school under her supervision and within a week's time, more posters were made for Pam, a campaign song was developed, and a cheerleading team was developed. The black history teacher allowed Pam to hand out brochures and candy cigars to all her classes (although this was against school regulations) in lieu of the parties. The teacher also tried to initiate some discussions among Susanne and her white friends about how to make the black students feel more welcomed. Some suggestions were made.

Pam lost the election by 30 votes. However, her parents had decided to send her to a Northern boarding school.

Susanne never followed through on initiating a program to welcome new students; as she confided to one of the white students, she was afraid that the other students would call her "a nigger lover."

In an interview with a black mother who had a six-year-old son in a desegregated school the following story was related:

"Last year Jimmy was in kindergarten at an all-black school where I was teaching. The kindergarten class was overcrowded, 33 students, and the first grade that he was scheduled to enter was going to have 40. When I got reassigned to teach English at a desegregated junior high school, I decided to put Jimmy in a desegregated elementary school near where I was to work. In the first-grade class at the desegregated school there were 28 children plus new reading methods were also going to be introduced. Jimmy was already reading at second-grade level and I knew at the all-black school they would not have an advanced reading group for him. My husband and I also thought that it was not a good idea for Jimmy to be at the same school where I taught and by transferring him we would solve several problems. We realized that the school had only one black teacher and about 12 black students, but Jimmy is very bright, has always been very outgoing, and has played with white children in the summer in Pittsburgh when we visit my sister. As a matter of fact, he went to a three-day interracial summer nursery school program last summer in Pittsburgh and loved it.

"Well, when fall came and Jimmy went to his new school, he was very excited about going to the new school. I had taken him there for a visit so that the school would not seem so strange to him. Shortly after school began, Jimmy began to have nightmares; some white man was chasing him with a knife. This went on, off and on, for about the first term and then subsided. Then he began to develop stomachaches and several times I was called to come get him from school because he had vomited. The stomachaches occurred every morning and he would refuse to go to school. At first we thought he was faking, but when the vomiting started we took him to see our family doctor and he had every test in the book. Nothing could be found. Then he started to say he hated black people and wished he were white. The nightmares began to occur again, but this time there were always big black monsters with white teeth. When I talked with his teacher, she said he was a good student but very, very quiet and preferred to stay indoors at recess.

"At Easter vacation he went to Pittsburgh to visit my sister with my husband and me. My sister has a boy who is a Cub Scout at their church, which is interracial, where Jimmy had gone to summer nursery school. The church was having several activities for children during the Easter vacation. He went to an Easter Egg Hunt with my nephew, stayed 15 minutes and then ran home in terror. When I asked him what was the matter, he said he was afraid of all those white people. He was certain they were going to kill him. During the rest of the visit he would only go out with me or my husband and whenever he saw a white person he cried out with fear. Now my husband and I don't know what to do. We went up to school and talked with his teacher and the principal. We just couldn't understand what was happening.

"Three days ago we got a call from the black teacher at the school. She said that Jimmy has the most bigoted teacher in the school. This white teacher still doesn't speak to this black teacher who has been there two years. The principal and the other teachers apologize for her. One day the black teacher just happened to come into the teacher's lounge unnoticed and heard Jimmy's teacher say 'That nigger kid vomited in my class again, so I made him get the mop and clean it up himself. The janitor told me that he wasn't going to clean up after any nigger kid and I don't blame him.'

"One day after school when I was a little late picking him up, the black teacher happened to come out of the school and see six fifth- and sixth-grade boys holding Jimmy; they ran when they saw her. Jimmy told her that they said that if he told on them that they'd get their fathers to kill his dad just the way Ray had killed Martin Luther King.

"The black teacher told him to be sure to tell his mother and reported the incident to the principal whose response was 'Now, Ada, don't go get touchy; boys will be boys.' When the black teacher asked Jimmy if he had told us, he lied and said yes. When we asked him about it, he started to cry and said, 'Now they'll kill Daddy?' (By this time the mother was in tears) He said that one of the older boys had told him, 'If any of the white kids do anything to you, don't report it because the principal said that he did not want any racial fighting. If you tell on a white kid and get him in trouble, he'll go tell his father and then his father will get your dad. That's what had happened to a black student at the school last year.'"

Greensboro is a pretty town. The white people are proud of the prosperity and the progressive moves made by the state. They feel that it is different in Greensboro than in other parts of the South and that given time the racial problem will solve itself.

1. Greensboro Daily News. Wednesday, April 30, 1969, p. B5.

15

Self-Concept Scores in Greensboro

Four hundred and seventy white and black students in seventh, eighth, and ninth grades from five public schools in Greensboro participated in the study. The number of males represented was 238; 163 were white and 75 were black. Among the 232 females who participated, 147 were white and 85 were black. Of the five schools participating three schools were desegregated schools: (1) a 10 percent black school which had been desegregated for four years; (2) a 10 percent black school which had been desegregated for six years; (3) a 10 percent black school which had been desegregated for eight years.

Among the segregated schools participating, one was a totally black segregated school and the other was a predominantly white segregated school, which had less than 10 percent black students enrolled. Ninety-four of the black students were in segregated or black schools, and 66 of the black students were in desegregated schools. Among the white students, 82 were in segregated schools and 228 were in desegregated schools (see Table 1).

Of the 470 students tested, 160 students were black and 310 were white. The mean total positive score for all students participating in the study was 335.5 which falls into the 35th percentile for the self-concept scale. Nineteen percent of all students tested scored below 300, or below the 7th percentile for the self-concept scale. Twenty-eight percent scored 350 or above, which is in the 50th percentile for the test. Some 6 percent of the students scored above 400 or above the 97th percentile. The mean self-criticism score for the entire group of students tested was 36.3, indicating a general capacity for some openness in analyzing the self. The mean vari-

TABLE 1

Population Sample According to Sex, Race, and Type of School in Greensboro

Males 238				Females 232			
White 163		Black 75		White 147		Black 85	
Segregated 41	Desegregated 122	Segregated 46	Desegregated 29	Segregated 41	Desegregated 106	Segregated 48	Desegregated 37

Number of Public Schools = 5

Segregated or Predominantly White Schools = 1
Segregated Black Schools = 1
Desegregated Schools = 3

ability score for the Greensboro students was 54.7, indicating a moderate degree of variability from one area of self-perception to the other. The Greensboro students achieved a mean distribution score of 126.4, reflecting some uncertainty about the self-picture (see Table 2).

GREENSBORO'S BLACK STUDENTS

The black students who participated were 75 boys and 85 girls. These 160 black students achieved a total positive mean score of 337 with 18 percent scoring below 300, 23 scoring 350 and above, and 6 percent scoring above 400 (see Table 2). The students demonstrated average ability for openness and defensiveness as reflected by their mean self-criticism score of 35.2. They had a tendency for great variability from one area of self-perception to the other as reflected by their mean variability score of 56.9. The black students felt very definite and certain about their self-concepts as reflected by the mean distribution score of 130.

THE BLACK GIRLS IN GREENSBORO

Of the 85 black girls, more than half (48) came from the 100 percent black public school. Although the mean total positive score for the entire group of black girls is 341, the mean total positive score for the 48 girls in the all-black school is 352, falling within the 56th percentile for the self-concept scale (see Table 3). Among the 48 segregated black girls, 52 percent scored 350 or above, with only 10 percent scoring below 300 (7th percen-

TABLE 2
Black and White Students in Greensboro
Grades 7-8-9

Students	Number	TP Mean	TP Percentages	SC Mean	V Mean	D Mean
White	310	334	<300 = 20% >350 = 34% >400 = 5%	37.4	52.6	122
Black	160	337	<300 = 18% >350 = 23% >400 = 6%	35.2	56.9	130
Total	470	335.5	<300 = 19% >350 = 28% >400 = 6%	36.3	54.7	126.4

TABLE 3
Black Girls in Greensboro Grades 7-8-9

Racial Composition of School	Number of Students	TP (Mean)	TP Percentages	SC (Mean)	V (Mean)	D (Mean)
100% Black	48	352	$<300 = 10\%$ $>350 = 52\%$ $>400 = 14\%$	32	55	139
10% Black (4 yrs.)	26	322	$<300 = 34\%$ $>350 = 24\%$ $>400 = 8\%$	39	61	133
Under 10% Black	3	350	$<300 = 0\%$ $>350 = 33\frac{1}{3}\%$ $>400 = 0\%$	39	49	133
10% Black (8 yrs.)	7	333	$<300 = 14\%$ $>350 = 28\%$ $>400 = 0\%$	37	55	124
10% Black (6 yrs.)	1	344	——	25	56	140
Mean Scores for Girls	85	341.0	$<300 = 12\%$ $>350 = 17\%$ $>400 = 5.5\%$	34.5	55	134.5

tile), and as much as 14 percent scoring above 400. The mean self-criticism score for the segregated black girl (32) is low, indicating an inability to be open and critical about the self. The mean variability score (55), however, indicates moderate variability in the self-picture while the mean distribution score (139) indicates that these girls feel very definite and certain about how they think and feel about themselves.

The next largest sampling of black girls came from the 10 percent black public school which had been desegregated for four years. These 26 black girls achieved a mean total positive score of 322. falling within the 20th percentile for the self-concept scale and below the normative mean. It should also be noted that as many as 34 percent of the girls scored below 300 (7th percentile), and only 24 percent achieved a score of 350 or better, while 8 percent scored above 400 (97th percentile). The mean self-criticism score is rather high, 39 (above the normative mean), indicating a healthy openness about the self and the ability to be critical and analytical about the self-picture. However, the very high mean variability score of 61 (above the normative mean), indicates a great deal of variability and inconsistency from one area of self-perception to the other. The mean distribution score of 133 is high, indicating definiteness and certainty about the self-picture.

It is difficult to interpret with certainty the test scores of the black girls in the remaining three schools, the three black students in the less than 10 percent black school, the seven black girls in the 10 percent black school that had been desegregated for eight years, or the one black girl in the 10 percent black school that had been desegregated for six years (see Table 3).

In general, the 85 black girls achieved a total mean positive score of 341, with 12 percent scoring below 300, 17 percent achieving 350 or above, and 5.5 percent scoring above 400. The mean self-criticism score of 34.5 is just below the normative mean score for the test. The mean variability score of 55, which is above the normative mean, indicates average inconsistency in variability from one self-picture to another, and the mean distribution score of 134.5, which is also above the normative mean, indicates relative certainty and definiteness about the self.

The self-concept profile of the 85 black girls find them scoring below the TSCS normative means on the following items:

1. Identity, 117.19
2. Moral-ethical self, 65.60
3. Personal self, 62.92
4. Social self, 67.11 (See Table 8)

THE BLACK BOYS IN GREENSBORO

The majority of the black boys who participated in the study were enrolled in a 100 percent black public school. These 46 black boys achieved a mean total positive score of 334, below the normative mean and in the 30th percentile, with 21 percent scoring below 300, 6 percent scoring above 400, and 36 percent scoring 350 or above. The mean self-criticism score of 35 is equivalent to the TSCS normative mean score. The mean variability score of 56, above the normative mean, indicates some inconsistency from one area of self-perception to another. The mean distribution score of 127, above the normative mean, indicates some uncertainty and indefinitess about the self-perception (see Table 4).

The second largest sampling of black boys came from the 10 percent black public school which had been desegregated for four years. These 19 black boys achieved a mean total positive score of 323, below the normative mean and in the 25th percentile, with 26 percent scoring below 300, five percent scoring above 400, and 20 percent scoring 350 or above. It is interesting to note that this group of black boys achieved a mean self-criticism score of 37, indicating a healthy openness about the self, and an extremely high mean variability score of 62, indicating a great deal of inconsistency about how they felt about themselves. The mean distribution score of 128 indicates some uncertainty about the self-picture.

The number of black boys at the other three schools is relatively small: three at the less than 10 percent black school, four at the 10 percent black

TABLE 4
Black Boys in Greensboro Grades 7-8-9

Racial Composition of School	Number of Students	TP (Mean)	TP Percentages	SC (Mean)	V (Mean)	D (Mean)
100% Black	46	334	<300 = 21% >350 = 36% >400 = 6%	35	56	127
10% Black (4 yrs.)	19	323	<300 = 26% >350 = 20% >400 = 5%	37	62	128
Under 10% Black	3	314	<300 = 2 boys >400 = 1 boy	35	50	126
10% Black (8 yrs.)	4	349	300 to 350 = 3 boys 350 to 400 = 1 boy	35	52	123
10% Black (6 yrs.)	3	353	<300 = 0% 300 to 350 = 1 boy 350 to 400 = 2 boys	36	59	128
Mean Scores for Boys	75	334.6	<300 = 24% >350 = 28% >400 = 6%	36	57	126

school that had been desegregated for eight years, and only three at the 10 percent black school that had been desegregated for six years. The group of 75 black boys achieved a mean total positive score of 334.6 which falls into the 35th percentile for the self-concept scale, and below the normative mean. Twenty-four percent scored below 300, 6 percent scored above 400, and 28 percent scored 350 or above. The mean self-criticism score is 36, the mean variability score is 57, and the mean distribution score is 126. As a whole the black boys demonstrate some capacity for openness, some inconsistency from one area of self-perception to another, and less certainty about how they perceive themselves (see Table 4).

The self-concept profile of the 75 black boys (see Table 9), indicates that the black boys scored below the TSCS normative mean on the following items:

1. Identity, 113.35
2. Behavior, 113.48
3. Moral-ethical self, 62.27
4. Personal self, 61.29
5. Social self, 65.45

WHITE STUDENTS IN GREENSBORO

The 310 white students who participated in the study obtained a mean total positive score of 334, which falls below the TSCS normative mean and in the 35th percentile, with 34 percent achieving a score of 350 or above, 20 percent scoring below 300, and 5 percent above 400. The mean self-criticism score (37.4) is above the normative mean, as is the mean variability score (52.6). The mean distribution score (122) is just above the TSCS normative mean. It would seem that white students in Greensboro have a self-concept of themselves below the normative group but are very critical of themselves, with some variability from one area of self-perception to another, and average certainty about the self (see Table 2).

WHITE BOYS IN GREENSBORO

The 163 white boys who participated in the study were enrolled in five public junior high schools. The mean total positive score achieved by the boys was 333, which falls into the 35th percentile for the self-concept scale and below the normative mean. Thirty-four percent of the boys achieved a score of 350 or more, 18 percent scored under 300, and 4 percent scored over 400. The mean self-criticism score (37.3) is high, above the normative mean, indicating the capacity for openness and the acceptance of mildly derogatory statements about themselves. The mean variability score of 51.2 indicates moderate to little inconsistency from one area of self-perception to the other. However, the mean distribution score of 121.2 indicates some uncertainty about self-perception.

The highest mean total positive score among the white boys was achieved by 47 white boys at the 10 percent black public school which had been desegregated for six years. These boys achieved a mean total positive score of 343, the 45th percentile and below the normative mean, with 45 percent scoring 350 or above, 8 percent scoring above 400, and 14 percent scoring below 300. This group of boys also has the highest mean distribution score of the white boys, achieving a score of 133, indicating definiteness and certainty about the self-perception (see Table 5).

On the self-concept profile, 163 white boys fall behind the TSCS normative mean scores on the following items:

1. Identity, 118.17
2. Behavior, 111.65
3. Moral-ethical self, 67.63
4. Personal self, 60.44
5. Social self, 65.58 (See Table 9)

TABLE 5
White Boys in Greensboro Grades 7-8-9

Racial Composition of School	Number of Students	TP (Mean)	TP Percentages	SC (Mean)	V (Mean)	D (Mean)
10% Black (4 yrs.)	29	334	<300 = 20% >350 = 31% >400 = 0%	39	51	118
Under 10% Black	41	328	<300 = 17% >350 = 31% >400 = 6%	38	50	119
10% Black (6 yrs)	47	343	<300 = 14% >350 = 45% >400 = 8%	36	53	133
10% Black (8 yrs.)	46	323	<300 = 21% >350 = 27% >400 = 4%	37	51	118
Mean Scores for Boys	163	333*	<300 = 18% >350 = 34% >400 = 4%	37.3*	51.2*	121.1*

No statistical significance between white boys and girls on any scores.

WHITE GIRLS IN GREENSBORO

All of the white girls (147) who participated in the study were enrolled in public schools. The group achieved a mean total positive score of 334, below the normative mean and in the 35th percentile, with 22 percent scoring below 300, 6 percent scoring above 400, and 34 percent scoring 350 or above. The mean self-criticism score of 37.5 is high (above the normative mean), indicating a healthy openness and the ability to analyze how one thinks and feels about the self. The mean variability score of 56 is high, indicating some variability from one area of self-perception to the other, and the mean distribution score of 124 indicates some uncertainty about self-perception (see Table 6).

Of the 147 girls tested, those achieving the highest total positive mean score are 33 girls at the 10 percent black school that had been desegregated for eight years and 48 girls at the 10 percent black school that had been desegregated for six years (see Table 6). The 33 girls at the school that had been desegregated for eight years achieved a mean total positive score of 343, the 45th percentile, while those at the school that had been desegregated for six years achieved a mean total positive score of 341, the 40th percentile. The higher mean self-criticism score among the white girls tested was achieved by the 41 girls at the less than 10 percent black school. Their mean self-criticism score of 40, which is above the normative mean, is extremely high, indicating a high degree of self-criticism and openness. Like-

TABLE 6
White Girls in Greensboro Grades 7-8-9

Racial Composition of School	Number of Students	TP (Mean)	TP Percentages	SC (Mean)	V (Mean)	D (Mean)
10% Black (4 yrs.)	25	323	<300 = 32% >350 = 24% >400 = 8%	39	62	133
Under 10% Black	41	329	<300 = 23% >350 = 33% >400 = 0%	40	57	118
10% Black (6 yrs.)	48	341	<300 = 16% >350 = 44% >400 = 6%	35	55	123
10% Black (8 yrs.)	33	343	<300 = 15% >350 = 30% >400 = 12%	37	50	123
Mean Scores for Girls	147	334*	<300 = 22% >350 = 34% >400 = 6%	37.5*	56*	124*

No statistical significance between white boys and girls on any scores.

wise, the 25 white girls at the 10 percent black school that had been desegregated for four years had a mean self-criticism score of 39. This group of 25 white girls achieved the highest mean variability score for the white girls, that of 62, which represents a high degree of inconsistency in self-perception. This same group of 25 white girls also achieved the highest mean distribution score among the white girls tested, that of 133, indicating more definiteness and certainty about the self than the other three groups of white girls (see Table 6).

The self-concept profile of the 147 white girls tested indicates that they fall behind the TSCS normative mean scores on the following items:
1. Identity, 117.32
2. Moral-ethical self, 68.45
3. Personal self, 59.82
4. Social self, 67.07 (See Table 8)

THE COMPARISON OF WHITE AND BLACK STUDENTS IN GREENSBORO

Although TSCS mean scores and profile scores have been discussed for black students and white students in the previous paragraph, a comparison of each group reveals some significant differences in scores. The 160 black junior high school students tested achieved a total positive mean score of

337.32, but it is not statistically significantly different from the score of 333.79 achieved by the 310 white students. (See Table 7.) A comparison of the mean self-criticism score between the black and white students shows the white students with a score of 37.35 and the black students with a score of 35.21; the difference is statistically significant ($p < 0.002$). On the mean variability score, the black students score higher (56.91) than the white students (52.68); the difference is statistically significant ($p < 0.001$). Likewise, on the mean distribution score the black students again scored significantly higher than the white students with a score of 130.98 compared with that of 122.26 for the white students ($p < 0.001$). Thus, on three of the four major TSCS scores the black students achieved higher means than the white students, and the differences are statistically significant except for the total positive score. The white students, however, seem to be more critical of themselves than the black students, and this difference in the ability to

TABLE 7

Comparison of White and Black Students in Greensboro

TSCS Scores		Black Students n = 160	White Students n = 310	Significance
TP	Mean	337.32	333.79	N.S.
	SD*	45.76	39.30	
SC	Mean	35.21	37.35	$p < 0.002$
	SD	6.48	6.20	
V	Mean	56.91	52.68	$p < 0.001$
	SD	13.39	13.38	
D	Mean	130.98	122.26	$p < 0.001$
	SD	25.82	26.15	
Identity	Mean	115.35	117.76	N.S.
	SD	15.69	47.53	
Self-Satisfaction	Mean	106.18	104.93	N.S.
	SD	21.85	18.12	
Behavior	Mean	115.65	113.58	N.S.
	SD	15.33	14.95	
Physical Self	Mean	72.01	72.96	N.S.
	SD	9.66	30.18	
Moral-Ethical Self	Mean	64.01	68.03	N.S.
	SD	11.41	36.40	
Personal Self	Mean	62.14	60.14	N.S.
	SD	12.09	10.34	
Family Self	Mean	72.82	70.47	$p < 0.05$
	SD	12.80	12.14	
Social Self	Mean	66.32	66.30	N.S.
	SD	10.92	9.02	

SD means standard deviation.

analyze and criticize the self is statistically significant. However, the black students indicate differences in perception of themselves from one area to another area, more so than white students, and this difference is statistically significant. In addition, they feel more definite and certain about themselves than do the white students, a difference which is also statistically significant. (See Table 7.)

A comparison of black and white students on the TSCS profile scores shows that both groups fall behind the self-concept mean scores on such items as identity, moral-ethical self, personal self, and social self. Only the white students fall behind the TSCS normative mean score on behavior. A closer look at the profile scores indicates that white students score higher (117) than black students (115) on identity, but the difference is not statistically significant. On the behavior score, black students score higher (115) than white students (113), but the difference is not significant. Both groups score about the same on physical self, but on moral-ethical self the white students achieve a mean score of 68 compared with the mean score of 64 for black students; this difference is not statistically significant. On personal self black students (62.14) score higher than white students (60.14); the difference is not statistically significant. However, on the family-self mean score, the difference is statistically significant ($p < 0.05$), with black students achieving a mean score of 72.82 compared with a mean score of 70.47 for white students. Both groups achieve identical mean scores on the social self (see Table 7).

When sex is considered as well as race some differences are revealed. When black girls are compared to white girls (see Table 8), black girls achieve a higher mean total positive score (341) than the white girls (326); the difference is not statistically significant. The difference between the mean self-criticism score of the black girls and white girls is statistically significant ($p < 0.03$), with the white girls achieving a mean score of 36.82 compared with that of 34.84 for the black girls. There is no significant difference between the mean variability score of black and white girls, but there is a significant difference between the two groups on the mean distribution scores ($p < 0.001$). In this instance, the black girls achieve a mean distribution score of 135.20 compared with 121.53 for the white girls. Although both groups score below the TSCS mean profile scores on identity, moral-ethical self, personal self, and social self, there is a significant difference between black and white girls on the moral-ethical mean scores ($p < 0.04$) with the white girls achieving a mean score of 68.45 compared with a mean score of 65.60 for the black girls. On the personal-self mean score, however, the black girls achieve a mean score of 62.92 compared with a mean score of 59.82 for the white girls; the difference is statistically significant ($p < 0.04$).

A comparison of black and white boys in Greensboro (see Table 9) shows that there is no significant difference between the two groups on the

TABLE 8
Comparison of Black and White Girls in Greensboro

TSCS Scores		Black n = 85	White n = 147	Significance
TP	Mean	341.00	336.25	N.S.
	SD*	47.94	36.65	
SC	Mean	34.84	36.82	p < 0.03
	SD	7.35	6.36	
V	Mean	56.79	54.32	N.S.
	SD	13.83	13.23	
D	Mean	135.20	121.53	p < 0.001
	SD	25.67	23.38	
Identity	Mean	117.19	117.32	N.S.
	SD	16.67	12.63	
Self-Satisfaction	Mean	106.17	103.85	N.S.
	SD	23.02	17.54	
Behavior	Mean	117.65	115.66	N.S.
	SD	14.68	13.02	
Physical Self	Mean	72.44	71.07	N.S.
	SD	9.28	9.05	
Moral-Ethical Self	Mean	65.60	68.45	p < 0.04
	SD	11.62	9.36	
Personal Self	Mean	62.92	59.82	p < 0.04
	SD	12.53	10.40	
Family Self	Mean	72.95	70.86	N.S.
	SD	12.97	11.11	
Social Self	Mean	67.11	67.07	N.S.
	SD	11.64	8.96	

*SD means standard deviation.

mean total positive score or the mean distribution score. However, there is a significant difference between the mean self-criticism scores of the black and white boys ($p < 0.03$), with the white boys achieving a mean score of 37.37, compared with a mean score of 35.62 for the black boys. When the mean variability scores are compared, the black boys score higher (57.05) than the white boys (51.15) and the difference is statistically significant ($p < 0.001$). Although black boys and white boys score below the TSCS normative mean scores for profile items such as identity, behavior, moral-ethical self, personal self, and social self, the black boys score higher than the white boys on self-satisfaction, behavior, personal self, and family self. None of these differences is statistically significant. On the other hand, the white boys score higher than the black boys on profile items such as identity, physical self, and moral-ethical self; but none of these differences is statistically significant (see Table 9).

TABLE 9
Comparison of Black and White Boys in Greensboro

TSCS Scores		Black n = 75	White n = 163	Significance
TP	Mean SD*	333.31 43.25	331.52 41.61	N.S.
SC	Mean SD	35.62 5.38	37.37 6.06	p < 0.03
V	Mean SD	57.05 12.99	51.15 13.37	p < 0.001
D	Mean SD	126.37 25.35	122.94 28.54	N.S.
Identity	Mean SD	113.35 14.38	118.17 64.94	N.S.
Self- Satisfaction	Mean SD	106.19 20.65	105.94 18.64	N.S.
Behavior	Mean SD	113.48 15.81	111.65 16.35	N.S.
Physical Self	Mean SD	71.54 10.09	74.72 40.96	N.S.
Moral- Ethical Self	Mean SD	62.27 10.99	67.63 49.79	N.S.
Personal Self	Mean SD	61.29 11.61	60.44 10.31	N.S.
Family Self	Mean SD	72.68 12.69	70.11 13.04	N.S.
Social Self	Mean SD	65.45 10.18	65.58 9.04	N.S.

SD means standard deviation.

When boys and girls of the same race are compared, it is interested to note that the 85 black girls have a higher mean total positive score (341) than do the 75 black boys (333.31). The difference is statistically significant (p < 0.05). (See Tables 8 and 9.) It is also interesting to note that the 147 white girls have a higher mean total positive score (336.25) than do the 163 white boys (331.52); the difference, however, is not statistically significant. There is no significant difference between the black boys and girls on the mean self-criticism score or the mean variability score (black girls have a SC mean of 34.84 and a V mean of 56.79; black boys have a SC mean of 35.62 and a V mean of 57.05). However, there is a statistically significant difference between the black girls and the black boys on the mean distribution score; the black girls achieve a mean score of 135.20 compared with a mean score of 126.37 for the black boys (p < 0.001). A comparison of the white girls and white boys on the mean self-criticism score, the mean variability score, and the mean distribution score shows no significant difference (see Tables 8 and 9).

When black girls are compared to black boys on the profile scores, black girls score higher than black boys on such items as identity, (117.19 for black girls and 113.35 for black boys); behavior (117.65 for black girls, 113.48 for black boys); physical self (72.44 for black girls and 71.54 for black boys); moral-ethical self (65.60 for black girls and 62.27 for black boys); personal self (62.92 for black girls and 61.29 for black boys); and social self (67.11 for black girls and 65.45 for black boys). However, none of these differences is statistically significant.

A comparison of the 147 white girls with the 163 white boys on the self-concept profile score shows that the white boys score slightly higher than the white girls on such profile items as identity, self-satisfaction, physical self, and personal self; but none of these differences is statistically significant. On the other hand, the white girls score slightly higher than the white boys on such profile items as behavior, moral-ethical self, and social self; none of these differences is statistically significant. (See Tables 8 and 9.)

A COMPARISON OF STUDENTS IN SEGREGATED AND DESEGREGATED SCHOOLS

When black students in segregated schools are compared with black students in desegregated schools, the following differences can be noted (see Table 10):

1. Black students in segregated schools achieve a higher mean total positive score (343.43) than do black students in desegregated schools (327.55). The difference is statistically significant ($p < 0.02$).
2. Black students in segregated schools score lower on the self-criticism score (33.81) than do those in desegregated schools (37.29). The difference is statistically significant ($p < 0.001$).
3. Black students in segregated schools score lower on the variability score (55.42) than do those in desegregated schools (59.12). The difference is not statistically significant.
4. Black students in segregated schools achieve a higher mean distribution score (132.06) than do those in desegregated schools (129.38). The difference is not statistically significant.

A comparison of the 94 black students in segregated schools with the 66 black students in desegregated schools on the self-concept profile scores shows that the black students in segregated schools not only score higher on

TABLE 10

Comparison of Black Students in Segregated and Desegregated Schools in Greensboro

TSCS Scores		Segregated n = 94	Desegregated n = 66	Significance
TP	Mean	343.93	327.55	p < 0.02
	SD*	45.22	45.14	
SC	Mean	33.81	37.29	p < 0.001
	SD	6.53	5.86	
V	Mean	55.42	59.12	N.S.
	SD	13.29	13.35	
D	Mean	132.06	129.38	N.S.
	SD	26.26	25.28	
Identity	Mean	117.56	112.09	p < 0.03
	SD	15.48	15.55	
Self-Satisfaction	Mean	108.65	102.53	N.S.
	SD	21.94	21.37	
Behavior	Mean	117.44	113.01	N.S.
	SD	15.54	14.73	
Physical Self	Mean	72.78	70.87	N.S.
	SD	8.47	11.16	
Moral-Ethical Self	Mean	65.05	62.47	N.S.
	SD	11.61	11.02	
Personal Self	Mean	63.12	60.70	N.S.
	SD	12.18	11.90	
Family Self	Mean	75.12	69.43	p < 0.005
	SD	12.27	12.90	
Social Self	Mean	67.62	64.40	N.S.
	SD	10.91	10.85	

SD means standard deviation.

the three major profile scores such as identity, self-satisfaction, and behavior, but also score higher on the sub-profile scores measuring physical self, moral-ethical self, personal self, family self, and social self. Those differences which are statistically significant are the mean identity scores ($p < 0.03$) in which the segregated black students achieved a mean score of 117.56, compared with a mean score of 112.09 for the desegregated group. The difference between the segregated and desegregated group is also statistically significant ($p < 0.005$) on the family-self item on which the segregated black students achieved a mean score of 75.12 compared with a mean score of 69.43 for the desegregated black students. (See Table 10.)

When black girls in segregated schools are compared with black girls in desegregated schools, the following differences emerge (see Table 11):

TABLE 11

Comparison of Black Girls in Segregated and Desegregated Schools in Greensboro

TSCS Scores		Segregated n = 48	Desegregated n = 37	Significance
TP	Mean SD*	351.93^2 46.47	326.41 46.56	$p < 0.01$
SC	Mean SD	32.35 7.22	38.16 6.19	$p < 0.001$
V	Mean SD	54.89 14.54	59.33 12.56	N.S.
D	Mean SD	138.10^2 27.05	131.33 23.52	N.S.
Identity	Mean SD	120.41^1 15.72	112.88 17.14	$p < 0.04$
Self- Satisfaction	Mean SD	110.75 24.18	100.08 20.12	$p < 0.03$
Behavior	Mean SD	120.77^1 13.84	113.50 14.93	$p < 0.02$
Physical Self	Mean SD	73.41 7.88	71.13 10.85	N.S.
Moral- Ethical Self	Mean SD	68.18^1 11.08	62.16 11.57	$p < 0.01$
Personal Self	Mean SD	64.41 13.34	60.94 11.24	N.S.
Family Self	Mean SD	76.16 12.31	68.66 12.74	$p < 0.008$
Social Self	Mean SD	69.58 11.19	63.83 11.57	$p < 0.02$

*SD means standard deviation.
[1] Significant at the 5 percent level between segregated black girls and boys.
[2] Significant at the 1 percent level between segregated black girls and boys (see Table 12).

1. The 48 black girls in segregated schools achieved a mean total positive score of 351.93 compared with that of 326.41 for the 37 black girls in desegregated schools. The difference is statistically significant ($p < 0.01$).
2. The black segregated girls achieved a lower mean self-criticism score than did the black desegregated girls, the former having a mean score of 32.35, the latter one of 38.16. The difference is statistically significant ($p < 0.001$).
3. The black segregated girls have a lower mean variability score (54.89) than do the black desegregated girls (59.33). The difference is not significant.

4. The black segregated girls had a higher mean distribution score (138.10) than the black desegregated girls (131.33). The difference is not statistically significant.

On the three major profile items, i.e., identity, self-satisfaction, and behavior, the black girls in segregated schools have higher mean scores on all three items than the black desegregated girls. The differences on all three profile items are statistically significant (identity, $p < 0.04$; self-satisfaction, $p < 0.03$; behavior, $p < 0.02$). Likewise, on the five sub-profile items, i.e., physical self, moral-ethical self, personal self, family self, and social self, the black segregated girls score higher on all five items than the black desegregated girls. The difference is statistically significant for the mean scores on moral-ethical self ($p < 0.01$), family self ($p < 0.008$), and social self ($p < 0.02$) (see Table 11).

In comparing black boys in segregated schools with those in desegregated schools, there is no statistical significance in the total positive mean scores of the black segregated boys (335.93) and the black desegregated boys (328.96). Also, there is no statistically significant difference between the mean self-criticism scores of the segregated (35.27) and the desegregated (36.20); the mean variability scores of the segregated (55.95) and the desegregated (58.85); and the mean distribution scores of the segregated (126.02) and the desegregated (126.96). Likewise, on the three major profile scores and five sub-profile scores, the black boys in segregated schools have a tendency to score slightly higher than the desegregated black boys on all items with the exception of the moral-ethical self (the desegregated groups score slightly higher) and the social self (both groups score the same). However, none of these differences is statistically significant (see Table 12).

When the 29 black boys in desegregated schools are compared with the 37 black girls in desegregated schools, there is little difference between the two groups on any of the self-concept scores. The black desegregated girls achieved a total positive mean score of 326.41 and the black desegregated boys achieved a TP mean score of 328.96. This difference is not statistically significant and there is no significant difference between the two groups on the TSCS profile scores (see Tables 11 and 12).

When the 48 black girls in the segregated schools are compared with the 46 black boys in the segregated schools the differences in their total positive mean score are statistically significant at the 1 percent level; the boys have a TP mean of 335.93 and the girls have a TP mean of 351.93. The other significant difference is in the mean distribution score, where the black segregated girls achieve a mean distribution score of 138.10 compared with that of the black segregated boys of 126.02; the level of significance is at the

TABLE 12

Comparison of Black Boys in Segregated and Desegregated
Schools in Greensboro

TSCS Scores		Segregated n = 46	Desegregated n = 29	Significance
TP	Mean	335.93[2]	328.96	N.S.
	SD*	42.94	44.08	
SC	Mean	35.27	36.20	N.S.
	SD	5.44	5.32	
V	Mean	55.95	58.86	N.S.
	SD	12.03	14.48	
D	Mean	126.02[2]	126.96	N.S.
	SD	24.23	27.54	
Identity	Mean	114.70[1]	111.10	N.S.
	SD	14.85	13.53	
Self-Satisfaction	Mean	106.56	105.58	N.S.
	SD	19.47	22.80	
Behavior	Mean	114.12[1]	112.41	N.S.
	SD	16.56	14.72	
Physical Self	Mean	72.14	70.55	N.S.
	SD	9.06	11.71	
Moral-Ethical Self	Mean	61.91[1]	62.86	N.S.
	SD	11.38	10.48	
Personal Self	Mean	61.83	60.41	N.S.
	SD	10.89	12.86	
Family Self	Mean	74.08	70.37	N.S.
	SD	12.27	13.26	
Social Self	Mean	65.66	65.10	N.S.
	SD	10.37	10.03	

*SD means standard deviation.
[1]Significant at the 5 percent level between segregated black girls and boys.
[2]Significant at the 1 percent level between segregated black girls and boys (see Table 11).

1 percent level. Other significant differences are in the mean identity score, with a significance at the five percent level (segregated black girls, 120.01; segregated black boys, 114.70). The difference in the mean behavior score is significant at the five percent level, with the black segregated girls having a mean score of 120.77 and the black boys having a mean score of 114.12. On the moral-ethical-self items, the black segregated girls have a mean score of 68.18 compared with that of 61.91 for the segregated black boys. The level of significance is at the five percent level.

A comparison of white students in desegregated and segregated schools in Greensboro shows that the 228 white students in desegregated schools achieve a total positive mean of 334.5 compared with a total positive mean of 328.9 for the 82 white students in segregated schools. The difference, however, is not statistically significant. The mean self-criticism scores and the mean variability scores for the two groups are quite similar: the desegregated group achieves a mean SC of 37, the segregated group a mean SC of 39; the desegregated group achieves a mean V score of 54, and the segregated group achieves a mean V of 53.5. The desegregated white students achieve a mean distribution score of 124.5 compared with a mean distribution score of 118.5 for the segregated white group; the difference, however, is not statistically significant. (See Tables 13 and 14.)

TABLE 13

White Students in Segregated Schools in Greensboro†

Number of Students	Sex	TP (Mean)	TP Percentages	SC (Mean)	V (Mean)	D (Mean)
41	*Boys	328	<300 = 17% >350 = 31% >400 = 6%	38	50	119
41	*Girls	329	<300 = 23% >350 = 33% >400 = 0%	40	57	118
82		328.9	<300 = 20% >350 = 32% >400 = 3%	39	53.5	118.5

*No statistical significance on TSCS scores between boys and girls.
†No statistical significance between segregated and desegregated students on any scores.

TABLE 14

White Students in Desegregated Schools in Greensboro†
Grades 7-8-9

Number of Students	Sex	TP (Mean)	TP Percentages	SC (Mean)	V (Mean)	D (Mean)
122	*Boys	333	<300 = 25% >350 = 34% >400 = 4%	37	52	123
106	*Girls	336	<300 = 21% >350 = 33% >400 = 9%	37	56	126
228		334.5	<300 = 23% >350 = 34% >400 = 7%	37	54	124.5

*No statistical significance between boys and girls on any scores.
†No statistical significance between segregated and desegregated students on any scores.

Comparison of white boys and white girls in desegregated schools shows that the white girls score slightly higher than the white boys on the mean total positive scores, mean variability scores, and mean distribution scores; but their differences are not statistically significant. The profile scores of white girls in desegregated schools compared with white boys in desegregated schools are very similar, with no significant differences (see Tables 15 and 16).

A comparison of the self-concept scores of white boys and girls in segregated schools reveals great similarity, with the exception of the variability score where the white girls score higher than the white boys. This difference, however, is not statistically significant (see Table 13). The self-concept profiles of white boys and girls in segregated schools reveal no significant differences.

TABLE 15

White Girls in Segregated and Desegregated Schools in Greensboro Grades 7-8-9

Number of Students	Type of School	TP (Mean)	TP Percentages	SC (Mean)	V (Mean)	D (Mean)
41	Segregated	329*	<300 = 23% >350 = 33% >400 = 0%	40	57	118
106	Desegregated	336*	<300 = 21% >350 = 33% >400 = 9%	37	56	126*

Significant difference at the 5 percent level.

TABLE 16

White Boys in Segregated and Desegregated Schools in Greensboro Grades 7-8-9

Number of Students	School	TP (Mean)	TP Percentages	SC (Mean)	V (Mean)	D (Mean)
41	*Segregated	328	<300 = 17% >350 = 31% >400 = 6%	38	50	119
122	*Desegregated	333	<300 = 25% >350 = 34% >400 = 4%	37	52	123

No statistical significance in any of scores between the two groups.

A comparison of white girls in segregated schools with white girls in desegregated schools indicates that the 106 white girls in desegregated schools achieve a total mean positive score of 336, while the 41 white girls in segregated schools achieve a total positive mean score of 329. The difference is significant at the 5 percent level. Likewise, the white girls in desegregated schools achieve a higher mean distribution score (126) than the white girls in segregated schools (118); the difference is significant at the 5 percent level. There is no significant difference between the self-concept profile scores when white girls in desegregated schools are compared with white girls in segregated schools (see Table 15).

When white boys in segregated schools are compared with white boys in desegregated schools, the desegregated group achieves a higher total positive mean score than the segregated group, but the difference is not statistically significant (see Table 16). The mean self-criticism scores and the mean variability scores are very similar for the two groups. The white boys in desegregated schools have a higher mean distribution score (123) than white boys in segregated schools (119), but the difference is not statistically significant.

Although white students in desegregated schools (228) have a tendency to score higher on the self-concept scale than white students in segregated schools (82), the difference is not statistically significant. It is also interesting to note that white students in desegregated schools tend to score higher on the distribution score (124.5) than do white students in segregated schools (118.5), but the difference is not statistically significant (see Table 13).

PART FIVE

Black Monday's Children

16

The Three Cities:
A Summary of the Findings

THE SAMPLE OF STUDENTS TESTED

The three cities studied included 1,720 students—634 from New Orleans, 616 from Nashville, and 470 from Greensboro. Of the 1,720 students participating, 775 were black and 945 were white; 760 were boys and 960 were girls. A total of 21 junior high schools participated, including 15 public schools and 6 parochial schools. Among the schools participating five were segregated or predominantly white, six were segregated or predominantly black, and ten were desegregated schools. In the ten schools classified as desegregated the black enrollment ranged from 10 to 59 percent. Those schools classified as segregated or predominantly white included two 100 percent white schools in Nashville, two less than 10 percent black schools in New Orleans, and one school in Greensboro with less than 10 percent black enrollment. The six segregated or predominantly black schools consisted of five 100 percent black schools and one school with over 80 percent black enrollment. Thus, the definition of segregated or desegregated was dependent on what would constitute racial balance or imbalance according to HEW guidelines. (See Table 1.)

The number of students in segregated schools in the three cities numbered 800 compared with 920 students in desegregated schools. Of the segregated students, 455 were black, attending segregated or predominantly black schools, and 370 were white, attending white segregated or predominantly white schools. The desegregated group consisted of 320 black students at desegregated schools and 575 white students at desegregated schools (including 50 white students at the more than 80 percent black school in Nashville classified as a segregated black school and 6 black students at a less than 10 percent black school in Greensboro classified as a segregated white school).

The 760 male participants consisted of 162 white boys at segregated schools, 260 white boys in desegregated schools, 202 black boys at segregated schools, and 136 black boys at desegregated schools. The 960 girls represented consisted of 208 white girls in desegregated schools, 315 white girls in desegregated schools, 253 black girls in segregated schools, and 184 black girls in desegregated schools. Thus, the total number of white boys in the sample was 422 and the total number of white girls was 523. Among the black students 338 were boys and 437 were black girls.

The study was conducted in junior high schools in the three cities. In the seventh grade 605 students were tested, 272 black and 333 white. The eighth-grade students numbered 613; 289 black and 324 white. Among the ninth grade students 217 were black and 280 were white, totaling 497 in all (See Tables 2 and 3). For further breakdown by sex see Table 4.

The age range in New Orleans was from 11 to 18 years; in Greensboro, from 11 to 16 years; and in Nashville, from 11 years to 17 years. There were many students who neglected to include their ages but number of students per age group was as follows: 20 eleven-year-olds, 306 twelve-year-olds, 516 thirteen-year-olds, 490 fourteen-year-olds, 275 fifteen-year-olds, 67 sixteen-year-olds, 17 seventeen-year-olds, and 3 eighteen-year-olds. Most of the older students were in the New Orleans sample.

TABLE 1
Number of Schools

Segregated Schools n = 11
White = 5
 Public = 3
 Parochial = 2
Black = 6
 Public = 4
 Parochial = 2

Desegregated Schools n = 10
Public = 8
Parochial = 2

TABLE 2
Number of Students Per Age Group

11 yrs.	12 yrs.	13 yrs.	14 yrs.	15 yrs.	16 yrs.	17 yrs.	18 yrs.
20	306	516	490	275	67	17	3

TABLE 3

Number of Students Per Grade

	7th	8th	9th
Black	272	289	217
White	333	324	280
Totals	605	613	497

TABLE 4

Distribution of Sample According to City, Race, Sex, and Type of School

Students Per City:

Greensboro	470
Nashville	616
New Orleans	634
Total	1,720

Number of Students According to Race and Sex:

Black	775	(438 boys, 437 girls)
White	945	(422 boys, 523 girls)
Total	1,720	

Number of Students According to Type of School and Race:

Segrated Schools	800	(320 black, 575 white)
Desegregated Schools	920	(455 black, 370 white)
Total	1,720	

Number of Students According to Sex and Type of School:

Boys	Girls
162 white segregated	208 white segregated
260 white desegregated	315 white desegregated
202 black segregated	253 black segregated
136 black desegregated	184 black desegregated

THE SOCIOECONOMIC AND FAMILIAL DATA

The items on the questionnaire designed to elicit socioeconomic status were related to occupation of mother and father, income of family, as well as father and mother's educational attainment. There was very little success in obtaining incomes of parents; most students were not knowledgeable about family income. Income data were obtained primarily from census tract information as well as from interviews with school personnel. Some students did not know the educational levels of their parents and made "educated guesses"; and some students were uncertain as to occupation. Consequently, the Hollingshead Index or the Warner Index were not used. The socioeconomic data derived is dependent on the students' responses and general categories of lower-, middle-, and upper-class status are assigned according to the responses received.

The degree of family stability was determined by responses of the students as to whether parents were separated, divorced, or together, as well as data regarding with whom students were living. However, many of the questions regarding family life proved to be embarassing to many students and the responses are not completely reliable. In general, information from cum files and school personnel proved to be more reliable. Since the main concern of the research was school desegregation, no attempt was made to interview parents or have parents fill our questionnaires. It was important to keep the nature of the research confidential because school authorities felt that if the true nature of the study were known, or there would be either great resistance a tendency to "put up the best front." In most instances the socioeconomic status of the student body and the general area corresponded with the responses obtained from the students.

In regard to educational attainment of fathers, 55.6 percent of the black students indicated that their fathers had completed high school, compared with 54.3 percent of the white students; 16.6 percent of the black students and 16.6 percent of the white students indicated that their fathers had completed college; and 9.6 percent of the black students and 10 percent of the white students indicated that their fathers had had some college, but had not completed college. Only in Nashville was there a decided difference in educational attainment of black and white fathers with more black fathers completing high school and college (see Chapter 5).

It should be noted that in Nashville the percentage of black fathers in professions is higher than that for whites. In Greensboro and New Orleans the reverse is true. In the entire sample 14.6 percent of the black students report that their fathers are in professions while 22 percent of the white students do; 54.3 percent of black fathers and 47 percent of white fathers are reported to be in the technician-trade category; and 12 percent of black fathers and 13.6 percent of white students have fathers working as laborers.

In comparing educational and occupational status of mothers in the three cities, the black students' mothers have more education, are in more professional jobs, and more often work than do the mothers of white students. Among the total sample from the three cities, 63.3 percent of black mothers and 59.3 percent of white mothers were reported to have finished high school; 14.6 percent of black mothers and 10.3 percent of white mothers had finished college; 7.3 percent of black mothers and 12 percent of white mothers had had some college. Black students reported 57.6 percent of their mothers working, and 45 percent of white mothers were working.

In New Orleans more parents were reported to be separated or divorced than in the other two cities. Also, the families in New Orleans tended to be larger than in the other two cities. No students in Greensboro reported having more than six children in the family. In the entire sample, 75 percent of the black students reported their parents living together and 78.6 percent of the white students reported the same. The percentage of white parents separated or divorced was 20 percent and of black parents, 20.3 percent.

In Nashville the 616 students tested obtained a TP mean score of 340.4, below the normative mean and in the 40th percentile. Sixteen percent of the students scored below the 7th percentile (300), and 8 percent scored above the 97th percentile. Forty-five percent obtained a score of 350 or above. Thus, it would seem that at least 53 percent of the Nashville students have adequate to high self-concepts and score above the normative mean. The V mean score of 53.8 and D mean score of 126.9 are above the normative means, but the mean SC score of 34.6 is below the normative mean. (See Chap. 7, Table 15.)

The TSCS mean scores of the 634 students tested in New Orleans are similar in some respects to those of Nashville. The New Orleans students obtained a TP mean score of 340.3, below the normative mean and in the 40th percentile. Sixteen percent scored below 300, 6 percent scored above 400, and 43 percent obtained a score of 350 or above. At least 49 percent of the New Orleans students have adequate or high self-concepts and score above the normative mean. The mean SC score of 36.1, the mean V score of 56.1, and the mean D score of 132.2 are all above the normative mean and higher than those scores in Nashville. (See Chap. 11, Table 1.)

Greensboro's 470 students do not score as high as the Nashville and New Orleans students on the TP mean score. Their TP mean score of 335.5 is below the normative mean and in the 30th percentile. Nineteen percent of the students score below 300, 6 percent score above 400, and only 28 percent obtained a score of 350 or above. Thus, the majority (about 60 percent) of the Greensboro students have low self-concepts or score below the normative mean. The mean SC score of 36.3 is higher than in Nashville, the same as in New Orleans, and above the normative mean; the mean V score of 54.7 is above the normative mean, higher than in Nashville but lower than in New Orleans; the mean D score of 126.4 is above the normative mean, similar to that in Nashville, but lower than that in New Orleans. (See Chap. 15, Table 2.)

The mean profile scores for the students from each city are as follows:

	Nashville	New Orleans	Greensboro
Identity	117.05	111.55	115.06
Self-Satisfaction	107.51	105.05	110.40
Behavior	118.11	114.61	115.54
Physical Self	72.27	72.48	72.11
Moral-Ethical Self	66.06	66.02	67.92
Personal Self	64.35	61.14	67.16
Family Self	74.49	71.64	72.60
Social Self	67.53	66.31	66.06

It should be noted that the students from all three cities score below the normative mean for identity (127.10), for moral-ethical self (70.33), and for social self (68.14). There is a tendency in all the subgroups compared for students to score below the normative mean on these three scores. The three groups of students scored above the normative means on self-satisfaction, physical self, and family self. The groups tend to vary in whether they scored above, below, or equal to the normative means on behavior (Nashville above, Greensboro below, and New Orleans equal) and personal self (Nashville equal, Greensboro below, and New Orleans above).

COMPARISON OF BLACK STUDENTS IN EACH CITY

The results of the TSCS scores for black students have been discussed in Chapter 7 for Nashville (see Chap. 7, Table 15), Chapter 11 for New Orleans (see Chap. 11, Table 1), and Chapter 15 for Greensboro (see Chap. 15, Table 2). For a full scale comparison parts of Chapter 8, Table 1; Chapter 12, Table 8; and Chapter 15, Table 7, will be reproduced here for convenience in comparing the TSCS scores:

	Nashville	New Orleans	Greensboro
TP	348.36	348.88	337.32
SC	34.30	36.12	35.21
V	54.20	58.33	56.91
D	129.72	140.19	130.98

The Nashville and New Orleans black students score the same on the mean TP score, about the normative mean of 345.57, and in the 55th percentile; but the Greensboro students score below the normative mean and in the 37th percentile. On the mean V and D scores each city scores above the normative means, but New Orleans has the highest mean scores. On the SC mean score, Nashville scores below the normative mean, Greesboro equal to the normative mean, and New Orleans above the normative mean (35.54).

On the profile scores some interesting differences among cities can be noted:

	Nashville	New Orleans	Greensboro
Identity	118.75	117.52	115.35
Self-Satisfaction	110.76	113.97	106.15
Behavior	119.03	117.54	115.65
Physical Self	72.53	74.73	72.01
Moral-Ethical Self	67.12	69.41	64.01
Personal Self	65.70	63.79	62.14
Family Self	75.12	74.86	72.82
Social Self	68.03	66.31	66.32

On the mean identity and mean moral-ethical-self scores, the black students in each city score below the normative mean for each score, although Nashville scores the highest on identity, New Orleans the highest on moral-ethical self, and Greensboro the lowest on both. The black students in all three cities score above the normative mean scores on self-satisfaction, physical, and family self. However, on behavior Nashville and New Orleans black students score above the normative mean, Greensboro black students equal to the normative mean; on personal self only Nashville scores above the normative mean, the other black students in the other two cities below; on social self Nashville black students score equal to the normative mean, New Orleans and Greensboro below.

For a comparison of black girls in each of the three cities see Table 3 in Chapter 8, Table 9 in Chapter 12, and Table 8 in Chapter 15. For a discussion of their scores see Chapters 7 and 8 for Nashville, Chapters 11 and 12 for New Orleans, and Chapter 15 for Greensboro. Black girls in Nashville (346.97) and in New Orleans (352.94) have TP mean scores above the normative mean of 345.57 falling into the 50th and 55th percentile respectively. The black girls in Greensboro have a TP mean score of 341.00, below the normative mean, and in the 40th percentile. Only the black girls in New Orleans score above the normative mean on the SC score, but the black girls in all three cities score above the normative mean for the scale on the mean V and mean D scores, with New Orleans scoring highest for both scores and Nashville lowest for both scores. In all three cities the black girls score below the normative mean on identity and social self, obtaining the same scores on identity (117) and very similar scores on social self. The black girls in Nashville and Greensboro score below the normative mean on moral-ethical self, but the New Orleans black girls score above the normative mean. On self-satisfaction, behavior, physical self, and family self the black girls in all three cities score above the normative means, with Nashville or New Orleans scoring higher than the girls in Greensboro on each score. On the mean personal-self score the black girls in Nashville and New Orleans score equal to the normative mean, but the Greensboro girls score below.

In comparing the black boys from the three cities Table 9 in Chapter 15, Table 2 in Chapter 8, and Table 10 in Chapter 12 should be reviewed for exact scores. Only major differences will be mentioned here inasmuch as detailed discussions have already been presented in Chapters 8, 12, and 15. For TP mean scores the rank order from highest to lowest is

1. Nashville black boys TP mean = 350.20
2. New Orleans black boys TP mean = 348.38
3. Greensboro black boys TP mean = 333.31

Only the New Orleans and Greensboro black boys obtained a SC mean score equal to the normative mean, the Nashville black boys fall behind with a SC mean score of 34.62. On the mean V and D scores all the boys score above the normative means with New Orleans in the lead. The three groups of black boys score below the normative means on identity and moral-ethical self, with the black boys in Nashville obtaining a higher score on identity than the other two groups. On social self both the Greensboro and New Orleans black boys score below the normative mean, while the Nashville boys score equal to the normative mean. On only two other scores are the three groups of black boys all above the normative mean, self-satisfaction and family self, with the black boys from Nashville having a slight lead on both scores. On behavior and physical self the black boys in Nashville and New Orleans score above the normative mean, with the black boys in Greensboro trailing behind the normative mean on behavior and scoring equivalent to the normative mean on physical self. On personal self both the New Orleans and Greensboro black boys score below the normative mean, while the black boys in Nashville score above the normative mean. There is no significant difference on any TSCS scores between black boys and black girls although the black girls have a tendency to score higher on the TP mean score and the profile scores. There are, however, some differences within cities, e.g., in New Orleans the black girls score significantly higher than the black boys on mean TP score, mean self-satisfaction, and mean moral-ethical self.

COMPARISON OF WHITE STUDENTS IN EACH CITY

The TSCS scores of white students in each of the three cities have been presented in previous chapters. An abbreviated form of Chapter 8, Table 1; Chapter 12, Table 8; and Chapter 15, Table 7 is presented for comparison of the scores of white students in each of the three cities. Many more similarities than differences can be noted:

	Nashville	New Orleans	Greensboro
TP	332.56	332.96	333.79
SC	34.97	36.21	37.35
V	53.47	53.95	52.68
D	124.03	124.34	122.26
Identity	115.32	112.60	117.76
Self-Satisfaction	104.26	106.84	104.93
Behavior	117.18	113.54	113.58
Social Self	67.03	65.81	66.30

The white students in all three cities score below the normative mean on the following scores: total positive, identity, moral-ethical self, personal self, and social self. They score above the normative mean on the following scores: variability, distribution, self-satisfaction. The white students from Nashville score above the normative mean on behavior, physical self, and family self; those from New Orleans score below the normative mean on behavior and physical self and equal to the normative mean on family self; the whites from Greensboro score below on behavior, above on physical self, and equal to the normative mean on family self. The white students in New Orleans and Greensboro score above the norm on SC, but those from Nashville score below the norm.

The TSCS scores of white boys in the three cities have been presented in previous chapters. The scores of the white boys are very similar to the scores of the entire sample of white students. The white boys in all three cities score below the normative mean on the following: total positive, identity, moral-ethical self, and social self. They score above the normative mean on the following scores: variability, distribution, and self-satisfaction. In Nashville they score above the normative mean on behavior, physical self, personal self, and family self, and below on SC. In New Orleans they score below the normative mean on behavior, physical self, personal self, and family self, but equal to the normative mean on SC. In Greensboro they score above the norm on SC and physical self, below on personal self, and equal to the norm on family self.

In general the white girls in all three cities tend to score a few points higher than the boys. Like the white boys, they score below the normative mean scores on total positive, identity, moral-ethical self, social self, and personal self. The white girls score equal to, but mostly above the normative means on SC, V, D, and family self. In Nashville they score below the norm on self-satisfaction and physical self, but equal to the norm on behavior; in New Orleans they score below the norm on behavior and physical self and above the norm on self-satisfaction; and in Greensboro they score equal to the norm on self-satisfaction, behavior, and physical self. (See Chap. 8, Table 3; Chap. 12, Table 9; Chap. 15, Table 8.) In general, there are no significant differences between white boys and white girls on any of the TSCS scores in all the cities.

COMPARISON OF WHITE AND BLACK STUDENTS

Finally, in comparing the TSCS scores of the 775 black students with those of the 945 white students, some significant differences can be noted. First of all, the black students score higher on the TP mean score (344.85) than the white students (333.13), and the difference is significant at the 1 percent level (see Table 5). The black students score lower (35.21) than the whites (36.18) on the SC score, but the difference is not significant. On the mean V and D scores (58.48 and 133.63 respectively) blacks score significantly higher than whites (53.37 and 123.54); and the differences in the means are significant at the 5 percent and 1 percent levels respectively. The black students also score significantly higher than the white students on self-satisfaction (110.29 and 105.34 respectively) as well as on family self (74.27 and 71.55 respectively), with a significance at the 5 percent level for both scores.

The 337 black girls score significantly higher than the 523 white girls on TP mean score (significance at the 1 percent level); mean D score (significance at the 1 percent level); mean self-satisfaction score (significance at the

TABLE 5

Comparison of White and Black Southern Children

TSCS Scores		Black n = 775	White n = 945	Significance
TP	Mean SD*	344.85 41.46	333.10 42.57	1%
SC	Mean SD	35.21 6.34	36.18 6.61	N.S.
V	Mean SD	58.48 13.75	53.37 13.33	5%
D	Mean SD	133.63 27.36	123.54 27.84	1%
Identity	Mean SD	117.20 15.26	115.22 26.21	N.S.
Self- Satisfaction	Mean SD	110.29 18.27	105.34 18.78	5%
Behavior	Mean SD	117.40 15.41	114.76 23.40	N.S.
Physical Self	Mean SD	73.09 9.40	71.48 28.53	N.S.
Moral- Ethical Self	Mean SD	66.84 10.40	66.49 19.28	N.S.
Personal Self	Mean SD	63.87 11.67	61.47 18.68	N.S.
Family Self	Mean SD	74.27 12.02	71.55 24.95	5%
Social Self	Mean SD	66.88 10.53	66.38 10.45	N.S.

SD means standard deviation.

1 percent level); mean behavior score (significance at the 1 percent level); mean personal-self score (significance at the 5 percent level); and the mean family-self score (significance at the 5 percent level). (See Table 6.)

The 508 black boys score significantly higher than the 605 white boys on TP mean score (significance at the 1 percent level); mean V score (significance at the 5 percent level); mean D score (significance at the 1 percent level); and mean identity score (significance at the 1 percent level). (See Table 7.)

It should also be noted that in general, regardless of sex or type of school, black students score significantly higher than white students except in the case of desegregated white and black girls in Nashville and Greensboro.

TABLE 6

Comparison of Black and White Girls

TSCS Scores		Black n = 437	White n = 523	Significance
TP	Mean	346.97	335.09	1%
	SD*	41.76	40.04	
SC	Mean	35.15	36.19	N.S.
	SD	6.64	6.46	
V	Mean	55.94	54.14	N.S.
	SD	13.68	12.82	
D	Mean	134.43	122.12	1%
	SD	26.91	25.24	
Identity	Mean	116.96	113.44	5%
	SD	16.22	15.85	
Self- Satisfaction	Mean	110.86	104.35	1%
	SD	18.75	17.48	
Behavior	Mean	118.37	115.40	N.S.
	SD	14.96	13.83	
Physical Self	Mean	73.25	69.91	1%
	SD	9.28	9.07	
Moral- Ethical Self	Mean	68.20	67.73	N.S.
	SD	10.32	9.55	
Personal Self	Mean	63.94	60.41	5%
	SD	11.62	10.91	
Family Self	Mean	74.55	71.46	5%
	SD	12.22	11.58	
Social Self	Mean	66.92	66.50	N.S.
	SD	10.82	9.34	

SD means standard deviation.

TABLE 7

Comparison of Black and White Boys

TSCS Scores		Black n = 338	White n = 422	Significance
TP	Mean	342.29	330.61	1%
	SD*	40.98	44.25	
SC	Mean	35.26	35.90	N.S.
	SD	5.94	6.83	
V	Mean	57.15	52.58	5%
	SD	13.85	13.94	
D	Mean	133.24	125.56	N.S.
	SD	27.72	30.69	
Identity	Mean	116.84	114.08	N.S.
	SD	15.09	33.46	
Self-Satisfaction	Mean	109.53	106.55	N.S.
	SD	17.65	20.26	
Behavior	Mean	116.27	114.30	N.S.
	SD	15.80	30.70	
Physical Self	Mean	72.90	73.32	N.S.
	SD	9.56	40.26	
Moral-Ethical Self	Mean	65.15	64.77	N.S.
	SD	10.30	24.44	
Personal Self	Mean	63.84	62.90	N.S.
	SD	11.70	23.86	
Family Self	Mean	73.89	71.65	N.S.
	SD	11.79	33.97	
Social Self	Mean	66.89	66.35	N.S.
	SD	10.16	11.94	

*SD means standard deviation.

COMPARISON OF SEGREGATED AND DESEGREGATED STUDENTS

COMPARISON OF THE BLACK STUDENTS IN SEGREGATED AND DESEGREGATED SCHOOLS

A comparison of black students in segregated (437) and desegregated (314) schools for Nashville, New Orleans, and Greensboro are given in Chapter 8, Table 4; Chapter 12, Table 2; and Chapter 15, Table 10, respectively. When the entire sample of 437 black students in segregated schools are compared with the 314 black students in desegregated schools, the significant difference in TP means remains. (See Table 8.) The 437 segregated black students score higher on identity, self-satisfaction, and behavior than the 314 black desegregated students but none of the differences are statis-

TABLE 8

Comparison of Black Students in Segregated
and Desegregated Schools

TSCS Scores		Segregated n = 437	Desegregated n = 314	Significance
TP	Mean	349.65	337.81	5%
	SD*	40.27	42.83	
SC	Mean	34.78	35.80	N.S.
	SD	6.48	5.90	
V	Mean	56.04	57.36	N.S.
	SD	13.40	14.21	
D	Mean	133.74	133.50	N.S.
	SD	27.08	28.33	
Identity	Mean	118.84	115.19	N.S.
	SD	15.20	16.25	
Self-Satisfaction	Mean	111.64	107.57	N.S.
	SD	16.34	13.48	
Behavior	Mean	118.66	115.07	N.S.
	SD	22.63	13.09	
Physical Self	Mean	73.57	72.17	N.S.
	SD	7.34	8.33	
Moral-Ethical Self	Mean	67.52	65.89	N.S.
	SD	9.07	9.85	
Personal Self	Mean	67.86	64.44	N.S.
	SD	9.13	10.36	
Family Self	Mean	75.35	72.20	N.S.
	SD	9.95	10.96	
Social Self	Mean	67.59	65.78	N.S.
	SD	9.04	9.50	

*SD means standard deviation.

tically significant. Likewise on the five sub-profile scores the segregated black students score higher than the desegregated students but the differences are not statistically significant.

Within each of the three cities, although the black segregated students score higher than the black desegregated students, the statistical significance for any score is not consistent.

For instance, in Greensboro, Nashville, and New Orleans the segregated black students score higher than the desegregated black students and in Greensboro and New Orleans the difference was significant at the 5 percent level for each (both had $p < 0.02$). In Nashville, however, there was no significant difference between mean TP scores of the two groups.

In Greensboro, not only is there a significant difference between the segregated and desegregated black students on mean TP scores, but also on mean SC score, the desegregated group scoring higher with a significance at the 1 percent level. On identity and family-self mean scores, the segregated black students score higher with a significance at the 5 percent and 1 percent levels respectively.

In New Orleans not only do the segregated black students score significantly higher on the mean TP scores, but also on the mean behavior and mean moral-ethical-self scores with a significance at the 5 percent and 1 percent levels respectively. In Nashville the segregated black students score significantly higher on the mean self-satisfaction and mean personal-self scores with a significance at the 5 percent level for each.

A comparison of the 253 black girls in segregated schools with the 184 black girls in desegregated schools in the three cities reveals that the segregated black girls score higher on the mean TP, D, identity, self-satisfaction, behavior, physical self, moral-ethical self, personal self, family self, and social self scores with a significance at the 5 percent level for the mean TP and self-satisfaction scores. The 184 black desegregated girls score higher on the mean SC and V scores than the 253 black segregated girls but the differences are not statistically significant. (See Table 9.)

In addition to the 253 black girls in segregated schools scoring significantly higher than the 184 black girls in desegregated schools on mean TP score (with a significance at the 5 percent level), the black segregated girls score significantly higher on self-satisfaction, moral-ethical self, and family self (with a significance at the 5 percent level for each mean score).

In Greensboro the desegregated black girls score significantly higher on the mean SC score, a significance at the 1 percent level. The black segregated girls score significantly higher than the black desegregated girls on total positive, identity, self-satisfaction, behavior, moral-ethical self, social self, and family self; the difference is significant at the 5 percent level for each mean score with the exception of family self, which is significant at the 1 percent level.

In Nashville the black segregated girls score significantly higher than the black desegregated girls on self-satisfaction, physical self, and personal self, with a significance at the 5 percent level for each.

In New Orleans the black segregated girls score significantly higher than the black desegregated girls on moral-ethical self, with a significance at the 5 percent level.

There is no significant difference on any TSCS scores between the 202 black boys in segregated schools and the 136 black boys in desegregated

TABLE 9

Comparison of Black Girls in Segregated
and Desegregated Schools

TSCS Scores		Segregated n = 253	Desegregated n = 184	Significance
TP	Mean	353.94	337.66	5%
	SD*	40.32	41.81	
SC	Mean	34.29	36.27	N.S.
	SD	6.76	6.03	
V	Mean	55.56	56.36	N.S.
	SD	13.72	13.70	
D	Mean	135.79	131.59	N.S.
	SD	26.50	27.68	
Identity	Mean	120.02	116.10	N.S.
	SD	15.19	16.63	
Self- Satisfaction	Mean SD	113.30 16.94	106.30 16.10	5%
Behavior	Mean	120.08	115.33	N.S.
	SD	16.76	12.12	
Physical Self	Mean SD	73.78 7.04	71.83 8.09	N.S.
Moral- Ethical Self	Mean SD	69.19 8.66	66.45 9.69	N.S.
Personal Self	Mean SD	65.93 9.92	62.11 9.69	N.S.
Family Self	Mean SD	75.95 9.93	71.72 10.76	N.S.
Social Self	Mean SD	68.45 9.58	65.65 9.18	N.S.

SD means standard deviation.

schools. (See Table 10.) There is no significant difference in Nashville, in New Orleans, or in Greensboro. There are no significant differences when the 136 black boys in desegregated schools are compared with the 184 black girls in desegregated schools, or when the 202 black boys in segregated schools are compared with the 233 black girls in segregated schools. It should be noted, however, that in each of the three cities the black girls in segregated schools tend to score higher than black boys in segregated schools, but black boys in desegregated schools in Nashville and Greensboro tend to score higher than black girls in desegregated schools. In New Orleans, however, the black desegregated girls score higher than the black desegregated boys.

TABLE 10

Comparison of Black Boys in Segregated and Desegregated Schools

TSCS Scores		Segregated n = 202	Desegregated n = 136	Significance
TP	Mean	344.66	337.80	N.S.
	SD*	39.43	43.99	
SC	Mean	35.15	35.22	N.S.
	SD	6.00	5.75	
V	Mean	56.56	58.00	N.S.
	SD	13.14	14.92	
D	Mean	131.90	135.39	N.S.
	SD	26.92	29.19	
Identity	Mean	117.56	114.89	N.S.
	SD	15.24	15.75	
Self-Satisfaction	Mean	109.61	108.96	N.S.
	SD	15.57	17.59	
Behavior	Mean	117.19	114.72	N.S.
	SD	11.97	14.24	
Physical Self	Mean	73.35	72.15	N.S.
	SD	7.67	8.69	
Moral-Ethical Self	Mean	65.58	65.08	N.S.
	SD	9.20	9.92	
Personal Self	Mean	63.71	62.71	N.S.
	SD	9.05	10.97	
Family Self	Mean	74.62	72.71	N.S.
	SD	9.98	11.20	
Social Self	Mean	67.10	66.00	N.S.
	SD	8.09	6.65	

*SD means standard deviation.

COMPARISON OF WHITE STUDENTS IN SEGREGATED AND DESEGREGATED SCHOOLS

A comparison of the 370 white students in segregated schools with the 575 white students in desegregated schools reveals no significant differences on any of the TSCS scores, although the desegregated white students tended to have higher mean TP scores. (See Table 11.) There were some intracity differences, especially in New Orleans where desegregated white students were significantly higher than segregated white students on many scores.

There are no significant differences on any of the TSCS scores between the 208 white girls in segregated schools and the 315 white girls in desegregated schools, although the desegregated girls tend to score higher, especially in Greensboro and New Orleans, on most scores. There are no significant differences on any TSCS scores between 162 white segregated males and the

TABLE 11

Comparison of White Students in Segregated and Desegregated Schools

TSCS Scores		Segregated $n = 370$	Desegregated $n = 575$	Significance
TP	Mean	328.52	334.53	N.S.
	SD*	47.39	41.95	
SC	Mean	36.77	36.05	N.S.
	SD	6.82	6.66	
V	Mean	52.29	54.84	N.S.
	SD	13.38	13.06	
D	Mean	118.45	125.96	5%
	SD	26.61	29.34	
Identity	Mean	112.33	115.25	N.S.
	SD	15.40	25.92	
Self-Satisfaction	Mean	103.37	105.68	N.S.
	SD	21.45	17.66	
Behavior	Mean	112.33	114.23	N.S.
	SD	28.96	14.92	
Physical Self	Mean	69.02	70.86	N.S.
	SD	29.21	16.52	
Moral-Ethical Self	Mean	64.06	66.61	N.S.
	SD	10.68	19.30	
Personal Self	Mean	60.50	61.22	N.S.
	SD	23.87	10.94	
Family Self	Mean	69.38	70.59	N.S.
	SD	31.66	12.84	
Social Self	Mean	65.53	66.20	N.S.
	SD	11.32	9.70	

*SD means standard deviation.

260 white desegregated males although the desegregated students tend to score higher on the mean TP score. In New Orleans, however, there are many significant differences between the desegregated and segregated white boys on many TSCS scores, with the desegregated group scoring higher.

SUMMARY

The following findings should be noted:

1. The 1,720 students score below the normative mean for the scale on identity, moral-ethical self, and social self. This finding does not hold true for all groups but is true for the majority of the groups.

2. The 775 black students score significantly higher than the 945 white students on the TSCS.
3. The 320 black students in segregated schools score significantly higher on the TSCS than the 455 black students in desegregated schools and the significance is decidedly pronounced when sex is considered, for black girls in segregated schools score significantly higher than black girls in desegregated schools.
4. Although white students in segregated and desegregated schools show no significant difference on the TSCS scores, the desegregated students tend to score higher.

The discussion of "Black Monday's Children," the fifth part of this study of school desegregation and self-concept, will include not only a review of the pertinent findings as presented in Chapter 16, but some historical, philosophic, and psychologic concepts that may help the reader understand the "what," "why," and "how" of the impact of school desegregation. No discussion of the results of school desegregation would be complete without an historical review of the implementation decision and the role of the behavioral scientists in outlining some guidelines for implementation. So, once again, the pages of history are turned back in an effort to help us understand the present. An exploration into some of the reasons for high self-concepts among the black students will be presented, followed by a discussion of the low self-concepts among white students. Finally, an attempt will be made to review the current school desegregation process and its implication for the development of America and her children.

17

Behavioral Science and the Law: The Psychosocial Effects of Segregation and Implications for Desegregation

When Chief Justice Earl Warren delivered the opinion of the U.S. Supreme Court on school desegregation on May 17, 1954, he reviewed briefly the doctrine of "separate but equal," which had made its mark on legal history vis-à-vis the 1896 case of *Plessy* v. *Ferguson*. The subsequent impact of that decision on public education, which was noted in the text of his statement as footnotes 6 and 7, has been reviewed in Chapter 2 of this book. He then proceeded to state and answer the basic question before the court:

> Does segregation of children in public schools solely on the basis of race, even though the physical facilities and other "tangible" factors may be equal, deprive the children of the minority of equal education opportunities? We believe that it does.

To support the court's belief that segregated educational facilities deprived minority children of equal educational opportunities, Chief Justice Warren referred to the finding of the Kansas court which had stated:

> Segregation of white and colored children in public schools has a detrimental effect upon the colored children. The impact is greater when it has the sanction of the law; for the policy of separating the races is usually interpreted as denoting the inferiority of the Negro group. A sense of inferiority affects the motivation of a child to learn. Segregation with the sanction of law, therefore, has a tendency to retard educational and mental development of Negro children and to deprive them of some of the benefits they would receive in a racially integrated school system.

This quotation from the Kansas court which was included in the body of the text was noted by footnote 10.

The 11th footnote, and perhaps the most controversial one of the text, made reference to findings of social scientists and is preceded by the following statement:

> Whatever may have been the extent of psychological knowledge at the time of *Plessy* v. *Ferguson*, this finding [referring to the above quotation from the Kansas court] is simply supported by modern authority. Any language in *Plessy* v. *Ferguson* contrary to this finding is rejected.

Who were the modern authorities to which the court made reference in footnote 11 and what kind of data had they presented that the Court had considered so carefully in making its decision? In the famous footnote 11 the following references are cited:

1. K.B. Clark, "The Effects of Prejudice and Discrimination on Personality Development" Mid-Century White House Conference on Children and Youth, 1950.
2. Witmer and Kotinsky, *Personality in the Making*, 1952, Chapter 6.
3. Deutscher and Chein, "The Psychological Effects of Enforced Segregation: A Survey of Social Science Opinion," 26 Journal of Psychology, 259, 1948.
4. Chein, "What are the Psychological Effects of Segregation Under Conditions of Equal Facilities?" 3 International Journal of Opinion and Attitudes Research, 229, 1949.
5. Brameld, *Educational Costs in Discrimination and National Welfare*, McIver, ed., 1949, pp. 44-48.
6. E.F. Frazier, *The Negro in the United States*, 1949, pp. 674-681.
7. Myrdal, *An American Dilemma*, 1944.

It would seem from the lengthy list of references above that the Court had done its homework in considering the psychologic as well as legal aspects of the school desegregation issue. Justice Warren made reference to the extent or rather lack of psychologic knowledge at the time of *Plessy* v. *Ferguson* and at the time of subsequent school issues that had been brought before the Court.[1] One may well ask what was the extent of psychologic knowledge at the time of the decision regarding the effects of segregation on minority children? Perhaps it would be well to review the data as presented in the references cited by the Court on this issue written by the "modern authorities" cited at the same time of the decision before considering the effects of desegregation on minority children as uncovered by the data presented in this research, for that data has many implications on the psychologic effect of present-day school desegregation.

THE APPENDIX TO THE APPELLANTS' BRIEF

That the U.S. Supreme Court gave careful consideration to the findings of social science in the crucial desegregation cases is supported by the emphasis placed in the text of the May 17, 1954, decision on the psychologic damage inherent in racial segregation, as been quoted in previous paragraphs. The first six social science documents noted in footnote 11 came from the social scientists' appendix to the appellants' brief submitted in the October, 1952, term of the Court by 32 social scientists. The appendix supported the argument that separate school facilities for whites and blacks were unequal. It included evidence by professional educators, as well as data from social psychologists and other social scientists, to support the argument that segregation itself is an inequality and that state-imposed racial segregation inflicts injuries upon the black child. This appendix could have occurred only through the close collaboration and cooperation of the social scientists and psychologists with the NAACP legal staff. The history of that collaboration between the social psychologists and the NAACP is given by Dr. Clark:

In February, 1951, Robert L. Carter, one of the lawyers of the National Association for the Advancement of Colored People visited me to inquire whether psychologists had any findings which were relevant to the effects of racial segregation on the personality development of Negro children. He stated that the legal staff of the NAACP had decided to challenge the constitutionality of state laws which required or permitted racial segregation in public schools. Their proposed cases would be tried in an attempt to overrule the *Plessy* v. *Ferguson* "separate but equal" doctrine and to demonstrate that segregated facilities are inherently unequal. Carter and his legal colleagues believed that in order to increase the chances of successfully demonstrating before the federal courts that segregation violated the equal protection clause of the Fourteenth Amendment of the Constitution, the help of psychologists was necessary to evaluate "that racial segregation inflicts psychological damage on its victims." He invited me to collaborate with the lawyers in planning for the most effective use of social psychologists and other social scientists in the courts of first instance and appeal when these cases were heard. On the trial level social scientists participated as expert witnesses giving testimony on the nature of racial segregation, its psychological and personality consequences, and the probable consequence of desegregation. The first of these cases was heard before a federal court in Charleston, South Carolina, on May 28 and 29, 1951. The last of four cases which challenged the constitutionality of state laws requiring or permitting segregated public schools was held in the federal court at Richmond, Virginia, starting on February 25, 1952. On the appeal of these cases to the United States Supreme Court the role of the social scientist was restricted to the preparation of material related to the psychological effects of segregation, the consequences of desegregation, and finally an empirical analysis of techniques for desegregation. The data were collected and analyzed by social scientists and presented to the NAACP attorneys to be used in whatever ways they believed most effective in the presentation of their cases. For the first argument in the October, 1952, term of the Supreme Court the lawyers decided that the social-psychological data should be presented in the form of a special social science brief as an appendix to the regular legal appellant brief. This precedent-setting document entitled "The Effects of Segregation and the Consequences of Desegregation; A Social Science Statement" was prepared by Stuart Cook, Isidor Chein, and me. Thirty-two outstanding American social scientists reviewed and endorsed it for presentation to the highest court of our land.[2]

The role of the social scientists in the 1954 decision has been an issue of great controversy in legal circles. The circuit courts of appeal in Virginia and South Carolina rejected the sociologic evidence as irrelevant. Senator Eastland from Mississippi responded to the decision before the Senate: "Mr. President, in the long history of this country there has never before been a time when an Appellate Court or Supreme Court of the United States relied solely and alone on scientific authority to sustain a legal decision."[3]

Professor Cahn, one of the most ardent critics of the social scientists' role, writes that the social scientist merely testified to the obvious: "For at least twenty years hardly a cultivated person has questioned that segregation is cruel to Negro school children."[4] He caustically contends that it would not be wise "to have the constitutional rights of Negroes—or of other Americans—rest on such flimsy foundation as some of the scientific demonstrations in the records."[5]

He also states, "It is quite another thing to have our fundamental rights rise, fall, or change along with the latest fashions of psychological literature."[6]

On the other side, Jack Greenberg, an assistant NAACP lawyer writes

Social scientists' testimony was used in a wholly different and new way in the recent school segregation cases. There, by placing before the court authoritative scientific opinions regarding the effect of racial classification and of "separate but equal" treatment, the plaintiffs helped persuade the Court in the shaping of a judge-made rule of law.[7]

Just prior to the 1954 decision Kenneth Clark wrote, "Proof of the argument that segregation itself is inequality and that state-imposed racial segregation inflicts injuries upon the Negro had to come from the social psychologists and other social scientists."[8]

Thus, there were many who considered the 1954 decision a "sociological decision."[9]

When the Supreme Court adopted the findings of the lower courts in Kansas and Delaware, it was accepting what these tribunals had adjudged to be truth in the evidence presented before them. And this meant that the Supreme Court had adopted the findings of the lower courts that the psychological and sociological experts were right in declaring that school segregation had a detrimental effect upon the Negro.[10]

THE MID-CENTURY WHITE HOUSE CONFERENCE REPORT

The Mid-Century White House Conference Report on the Effects of Prejudice and Discrimination was largely the responsibility of Dr. Kenneth Clark. That report noted that although there was an abundance of material on the existence of prejudice and discrimination in regard to their origins, as well as techniques to reduce bigoted attitudes, there was little in the scientific literature on the precise effects of prejudice and discrimination on healthy personality development. Nonetheless the report stressed the fact that it was highly probable that prejudice and discrimination had many detrimental effects on the personality development of most minority children in one way or another. The report pointed out that the effects of prejudice and discrimination manifest themselves at an early age, as early as nursery school and kindergarten, and the investigations of Radke, Trager, and Davis; Goodman; Horowitz; and Clark and Clark were used to support this statement.[11]

According to the report, the way in which prejudice and discrimination affect personality development depended on (a) whether the individual lived within a self-contained group of his own or (b) whether he was exposed daily to the contrast between himself and others. The child who is reared in a racially insulated environment passes through the early stages of personality development with little difficulty as far as prejudice is concerned. However, once he leaves that insulated environment "the sudden exposure to the fact that he is not as good as other people is very disrupting to personality development."[12] "It is a shock to the sense of trust, an incitement to feelings of doubt and shame" especially if such a change takes place during adolescence when a sense of identity is in the making.[13]

For those children who have been exposed daily to the fact of their differences, early personality development is more likely to be disturbed. It may be difficult for them to achieve trust. The development of a sense of autonomy may be retarded because of parental fears that independent action will expose the child to danger, and initiative may be curbed by external circumstances because the Negro mother may feel her children must be warned to avoid offending whites. If initiative is curbed too much, then feelings of shame and doubt may be aroused in the children and reinforced by the aspersions they eventually encounter in school or in the community.

> In any case, [the child] who is surrounded by pervasive hostility and rejection and who has become ambivalent in his feelings about himself is likely to react to both the ambiguous and the objectively nonthreatening aspects of his experiences with defensiveness and hypersensitivity. [These children] exhibit a generalized pattern of personality difficulties that seem to be associated with the humiliation to which they are subjected. Not that all of them are obviously emotionally maladjusted. The majority pulls through somehow or other, but with what burdens of resentment and bitterness few know.[14]

To support the kinds of personality reactions that develop in black children the report cited the autobiography of Richard Wright (*Black Boy*) and referred to the writings of Hortense Powdermaker on patterns of aggression among blacks as well as the dynamic formulations on black personality development as formulated by C.V. Quarles; Kardiner and Ovessy; John Dollard; and Warner, Junker and Adams.[15] The report concluded:

> Summing up the evidence in regard to the effects of prejudice, discrimination, and segregation on the personality of Negro children in the United States, we may conclude, then as follows:
> 1. There is a pattern of personality disabilities which seems to be associated with the inferior and rejected minority status of the Negro.
> 2. This pattern includes not only subjective feelings of inferiority, low self-esteem, ambivalent attitudes toward his own group, but also either overt or indirect hostility against both whites and Negroes.
> 3. The particular structure of this pattern does not appear to be the same for, nor is it found to the same degree in, all Negroes.
> 4. Factors such as degree of stability of family and security of the individual within the family setting, individual differences of a constitutional nature, and social and economic level appear to be relevant to the particular kind of personal adjustment made to minority status.[16]

In regard to the personality of the prejudiced person, the report concluded that there was some complex relationship between the total personality structure of an individual and the amount and quality of his prejudices. The studies done up until that time did not show a relationship between amounts of prejudice and personality disturbances.

> Extreme prejudice in an individual may reflect many factors, either acting in aggregate or in different constellations. It may indicate displaced hostility from some nonrelevant source of frustration (e.g., deflected hostility from frustrating parents), or it may be an expression of unresolved guilt, anxiety, and emotional conflicts which arise from sources related or unrelated to the actual objects of prejudice.[17]

The report then goes on to suggest that prejudice may be initiated from basic needs which differ among human beings depending on whether they have a stable or unstable personality structure. The basic needs that might be involved in the etiology of prejudice were enumerated as status needs, hostility needs, in-group identity needs, and conformity needs.

The White House Conference report reviewed some methods that had been used to reduce prejudice and discrimination as well as the effectiveness and obstacles encountered in the various methods used. Particular reference is made to Robin William's comprehensive survey of the chief methods used by various intergroup relations organizations as well as to Arnold Rose's summary of the net results in the reduction of prejudice.[18]

The views of Bettelheim and Janowitz were presented, who maintained that prejudice has its roots based in anxiety and insecurity and consequently can't be dispelled by rational propaganda. According to their theory, the elimination of prejudice must be done on an individual and social level— individuals must be helped to achieve greater personal integration in a social climate of social and economic security.[19]

The famous footnote 11 also referred to the 1947 research of Max Deutscher and Isidor Chein, who questioned over 500 anthropologists, social psychologists, and sociologists regarding the psychologic effects of enforced segregation on the segregated group as well as the group that enforces the segregation.[20] The majority of social scientists polled stated that it was their opinion that segregation had detrimental psychologic effects on the segregated group even if equal facilities are provided. This study was also cited in the appendix to the appellants' brief presented before the Supreme Court. The major comments of those social scientists polled who based their opinions on professional experience and scientific research are summarized succinctly in the Mid-Century White House Conference Report. That summary was as follows:

1. Special stresses are created for individuals by the discrepancy between democratic teachings with respect to equality and the practice of enforced segregation.
2. Segregation is a special source of frustration.
3. Feelings of inferiority and of not being wanted are induced by segregation.
4. Submissiveness, martyrdom, feelings of persecution, withdrawal tendencies, self-ambivalence, and aggression are likely to develop.
5. Distortion in the sense of reality may occur as a consequence of enforced segregation.
6. A few individuals gain psychologically from being members of segregated groups, but more are harmed thereby.[21]

However, it is important to note that the Conference Report, in evaluating some of the research findings, took into account the fact that completely satisfactory research in the field of Negro personality had not been done. Some of the tests used up until that point of time were not completely valid.

MYRDAL'S STUDY

Footnote 11 of Justice Warren's text of the school desegregation decision also made reference to one of the most outstanding and controversial
studies done prior to the Court's decision—Gunnar Myrdal's *An American
Dilemma*. In order to understand the significance of that reference in the
footnote, the nature of that study, and the controversy that grew up around
it, it should be reviewed briefly.

In 1937 the Board of Trustees of the Carnegie Foundation authorized a
comprehensive study of the Negro in America. The decision of who the
director of such a study should be was a serious question, for the whole issue
of the Negro in America was so charged with emotion that it would be
difficult to find an American who was not influenced by traditional attitudes
or preformed conclusions. And, so it was that in August of 1937 Frederick
P. Keppel, President of the Carnegie Corporation of New York, invited Dr.
Gunnar Myrdal of Sweden to be director of the comprehensive study of the
Negro in the United States. Dr. Myrdal was chosen for several reasons: (a) he
came from a country of "high intellectual and scholarly standards but with
no background or traditions of imperialism" and thus would be more able to
lend impartiality and validity to the study; (b) he was a scholar with an
international reputation as a social economist—professor in the University of
Stockholm, economic advisor to the Swedish Government, a member of the
Swedish Senate, a lecturer at Harvard University.[22] The study was to be
comprehensive and to be undertaken in a wholly objective way as a social
phenomenon.

> The study, thus conceived, should aim at determining the social, political,
> educational, and economic status of the Negro in the United States as well as
> defining opinions held by different groups of Negroes and whites as to his
> "right" status. It must, further, be concerned with both recent changes and
> current trends with respect to the Negro's position in American society. Atten-
> tion must be given to the total American picture with particular emphasis on
> relations between the two races. Finally, it must consider what changes are being
> or can be induced by education, legislation, interracial efforts, concerted action
> by Negro groups, etc.[23]

The Foundation was to place at the director's disposal a group of American scholars who were experts in anthropology, economics, education,
sociology, public health, and public administration. The study, which began
in September, 1938, with a trip through the Southern states, was completed
in 1942 and was available for distribution publicly by 1944 as *An American
Dilemma*. In the book Myrdal pointed out the gulf that existed between the

American ideals of democracy and brotherhood on the one hand, and the existence of racial prejudice, discrimination, and segregation of the Negro on the other. He began the introduction to the book by stating that there is a Negro problem in the United States and for white America this problem has distinctly negative connotations—it is embarrassing, it creates a feeling of moral uneasiness, it produces anxiety and guilt.

> The American Negro problem is a problem in the heart of the American. It is there that the interracial tension has its focus. It is there that the decisive struggle goes on. This is the central viewpoint of this treatise. Though our study includes economic, social, and political race relations, at bottom our problem is the moral dilemma of the American—the conflict between his moral valuations on various levels of consciousness and generality. The "American Dilemma" referred to in the title of this book is the ever-raging conflict between, on the one hand, the valuations preserved on the general plane which we shall call the "American Creed," where the American thinks, talks, and acts under the influence of high national and Christian precepts, and, on the other hand, the valuations on specific planes of individual and group living, where personal and local interests; economic, social and sexual jealousies; considerations of community prestige and conformity; group prejudice against particular persons or types of people; and all sorts of miscellaneous wants, impulses, and habits dominate his outlook.[24]

A second issue or insight on which Myrdal focused in the book and highlighted in its introduction is the nature of American valuations and beliefs, one aspect of which is that "the moral struggle goes on within people and not only between them."[25] He pointed out that even the American Negroes shared in this community of valuations—i.e., the American Creed, the Christian ethic, and even the majority prejudice against their own kind.

A third point of view presented by Myrdal was that the "dilemma" is the white man's problem. He concluded that a study of the Negro problem revealed little if any evidence that could explain the problem in terms of "the peculiarities" of the Negroes themselves. He found that the Negroes did not have even "one tenth of the things worth having in America" and that thus, the white American determined the Negro's status.[26]

The fourth thesis analyzed is that the Negro problem is part of the whole complex of problems in the larger American society and therefore cannot be treated in isolation.

> The relationship between American society and the Negro problem is not one-sided. The entire structure of American society is itself greatly conditioned by the presence of 13 million Negro citizens. . . . While primary attention will be focused on the Negro people and on the influences from the larger society working on them, their influence back on white society will not be ignored.[27]

In re-reading Myrdal's monumental work one is struck by the scholarship of the research, the humanism of a sensitive person, as well as the insight of a philosopher. In the last paragraph of his first chapter, a summary of the essence of the great American dilemma is presented:

> From the point of view of the American Creed, the status accorded the Negro in America represents nothing more and nothing less than a century-long lag of public morals. In principle, the Negro problem was settled long ago; in practice, the solution is not effectuated. The Negro in America has not yet been given the elemental civil and political rights of formal democracy including a fair opportunity to earn his living upon which a general accord was already won when the American Creed was first taking form. And to this anachronism constitutes the contemporary "problem" both to Negroes and to whites.[28]

Having struck at the very heart of the matter in his first chapter, Myrdal presents a challenge to American society in the final paragraph of the last chapter.

> What America is constantly reaching for is democracy at home and abroad. The main trend in its history is the gradual realization of the American Creed. In this sense the Negro problem is not only America's greatest failure, but also America's incomparably great opportunity for the future. If America should follow its own deepest conviction, its well-being at home would be increased directly. At the same time America's prestige and power abroad would rise immensely. The century-old dream of American patriots that America should give to the entire world its own freedom and its own fate would come true. America can demonstrate that justice, equality and cooperation are possible between white and colored people. In the present phase of history, this is what the world needs to believe. Mankind is sick of fear and disbelief, of pessimism, and cynicism. It needs the youthful, moralistic optimism of America. The empty declarations only deepen cynicism. Deeds are called for. If America in actual practice could show the world a progressive trend by which the Negro became finally integrated into modern democracy, all mankind would be given faith again—it would have reason to believe that peace, progress, and order are feasible, and America would have a spiritual power many times stronger than all her financial and military resources—the power of the trust and support of all the people on earth. America is free to choose whether the Negro should remain her liability or become her opportunity.[29]

If indeed the nine men who set forth to make that decision on May 17, 1954, read Gunnar Myrdal's words, they had done their homework well, for within Myrdal's text was presented the essence of the problem posed by the decision those nine men had to make.

THE IMPLEMENTATION DECISION: MAY 31, 1955

At the time of the May 17, 1954, decision, the Court had announced that segregation was "denial of the equal protection laws." However, the Court had made no statements regarding how school desegregation should be implemented. Instead, it stated:

> Because these are class actions, because of the wide applicability of this decision, and because of the great variety of local conditions, the formulation of decrees in these cases presents problems of considerable complexity. On reargument, the consideration of appropriate relief was necessarily subordinated to the primary question—the constitutionality of segregation in public education. . . . In order that we may have full assistance of the parties in formulating decrees, the cases will be restored to the docket, and the parties are requested to present further argument on Questions 4 and 5 previously propounded by the court for re-argument this term.

Question 4 was to be reargued and presented in two questions:

> (a) would a decree necessarily follow providing that within the limits set by normal geographic school districting, Negro children should forthwith be admitted to schools of their choice or (b) may this Court, in the exercise of its equity powers, permit an effective gradual adjustment to be brought about from existing segregated systems to a system not based on color distinctions?"

This question in particular suggested there was a concern by the Court that important social problems would arise if the Court decided segregation in public schools was unconstitutional.

The fifth question concerned itself with four questions:

> (a) should this Court formulate detailed decrees in these cases; (b) if so, what specific issues should the decrees reach, (c) should this Court appoint a special master with a view to recommending specific terms for such decrees, (d) should this Court remand to the courts of first instance with directions to frame decrees in these cases, and if so what general directions should the decrees of this Court include and what procedures should the courts of first instance follow in arriving at the specific terms of more detailed decrees?

Questions 4 and 5 had been propounded for counsel in 1953 and the request was repeated on May 17, 1954. Dr. Ernest Borinski described the process: "We have here the rather unique situation that the Court hands down a decision in principle but refrains from formulating the decree to implement this decision."[30]

The social scientists and psychologists tried to answer this question in the light of empirical evidence. In order to do this they had to collect and analyze all of the available data, primarily in the South, as to whether and how a change from a segregated to a nonsegregated situation could be smoothly accomplished. Then too, they had to present this evidence in a specific and concrete way in order to clarify the circumstances under which desegregation could be accomplished without severe or permanent disruption of a community. Information was obtained by examination of the available literature, by direct reports from individuals who observed directly or participated in change patterns of segregation, and by reading relevant, unpublished research manuscripts and unpublished research data. Under the leadership and direction of Kenneth Clark, noted social scientists, psychologists, and psychiatrists "combed reports published in the most scattered corners, corresponded, traveled and interviewed to gather together a record of evidence which formed an important resource for guiding an enlightened decision in this critical area of social policy."[31]

The detailed documentation produced by the social scientists must be regarded as a significant contribution to social psychology. The culmination of the research findings of the social scientists was published in a monograph entitled "Desegregation; An Appraisal of the Evidence" by S.P.S.S.I. In this article Kenneth Clark presented the evaluation of the available evidence dealing with known incidences of desegregation at the time as well as the consequences of segregation and some of the factors involved in changing from segregated to nonsegregated facilities. Some of the observations presented in that in-depth research paper are very useful to those who are involved in facilitating and evaluating the process of desegregation today. Many of the statements and judgments are prophetic and insightful and may help explain why school desegregation has or has not proceeded smoothly in many instances. The article also provided guidelines for educators and administrators who would be involved in the process of school desegregation.

In 1952 a trend toward desegregation could be found in many areas of community life involving various social institutions such as the church, the armed forces, housing, interstate transportation, hospital and health services, public accommodations and recreation, organized sports, labor unions and industrial employees unions, as well as in politics and government. While the majority of instances of desegregation came from Northern, border, Midwestern and Southwestern states, there were examples of successful desegregation in Southern states prior to the *Brown* v. *Board of Education* decision. The factors involved in the desegregation process varied from situation to situation and from institution to institution. Some of the major factors were population changes; voluntary public opinion pressure; referendum of the

electorate; the threat of publicity; moral argument; the activity of commu-
nity-action agencies; the personal decision of responsible people in authority;
nonjudicial governmental action; legislative action; the threat of court
action; pending court decisions as well as court action.

Clark's report emphasized that desegregation resulting from litigation
and judicial decision was just as effective as desegregation resulting from
other causes. In those instances in which desegregation had been accomplished by a gradual process several methods had been used, such as dead-
lines, time for preparation, progressive desegregation, or quota desegregation.
On the other hand, the process of immediate desegregation had utilized
other approaches, such as (1) abolishing segregated black facilities and admitting blacks into previously all-white facilities, (2) opening all facilities
without regard to race or color, (3) decreeing that white facilities cannot
exclude blacks and then allowing blacks to decide whether they will seek
admission or not, (4) a combination of (1) and (2) with specific time limits
involved, and (5) a nonsegregation policy instituted at the founding of the
institution.

When immediate desegregation processes were compared with the gradual process of desegregation, it was found that gradual desegregation did not
necessarily ensure effectiveness of the desegregation process, nor did it increase the chances of acceptance by those who were opposed to the desegregation process. It is important to note that Clark and his staff found that
time itself did not seem to be related to the effectiveness of the desegregation process, nor was opportunity and time for preparation of the public
for change necessarily related to the effectiveness and smoothness of change.
A review of desegregation processes in the country in 1952 revealed that
segmentalized, gradual desegregation did not ensure the effectiveness of desegregation but it had been found to increase the chances of resistance and
resentment of those whites who would be immediately involved in the desegregation process.

The research data also revealed that various types of immediate desegregation were no more prone to lead to nonviolent resistance than the gradual
methods of desegregation. In fact, there was evidence to support the fact
that a directive abolishing Negro facilities and the immediate admission of
Negroes into previously all-white facilities had been an especially effective
method of desegregation. Such a process had resulted in the accomplishment
of desegregation in a shorter time, the involvement of a larger number of
Negroes and whites who would be involved in the desegregation process, and
a more rapid acceptance by the community with little overt resistance or
controversy. Active resistance and violence following desegregation had been
found to be rare, and where they had occurred had been associated with
ambiguous or inconsistent policy or ineffective policy action or conflict

between competing governmental authorities or officials. It was well documented that the accomplishment of effective desegregation with a minimum of social disturbance depended upon (1) a clear statement of policy by leaders with prestige and other authority, (2) firm enforcement by official authorities and persistance in the execution of the enforcement, (3) willingness to deal with violations by law, strong enforcement, and by action, (4) refusal of authority to resort to subterfuge or other evading devices, and (5) an appeal to individuals in terms of their religious or democratic principles. The report concluded that whenever desegregation had occurred under the above conditions, it had been evaluated as socially beneficial or otherwise successful. The size or the scope of the institution does not necessarily determine the success or failure of desegregation. In fact, the larger the scale of desegregation, the greater the likelihood of general acceptance.

On Monday, May 31, 1955, the Supreme Court rendered the implementation decision in *Brown* v. *Board of Education.* Once again the decision was unanimous and proved to be historic:

> Full implementation of these constitutional principles may require solution of varied local school problems. School authorities have the primary responsibility for elucidating, assessing, and solving these problems; courts will have to consider whether the action of school authorities constitutes good-faith implementation of the governing constitutional principles. Because of their proximity to local conditions and the possible need for further hearings, the courts which originally heard these cases can best perform this judicial appraisal. Accordingly, we believe it appropriate to remand the cases to those courts.

The Supreme Court in its implementation decision chose to ignore the guidelines furnished by the NAACP as researched by the social scientists. It chose the course of compromise and delay. It gave covert approval to decisions permitting gradual desegregation. It set a historic course for "a generation of litigation."

The famous "with all deliberate speed" clause was coined when *Briggs* v. *Elliot* was remanded to the United States Court of Appeals, Fourth Circuit, in South Carolina which declared that the South Carolina school board was to discontinue its discriminatory practices after it makes "necessary arrangements . . . with all deliberate speed." Not until the Civil Rights Act of 1964 did any semblance of consistent guidelines for school desegregation emerge.

1. See Chapter 2 for the school segregation cases presented to the Court following *Plessy* v. *Ferguson.*
2. Clark, K.B. Op. cit., 1966, pp. 210-211.
3. Blaustein and Ferguson. 1962, p. 135.
4. Cahn, E. Jurisprudence. New York University Law Review, 30:150-159. Jan. 1955.
5. Ibid.
6. Ibid.

7.Greenberg, J. Social scientists take the stand: A review and appraisal of their testimony in litigation. Michigan Law Review, 54:953, May, 1956.

8.Clark, K.B. Desegregation: An appraisal of the evidence. Journal of Social Issues, 9:2, Oct., 1953.

9.Blaustein and Ferguson. Op. cit., p. 134.

10. Ibid., p. 131.

11. Witmer, H.L., and Kotinsky, R. Personality in the Making. New York, Harpers, 1952, p. 141.

12. Ibid., p. 137.

13. Ibid., p. 137.

14. Ibid., p. 138.

15. Ibid., p. 144.

16. Ibid., p. 145.

17. Ibid., p. 152.

18. Ibid., p. 154-155.

19. Ibid., p. 156.

20. Deutscher, I., and Chein, I. The psychological effects of enforced segregation: A survey of social science opinion. Journal of Psychology, 26, Oct., 1948, pp. 259-287.

21. Witmer and Kotinsky. Op. cit., p. 139.

22. Myrdal, G. An American Dilemma. Forward, p. xlviii-xlix.

23. Ibid., Preface, pp. lii-liii.

24. Ibid., p. lxxxi.

25. Ibid., p. lxxii.

26. Ibid., p. lxxv.

27. Ibid., p. lxxvii.

28. Ibid., p. 24.

29. Ibid., p. 27.

30. Borinski, E. A legal and sociological analysis of the segregation decision of May 17, 1954. University of Pittsburgh Law Review, 15:622-627, 1954.

31. Clark. Op. cit., 1953, p. 3.

18

"Black Is Beautiful"

THE CORRELATES OF SELF-CONCEPT FOR BLACK STUDENTS

Seven hundred and fifty-eight black boys and girls in 21 junior high schools in three different Southern cities obtained a mean total positive score of 344.52 compared with 945 white students from the same cities and the same schools who obtained a mean total positive score of 333.10; The difference is highly significant (1 percent level). (See Chapter 16, Table 5.) The black students score in the 48th percentile, the white students in the 30th percentile.

The black students also score significantly higher than the white students on variability, distribution, identity, self-satisfaction, moral-ethical self, and family self. On the self-criticism score the two score about the same, 35.31 for the black students and 36.18 for the white students. Thus, it can be said that black students have adequate self-concepts, that they are open in admitting negative statements about themselves, that they vary in the different sub-profile groups in how positive they feel about themselves, and that they feel very definite and certain about their self-perceptions. Although they score below the mean on identity and moral-ethical self, they nonetheless indicate that they feel significantly more positive about themselves in these two areas than white students do. They score above the normative mean on self-satisfaction and family self and feel significantly more positive about themselves in these two areas than do the white students.

What explanation can be offered for higher self-concepts among black students? What are the variables involved? Analysis of variance and multiple regression of all the data show that the three most important correlates of

277

positive self-concept among the 758 black students are (1) segregation, (2) occupation of the parents, and (3) sex of the student. Additional variables such as college education of the father, income of the family, number of children in the family, a working mother, and college education of the mother are not as important. The variables that are important for black girls in relationship to positive self-concept are two: (1) segregation and (2) occupation of parents. For black boys the most important variables are (1) occupation, (2) high school education of the mother, and (3) college education of the mother. However, there are many interesting differences among the black students in the three cities that should be pointed out.

In Nashville, the black students obtained a mean total positive score of 348.86 compared with a score of 332.56 for the white students; the difference is significant at the $(p < 0.01)$. Likewise, black girls (346.97) score significantly higher than white girls (333.69) $(p < 0.004)$ and black boys (350.20) score significantly higher than white boys (331.036) $(p < 0.001)$.

The Nashville black students (299) score significantly higher than the white students (317) on distribution, identity, self-satisfaction, and moral-ethical self. They also score higher than the white students on behavior, personal self, and social self, but the differences are not significant. Thus, the Nashville black students have adequate to high self-concepts. Although they score below the normative mean on identity and moral-ethical self, they nonetheless feel significantly more positive about themselves in these two areas than white students do and feel especially positive about themselves in terms of self-satisfaction. They vary in how they perceive themselves in different areas and are not always consistent in how positive they feel about their total self. Nonetheless, they indicate that they are certain how they feel and think about themselves. When sex is considered, the black boys feel more positive about themselves than the black girls and significantly so in the area of personal self. The black boys also tend to be more inconsistent in how they view the total self than do the black girls.

Inasmuch as more black students in Nashville have parents with higher educational and occupational status than do the white students, could these factors explain the higher self-concept among blacks and the lower among whites? Analysis of variance and multiple regression of the Nashville data reveals that the four most important correlates of self-concept among the black students are (1) college education of the father, (2) occupation of the parents, (3) number of children, and (4) family stability.

For the black boys in Nashville the four most important correlates of self-concept are (1) occupation of parents, (2) college education of the mother, (3) segregation, and (4) college education of the father. The most important correlates for the black girls are (1) college education of the father, (2) occupation of the parents, (3) high school education of the father, and (4) family income, in that order. College education of the mother and number of children are also factors, but not as important. The correlates for positive self-concept among Nashville black students seem to differ from those for the black group as a whole.

In New Orleans a different picture emerges. The 316 black students score higher than the white students on every TSCS score, with the exception of the SC score, and they score significantly higher than the white students on the remaining scores (with a significance at the 1 percent level) with the exception of social self. (See Chap. 12, Table 8). Thus, it can be said that the New Orleans black students have adequate to high self-concepts, are open and not defensive, demonstrate a great deal of variability in how they feel about themselves on the profile items, and are very certain about their self-perceptions. Although they score below the normative mean score on identity and moral-ethical self, they nonetheless feel significantly more positive about themselves on these items than do the white students. They also feel significantly more positive about themselves in regard to self-satisfaction, behavior, physical self, and personal self. The black students in New Orleans, unlike the black students in Nashville, had parents with lower educational and occupational achievements than the white students, and black students reported a little more family instability than white students. What, then, accounts for their high self-concept scores? Analysis of the data shows that the most important correlates of positive self-concepts among black students in New Orleans are (1) segregation, (2) sex of the student, and (3) number of children in the family, in that order of importance. College education of the mother and family income are also factors, but not as important as the others. It is interesting to note that segregation and sex are two of the most important variables related to positive self-concept for the entire black student group.

The 182 black girls in New Orleans present a picture quite similar to the one described for the total group of black students in New Orleans (see Chap. 12, Table 9), except that they obtain a total positive mean score of 352.94, which is higher than that for the group of New Orleans black students (348.88). All their scores are statistically and significantly different from those of the white girls with the exception of self-criticism (two groups score the same) and social self (black girls score higher, but not significantly so).

The 134 black boys in New Orleans score higher on every TSCS score than the white boys and significantly so on total positive, variability, distribution, identity, behavior, physical self, moral-ethical self, and family self. They score the same as the white boys on self-criticism (35+) and higher on social self, but not significantly so.

The black girls score significantly higher than the black boys on the total positive mean score, self-satisfaction mean score, and moral-ethical-self mean score. It should be noted that the black girls in New Orleans are the only group in the entire sample of students tested who score above the normative mean (70.33) on moral-ethical self.

For the black boys in New Orleans the three most important correlates for high self-concept are (1) segregation, (2) college education of father, and (3) family size or number of children. For the black girls the most important correlates are (1) segregation, (2) income of family, and (3) high school education of the mother.

In Greensboro black students have low self-concepts (TP mean score 337.32)[1] They score significantly higher than white students on variability, distribution, and family self. At the very most, the Greensboro black students demonstrate a great deal of variability and certainty about the self picture. The black boys and girls in Greensboro both have low self-concepts although the girls are more positive than the boys. The only significant difference between the black girls and black boys is the mean distribution score; the girls score higher indicating they are more certain about themselves than the black boys. The most important variables for positive self-concept for black students in Greensboro are (1) working mother, (2) segregation, and (3) family size or number of children. For the black boys the four most important variables for positive self-concept are (1) income level, (2) family size, (3) high school education of mother, and (4) high school education of the father. For the black girls the two most important variables are (1) segregation, and (2) working mother.

It has already been noted that black students in segregated schools have higher self-concepts than those in desegregated schools and in Greensboro and New Orleans the difference is statistically significant. In all three cities, black girls in segregated schools score significantly higher than black girls in desegregated schools. However, this significant difference between segregated and desegregated black students does not hold up for black boys in any of the three cities. Although segregated black boys have more positive self-concepts than desegregated black boys, the difference is not significant. Added to these facts is the fact that when the correlates for positive self-concept for all the 1,720 students tested are examined the most significant variable is race. Thus, it would seem that the prototype of a student with high self-concept in this sample would be a *black girl* in a *segregated school.*

How is it that being black is *the* most important and significant correlate for positive self-concept among a group of adolescents in three Southern cities and that segregation is the most important variable for positive self-concept among black adolescents? These findings belie the findings of Coopersmith and Rosenberg that educational and occupational status and family stability are the most important correlates of self-esteem. Rosenberg did note, however, that in considering ethnic groups the adolescents of "Old Yankee" stock had a self-esteem level slightly lower than the other groups, and "the self-esteem of these youngsters [Negroes] is slightly below that of white—33 percent of the Negroes and 45 percent of the whites had high self-esteem—but it is not nearly as low as one might expect if general societal status were an important determinant of self-esteem."[2] He goes on to state that "the Negroes in our sample are considerably more likely to come from the lowest classes and to have poorly educated parents, and are less likely to be taking academic course programs and to come from small towns."[3] Baughman and Dahlstrom in their study of black and white rural eighth-graders also noted that the damaged self-percept concept which is so prevalent throughout the literature did not seem to be so among their sample of black students.[4]

THE DESEGREGATION PROCESS: WHITE IS STILL RIGHT?

That segregation should be an important and significant correlate of positive self-concept among Southern black adolescents is ironic in the face of the push on the federal level for further desegregation in Southern schools. Perhaps these findings have some implications about the desegregation process in the South. This would seem to be supported by the fact that black students in desegregated schools have lower self-concepts than those in segregated schools. What are the harmful psychologic effects of school desegregation? (There is no indication that the sampling of students in desegregated schools had social, economic, or emotional factors that were different from the sample in segregated schools).

First of all, it is very necessary to define desegregation as distinct from integration. The two words cannot or should not be used interchangeably for they describe two very separate processes. Desegregation is the elimination of laws, customs, or practices under which different races or groups are restricted to separate facilities, schools, organizations, or the like; it is the elimination of racial separation. Integration is the process of incorporating parts into a whole, the process of becoming part of the dominant culture, the process of combining separate groups into a harmonious organization. Integration may follow segregation or desegregation depending on the rate of and resistance to change. When a facility has been desegregated, in that the physical separation of groups has been eliminated, it does not mean that harmonious incorporation of a group into the organization has occurred. That is a psychologic process.

Let is be said at the outset that none of the eight desegregated schools in the three Southern cities that participated in this study were integrated schools. Black and white students and teachers shared the same physical facilities, but not the same cultural or psychologic facilities. Black and white students occupied the same classrooms, but blacks were separate and considered unequal to whites. They were separated by invisible walls of resistance, dislike, and racism, by the whites, and fear, anger, defensiveness, and feelings of alienation by the blacks. The schools did not represent or pretend to represent the harmonious incorporation of black students into the total life of the school, rather there was a dissonance, alienation, and separation far greater than that in any segregated black school. When the overt hostility disappears it is replaced by indifference and withdrawal. In such a system of exclusion, hostility, and racism how does a black adolescent begin to define or conceptualize himself?

Mead has defined the self in all its dimensions as being socially determined and Sullivan has stressed the importance of significant others in the formation of self-perception. During adolescence the peer group assumes great importance in formulating attitudes about the self. For black adolescents in a desegregated school the hostile racial attitudes of their peers and their teachers become incorporated into negative self-attitudes.

It is interesting to note the difference in TSCS profiles of desegregated black students in the various cities. For instance in Nashville the black desegregated group scored significantly lower than the black segregated group on the self-satisfaction and personal-self items. Under the daily critical hostile scrutiny of white racists it would be difficult for an adolescent to be satisfied with himself or content with his personal self. In New Orleans the black desegregated group scored particularly low on the behavior and moral-ethical-self items. This is particularly interesting in view of the fact that the black segregated students in New Orleans are the only group in the entire sample who scored equal to the normative mean on moral-ethical self. The low scores on these two items may reflect the cultural and ethnic differences in mores whereby in white racist environment the black way is considered the deviant way. In Greesboro the black desegregated group is much more critical of themselves and score extremely low on identity and family self. The low scores on these two items would seem to reflect some intense conflict concerning "Who am I?" or "Who should I become?" and "Should I follow my family's way or the school's way?"—the clash of culture in the classroom as described by Clark.

Among the black girls in desegregated schools, there are negative self-attitudes in many areas. Among the Greensboro black desegregated girls there are negative attitudes toward the self in many areas, e.g., identity, self-satisfaction, behavior, moral-ethical self, family self, social self, as well as total self-concept. In New Orleans in addition to a low self-concept, the black desegregated girls score much lower than the segregated black girls on the moral-ethical-self items. (The segregated black girls score above the normative mean on moral-ethical self.) In Nashville, besides the low self-concept, the black desegregated girls score particularly low on self-satisfaction, physical self, and personal self.

In all three cities, although the black desegregated boys score lower than the segregated boys, there are no significant differences. The black boys tested in this sample were junior high school boys, the majority between the ages of 12 and 15 years. Their maturation in terms of self-concept, as in some other areas, may be slower than the girls. A second explanation offered is that more often that not the black boys in the desegregated schools sublimated through sports in which they excelled and gained some positive recognition.

It would seem that desegregated black students in the three cities differ in the way desegregation affects their self-concept. This fact can be explained in part by the degree of desegregation in the schools from whence they come. For instance in Greensboro, all the black students in desegregated schools come from schools with only 10 percent black enrollment and schools to which they had to be transported. Thus, not only are they a definite minority, not only are they unwanted black students coming to desegregate and defile the white schools, but they are also the outsiders from the other part of town. This kind of attitude of being "the outsiders" who are bused to white schools has often been expressed by the white "neighborhood" children in many cities. The self-concepts of the black desegregated students are very low (about the 25th percentile).

The New Orleans desegregated schools had the highest black enrollment of all the three cities (see Chapters 7, 11, and 15), with the four desegregated schools having 18 percent, 50 percent, 58 percent, and 59 percent black enrollment. In Nashville among the desegregated schools there were two with 10 percent black enrollment and one with 20 percent enrollment. The effect of percent of black enrollment in a desegregated school is clearly seen when one examines the TSCS scores of the black desegregated girls in the three cities, inasmuch as the black boys do not seem to be so adversely affected by desegregated schools as black girls. The black girls in desegregated schools in New Orleans, where the black enrollment is higher, have the highest mean TP score (347.38) compared with Nashville (339.2) and Greensboro (326.41). There are some exceptions; for instance, in Nashville the black students at the 10 percent black public school score higher than the black students at the 20 percent black public school, but lower than the students at the 10 percent black parochial school (that school was a new school and had been opened for three months prior to the testing). Secondly, in New Orleans the black students at the 18 percent black public school scored higher than the black students at the 50 percent black parochial school. These differences could be explained by sampling techniques or by certain variables that have not been considered.

IMPLEMENTATION AND COMPLIANCE

The difference in the scoring patterns of the black students in the three cities raises some interesting questions. First of all, if socioeconomic factors and educational attainment are the most important correlates for self-esteem for the black students in Nashville, why is it not so in New Orleans? Secondly, if socioeconomic status and education of parents are important correlates of self-concept, why do the black students in New Orleans have as high self-concept scores as those in Nashville when black parents in New Orleans are not as well educated and do not have as high a socioeconomic status as those black parents in Nashville? Thirdly, if segregation and occupation of parents and/or working mother are the most important correlates of high self-concept in New Orleans and Greensboro, why do New Orleans' black students have significantly higher self-concepts than Greensboro black students whose socioeconomic and educational attainment of parents are similar? In order to answer these questions, the history of race relations of each city as well as the implementation of school desegregation has to be compared. These subjects have been discussed at length for each city; only a few landmarks will be reviewed here.

Southern state statistics of 1967 show that the Southern states remain grouped as before as to the extent of desegregation.[5] Alabama, Georgia, Louisiana, Mississippi, and South Carolina have the smallest percentage of Negroes desegregated, ranging from 3 to 10 percent. Arkansas, Florida, North Carolina are a middle group, with 10 to 20 percent of their Negroes in desegregated schools. Leading the group with the largest percentage of desegregation are Tennessee with 31.7 percent, Texas with 47.3 percent, and Virginia with 24.8 percent. In terms of compliance there are basically four groups of states: (1) those who complied immediately and desegregated rapidly, (2) those who complied and after two or three years began to desegregate, (3) those who complied but delayed in actual implementation, and (4) those who resisted and who were finally forced to comply under court order. The first group is represented by the border states and the District of Columbia; the second group by Texas, Tennessee, and Arkansas; the third group by Florida, North Carolina, and Virginia; and the fourth group by Alabama, Georgia, Louisiana, Mississippi, and South Carolina. (Actually, Virginia and Louisiana could be put in a class of resisted, complied, and delayed.)

In many respects Nashville, Greensboro, and New Orleans are characteristic of the states where they are located. Nashville had and has an active cohesive militant black community with many impressive black leaders. It is a black educational center and has a fairly cosmopolitan white community as a result of a large white educational center and many publishing houses. Nashville began its desegregation process during the school year 1956-1957 with minimal violence.

Greensboro has a black population about the size of Nashville. However, in spite of its industry and educational institutions desegregation has proceeded slowly on a freedom-of-choice basis without violence, but in 1969 the school board was subject to have funds cut off for noncompliance with the Civil Rights act of 1964. Desegregation was minimal. New Orleans has a large black population which is divided in leadership. Resistance to school desegregation was strong with a great deal of violence and reluctant compliance.

BEAUTIFUL MONDAY

Before 1954, 17 Southern and border states plus the District of Columbia operated completely separate schools for whites and blacks. On May 17, 1954, the Supreme Court held that such schools were inherently unequal. The decision ushered in an era of American school revolution. It was the first major recognized victory of black people in this country. It said, in effect, second-class citizenship is illegal and immoral. It said, black people in this country deserve all the privileges, rights, and responsibilites that other citizens enjoy. It said segregation and discrimination are not only unconstitutional and illegal, but also immoral. That moral victory for black people served as an impetus for black people to demand other rights. No longer were they a passive lot; they could, in effect, actively affect their destiny and they did. For Southern blacks for whom oppression and racism were more overt, indeed the walls of Jericho had come tumbling down.

The nonviolent movement of Martin Luther King stressed Christian love and nonviolence. But, more than that, King constantly preached that it was the black man's Christian duty to show the white man the error of his ways; this was the ultimate of Christian love. In psychologic terms, what King was saying was that we have truth and justice, the Supreme Court, and the Lord on our side. The white man is sinful and we as black people in our ultimate mercy, goodness, and love must help these wayward people. King perpetuated a position of ultimate strength and self-esteem that made the black oppressed in the South feel hopeful but, more especially, proud. The student nonviolent movement among young blacks operated with the ideology that "right, good, justice, and strength are on our side." Thus these young blacks operated from a position of high self-esteem and a belief that they could and would affect the destiny of black and white people. Those communities that participated actively in Civil Rights activities shared in this new elitism and helped to perpetuate it in their communities.

Nashville represents such a community which may in part explain why the desegregated black students, although scoring lower than the segregated black students, nonetheless score at least at the 40th percentile. The cohesiveness of the black community, their power base, and their elitism in terms of self-esteem and pride can extend to the adolescent in the desegregated school, and affect some of the noxious elements of a desegregated school. A black student in a desegregated school still belongs to a powerful, proud black community. This is a given for the black adolescent in Nashville and, thus, other variables come into play to increase self-concept.

In New Orleans within the black school and community one can find solace and comfort. Outside it there is a hostile white community who continues to reject and erode the power of the black community. New Orleans black students also participate in the new black elitism, but without a cohesive, strong black community such self-esteem cannot be maintained in a hostile environment. In such a society it is more difficult for the black male adolescent to find his place, because he poses the greatest threat in the white racist hostile environment. Desegregated black girls score higher than desegregated black boys (TP mean score—347); desegregated black boys have a TP mean score of 340.

In New Orleans and Greensboro black girls do better on the self-concept score than black boys whether the school be segregated or desegregated. It is interesting to note that black desegregated boys in Nashville score higher than the desegregated girls and black boys in general score higher than black girls. In Nashville the new black elitism proclaims the power and leadership of the black male.

In Greensboro, in spite of May 17, 1954, very little has happened. Black leadership is divided. Desegregation has proceeded slowly; blacks are not wanted in white schools and have not been able to affect change in this area; the powerlessness pervails.

The desegregation process itself is not a factor in positive self-concept among black students, for in actuality at the time of the testing 83.1 percent of black students in the South attend schools with all-black enrollments. Ironically, segregation is the major factor in positive self-concepts for black students.

However, in spite of everything, May 17, 1954, is a major landmark in black history. It represented, and still does, a major moral victory for black people. It represented "Black Monday" to the whites in the South, black meaning "despair," "death," "evil" to the white Southerner. Ironically, the day was fittingly named because for black people, it was also a "Black Monday," a "Beautiful Monday." Because of that day "black is beautiful."

Frantz Fanon expresses the essence of the dynamics of the effects of the school desegregation decision on self-concept of black Southern adolescents in a passage from his *Wretched of the Earth*:

> Thus, the native discovers that his life, his breath, his beating heart are the same as those of the settler. He finds out that the settler's skin is not of any more value than the native's skin; and it must be said that this discovery shakes the world in a very necessary manner. All the new revolutionary assurance of the native stems from it.[6]

1. It should be noted that the 48 black girls in segregated schools obtain the highest TP mean score (351.98) of any group of students tested in Greensboro (See Chap. 15, Table 11).
2. Rosenberg. Op. cit., 1965, p. 303.
3. Ibid.
4. Baughman and Dahlstrom. Op. cit., 1970.
5. Southern Education Report. Feb., 1967, p. 30.
6. Fanon, F. The Wretched of the Earth. New York, Grove Press, 1966, p. 36.

19

The Sins of the Father

CORRELATES FOR SELF-CONCEPT AMONG WHITE STUDENTS

As striking as the finding that black students in Southern urban communities have higher self-concepts than whites is the finding that Southern white students score extremely low on the total positive mean score, indicating very low or negative self-concepts. They score in the 30th percentile for the scale, well below the normative mean. Although there is a tendency for the 1,720 students tested to score below the normative mean on identity, moral-ethical self, and social self, in many instances the white students score significantly lower on these items than black students. Thus, although the adolescents in general have some conflicts in the area of identity, moral-ethical self, and social self,[1] these areas are particularly troublesome for white adolescents. In addition to scoring very low on identity, moral-ethical self, and social self, the white students (but not the black students) also score very low on the personal-self score. In general, the white students score slightly higher on the self-criticism score than the black students, but the difference is not significant. But the white students score lower on the mean V and D scores. It would seem that white students have a tendency to be a little more critical about themselves than black students, to feel more consistent about themselves in the various areas of self-perception (which is generally negative), and demonstrate less certainty in how they think and feel about themselves.

288

In considering the variables for positive self-concept for white students, it would appear that the most important variables are family stability, college education of the father, and, to a lesser degree, college education of the mother. For white boys the most important variable is occupation of parents; segregation plays a minor role, but is the next important variable. For white girls family stability and size of family are the two most important variables. College education of the father and segregation have less importance.

In Greensboro for white boys the most important variables are family income, working mother, and college education of the father; for white girls, high school education of the mother and segregation have the highest correlation with positive self-concept. The most important correlate of self-concept for all the white students in Greensboro is working mother; income of family and college education of father have less importance.

In New Orleans none of the variables have any significant correlation, but sex of the student, high school education of the mother, and segregation are the most important correlates. For white males occupation, size of family and segregation are the most important correlates of all the variables. For white girls the only variable that has any important correlation is occupation of parents; income is second, but is not highly correlated.

In Nashville the most significant correlates of self-concept for white students are family stability, college education of the father, and income of the family. College education of the mother and family size are also important, but not as significant. The most significant correlates for the white girls are college education of the father, family size, and family stability. For white boys the most important variable is family stability; occupation and income of family are less important.

So, it would seem that the correlates of high self-concept for white students follow the usual ones reported in the literature but those for black students are very different, with segregation and sex being the most significant. It would also seem that there are more alienating forces affecting white adolescents than black adolescents, unless the assumption can be made that there were more sampling errors in the selection of white students than in the selection of black students. It might seem that Nashville is more atypical for blacks, which would account for the blacks excelling in self-concept, but New Orleans and Greensboro cannot be considered atypical. However, regardless of the differences or similarities among cities, the white students score the same in each city. Let us look beyond the cities to explain the phenomenon of low self-concepts of white students. It should be stressed that the importance of this finding lies not in the fact that blacks excel in self-concept when compared with whites, but that white students score so very low.

THE AMERICAN DILEMMA UNRESOLVED

What meaning did "Black Monday" have for Southern white children in spite of the resistance, violence, and noncompliance? It said to the white community, "You are immoral, inhumane, illegal, and unconstitutional. Because of you, our reputation abroad as a democratic nation has been seriously damaged. You have violated the very principles on which this country was founded. You have made a hypocrisy of the American Creed and the American Dream."

As schools begin to desegregate, sometimes with violence, some conflicts for white adolescents present themselves as to identity models. Basically believing in human decency and the American ideal, can one really identify with the cruel "red necks" abusing passive nonviolent children? To have federal troops in one's city to enforce the law of the land and the American Creed on which one was reared raises some puzzling questions. And, then, the final compliance and desegregation proceeds; does that not mean the white adults have admitted that they were wrong, that they were illegal and immoral? On the one hand one is taught the American Creed and on the other hand that blacks are inferior and whites are superior. But then the blacks, with dignity and strength, with courage and determination, one by one destroy all the symbols that stood for white superiority and black inferiority, and the nation and indeed the world applauds. In such a changing, inconsistent, hypocritical system one asks, "Who am I?" and "Where do I belong?" Black leaders talk about the injustices whites have imposed upon blacks, and many white people agree. White adults who at first clung to segregation are confused and do not know what to do. They say they believe in liberty and justice for all, but they resent blacks coming to their white schools. And, white America knows that even though they are black, they are proud to be black. They believe in what they are fighting for. There is courage and strength among them and even power, "black power." Are whites really superior to them?

That white adolescents have low self-concepts should not be surprising in the face of the social revolution of the 1960's. First of all, a system of self-esteem based on the degradation of other human beings is bound to collapse. Secondly, following the black student movement in the South there was the white student movement in the North with the same theme—liberty and justice for all. The white student movement augmented the civil rights movement in the South, but then moved North to concentrate on major issues there. Many adults called it an antiestablishment movement, but more exactly it was and still remains an antihypocrisy movement. The hippie phenomenon was an attempt on the part of white youth to reject the hypocrisy and materialistic values of the adult white world. The Vietnam War further demonstrated the hypocrisy and racism in this country, and students began to raise their voices in protest. The response to their protest can be witnessed by the events at Kent State and in Jackson, Mississippi. Then the drug scene which had started with LSD in the late 1950's began to reach alarming proportions—at first the hallucinogenics, then the uppers and the downers, the cocktails, and then the "hard stuff" which previously was a phenomenon prevalent in the poor Northern black ghetto subcultures. Now it reached into the very homes and lives of the great silent majority. It represented alienation, hopelessness, aimlessness, depression, and the ultimate of rebellion and rejection of the "white" way of life.

It is a curious sight indeed to see throngs of white students waiting to hear Eldridge Cleaver or Bobby Seale. How many black students go to hear Senator Eastland, or George Wallace, or John Casper? It is a curious sight indeed to walk through a Western college town and see the Afro's on white students. For white students the world today holds no place for them. They see a third world order of peace, sharing, and kinship; they wander about the country and the world looking for places to set up a commune.

The phenomenon of low self-concepts among white Southern students extends to the North also.[2] As a matter of fact, Northern white students score lower than Southern white students—white Southerners in the 30th percentile, white Northerners in the 20 to 25th percentile.[3] The phenomenon extends to white students in upper, middle, and lower social classes, those with high academic achievement, and those with low academic achievement.[4]

For a long while we have focused attention on the effects of white racism on black children; perhaps we need to take a closer look at its effects on white children as well. It would seem that the sins of the white fathers have been visited upon their white children.

~

"CELIA SAYS . . . "

The psychodynamics of white racism in low self-concepts of white children is illustrated by the following true story:

Annette is a 5-year-old black girl who has been attending an integrated nursery school in a large metropolitan city for two years. Her Parents, both professional (a teacher and a nurse), have selected this particular nursery school because of the quality of the program which helps the children develop cognitive skills and provides for fantasy play, as well as music and dramatics. The children who attend are mostly the children of university students and professors, and generally from upper socioeconomic backgrounds. Annette is one of six black children and 10 minority children (three Japanese and one Chicano) who attend the school.

At age three, when she entered, she thoroughly enjoyed herself and was always eager to go to school. After four months of school, she began to refer to herself as "icky brown." "The kids say that brown is an 'icky color'; I'm an icky brown." Another time, she returned home from school saying "Johnny says I should wash my face and hands because I'm dirty. He thinks I'm dirty just because I'm brown." The parents became concerned and requested a conference with the teacher who they felt with a little skillful intervention could begin to point out objects within the environment that were brown and black but also beautiful. It would provide an important lesson to Annette, but also to the other children. During the conference it was obvious that the teacher felt very threatened by the two black professional parents, who knew more about child development than she, and even more uncomfortable about dealing with any issue regarding race. Her ambivalence toward blacks was obvious; her self-confidence in teaching was shaky.

Instead of removing Annette from the classroom, the mother decided to visit regularly, twice a week, to provide support to Annette, to help her in dealing with a situation that was bound to occur frequently in her life, and to provide a learning experience for the teacher, Annette, and her classmates. At first the children treated Annette's mother like a visitor, but soon they began to come to her for help and to discuss things with her. Within the course of time the issue of color came up and Annette's mother handled it the way she had suggested the teacher handle it. One day a robin fell out of its nest and the children were very concerned. They surrounded the bird while Annette's mother talked to them about robins and other birds. One child remarked, "He's brown and feathery." Another said, "He's beautiful." They became interested in ants and discovered that there were green ants, and brown ants, and black ants. In the fish bowl was one striped black fish, which became the children's favorite, and of course the little brown hamster was everyone's favorite.

The following year a black principal was appointed to the school and Annette's parents requested that both Annette and her younger sister be assigned to her room. This teacher was very warm, an excellent teacher, and very skillful in helping children. Both Annette and her younger sister thrived in this classroom environment.

The following year when Annette turned five and a half she was placed in the first grade of the school. She loved school, had made many friends over the years, and felt very comfortable. However, the classroom was really ungraded and there were several children who were one year to one and a half years older than Annette. One such child was Celia, who became a good friend of Annette's. Every day Annette would report on her adventures with Celia and from the description of the tales, Celia sounded like a bright, innovative, imaginative child. The second older child that Annette frequently reported stories about was a seven-year-old-boy named Peter Slawson. It seemed that he was always getting into trouble, that he frequently swore, and he was the class bully. After Valentine's Day Peter began to direct his hostility toward Annette and there were stories about how Celia intervened. Peter became the villain and Celia the heroine. The day usually began or ended with some comment from Annette about "Celia says . . ." Any statement made by Annette's family was usually followed by Annette's observations that, "Well, Celia says . . . " and Celia's point of view was presented.

In March the escapades with Peter became more devasting for Annette. "Every day Peter calls me that fuck-it Negro girl." Ignoring the "fuck-it" for the moment, Annette's parents countered with "Why should you mind if he calls you 'that Negro girl,' after all isn't that what you are?" Annette replied with sadness, "Yes, but he says it in a mean way." She had picked up the hostility in his remarks and his efforts to insult her.

Early in May, Annette's mother decided to visit the class after having several conferences with Annette's teachers. Upon entering the classroom, she was greeted by a pert, pretty red-haired little girl who introduced herself, "I'm Celia. You must be Annette's mother, she said that you were going to visit today." Annette's mother and Celia conversed some more when another child joined them "Are you Annette's mother?" Discovering that this was so, he left and Celia said with all the dramatic vehemence that she could muster, "Do you know who that is? That's Peter Slawson." A group of children surrounded them as Celia continued "Everyday that God brings, Peter Slawson calls Annette that 'fuck-it Negro girl.' Now I do not think it is fair to make fun of anyone because of the color of their skin, the clothes they wear, or the color of their hair." It was very obvious that Celia's bright red hair had singled her out for some teasing. She continued her lecture with "People can't help the color of their skin or the color of their hair because that's what they're born with. And, some people can't afford fancy clothes because they are poor. So it's not fair to make fun of them." The group who had now surrounded Celia and Annette's mother all agreed and took turns offering their opinions. However, it was very clear that Celia was the leader.

Celia then said "Annette says that some mean white man killed this good black man Martin Luther King because he was trying to help black people all over the world. We cried when she told us. That's a very sad story." Annette's mother agreed. Celia then said, "Well, you know what we have decided? We have decided that it just must have been Peter Slawson's father who killed Martin Luther King."

It is fascinating to imagine the cognitive process that evolved in Celia's mind to reach that conclusion: (1) Peter Slawson is a mean boy. (2) Peter Slawson does not like black people and treats them in a mean way. (3) Why does Peter Slawson treat black people so mean? (4) Did his Daddy teach him to be mean to black people? (5) My daddy teaches me things about people and the world so maybe Peter's father taught Peter not to like blacks and to be mean to them. (6) Martin Luther King was a nice black man just like Annette is a nice black girl. (7) If Peter is mean to black kids because his daddy said so, his daddy is probably mean to black grown-ups. (8) A mean white man killed Martin Luther King because he was black. (9) What mean white man could have done that? (10) Peter Slawson's father is a mean white man and he doesn't like black people (knowing of only one white mean man who dislikes blacks in her small world). Ergo (11) Peter Slawson's father killed Martin Luther King.

    And Celia is right. All the mean white men did kill Martin Luther King
and all the silent good men also killed him. And that is the guilt that whites
parents and white children carry—because of the greed, hatred, bigotry, and
indifference, which are a part of their heritage, many black people suffered
and died. The conflict between the heritage of the American ideals as em-
bodied in the Constitution and the American Creed and the heritage of
greed, negrophobia, and racism has never been resolved. The American
Dilemma still exists, especially in the hearts and minds of young people who
are struggling to find a self in the midst of a chaotic changing world.

1. Many groups of black students score equal to the normative mean on social self which
would seem to indicate that the low mean score of the whites lowers the overall score for
the entire group.
2. Powell, G.J. Self-concepts among white and black children. Presented at the Conference on Racism and Mental Health, Syracuse University, April 21, 1971 (to be published
in Racism and Mental Health, Willie, C., and Kramer, M., eds. Pittsburgh Press).
3. Powell, G.J., and Fuller, M. Self-concept profiles of American adolescents in the
midst of socio-political changes in the U.S. Paper presented at the VII International
Congress of Child Psychiatry, Tel Aviv, Israel. August 2-6, 1970.
4. Tucker, A.B. The self-concepts of 7th and 8th grade students: A summary and comparative study. Unpublished thesis for master's in social work, Graduate School of University of Minnesota, June, 1971.

20

A Little Child Shall Lead Them? The Future of School Desegregation

THE EFFECTS OF SCHOOL DESEGREGATION

Among white and black educators, quality education has been equated with integrated education, and desegregated education with racial balance. Most people who believe in this creed point to the Coleman report, the 1966 research project sponsored by the U.S. Office of Education which reported that the racial balance of schools was one of the few factors that improved black students' educational achievement. What is it that Coleman really said?[1]

1. It is thus apparent that the tables must be studied carefully, with special attention paid to the regional breakdowns which often provide more meaningful information than do the nationwide averages. Such careful study will reveal that there is not a wholly consistent pattern—that is, minorities are not at a disadvantage in every item listed.
2. Usually greater than the majority-minority differences, however, are the regional differences.
3. Just as minority groups tend to have less access to physical facilities that seem to be related to academic achievement, so too they have less access to curricular and extracurricular programs that would seem to have such a relationship.
4. A constant difference in standard deviations over the various grades represents an increasing difference in grade-level gap. Thus, by this measure, the deficiency in achievement is progressively greater for the minority pupils at progressively higher grade levels. For most minority groups, then, and most particularly the Negro, schools provide no opportunity at all for them to overcome this initial deficiency . . . Whatever may be the combination of nonschool factors—poverty, community attitudes, low educational level of parents—which put minority children at a disadvantage in verbal and non-verbal skills when they enter the first grade, the fact is the schools have not overcome it.

295

5. A difference of one standard deviation in median scores means that about 84 percent of the children in the lower groups are below the median of the majority students—but 50 percent of the white children are themselves behind that median as well.

6. By grade 12, both white and Negro students in the South score below their counterparts—White and Negro—in the North. In addition, Southern Negroes score farther below Southern whites than Northern Negroes score below Northern whites.

7. The achievement of minority pupils depends more on the schools they attend than does the achievement of majority pupils. Thus, 20 percent of the achievement of Negroes in the South is associated with particular schools they go to, whereas 10 percent of the achievement of whites in the South is. The conclusion can then be drawn that improving the school of a minority pupil will increase his achievement more than will improving the school of a white child increase his. Similarly, the average minority pupil's achievement will suffer more in a school of low quality than will the average white pupil's. This indicates that it is for the most disadvantaged children that improvements in school quality will make the most difference in achievement.

8. An analysis was carried out to examine the affects of an achievement which might appear in the short run. This analysis of the test performance of Negro children in integrated schools indicates positive effects of integration though rather small ones. Comparing the averages in each row, in every case but one, the highest average score is recorded for the Negro pupils where more than half of their classmates were white. But in reading the rows from left to right, the increase is small and often those Negro pupils in classes with only a few whites score lower than those in totally segregated schools.

It should be noted that in Coleman's analysis of integration and achievement as quoted above the regions included were the metropolitan Northeast and metropolitan Midwest. No actual statistical data is presented on the effects of desegregation on achievement in the South. Nor is desegregation a certain factor for academic achievement even in the metropolitan Northeast and Midwest, for Coleman also noted that "in many cases the average for the Negro students in totally segregated classes is higher than the average for those in classes where half or less of the students were white" and "the average scores of Negroes who have only experienced segregated schooling may exceed the averages recorded for those students who first came to desegregated schools in the later grades."[2]

Consequently, the effects of desegregation on the achievement of black students is not consistent, in many instances is minimal, and indicates that the number of blacks in the desegregated school may be as important or more important than the number of white students.

A research study done by the Menninger Foundation found in studying one high school that desegregation produced social segregation and the solidification of racial stereotyping.[3] However, another report by Dr. Louis Damant, chairman of the Department of Psychology at the University of North Carolina in Charlotte, states that no matter how prejudicial a child's parents may be, a white child may develop relatively free of racial prejudice if he gets into an integrated school system at the kindergarten level.[4] Likewise, the Coleman report found that in schools in the metropolitan Northeast and Midwest white children who first attended desegregated schools early in their school careers were likely to value their associations with black students.[5] The findings of this study showed that the white students in desegregated schools tended to have higher self-concept scores than those in segregated or predominantly white schools. (See Chapter 16, Table 7.) In New Orleans, in particular, the differences on many TSCS scores between segregated and desegregated white students were statistically significant. (See Chapter 12, Tables 5, 6, and 7.)

In a study of more than 683 schools in 19 cities conducted by the Policy Institute of Syracuse University for the Office of Education a direct correlation was made between violence in the nation's high schools and integration.[6] The investigators felt that "short of a total moral conversion" of American society, school disturbances will continue for some time to come.

Hodgkins and Stakenas conclude from their study of self-concepts of black and white youth in segregated Southern environments that successful desegregation cannot occur without significant modification of white prejudice. Without this the consequences for the development of self-concepts of black students could be very negative especially for previously segregated blacks.[7] Likewise, Haggstrom in his study of blacks' personality in segregated and desegregated situations, states that desegregation is likely to work to the disadvantage of blacks' personalities and he quotes a study by Staten and Webster in which during desegregation whites became less accepting of blacks. "However, so long as Negroes in the broader society are assigned a lesser social status because of their race, the improvement of some segregated facilities cannot be psychologically beneficial to them."[8]

Needless to say, there are many diverse opinions on the effect of desegregation. What then are the alternatives? Christopher Jencks feels the best alternative to endless school crises in education is to follow the Catholic precedent and have blacks set up their own private schools. He feels that the present urban school crisis should be viewed as a political problem first and a pedagogic one second. "Given racial and economic segregation in housing, localism in education means *de facto* segregation in schooling."[9]

Black private controlled schools would help black students develop a sense of community, solidarity, and pride in the ghetto. For without a change in the social order of things there is little real evidence that improving black children's academic skills would help any appreciable number to escape poverty and powerlessness. Stephan Michelson at the Brookings Institution found that in order for a black to break out of poverty it is not enough for him to finish high school, he must at least finish college.[10]

Maurice R. Berube feels that blacks can learn a lesson from Catholic education inasmuch as there is evidence to support the fact that learning primarily depends on a student's attitude toward himself. "For if this theory of learning is accurate, and there are many reasons to believe it is, then the antidote to a long history of black failure in schools would be this new-found race consciousness. In short, black power holds the key to learning for the black man in America."[11]

Preston Wilcox, director of Afram Associates, Inc., a Harlem-based social research facility which engages in studies in educational, community, and human development, says that the kids will decide.

> "Pan-African students are increasingly resisting efforts to get them to cooperate in their own educational genocide. No longer can they be contained by white rhetoric; nor can they be seduced into rejecting the interests of their own people. They have learned what a large number of Pan-Africans are beginning to learn from our young people: the revolution is not over; and it is not just beginning; it's continually with us. Struggle is education is struggle. Blacks in the nation's high schools and colleges are searching for models which will link them integrally with the Pan-African experience."[12]

THE CHILDREN SPEAK

Dr. Mark A. Chesler of the Institute for School Research at the University of Michigan was a visiting instructor in 1960 at Tuskegee Institute in Alabama. While he was there he interviewed and recorded the comments of 20 teenagers who were among the first blacks to attend formerly all-white public schools in Alabama. Their comments were published by the Southern Regional Council in a booklet entitled *In Their Own Words*. The following comments are quotes from those students:[13]

THE SCHOOL STAFF

> "Some of the teachers will try to be funny. When they get to a word like Negro, they call it nigger or else try to make fun."
> "When we got in there, they started throwing rocks and crayons at us. I told the teacher and she went back there, and they all started laughing, she was laughing with them. And then they went outside and they brought more rocks and they started throwing them."
> I had this teacher who divided the class up into groups. The Negroes sit on one half of the class and then she would go over to the white kids. If we came to anything about communism or say something like relating to civil rights, she

would bring up [Dr. Martin Luther] King's name and say something like, 'In a little time our freedom will be gone.' Their freedom, the whites. She feels that just because she is a teacher she can talk about anything."

"Our teacher was always calling on us when we wouldn't have our hands up, and when we did have our hands up she wouldn't call on us; when we'd take them down, that's when she would call on us."

"The principal got a refrigerator and put it in there for you. He went and got drinks for us also. He would ask us in the morning what we would like to have and would go out of his way to get it for us. He was pretty nice."

ON WHITE CLASSMATES

"Sometimes we'd be going down the hall and if any of the white students was standing in the hall and they see us coming, they say here comes a black nigger, you better stand back or something. They would get back up against the wall. In the morning sometime we'd be standing by our locker and they would get off the bus and come in and try to walk close up by the wall or something, pretending they didn't want to get close to touch us or anything."

"[Kids with] real BB guns would stand around the bus and aim at us and threaten us. Boys would ride around on motorcycles and throw rocks at us from the outside. The elementary kids would throw rotten eggs at us. The police would ignore them."

"This is the first thing that comes over them, intermarriage. Well, it takes two to marry somebody. Nobody wants to marry them; you just want to be their friends, that's all."

"Well, before I went to the white school, I always did think that the white person was smarter than we are. I used to think that they were just born smarter, just because they were white, but I found out this year that this isn't true. There were a lot of them who had more trouble than I had in getting their lessons and they had been in this school and in this situation, maybe not in the same situation, but they had been around their friends and teachers for 11 years before then. Some of them couldn't do half as good as I could, and I don't see how some of them even graduated. They failed some subjects and took an extra subject and made D's in that subject and they still passed. I don't understand it. I think that maybe the reason we think we aren't as smart as they are is because they've made us feel like we don't know anything."

ON THE NEGRO COMMUNITY

"In our community, all of them were very encouraging. We had been having small mass meetings around our community to try and encourage people to try to enroll students in this school because you get a better education there. Everyone was very glad that I was chosen to go there and they were trying to encourage me as much as possible to continue."

"People in my neighborhood didn't like my going to the white school because they said that I was just trying to be popular and the white school wasn't any better than the Negro school. They said that the Negro school was the

newest school. They said that our house was going to be burned and the Ku
Klux Klan was going to get us and [when it happened] lots of people said,
'That's what I told you was going to happen.' "

"Well, the colored people in my community, well, some of the colored
anyway, the Uncle Toms, would tell me to stay in my place and that they
weren't going to sit near us over there and get throwed at and called nigger."

ON THE FUTURE

"I think the situation would be better if more Negro students went because a
lot of the students just pick on you because they think they can get by with it. I
don't think a student would hit a Negro student if he thought somebody was
behind him to give him just that much more. He wouldn't do it even if he
thought somebody was behind him that would see him and tell the student who
it was."

"You have to be in area where you can be accepted together. It's not like
that down here. That's what's wrong, and it'll take time, a long time, to change."

The October 15, 1970 issue of the *Wall Street Journal* reported on the
evasive action of schools in the deep South to decrease the pace of desegregation.

They are inspiring a growing wave of vocal black resentment and even pro-
voking some young blacks to yearn for what they view as the less degrading days
of total segregation . . .
In those cases where whites have ceased active resistance and admitted
Negroes to their classrooms, the going hasn't been easy for the black children.
Despite complaints by blacks, one Louisiana school has maintained its nickname
"The Rebels" and members of its marching band still wear Confederate uni-
forms. A favorite song at school assemblies is "Dixie."
Often blacks find the only way to erase such seemingly trivial slights is by
going to court . . . Civil Rights advocates are convinced such incidents are likely
to grow in number; and they are gloomy about even such court victories.
In Earle, Arkansas, 200 blacks walked out of the newly [desegregated]
integrated schools and marched through town stoning businesses.[14]

In Franklinton, Louisiana, the school board has used ability testing to
create all-white or all-black classes.

Ability grouping "has knocked the ambition out of the children . . ."When I
try to tell some of my own children to work, they won't, because they know
they're in the lowest sections and the school expects them to be bad." Black
students themselves say they find being assigned to low sections so degrading
that they would prefer outright segregation. "I don't like my new school", says
an 11-year-old black girl so assigned. "I'd rather go back to the old one." [She
recalls her segregated school fondly.] "In the old school, if we did something

wrong, we'd just get a warning," she explains, "but, in the new school we get a paddling."

But [her] mother is not so optimistic about the lessons her daughter is learning from her first taste of integration. "The kind of integration we're going through here may convince these children that integration is a hopeless cause and not worth fighting for," she says. "I hope that won't happen, but it sure looks like it is."[15]

SEPARATE BUT EQUAL Revisited

The greatest crises in American society today are focused on the issues of public school education, educational reform, quality education, but more especially, school desegregation and racial imbalance. These are issues confronting the North and South, but the final battleground will probably be in the North where the neglect of ghetto schools has gone unnoticed while the nation focused its attention on the drama of school desegregation in the Mansfields, the Clintons, and the Little Rocks of the South. In 1954, the U.S. Supreme Court ordered the Southern and border states to proceed "with all deliberate speed" to desegregate the schools and discontinue their dual school systems. Many children born in that momentous year of 1954 have completed their public school education. How many of them were actually part of the enactment of that famous decree? In the school year before the first Supreme Court ruling on segregation in public schools, the Southern states and border regions had 2.5 million black children in segregated schools.[16] By the school year 1966-67, there were 2.7 million black children in segregated schools. Less than one percent integration per year is neither speedy nor deliberate. It is less than a snail's pace. It may be said then that while making clear what it did not want, i.e., *de jure* segregation, the court was far less clear on what it did want. The implementation decision of May 31, 1955, was clearly an avoidance of how, when, and where school desegregation should take place. At the time, many felt that the justices were trying to accommodate the South and to be gradual and moderate. The Court's indecisiveness and lack of clarity on this issue led to years of litigation, excuses for delay, and noncompliance and removed the clout from the May 17, 1954 ruling. Since then, confusion has reigned. Many think that if the great change from segregated schools to desegregated schools had been made more swiftly and more decisively, there would have been less resistance and turmoil. Most certainly that was the evidence presented by the social scientists at the time. (See Chapter 17.)

The 1964 Civil Rights Act with the compliance procedures of Title VI placed the enforcement of desegregation on HEW who then had the power to decide when federal funds could be withdrawn from districts that failed to comply with the department's desegregation guidelines. The task fell upon Mrs. Ruby G. Martin, a young black lawyer who was appointed the director of HEW's Office for Civil Rights. Mrs. Martin's tough enforcement of Title VI aroused the wrath of some white Southern school officials. However, the 1964 Civil Rights Act helped to quicken the pace of desegregation in the South.

In 1966 the Fifth Circuit Court of Appeals allowed "freedom-of-choice" plans, but only as a means of ending segregated school systems. In 1968 the Supreme Court ruled that so-called freedom-of-choice desegregation plans were inadequate when they did not undo school segregation as rapidly as other available methods could. The Court warned that school systems that continued to resist desegregating classrooms by any methods such as "freedom of choice," school district gerrymandering, and other evasive devices were inviting the courts to desegregate for them. In 1969 the Burger Court decided that "all deliberate speed" for desegregation was no longer constitutionally permissible and ordered the immediate desegregation of all the schools throughout the region for the 1969-70 school term. The combined efforts of the Federal courts, the U.S. Justice Department, and HEW officials produced a substantial increase in school desegregation. By June of 1969, of the 4,529 school districts in the 17 Southern and border states, about two thirds or 3,004 districts were operating unitary or desegregated school systems.[17] The remaining 1,525 consisted of 360 desegregating under Federal court order, 655 desegregating under a voluntary plan approved by HEW, and 510 in noncompliance or in questionable compliance with the law (of those that had not complied, 121 had lost their funds, 103 had been cited for fund termination, and 286 were still negotiating with HEW).[18]

However, statistics can only tell part of the desegregation story. Although the record looked good, there were still some pesty questions to be answered. What constitutes a disparity between "technical" desegregation and "actual" desegregation? What constitutes racial balance and imbalance? Both state and lower Federal courts had ruled that the Constitution does not prohibit school boards from voluntarily adopting programs to reduce racial imbalance in the public schools for the purpose of providing equal educational opportunities for all students. The highest judicial authorities had stated that the Constitution does not require educational officials to take measures to alleviate racial imbalance.

> At least three Federal courts of appeals have concurred in the view that the decision in *Brown* and the many cases following it do not require a school system developed on the neighborhood school plan, even though it results in a racial imbalance in the schools, where . . . that school system has been honestly and conscientiously constructed with no intentions or purpose to maintain or perpetuate segregation.[19]

This stance by the judiciary had not been helpful in eliminating the majority black districts in the South. By 1970, in more than 300 of the 2,780 public school districts in the South, the majority of the district enrollment was black with percentages ranging from barely over 50 percent black to as high as 70 or 80 percent black to some instances of all black.[20]

Finally on April 20, 1971 the U.S. Supreme Court gave another unanimous decision on school desegregation which has major implications for the South but also the North. First of all, busing of students to schools outside their neighborhoods may be required if it is necessary to achieve "effective" desegregation. Secondly, neighborhood schools must go if they maintain segregation. Thirdly, a racial ratio is not constitutionally required in each school to match the racial composition of the entire school district, but limited use may be made of ratios as a "useful starting point in shaping a remedy to correct past constitutional violations." The fourth point was that "a small number of all black schools may be permissable under certain circumstances, but where they exist, authorities must be prepared to prove, that they are not the result of discrimination."

It is interesting to note that at the same time this decision on school desegregation was made the bill to provide for low-cost housing in suburban areas was defeated.

Since the 1971 decision, lower Federal courts have made decisions which have had major implications for Northern and Southern school districts. In Richmond, Virginia the Federal court approved a desegregation plan that entails busing to consolidate the predominantly black city school system with the predominantly white suburban school districts. In Detroit, Denver, Los Angeles, Las Vegas, and San Francisco, Federal courts have ruled on *de facto* segregation which has been reinforced by official action. The Denver and Richmond cases are being appealed but if the lower courts are upheld, mandatory public school desegregation will be the law of the land. The elimination of *de facto* segregation patterns by cross-district busing plans has raised a furor of antibusing protests in Northern and Southern communities. The arguments against busing include (1) that the Supreme court is tampering with an individual's basic right to decide where he wants his child to go to school, (2) that many children who are attending good schools will be forced to attend bad ones, (3) that busing is unsafe and may risk the health of the children, (4) that white children are being sent into ghetto areas where there is violence and drugs, and (5) that white children may suffer psychologically if they are a minority in a black ghetto school. Beneath the superficial concern for safety, educational quality, basic individual rights, and the value of the neighborhood school, the ugly spectre of negrophobia raises its head. The opposition of white parents to busing is based on the same old white racists' irrational fears and insecurities that maintained "the separate but equal" doctrine that the Supreme court declared illegal and immoral in 1954.

However, the ugliest spectre of all is the President's support of the anti-busing movement. During the presidential campaign of 1968, Mr. Nixon campaigned vigorously in the South, repeatedly coming out in favor of the neighborhood school, against busing, and exploiting white resentment of the Johnson administration's aggressive enforcement of Title VI. With Strom Thurmond's support he carried Virginia, both Carolinas, Tennessee, and Florida. After the election Southern senators anticipated some delays in court orders to desegregate. The initial ambivalence demonstrated by the Administration caused confusion and dismay, both in Southern circles hoping to delay and in civil rights circles where there was a committment to the continued enforcement of Title VI. Several subsequent events increased the dismay in civil rights circles. One was the forced resignation of Leon Panetta, director of HEW's Office for Civil Rights, the unit that enforces the Title VI fund cutoffs. The other was the Stennis and Whitten amendments—both from Mississippi—that sought to 1) require Federal legislation regarding desegregation policies to be applied uniformly throughout the nation, 2) permit freedom-of-choice plans to suffice everywhere, and 3) ban compulsory busing of students to achieve integration. The Stennis and Whitten amendments were eventually defeated but the antibusing forces gained momentum. With the President's approval, other attempts are being made to offset Federal court rulings requiring pupil busing to achieve desegregation. Now the President has asked the Congress to use its power under the 14th Amendment to halt further court-ordered busing until July 1, 1973. In the meantime more Federal aid is promised to those schools which have more than 30 percent poverty children enrolled. This last Presidential request and promise along with the defeat of the bill to provide low-cost housing in suburban areas are attempts to protect Nixon's white "silent majority" of middle class America from contamination with poor minorities. The message is clear: We must keep you blacks separate but we promise to keep things equal. In the midst of the legal debate what does the black community think about school desegregation?

Crain and Inger contend that since the 60s there have been indications of withdrawal from the school desegregation issue. Blacks who had been maintaining their interest in the schools were becoming less concerned about integration and more concerned about "better black schools" and "local control" over the neighborhood black school.[21]

For increasing numbers of black citizens and teachers school desegregation is no longer the magic formula that it was in the heady exultant day following the 1954 *Brown* decision. In the South where it has brought fundamental social change, many still advocate desegregation. Charles Evers, black mayor of Fayette, Mississippi, says, "Black people can fight better when they are pressured. We're on our way still. We're going to keep moving. We're not going back. Brother Nixon, Brother Mitchell, Brother Eastland, Brother Stennis—not one of them is going to stop us now."[22]

In the rural South whites have always had the best schools and blacks feel that the only way to get a decent education is to go to a white school. Preston Wilcox of Afram in New York states:

"Integrated education has largely been a subterfuge for white supremacy; little systematic effort has been undertaken to help black and white students relate as equals. Little has been done to help black and white students obtain the skills and desire to help solve the nation's problems without becoming part of the problem themselves."[23]

Rhody McCoy, administrator of the Ocean Hill-Brownsville school district in Brooklyn states: "Integration has never worked. What kind of hypocrite am I to tell black children to do their thing in school and college so that they can take their rightful place in society? Where is that place?"[24]

Ray Innis of CORE claims: "Integration came to be viewed by the civil rights aristocracy not as a means to an end but as an end in itself."[25]

Benjamin Holman, director of the Justice Department's community relations service considers integration "unrealistic and unwise" because most whites cannot accept it: "[My goal] is not some sort of vague illusory melting pot in which we're all mixed like salt and pepper, but a multiracial society in which we have black neighborhoods and black communities and still live as one nation."[26]

John Mansell of the NAACP concludes: "What we are up against is a concerted attempt by segregationists, black and white, North and South, with the blessing of the President, to turn back the clock and plant second class citizenship firmly and forever on us."[27]

And finally, in the face of all the legal debates and all the research studies how can black parents decide where to send their children to school? Black parents must always consider what will promote the emotional development of their children. Unless a child feels secure within himself, he cannot learn. When a child has the emotional security to meet the tasks that confront him, he can learn, he can play, he can work, and he can grow. As black parents we must ask ourselves, will this school program provide not only intellectual growth for my child but also further his emotional development? In order to answer that question we need to know not only how school desegregation will be implemented but also how the process of integration will be carried out? What are the attitudes of the teachers? What kind of in-depth preparation in the black and white communities is being done to pave the way? In addition to the three R's will children also be taught "liberty and justice for all?"

For too long, now, we the people of the United States have had the simplistic belief that the children will solve the problems of our multifacet society. School desegregation has been seen as the panacea for all our racial problems and having accomplished that, we have only to sit back and reap the benefits from a truly just multiracial, integrated society. Thus, in the name of quality education and racial equality black children became a political football, the cutting edge for social change, the infantry in the battle on racism—a battle that we adults have not been able to resolve. Although the nation could rejoice at the 1954 school desegregation ruling, the actual process has been less than encouraging. The mere placing of white and black children in the same school building has not lead to integration or quality education. Although the Court could decree the end of separate schools for black and white children, it could not legislate brotherly love and human kindness. Black parents must remember what more radical young blacks have pointed out—"education without dignity is invalid."

With the white racist attitudes of teachers and students, many inhumane acts which are committed in the name of compliance lead to psychologic problems for black students, as our study has shown. Who will monitor the schools to prevent such vengeance? The Supreme Court? The NAACP? HEW? How is the process of desegregation changed to a process of integration? How much learning can go on in a hostile desegregated school? How does a school system that tries to further desegregation prevent the flight of whites to the suburbs or private schools, leaving the inner city with a majority of minority children and poor whites and without a tax base to support the innovations and reforms needed for quality education? How can the children solve that problem for the adults?

Somehow, somewhere, sometime the American people must wake up to the great American nightmare and the sanguine unreality of the American dream. We are a racist society, and until we have solved that very basic problem school desegregation may produce more problems than it will solve. W.E.B. DuBois once said: "The Negro needs neither segregated schools nor mixed schools; what he needs is education."[28] In view of the results of this study, which clearly indicate that the psychologic development of black children is facilitated by segregated or predominantly black schools and hampered by present-day techniques of school desegregation in hostile white racist communities, maybe we as black parents need to consider more carefully the educational and psychologic consequences of school desegregation. In view of the fact that white Southern children, and indeed white children in other parts of the country, are having difficulty with self-concept development, maybe we as black parents need to look more carefully at the assets of a cohesive black community which provides positive black models for black children. White is not always right. Inasmuch as public school education in this country has failed to educate our black children and many white children as well, maybe we as black parents need to provide more relevant educational and psychologic experiences for our black children. To bus or not to bus? To segregate or not to segregate? These questions must be considered carefully not only from a political viewpoint, but also from a psychologic one for our children. While the antibusing movement among whites who would try to curtail the legal, social, economic, and moral gains attained by black Americans in the last decades should be fought, it must not be fought at the expense of black children. In the face of the prevailing resistance of white people in this country to integrate the black man into all phases of American life, it would seem that the energies of black people must be directed to securing their own power base. An education for black children with dignity and pride may be the only way that "we will reach the mountain top and see the promised land."

1. Coleman, J. Equality of educational opportunity. U.S. Dept. of HEW, Office of Education. U.S. Govt. Printing Office, Washington, D.C., 1966 (abridged form) OE-38000, p. 15-22.

2. Ibid.

3. Time Magazine. Op. cit., 1970, p. 14.

4. Early race integration cuts down prejudice. Los Angeles Times, Feb. 18, 1969.

5. Coleman. Op. cit., 1966, p. 331.

6. Foley, T.J. High School unrest related to racial mixing. Los Angeles Times, Sept. 4, 1970, p. 1.

7. Hodgkins, B.J., and Stakenas, R.G. A study of self-concepts of Negro and white youth in segregated environments. Journal of Negro Education 38 (Fall, 1969), pp. 370-377.

8. Haggstrom, W.C. Segregation, desegregation, and Negro personality. Integrated Education. 1 (October-November, 1963), pp. 19-23.

9. Jencks, C. Private schools for black children. The New York Times Magazine, Nov. 3, 1968, p. 133.

10. Jencks. Op. cit., 1968, p. 132.

11. Berube, M.R. Black power and the learning process: Learning a lesson from Catholic education. Commonweal, April 11, 1969, p. 98.

12. Wilcox, P. The kids will decide. Ebony, Vol. xxv, No. 10, Aug., 1970, p. 135.

13. Chesler, M.A. In Their Own Words. Atlanta: Southern Regional Council, 1967, p. 2.

14. Herman, T. Evasive action: Schools in deep South slow integration tide with subtler tactics. The Wall Street Journal, Vol. LI, No. 2, Oct. 15, 1970.

15. Ibid.

16. Southern Education Report. April, 1967, p. 34.

17. Ibid., June, 1969, pp. 27-28.

18. Ibid.

19. Ibid., p. 35.

20. Race Relations Information Center. Majority Black School Districts in the 11 Southern States, July, 1970, p. 1.

21. Crain, R.L., and Inger, M. Urban school integration: Strategy for peace. Saturday Review, Feb. 18, 1967.

22. Turn around on integration. Time Magazine, Vol. 95, No. 10, March 9, 1970, p. 14.

23. Wilcox, P. Integration or separatism in education: K-12. July, 1969 (unpublished manuscript).
24. Turn around on integration. Op. cit.
25. Ibid.
26. Ibid.
27. Ibid.
28. Quoted by Preston Wilcox in "The Kid's Will Decide." Ebony Magazine, Vol. XXV, No. 10, August 1970, p. 135.

Appendix I

TEXT OF NEWS CONFERENCE FOR
GREENSBORO DAILY NEWS, *APRIL 30, 1969*
by Dr. Wm. J. House, Superintendent of
Greensboro City Schools

After consultation with our attorneys, it appears that the gist of the hearing examiner's decision is contained in the following statement from his conclusions of law:

> Although significant progress has been made in student, faculty, and facility desegregation, the Respondent School District is not in compliance with the Civil Rights Act of 1964, and Regulations, for the school year 1968-69 under its 'freedom of choice' plan because there has been no diminution of the dual school structure.

While the examiner states that at this time "the existence of some schools in the system which have a student body of one race only, does not, of itself, render freedom of choice illegal," he does say, regardless of the fact that the Greensboro City Board of Education's freedom-of-choice plan has achieved results "superior" to those achieved in the cases upon which HEW relies, that still "the fact stands out that in 1965 there were eleven all-Negro schools . . . " and that "there is no evidence upon which a prognosis can be made that there will be less than eleven all-Negro schools . . . " in the coming school year. The only way to eliminate all-Negro schools other than through freedom of choice would be forced attendance by white students at what HEW refers to as all-Negro schools.

The opinion of the examiner characterizes the finding against the Board as a "difficult decision" because of the statistical evidence favorable to the Board. The unfavorable ruling relies upon the continued existence of schools currently attended exclusively by Negro students.

Taking into account the fact that 91 percent of the Negro population lives in the southeast quadrant of Greensboro, the examiner states:

> The March, 1968, revision of the Guidelines provides that the policies enunciated do not require the correction of racial imbalance resulting from private housing patterns. It appears that beginning within the Reconstruction Period, there was discrimination against Negroes in the South of varying degrees with respect to housing, schooling, and work, which gradually, over the years, became less and less effective, and less and less common, but it might well have been the cause of the location of Negro housing in the southeast quadrant, and it is quite apparent that the racial imbalance in the school population resulted from that private housing pattern. However, there is no specific evidence in the record other than history and location, of discrimination in the sale or rental of housing to Negroes.

He adds:

> The significant discrimination sprang from the attitude and action of private individuals in years past. No evidence appears in the record of recent examples of refusal to sell or rent to Negroes housing outside of the southeast quadrant upon which a finding of discrimination can be based.

What the hearing examiner appears to be saying is that, in spite of the Board's good faith and significant progress in desegregation of pupils and staff, we still have the obligation to eliminate the so-called dual school structure in spite of local residential patterns resulting from "the attitude and action of private individuals in years past" and over which the Board has no control.

Among his findings of fact are the following statements:

> During the 1964-65 and 1965-66 school years, of forty regular schools, there were thirteen all-white, eleven all-Negro and sixteen integrated schools, and during the 1968-69 school year of forty-six regular schools, there were five all-white, twelve all-Negro, and twenty-nine integrated schools.

> During the 1968-69 school year the system had 32,094 pupils enrolled, of which 10,025 were Negro, 70 American Indian, and 21,998 were white. Of the Negro children, 1,897 or 19 percent made the choice to attend schools with white children and did so attend, which represented an increase in number and percentage of the Negro school children who attended formerly white schools from the 1965 to 1968 school year.

> In the 1968-69 school year, 144 teachers, librarians, and other persons who dealt directly with the students, of a total of 1600, taught or performed their duties across racial lines which was an increase over prior years.

Eighteen of eighty-four school buses carried students on an integrated basis and the [sic] number of drivers are of a race different from the pupils carried on the bus.

Extra-curricular activities were carried out on an integrated basis.

It is also worth noting that the approaches to compliance suggested by the Office for Civil Rights prior to the hearing would have reduced the number of schools enrolling students of only one race *but would not have eliminated the dual school structure* as that structure is defined by HEW.

Although I cannot presume to speak out for the Board, I am convinced that our Board has acted in good faith, that significant progress in desegregation has occurred, and that an answer should be sought for the question of the Board's responsibility to overcome the effects of residential housing patterns over which it has no control.

Appendix II
Sample Questionnaires

Powell–Fuller Questionnaire

1. Age _____

2. Birthdate _____

3. Birthplace _____

4. Sex _____

5. Name of School _____ City _____

6. Grade in school _____

7. How long have you been in your present school? _____

8. Name of your previous schools (list) and where they are located

   1. _____

   2. _____

   3. _____

9. Birthplace of mother _____

10. Birthplace of father _____

11. Are your parents (check one)

      a. Separated _____

      b. Divorced _____

      c. Remarried _____

      d. Together _____

12. With whom do you live (check appropriate item)

      a. Mother _____

      b. Mother and father _____

      c. Father _____

      d. Grandmother _____

      e. Grandmother and mother _____

      f. Grandmother and grandfather _____

      g. Stepmother and father _____

      h. Stepfather and mother _____

      i. Another relative (specify) _____

13. Did your father finish high school? Yes _____ No _____

14. How many years of college has your father had? _____

15. What is your father's occupation? _____

16. What is your father's monthly income? _____

17. Did your mother finish high school? Yes _____ No _____

18. How many years of college has your mother had? _____

19. Does your mother work? _____

      What kind of work does she do? _____

20. How many children are there in your family? _____

21. What are the ages of your sisters and brothers? _____

22. I (like) (do not like) going to school because _____

_____

23. How well are you doing in school now? (check one)

       Excellent _____

       Good _____

       Fair _____

       Poor _____

24. Are you satisfied with how you are doing in school?   Yes _____   No _____

25. My favorite subject is _____ and my least

favorite is _____

26. What would you like to do upon finishing school? _____

_____

27. My friends after school are

       a. The same kids I know in school _____

       b. Different kids from the ones I know in school _____

       c. About half and half _____

28. After school I like to _____

29. I see myself as _____

_____

30. I would like to be _____

31. How do you sleep at night? _____

32. Do you (check those that apply)

   a. Walk in your sleep _____

   b. Wet the bed _____

   c. Have nightmares _____

   d. Dream a lot each night _____

   e. Fear of going to sleep at night _____

TDMH – Self-Concept Scale

Instructions: These statements are to help you describe yourself as you see yourself. Please respond to them as if you were describing yourself <u>to yourself</u>. <u>Do not omit any item</u>! Read each statement carefully; then select one of the following responses; and next record the number that represents that particular answer in the blank space at the beginning of that statement.

Responses	–	Completely true	Mostly true	Partly true and partly false	Mostly false	Completely false
Number	–	5	4	3	2	1

<u>Remember</u> you are <u>not</u> trying to describe yourself as others see you, but <u>only as you see yourself</u>.

_____ 1. I have a healthy body.

_____ 4. I am full of aches and pains.

_____ 7. I am neither too fat nor too thin.

_____ 10. I don't feel as well as I should.

_____ 13. I take good care of myself physically.

_____ 16. I do poorly in sports and games.

_____ 19. I am a decent sort of person.

_____ 22. I am a moral failure.

_____ 25. I am satisfied with my moral behavior.

_____ 28. I wish I could be more trustworthy.

_____ 31. I am true to my religion in my everyday life.

_____ 34. I sometimes use unfair means to get ahead.

_____ 37. I am a cheerful person.

_____ 40. I am a hateful person.

_____ 43. I am satisfied to be just what I am.

_____ 46. I am not the person I would like to be.

_____ 49. I can always take care of myself in any situation.

_____ 52. I change my mind a lot.

_____ 55. I have a family that would always help me in any kind of trouble.

_____ 58. I am not loved by my family.

_____ 61. I am satisfied with my family relationships.

_____ 64. I am too sensitive to things my family say.

_____ 67. I try to play fair with my friends and family.

_____ 70. I quarrel with my family.

_____ 73. I am a friendly person.

_____ 76. I am mad at the whole world.

_____ 79. I am as sociable as I want to be.

_____ 82. I should be more polite to others.

_____ 85. I try to understand the other fellow's point of view.

_____ 88. I do not feel at ease with other people.

_____ 91. I do not always tell the truth.

_____ 92. Once in a while I think of things too bad to talk about.

_____ 93. I get angry sometimes.

_____ 2. I like to look nice and neat all the time.

_____ 5. I consider myself a sloppy person.

_____ 8. I am neither too tall nor too short.

_____ 11. I would like to change some parts of my body.

_____ 14. I feel good most of the time.

_____ 17. I often act like I am "all thumbs."

_____ 20. I am a religious person.

Responses	–	Completely true	Mostly true	Partly true and partly false	Mostly false	Completely false
Number	–	5	4	3	2	1

_____ 23. I am a bad person.

_____ 26. I am as religious as I want to be.

_____ 29. I ought to go to church more.

_____ 32. I do what is right most of the time.

_____ 35. I sometimes do very bad things.

_____ 38. I have a lot of self-control.

_____ 41. I am a nobody.

_____ 44. I am as smart as I want to be.

_____ 47. I despise myself.

_____ 50. I solve my problems quite easily.

_____ 53. I do things without thinking about them first.

_____ 56. I am an important person to my friends and family.

_____ 59. My friends have no confidence in me.

_____ 62. I treat my parents as well as I should.

_____ 65. I should trust my family more.

_____ 68. I do my share of work at home.

_____ 71. I give in to my parents.

_____ 74. I am popular with women.

_____ 77. I am not interested in what other people do.

_____ 80. I am satisfied with the way I treat other people.

_____ 83. I am no good at all from a social standpoint.

_____ 86. I see good points in all the people I meet.

_____ 89. I do not forgive others easily.

_____ 94. Sometimes, when I am not feeling well, I am cross.

_____ 95. I do not like everyone I know.

_____ 96. I gossip a little at times.

_____ 3. I am an attractive person.

_____ 6. I am a sick person.

_____ 9. I like my looks just the way they are.

_____ 12. I should have more sex appeal.

_____ 15. I try to be careful about my appearance.

_____ 18. I am a poor sleeper.

_____ 21. I am an honest person.

_____ 24. I am a morally weak person.

_____ 27. I am satisfied with my relationship to God.

_____ 30. I shouldn't tell so many lies.

_____ 33. I try to change when I know I'm doing things that are wrong.

_____ 36. I have trouble doing the things that are right.

_____ 39. I am a calm and easygoing person.

_____ 42. I am losing my mind.

_____ 45. I am just as nice as I should be.

_____ 48. I wish I didn't give up as easily as I do.

_____ 51. I take the blame for things without getting mad.

_____ 54. I try to run away from my problems.

_____ 57. I am a member of a happy family.

_____ 60. I feel that my family doesn't trust me.

_____ 63. I understand my family as well as I should.

_____ 66. I should love my family more.

Responses	–	Completely true	Mostly true	Partly true and partly false	Mostly false	Completely false
Number	–	5	4	3	2	1

_____ 69. I take a real interest in my family.

_____ 72. I do not act like my family thinks I should.

_____ 75. I am popular with men.

_____ 78. I am hard to be friendly with.

_____ 81. I try to please others, but I don't overdo it.

_____ 84. I ought to get along better with other people.

_____ 87. I get along well with other people.

_____ 90. I find it hard to talk with strangers.

_____ 97. Once in a while, I laugh at a dirty joke.

_____ 98. At times I feel like swearing.

_____ 99. I would rather win than lose in a game.

_____ 100. Once in a while I put off until tomorrow what I ought to do today.

Bibliography

Allport, G.W. Pattern and Growth in Personality. New York, Holt, Rinehart, and Winston, Inc., 1963.

Ausubel, D.P. Ego development among segregated Negro children. Ment. Hyg., 42:362-369, 1958.

Baldwin, J. Nobody Knows My Name. New York, Dell Publishing Co., Inc., 1961.

Baughman, E.E., and Dahlstrom, W.G. Negro and White Children: A Psychological Study in the Rural South. New York, Academic Press, 1968.

Blaustein, A., and Ferguson, C.C. Desegregation and the Law: The Meaning and Effect of the School Segregation Cases. New York, Vintage Books, 1962.

Brody, E. Minority Group Adolescence. Baltimore, Williams and Wilkins, 1968.

Butts, H.F. Skin color perception and self-esteem. Journal of Negro Education, 32:122-128, 1963.

Chethik, M., Fleming, E., and Mayer, M.F. A quest for identity: treatment of disturbed Negro children in a predominantly white treatment center. Amer. J. Orthopsychiat., 37:71-7, January, 1967.

Clark, K.B., and Clark, M.K. The development of consciousness of self and the emergence of racial identification in Negro pre-school children. J. Soc. Psychol., 10:591-599, 1939.

Clark, K.B., and Clark, M.R. Racial identification and preference in Negro children. In Readings in Social Psychology. MacCoby, E., ed., New York, Holt, Rinehart, and Winston, Inc., 1958.

Clark, K. Prejudice and Your Child. Boston, Beacon Press, 1963.

Clark, K.B. Dark Ghetto: Dilemmas of Social Power. New York, Harper Torchbooks, Harper and Row, Publishers, 1967.

Clausen, J.A., and Williams, J.R. Sociological correlates of child behavior. Child Psychology: the 62nd Yearbook of the National Society for the Study of Education, University of Chicago Press, 1963, pp. 62-107.

321

Coleman, J. The Equality of Educational Opportunity, HEW Office of Education, U.S. Government Printing Office: 1966. (OE-38000 and OE-38001)

Coopersmith, S. The Antecedents of Self-Esteem. San Francisco, W.H. Freeman and Company, 1967.

Crain, R.L. The Politics of School Desegregation. Chicago, Aldine Publishing Co., 1968.

Davis, A., and Dollard, D. Children of Bondage: The Personality Development of Negro Youth in the Urban South. New York, Harper Torchbooks, Harper and Row Publishers, 1964.

Dixon, J.C. Development of self-recognition. J. Genet. Psychol., 91:251-256, 1957.

Dollard, J. Caste and Class in a Southern Town. New Haven, Yale University Press, 1937.

Dreger, R.M., and Miller, K.S. Comparative psychological studies of Negroes and whites in the United States. Psychol. Bull., 57:361-402, 1960.

Dreger, R.M., and Miller, K.S. Comparative psychological studies of Negroes and whites in the United States: 1959-1965. Psychol. Bull., 70: Supplement: 1-58, Sept., 1968.

Erikson, E. The concept of identity. Daedalus, The American Academy of Arts and Sciences, Winter, 1966, pp. 150-151.

Erikson, E. Identity, Youth, and Crisis. New York, W.W. Norton and Co., 1968.

Fanon, F. Wretched of the Earth. New York, Grove Press, Inc., 1966.

Fishman, J.A. Childhood indoctrination for minority-group membership. Daedalus, Vol. 90, 2:329-349, Spring, 1961.

Fitts, W. Tennessee Self-Concept Scale Manual. Counselor Recordings and Tests, Box 6184, Acklen Station, Nashville, Tenn. 37212.

Franklin, J.H., and Isidore, S., eds. The Negro in the 20th Century. New York, Vintage Books, 1967.

Franklin, J.H. From Slavery to Freedom: A History of Negro Americans. New York, Vintage Books, 1969.

Frazier, E.F. The Negro Family in the United States, (revised edition). New York, Dryden Press, Inc., 1951.

Frazier, E.F. Negro Youth at the Crossways: Their Personality Development in the Middle States. American Council on Education: Washington, D.C., 1940.

Friedman, M., ed. The Worlds of Existentialism: A Critical Reader. New York, Random House, 1964.

Gibby, R.J., and Gabler, R. The self-concept of Negro and white children. J. Clin. Psychol., 1967, 23:144-150.

Glazer, N., and Moynihan, D.P. Beyond the Melting Pot. Cambridge, Mass., MIT Press and Harvard University Press, 1963.

Goodman, M.E. Race Awareness in Young Children. Cambridge, Addison-Wesley Press, 1952.

Greenwald, H.J., and Oppenheim, D.B. Reported magnitude of self-misidentification among Negro children—artifact. J. Personality Soc. Psychol., 8:49-52, Jan., 1968.

Harrington, M. The Other America: Poverty in the United States. New York, MacMillan Company, 1963.

Helmuth, J., ed. Disadvantaged Child, Volume 1. Special Child Publications of the Seattle Seguin School, Inc. Seattle, Wash. Bernie Straub and Jerome Helmuth, co-publishers, 1967.

Hsu, F.L., ed. Psychological Anthropology: Approaches to Culture and Personality. Homewood, Ill., The Dorsey Press, Inc., 1961.

Jersild, A.T. Child Psychology, 6th Ed. Englewood Cliffs, N.J., Prentice-Hall, Inc., 1963.

Johnson, C.S. Growing Up in the Black Belt. New York, Schocken Books, 1967.

Kardiner, A., and Ovesey, L. The Mark of Oppression: Explorations in the Personality of the American Negro. Cleveland, Meridian Books (The World Publishing Company), 1968.

Kierkegaard, S. Fear and Trembling and Sickness Unto Death. Garden City, N.Y., Doubleday and Company, Inc., 1955.

Kluckhohn, C., Murray, H.A., and Schneider, D. Personality in Nature, Society and Culture, 2nd ed. New York, Alfred Knopf, 1953.

Kvaraceus, W.C., et al. Negro Self-Concept: Implications for School and Citizenship, The report of a conference sponsored by the Lincoln Filene Center for Citizenship and Public Affairs. Tufts University: Medford, Massachusetts, 1964.

Linton, R. Culture and Mental Disorders. Springfield, Ill., Charles C Thomas Publishers, 1965.

Long, B.H., and Henderson, E.H. Self-social concepts of disadvantaged school beginners. J. Genet. Psychol., 113:41-51, September, 1968.

McDonald, R.L. Effects of sex, race, and class on self, ideal self and parental ratings in southern adolescents. Percept. Motor Skills, 27:15-25, 1968.

McDonald, R.L., and Gynther, M.D. MMPI differences associated with sex, race, and class in two adolescent samples. J. Consult. Psychol., 27:112-116, 1963.

Mead, G.H. Mind, Self, and Society. Chicago, University of Chicago Press, 1934.

Morland, J.K. Racial recognition by nursery school children in Lynchburg, Virginia. Social Forces, 37:132-137, 1958.

Morland, J.K. A comparison of race awareness of northern and southern children. Amer. J. Orthopsychiat., 36:22-31, 1966.

Myrdal, G. An American Dilemma, Vols. 1 and 2. New York, McGraw-Hill Paperback Edition, 1964.

Renninger, C.A., and Williams, J.E. Black-white color connotations and racial awareness in pre-school children. Percept. Motor Skills, 22:771-785, June, 1966.

Report of The Joint Commission on Mental Health of Children, Crisis in Child Mental Health: Challenge for the 1970's. New York, Harper and Row, 1970.

Riese, H. Heal the Hurt Child. Chicago, University of Chicago Press, Ill., 1962.

Rohrer, J.H., and Edmonson, M.S., eds. The Eighth Generation Grows Up. New York, Harper Torchbooks, 1964.

Rosenberg, M. Society and the Adolescent Self-Image. Princeton, N.J., Princeton University Press, 1965.

Silberman, C.E. Crisis in Black and White. New York, Vintage Books, 1965.

Spurlock, J. Problems of identification in young black children—static or changing? Read at the 74th Annual Meeting of the National Medical Association in San Francisco, August, 1969.

Strunk, O. Attitudes towards one's name and one's self. J. Individ. Psychol., 14:64-67, 1958.

Witmer, H.L., and Kotinsky, R. Personality in the Making. New York, Harpers, 1952.

Woodward, C. V. Clio with soul. *In* Black Studies: Myths and Realities. A. Philip Randolph Educational Fund, Sept., 1969.

Wynes, C.E., ed. The Negro in the South Since 1865. New York, Harper Colophon, 1968.

Index

Page numbers in italics refer to tables.